Ian Allan abc

Mi[illegible]
Ai[illegible]
Markings
1987

Peter R. March

LONDON

IAN ALLAN LTD

Contents

Introduction	3
Abbreviations	4
British Military Aircraft Serials	6
British Military Aircraft Markings	7
Deletions	97
RAF Maintenance/Support Command Cross Reference	98
RN Engineering Cross-Reference	101
RAF Gliding and Soaring Association Markings	102
RN Gliding and Soaring Association Markings	103
RN Landing Platform and Shore Station code-letters	104
Ship's Numeric Code-Deck Letters Analysis	106
RN Code-Squadron-Base-Aircraft-Crosscheck	106
British-based Historic Aircraft in Overseas Markings	107
Irish Army Air Corps Military Aircraft Markings	113
Overseas Military Aircraft Markings	114
US Military Aircraft Markings	139
UK Based USAF Aircraft	139
UK Based US Navy Aircraft	142
European Based USAF Aircraft	143
European Based US Army Aircraft	146
European Based US Navy Aircraft	149
US Based USAF Aircraft	150
Civil-Registered Aircraft in Military Service	160

Photographs by Andrew March (APM), Daniel March (DJM), and Peter R. March (PRM)

This eighth edition published 1987

ISBN 0 7110 1684 4

Published by Ian Allan Ltd
and printed by Ian Allan Printing Ltd at their works
at Coombelands in Runnymede, England

Cover: HS Hawk T1A XX297; RAF Red Arrows. *PRM*

Introduction

This eighth edition of *abc Military Aircraft Markings*, a companion to *abc Civil Aircraft Markings*, again sets out to list in alphabetical and numerical order all the aircraft which carry a United Kingdom military serial, and which are based, or might be seen, in the UK. The term 'aircraft' used here covers powered, manned aeroplanes, helicopters and gliders. It does not include un-manned target drones. Included are all the current Royal Air Force, Royal Navy, Army Air Corps, Ministry of Defence (Procurement Executive), manufacturers' test aircraft and civilian-owned aircraft with military markings, together with gliders of the private RAF and RN Gliding and Soaring Associations.

Aircraft withdrawn from operational use but which are retained in the UK for ground training purposes or otherwise preserved by the Services and in museums and collections are listed. The serials of some incomplete aircraft have been included, such as the cockpit sections of machines displayed by the RAF Exhibition Flight, aircraft used by airfield fire sections and for service battle damage repair training (BDRT), together with significant parts of aircraft held by preservation groups and societies. Many of these aircraft are allocated, and sometimes wear, a secondary identity, such as an RAF Support Command 'M' or a Royal Navy 'A' maintenance number. These numbers are listed against those aircraft to which they have been allocated, and cross-references are included.

A serial 'missing' is either because it was never issued as it formed part of a 'black-out block', or because the aircraft is written off, scrapped, sold, abroad or allocated an alternative marking. Aircraft used as targets on MoD ranges to which access is restricted, and un-manned target drones, are omitted.

In the main, the serials listed are those markings presently displayed on the aircraft. The manufacturer and aircraft type are given, together with any alternative, previous, secondary or civil identity shown in brackets. The operating unit and its based location, along with any known unit and base code markings in square brackets, are given as accurately as possible. The unit markings are normally carried boldly on the sides of the fuselage or on the aircraft's fin. In the case of RAF and AAC machines currently in service, they are usually one or two letters or numbers, while the RN continues to use a well-established system of three-figure codes between 000 and 999 together with a fin letter code denoting the aircraft's operational base. RN squadrons, units and bases are allocated blocks of numbers from which individual aircraft codes are issued. To help identification of RN bases and landing platforms on ships, a list of tail-letter codes with their appropriate name, helicopter code number, ship pennant number and type of vessel is included; as is a helicopter code number/ships' tail-letter code grid cross-reference as a new feature in this edition.

Codes change, for example when aircraft move between units, and therefore the markings currently painted on a particular aircraft might not be those shown in this edition because of subsequent events. There is also a list of aircraft which appeared in the last edition but which have now been removed, giving their fates where known.

The Irish Army Air Corps fleet is listed, together with the serials of other overseas air arms whose aircraft might be seen visiting the UK from time to time. The serial numbers are as usually presented on the individual machine or as they are normally identified. Where possible, the aircraft's base and operating unit have been shown.

USAF, US Army and US Navy aircraft based in the UK and in Western Europe, and of types which regularly visit the UK from the USA, are listed in separate sections by type. The serial number actually displayed on the aircraft is shown in full, with additional Fiscal Year (FY) or full serial information also provided. Where appropriate, details of the operating wing, squadron allocation and base are added. Veteran and Vintage aircraft which carry overseas military markings but which are based in the UK have been separately listed showing the identity carried as a principal means of identification.

Information shown is believed to be correct at 31 January 1987, and significant changes can be monitored through the monthly 'Military Markings' column in *Aircraft Illustrated*.

Acknowledgements

The compiler wishes to thank the many people who have taken trouble to send comments, criticism and other useful information following the publication of the previous edition of *abc Military Aircraft Markings*. In particular the following correspondents: P. H. Butler, J. R. Cross, G. Hall, J. Lake, P.-J. Martin, P. C. Marygold, S. Newton, T. Poole, M. C. Powney, L. P. Robinson, K. Sloper, M. Thompson and G. Turner.

This compilation has relied heavily on the publications of the following aviation groups and societies: *Air* (West London Aviation Group), *Air North, British Aviation Review* (British Aviation Research Group), *Hawkeye* (Gatwick Aviation Society), *Humberside Air Review* (Humberside Aviation Society), *Irish Air Letter, Norfolk Air Review* (Norfolk Aviation Society), *Osprey* (Solent Aviation Society), *Prestwick Airport Letter* (Prestwick Airport Aviation Group), *Scottish Air News* (Central Scotland Aviation Group), *Skyward* (Westcountry Aviation Society), *South West Aviation News* (South West Aviation Society), *Stansted Aviation Newsletter* (The Stansted Aviation Society), together with these publications: *Euromil — Foreign Military Air Arms to Europe* (Seefive Publications); *NATO to the UK 1986* (West London Aviation Group); *United States Military Aircraft to Europe* (Seefive Publications) and *Wrecks and Relics* (Midland Counties Publications/Merseyside Aviation Society).

The new edition of *abc Military Aircraft Markings* would not have been possible without considerable research and checking by Stephen Byles, Howard Curtis, Wal Gandy and Daniel March.

PRM

Abbreviations

AAC Army Air Corps
A&AEE Aeroplane & Armament Experimental Establishment
AAS Aeromedical Airlift Squadron
ABS Air Base Squadron
ABW Air Base Wing
ACCGS Air Cadets Central Gliding School
ACCS Airborne Command and Control Squadron
ACR Armoured Cavalry Regiment
AEF Air Experience Flight
AES Air Engineering School
AETW Air Engineering Training Wing
AEW Airborne Early Warning
AFRES Air Force Reserve
AIU Accident Investigation Unit
AMS Air Movements School
ANG Air National Guard
APS Aircraft Preservation Society
ARF Aircraft Restoration Flight
ARG Air Refuelling Group
ARRS Aerospace Rescue and Recovery Squadron
ARS Air Refuelling Squadron
ARW Air Refuelling Wing
ARW/LCF Advanced Rotary Wing/Lynx Conversion Flight
ARWS Advanced Rotary Wing Squadron
AS Aggressor Squadron
ASF Aircraft Servicing Flight
AS&RU Aircraft Salvage and Repair Unit
ATC Air Training Corps
ATCC Air Traffic Control Centre
ATS Aircrewman Training Squadron
AvCo Aviation Company
AW Armstrong Whitworth Aircraft/Aircraft Workshops
AW&CW Airborne Warning & Control Wing
BAC British Aircraft Corporation
BAe British Aerospace Company
BAOR British Army of the Rhine
BAPC British Aircraft Preservation Council
BATUS British Army Training Unit Support
BDRF Battle Damage Repair Flight
BDRT Battle Damage Repair Training
BFWF Basic Fixed Wing Flight
BGA British Gliding Association
BHC British Hovercraft Corporation
BBMF Battle of Britain Memorial Flight
BP Boulton & Paul
B-V Boeing-Vertol
BW Bomber Wing
CARG Cotswold Aircraft Restoration Group
CATCS Central Air Traffic Control School
CBAS Commando Brigade Air Squadron
CCF Combined Cadet Force
CDE Chemical Defence Establishment
CFS Central Flying School
CinC Commander in Chief
CSDE Central Servicing Development Establishment
CTE Central Training Establishment
CTTS Civilian Technical Training School
CV Chance-Vought
D-BD Dassault-Breguet Dornier
DH De Havilland
DHC De Havilland Canada
D&TS Development and Trials Squadron
DTI Department of Trade and Industry
ECS Electronic Countermeasures Squadron
EE English Electric

EMA	East Midlands Airport
EoN	Elliot's of Newbury
ETPS	Empire Test Pilots School
ETS	Engineering Training School
EWAU	Electronics Warfare Avionics Unit
FAA	Fleet Air Arm/Federal Aviation Authority
FBW	Fly by wire
FCS	Facility Checking Squadron
FE	Further Education
FF&SS	Fire Fighting & Safety School
FGF	Flying Grading Flight
FI	Falkland Islands
FIS	Fighter Interceptor Squadron
Flt	Flight
FMA	Fabrica Militar de Aviones
FOL	Forward Operating Location
FONAC	Flag Officer Naval Air Command
FRADU	Fleet Requirements and Direction Unit
FRL	Flight Refuelling Ltd
FRSB	Fleet Reserve Storage Base
FSS	Flying Selection School
FTS	Flying Training School
FW	Foster Wickner
GAL	General Aircraft Ltd
GD	General Dynamics
HMS	Her Majesty's Ship
HP	Handley-Page
HQ	Headquarters
HS	Hawker Siddeley
IAM	Institute of Aviation Medicine
IWM	Imperial War Museum
JATE	Joint Air Transport Establishment
JMU	Jaguar Maintenance Unit
JTU	Joint Trials Unit
LCF	Lynx Conversion Flight
LTF	Lightning Training Flight
MAG	Military Airlift Group
MAAG	Military Air Advisory Group
MAS	Military Airlift Squadron
MAW	Military Airlift Wing
McD	McDonnell Douglas
MGSP	Mobile Glider Servicing Party
MH	Max Holste
MoD(PE)	Ministry of Defence (Procurement Executive)
Mod	Modified
MR	Maritime Reconnaissance
MS	Morane Saulnier
MU	Maintenance Unit
NA	North American
NAF	Naval Air Facility
NASU	Naval Air Support Unit
NE	North-East
NHTU	Naval Hovercraft Trials Unit
NI	Northern Ireland
OCU	Operational Conversion Unit
OEU	Operation Evaluation Unit
OPITB	Offshore Petroleum Industry Training Board
OTD	Overseas Training Division
PAX	Passenger procedural trainer
PRU	Photographic Reconnaissance Unit
RAE	Royal Aircraft Establishment
RAeS	Royal Aeronautical Society
RAF	Royal Aircraft Factory/ Royal Air Force
RAFC	Royal Air Force College
RAFGSA	Royal Air Force Gliding and Soaring Association
RAOC	Royal Army Ordnance Corps
RCAF	Royal Canadian Air Force
REME	Royal Electrical & Mechanical Engineers
RM	Royal Marines
RMC of S	Royal Military College of Science
RN	Royal Navy
RNAS	Royal Naval Air Station
RNAY	Royal Naval Aircraft Yard
RNEC	Royal Naval Engineering College
RNEFTS	Royal Naval Elementary Flying Training School
RNGSA	Royal Navy Gliding and Soaring Association
R-R	Rolls-Royce
RS	Reid & Sigrist
RS&RE	Royal Signals and Radar Establishment
RW	Reconnaissance Wing
SA	Scottish Aviation
SAC	Strategic Air Command
SAH	School of Air Handling
SAL	Scottish Aviation Limited
SAR	Search and Rescue
Saro	Saunders-Roe
SAREW	Search & Rescue Engineering Wing
SARTU	Search and Rescue Training Unit
SCF	Scout Conversion Flight
SEPECAT	Société Européenne de Production de l'Avion ECAT
SHSU	Sea Harrier Servicing Unit
SKTF	Sea King Training Flight
SNCAN	Société Nationale Aeronautique du Nord
SOS	Special Operations Squadron
SoTT	School of Technical Training
Sqn	Squadron
SRW	Strategic Reconnaissance Wing
SSF	Station Servicing Flight
SW	Strategic Wing
TAS	Tactical Airlift Squadron
TAW	Tactical Airlift Wing
TCW	Tactical Control Wing
Tech Coll	Technical College
TFS	Tactical Fighter Squadron
TFW	Tactical Fighter Wing
TMTS	Trade Management Training School
TOEU	Tornado Operational Evaluation Unit
TRS	Tactical Reconnaissance Squadron
TRW	Tactical Reconnaissance Wing
TTTE	Tri-national Tornado Training Establishment
TWCU	Tornado Weapons Conversion Unit
TWU	Tactical Weapons Unit
UAS	University Air Squadron
UK	United Kingdom
UKAEA	United Kingdom Atomic Energy Authority
US	United States
USAF	United States Air Force
USAREUR	US Army Europe
USN	United States Navy
VGS	Volunteer Gliding School
VS	Vickers-Supermarine
WO	Written off
WRG	Weather Reconnaissance Group
WRS	Weather Reconnaissance Squadron
WS	Westland
WW2	World War II

British Military Aircraft Serials

The Committee of Imperial Defence through its Air Committee introduced a standardised system of numbering aircraft in November 1912. The Air Department of the Admiralty was allocated the first batch 1-200 and used these to cover aircraft already in use and those on order. The Army was issued with the next block from 201-800, which included the number 304 which was given to the Cody Biplane now preserved in the Science Museum. By the outbreak of World War 1 the Royal Navy was on its second batch of serials 801-1600 and this system continued with alternating allocations between the Army and Navy until 1916 when number 10000, a Royal Flying Corps BE2C, was reached.

It was decided not to continue with five digit numbers but instead to start again from 1, prefixing RFC aircraft with the letter A and RNAS aircraft with the prefix N. The RFC allocations commenced with A1 an FE2D and before the end of the year had reached A9999 an Armstrong Whitworth FK8. The next group commenced with B1 and continued in logical sequence through the C, D, E and F prefixes. G was used on a limited basis to identity captured German aircraft, while H was the last block of wartime ordered aircraft. To avoid confusion I was not used, so the new postwar machines were allocated serials in the J range. A further minor change was made in the serial numbering system in August 1929 when it was decided to maintain four numerals after the prefix letter, thus omitting numbers 1 to 999. The new K series therefore commenced at K1000, which was allocated to an AW Atlas.

The Naval N prefix was not used in such a logical way. Blocks of numbers were allocated for specific types of aircraft such as seaplanes or flying boats. By the late 1920s the sequence had largely been used up and a new series using the prefix S was commenced. In 1930 separate naval allocations were stopped and subsequent serials were issued in the 'military' range which had by this time reached the K series. A further change in the pattern of allocations came in the L range. Commencing with L7272 numbers were issued in blocks with smaller blocks of serials between not used. These were known as blackout blocks. As M had already been used as a suffix for Maintenance Command instructional airframes it was not used as a prefix. Although N had previously been used for naval aircraft it was used again for serials allocated from 1937.

With the build-up to World War 2 the rate of allocations quickly accelerated and the prefix R was being used when war was declared. The letters O and Q were not allotted, and nor was S which had been used up to S1865 for naval aircraft before integration into the RAF series. By 1940 the serial Z9999 had been reached, as part of a blackout block, with the letters U and Y not used to avoid confusion. The option to recommence serial allocation at A1000 was not taken up; instead it was decided to use an alphabetical two-letter prefix with three numerals running from 100 to 999. Thus AA100 was allocated to a Blenheim IV.

This two-letter, three-numeral serial system which started in 1940 continues today with the current issue being in the ZG range. The letters C, I, O, Q, U and Y were, with the exception of NC, not used. For various reasons the following letter combinations were not issued: DA, DB, DH, EA, GA to GZ, HA, JE, JH, JJ, KR to KT, MR, NW, NZ, SA to SK, TN, TR and VE. The first postwar serials issued were in the VP range while the end of the WZs had been reached by the Korean War. At the current rate of issue the Z range should last out the remainder of this century.

Note: Whilst every effort has been made to ensure the accuracy of this publication, no part of the contents has been obtained from official sources. The compiler will be pleased to continue to receive comments, corrections and further information for inclusion in subsequent editions of *Military Aircraft Markings*. A monthly up-date of additions, amendments and cancellations is published in *Aircraft Illustrated*.

British Military Aircraft Markings

A serial in *italics* denotes that it is not the genuine marking for that airframe.

Serial	Type (alternative identity)	Owner, Operator or Location	Notes
164	Bleriot Type XI (BAPC 106)	RAF Museum, Hendon	
168	Sopwith Tabloid Scout Replica (G-BFDE)	Bomber Command Museum, Hendon	
304	Cody Biplane (BAPC 62)	Science Museum, South Kensington	
433	Bleriot Type XXVII (BAPC 107)	RAF Museum, Hendon	
2345	Vickers FB5 Gunbus Replica (G-ATVP)	RAF Museum, Hendon	
2699	RAF BE2C	Imperial War Museum, Duxford	
3066	Caudron GIII (G-AETA)	RAF Museum, Hendon	
5964	DH2 Replica (G-BFVH)	Privately owned, Duxford	
5984	DH2 Replica (BAPC 112)	Museum of Army Flying, Middle Wallop	
6232	RAF BE2C Replica (BAPC 41)	RAF St Athan Historic Aircraft Collection	
8151	Sopwith Baby Replica (BAPC 137)	Leisure Sport, Thorpe Park	
8359	Short 184	FAA Museum, RNAS Yeovilton	
A1325	RAF BE2e	Mosquito Aircraft Museum, London Colney	
A1742	Scout D Replica (BAPC 38)	RAF St Athan Historic Aircraft Collection	
A4850	RAF SE5A Replica (BAPC176)	South Yorkshire APS, Firbeck	
A8226	Sopwith 1½ Strutter Replica (G-BIDW)	RAF Museum, Hendon	
B1807	Sopwith Pup (G-EAVX) [A7]	Privately owned, Keynsham, Avon	
B4863	RAF SE5A Replica (BAPC 113) [G]	Leisure Sport, Thorpe Park	
B4863	Eberhardt SE5E (G-BLXT) [G]	Privately owned, Booker	
B6401	Sopwith Camel F1 Replica (G-AWYY/C1701)	FAA Museum, RNAS Yeovilton	
B7270	Sopwith Camel F1 Replica (G-BFCZ)	Privately owned, St Just	
C1381	Avro 504K Replica (BAPC177) [G]	RAF Museum Store, Henlow	
C1904	RAF SE5A Replica (G-PFAP) [Z]	Privately owned, Bicester	
C4912	Bristol M1c Replica (BAPC 135)	Leisure Sport, Thorpe Park	
D3419	Sopwith Camel F1 Replica (BAPC 59)	RAF St Athan Historic Aircraft Collection	
D5329	Sopwith Dolphin	RAF Museum Store, Cardington	
D7560	Avro 504K	Science Museum, South Kensington	
D8096	Bristol F2B Fighter (G-AEPH) [D]	Shuttleworth Collection, Old Warden	
E373	Avro 504K Replica (BAPC178)	RAF Museum Store, Henlow	
E449	Avro 504K (G-EBJE)	RAF Museum, Hendon	
E2466	Bristol F2b (BAPC165)	RAF Museum, Hendon	
E2581	Bristol F2b Fighter	Imperial War Museum, Duxford	
E6452	SNCAN Stampe SV4C (G-AXNW)	Privately owned, St Merryn	
F344	Avro 504K Replica	RAF Museum Store, Henlow	
F760	SE5A Microlight Replica [A]	Privately owned, Redhill	
F904	RAF SE5A (G-EBIA)	Shuttleworth Collection, Old Warden	
F938	RAF SE5A (G-EBIC)	RAF Museum, Hendon	
F939	RAF SE5A (G-EBIB) [6]	Science Museum, South Kensington	
F943	RAF SE5A Replica (G-BIHF) [S]	Privately owned, Booker (*Lady Di*)	
F943	RAF SE5A Replica (G-BKDT)	Privately owned, Elvington	
F1010	DH9A [19]	Bomber Command Museum, Hendon	
F3556	RAF RE8	Imperial War Museum, Duxford	
F4013	Sopwith Camel Replica	Privately owned, Coventry	
F5447	RAF SE5A Replica (G-BKER) [N]	Privately owned, Strathallan/ Strathallan Aircraft Collection	
F5459	RAF SE5A Replica (BAPC 142) [Y]	Cornwall Aero Park, Helston	
F-5459	RAF SE5A Replica (G-INNY)	Privately owned, Old Sarum	
F6314	Sopwith Camel [B]	RAF Museum, Hendon	
F8010	RAF SE5A Replica (G-BDWJ) [19]	Privately owned, Booker	
F8614	Vickers Vimy Replica (G-AWAU)	Bomber Command Museum, Hendon	

Notes	*Serial*	*Type (alternative identity)*	*Owner, Operator or Location*
	G1381	Avro 504K Replica [G] (BAPC 177)	RAF Museum store, Henlow
	H1968	Avro 504K Replica (BAPC 42)	RAF St Athan Historic Aircraft Collection
	H2311	Avro 504K (G-ABAA)	RAF Museum Store, Henlow
	H5199	Avro 504K (G-ACNB, G-ADEV, E3404)	Shuttleworth Collection, Old Warden
	J7326	DH Humming Bird (G-EBQP)	Privately owned, Hemel Hempstead
	J8067	Pterodactyl 1a	Science Museum, South Kensington
	J9941	Hawker Hart 2 (G-ABMR)	Bomber Command Museum, Hendon
	K1786	Hawker Tomtit (G-AFTA)	Shuttleworth Collection, Old Warden
	K1930	Hawker Fury Replica (G-BKBB)	Privately owned, Booker
	K2050	Hawker Fury Replica (G-ASCM)	Privately owned, Stapleford
	K2059	Isaacs Fury (G-PFAR)	Privately owned, Dunkeswell
	K2060	Isaacs Fury II (G-BKZM)	Privately owned, Huddersfield
	K2567	DH Tiger Moth (G-MOTH)	Russavia Collection, Duxford
	K2568	DH Tiger Moth (G-APMM)	Privately owned, Bedford
	K2571	DH Tiger Moth	Privately owned, Lutterworth
	K2572	DH Tiger Moth (G-AOZH)	Privately owned, Shoreham
	K3215	Avro Tutor (G-AHSA)	Shuttleworth Collection, Old Warden
	K3584	DH 82B Queen Bee (BAPC 186)	Mosquito Aircraft Museum, London Colney
	K3731	Hawker Fury Replica (G-RODI)	Privately owned, Exeter
	K4232	Avro Rota I (SE-AZB)	RAF Museum, Hendon
	K4235	Avro Rota I (G-AHMJ)	Shuttleworth Collection, Old Warden
	K4972	Hawker Hart Trainer IIA (1746M)	RAF Museum, Hendon
	K5054	Supermarine Spitfire Replica	Privately owned, Swindon
	K5457	Hawker Hind (G-AENP/ BAPC 78) [XV]	Shuttleworth Collection, Old Warden
	K6038	Westland Wallace II	RAF Museum Store, Cardington
	K7271	Hawker Fury II Replica (BAPC 148)	RAF Cosford Aerospace Museum
	K8042	Gloster Gladiator II (8372M)	Battle of Britain Museum, Hendon
	K9942	VS Spitfire IA (8383M) [SD-V]	RAF Museum, Hendon
	L1592	Hawker Hurricane I [KW-Z]	Science Museum, South Kensington
	L1592	Hawker Hurricane I Replica (BAPC 63) [KW-Z]	Torbay Aircraft Museum, Paignton
	L2301	VS Walrus I (G-AIZG)	FAA Museum, RNAS Yeovilton
	L2940	Blackburn Skua I	FAA Museum, RNAS Yeovilton
	L5343	Fairey Battle I	RAF St Athan Historic Aircraft Collection
	L6906	Miles Magister (G-AKKY) (BAPC 44)	Privately owned, Wroughton
	L7245	HP Halifax	Privately owned, Brough
	L7775	Vickers Wellington (fuselage)	South Yorkshire Aircraft Museum, Firbeck, Notts
	L8032	Gloster Gladiator (G-AMRK)	Shuttleworth Collection, Old Warden
	L8756	Bristol Bolingbroke IVT (RCAF 10001) [XD-E]	Battle of Britain Museum, Hendon
	N220	Supermarine S5 replica (G-BDFF)	Privately owned, Bodmin
	N248	Supermarine S6A	Southampton Hall of Aviation
	N1671	Boulton Paul Defiant I (8370M) [EW-D]	Battle of Britain Museum, Hendon
	N1854	Fairey Fulmar II (G-AIBE)	FAA Museum, RNAS Yeovilton
	N2078	Sopwith Baby	FAA Museum, RNAS Yeovilton
	N2276	Gloster Gladiator II (really N5903) [H]	FAA Museum, RNAS Yeovilton
	N2980	Vickers Wellington BA [R]	Brooklands Museum, Weybridge
	N3788	Miles Magister (G-AKPF) (really G-ANLT)	Privately owned, Bassingbourn
	N4172	Fairey Albacore I [5A]	FAA Museum at St Just
	N4877	Avro Anson I (G-AMDA) [VX-F]	Skyfame Collection, Duxford
	N5180	Sopwith Pup (G-EBKY)	Shuttleworth Collection, Old Warden
	N5182	Sopwith Pup Replica (G-APUP)	RAF Museum, Hendon
	N5195	Sopwith Pup (G-ABOX)	Museum of Army Flying, Middle Wallop
	N5419	Bristol Scout Type D Replica	RAF Museum restoration centre, Cardington
	N5445	DH Tiger Moth (really G-AIXH/DE722)	Privately owned, Little Gransden
	N5492	Sopwith Triplane Replica (BAPC 111)	Leisure Sport, Thorpe Park
	N5628	Gloster Gladiator II	RAF Museum, Hendon

Serial	Type (alternative identity)	Owner, Operator or Location	Notes
N5912	Sopwith Triplane (8385M)	RAF Museum, Hendon	
N6004	Short Stirling 1	Cotswold Aircraft Restoration Group, RAF Innsworth	
N6160	Sopwith Pup	Privately owned, Tattershall Thorpe	
N6452	Sopwith Pup Replica (G-BIAU)	FAA Museum, RNAS Yeovilton	
N6466	DH Tiger Moth (G-ANKZ)	Privately owned, Barton	
N6720	DH Tiger Moth (7014M) [RUO-B]	No 1940 Sqn ATC, Levenshulme	
N6812	Sopwith Camel	Imperial War Museum, Lambeth	
N6847	DH Tiger Moth (G-APAL)	Privately owned, Little Gransden	
N6848	DH Tiger Moth (G-BALX)	Privately owned, Sedlescombe	
N6985	DH Tiger Moth (G-AHMN)	Museum of Army Flying, Middle Wallop	
N9191	DH Tiger Moth (G-ALND)	Privately owned, Shipdham	
N9238	DH Tiger Moth (G-ANEL)	Privately owned	
N9389	DH Tiger Moth (G-ANJA)	Privately owned, Shipmeadow, Suffolk	
N9510	DH Tiger Moth (G-AOEL)	Royal Scottish Museum of Flight, East Fortune	
N9899	Supermarine Southampton I	RAF Museum Store, Cardington	
P2183	Fairey Battle I [36]	RAF St Athan Historic Aircraft Collection	
P2617	Hawker Hurricane I (8373M) [AF-F]	Battle of Britain Museum, Hendon	
P3175	Hawker Hurricane I	Battle of Britain Museum, Hendon	
P6382	Miles Magister (G-AJRS)	Shuttleworth Collection, Old Warden	
P7350	VS Spitfire IIA (G-AWIJ) [EB-Z]	RAF Battle of Britain Flight, Coningsby	
P7540	VS Spitfire IIA [DU-W]	Dumfries & Galloway Aviation Museum, Tinwald Downs	
P9390	VS Spitfire I Replica (BAPC 71) [KL-B]	Norfolk & Suffolk Aviation Museum, Flixton	
P9444	VS Spitfire IA [RN-D]	Science Museum, South Kensington	
R1914	Miles Magister (G-AHUJ)	Strathallan Aircraft Collection	
R3950	Fairey Battle I (RCAF 1899)	Strathallan Aircraft Collection	
R4907	DH Tiger Moth (G-ANCS)	Privately owned, Norwich	
R4959	DH Tiger Moth (G-ARAZ) [59]	Privately owned, Goodwood	
R5086	DH Tiger Moth (G-APIH)	Privately owned, Little Gransden	
R5250	DH Tiger Moth (G-AODT)	Privately owned, Swanton Morley	
R5868	Avro Lancaster I (7325M) [PO-S]	Bomber Command Museum, Hendon	
R6915	VS Spitfire I	Imperial War Museum, Lambeth	
R9125	Westland Lysander III (8377M) [LX-L]	Battle of Britain Museum, Hendon	
S1287	Fairey Flycatcher Replica (G-BEYB) [5]	Privately owned, Middle Wallop/ Yeovilton	
S1595	Supermarine S6B	Science Museum, South Kensington	
S1595	Supermarine S6B Replica (BAPC 156)	Leisure Sport, Thorpe Park	
S3398	Spad XIII Replica (G-BFYO)	FAA Museum, RNAS Yeovilton	
S4523	Spad XIII [I] (N4727V)	Imperial War Museum, Duxford	
T5424	DH Tiger Moth (G-AJOA)	Privately owned, Chiseldon	
T5493	DH Tiger Moth (G-ANEF)	Privately owned, Cranwell	
T5672	DH Tiger Moth (G-ALRI)	Privately owned, Chalmington	
T5854	DH Tiger Moth (G-ANKK)	Privately owned, Halfpenny Green	
T5968	DH Tiger Moth (G-ANNN)	Privately owned, Ayr	
T6099	DH Tiger Moth (G-AOGR/ XL714)	Privately owned, Clacton	
T6296	DH Tiger Moth (8387M)	RAF Museum, Hendon	
T6313	DH Tiger Moth (G-AHVU)	Privately owned, Denham	
T6553	DH Tiger Moth (G-APIG) [N]	Privately owned, Avignon	
T6645	DH Tiger Moth (G-AIIZ)	Privately owned, Redhill	
T6818	DH Tiger Moth (G-ANKT)	Shuttleworth Collection, Old Warden	
T7281	DH Tiger Moth (G-ARTL)	Privately owned, Egton, nr Whitby	
T7404	DH Tiger Moth (G-ANMV)	Privately owned, Booker	
T7909	DH Tiger Moth (G-ANON)	Privately owned, Sherburn-in-Elmet	
T7997	DH Tiger Moth (G-AOBH)	Privately owned, Benington	
T8191	DH Tiger Moth	RN Historic Flight, RNAS Yeovilton	
T9707	Miles Magister (G-AKKR/8378M)	Greater Manchester Museum of Science and Industry	
T9738	Miles Magister (G-AKAT)	Privately owned, Newark	
V3388	Airspeed Oxford (G-AHTW)	Skyfame Collection, Duxford	
V7767	Hawker Hurricane Replica (BAPC 72)	Air Museum, North Weald	
V9281	Westland Lysander III (G-BCWL) [RU-M]	Privately owned, Henstridge	

Notes	Serial	Type (alternative identity)	Owner, Operator or Location
	V9300	Westland Lysander II (G-LIZY)	British Aerial Museum, Duxford
	V9441	Westland Lysander IIIA (RCAF2355/G-AZWT) [AR-A]	Strathallan Aircraft Collection
	W1048	HP Halifax II (8465M) [TL-S]	Bomber Command Museum, Hendon
	W4041	Gloster E28/39 [G]	Science Museum, South Kensington
	W4050	DH Mosquito 1	Mosquito Aircraft Museum, London Colney
	W5856	Fairey Swordfish II (G-BMGC)	Strathallan Aircraft Collection
	W5984	Fairey Swordfish II (really HS618/A2001) [5H]	FAA Museum, RNAS Yeovilton
	X4590	VS Spitfire I (8384M) [PR-F]	Battle of Britain Museum, Hendon
	Z2033	Fairey Firefly I (G-ASTL)	Skyfame Collection, Duxford
	Z7015	Hawker Sea Hurricane IB (G-BKTH)	Shuttleworth Collection, Duxford
	Z7197	Percival Proctor III (G-AKZN/ 8380M)	RAF St Athan Historic Aircraft Collection
	Z7258	DH Dragon Rapide (G-AHGD) (really NR786)	Privately owned, Old Warden
	AB910	VS Spitfire VB [BP-O]	RAF BBMF, Coningsby
	AL246	Grumman Martlet I	FAA Museum, RNAS Yeovilton
	AP507	Cierva C30A (G-ACWP) [KX-P]	Science Museum, South Kensington
	AR213	VS Spitfire IA (G-AIST) [QG-A]	Privately owned, Booker
	AR501	VS Spitfire VC (G-AWII) [NN-D]	Shuttleworth Collection, Duxford
	BB807	DH Tiger Moth (G-ADWO)	Wessex Aviation Society, Wimborne
	BB814	DH Tiger Moth (G-AFWI)	RN Gliding Club, Lee-on-Solent
	BL614	VS Spitfire VB (4354M) [ZD-F]	Greater Manchester Museum of Science and Industry
	BM597	VS Spitfire VB (5713M) [PR-O]	RAF Church Fenton, on gate
	DE208	DH Tiger Moth (G-AGYU)	Privately owned, Nayland
	DE363	DH Tiger Moth (G-ANFC)	Mosquito Aircraft Museum, London Colney
	DE373	DH Tiger Moth T.2 (A680/ A2127)	Privately owned
	DE623	DH Tiger Moth (G-ANFI)	Privately owned, St Athan
	DE673	DH Tiger Moth (G-ADNZ/ 6948M)	Privately owned, Hampton
	DE992	DH Tiger Moth (G-AXXV)	Privately owned, Wellesbourne Mountford
	DF128	DH Tiger Moth (G-AOJJ) [RCO-U]	Privately owned, Abingdon
	DF130	DH Tiger Moth (G-BACK)	Privately owned, Laindon
	DF155	DH Tiger Moth (G-ANFV)	Privately owned, Lossiemouth
	DF198	DH Tiger Moth (G-BBRB)	Privately owned, Biggin Hill
	DG202	Gloster F9/40 Meteor (5758M) [G]	RAF Cosford Aerospace Museum
	DG590	Miles Hawk Major (G-ADMW/8379M)	RAF Museum Store, Henlow
	DP872	Fairey Barracuda II	FAA Museum, St Just on rebuild
	DR613	FW Wicko GM1 (G-AFJB)	Privately owned, Berkswell
	DR628	Beech D.17s (N18V) [PB-1]	Privately owned, Duxford
	DV372	Avro Lancaster I (nose only)	Imperial War Museum, Lambeth
	EE416	Gloster Meteor III (nose only)	Science Museum, South Kensington
	EE531	Gloster Meteor F4 (7090M)	Midland Air Museum, Coventry
	EE549	Gloster Meteor F4 (6372M/ 7008M)	RAF St Athan Historic Aircraft Collection
	EJ693	Hawker Tempest V [SA-J]	Privately owned
	EM727	DH Tiger Moth (G-AOXN)	Privately owned, Yeovil
	EM903	DH Tiger Moth (G-APBI)	Privately owned, Audley End
	EN398	VS Spitfire IX Replica (BAPC184) [JE-J]	Imperial War Museum, Duxford
	EP120	VS Spitfire VB (5377M/8070M) [QV-H]	RAF Wattisham
	EX280	NA Harvard IIA (G-TEAC) [G]	Privately owned, Bourn
	EX976	NA Harvard III	FAA Museum, RNAS Yeovilton
	EZ259	NA Harvard III (G-BMJW)	Privately owned, Bracknell
	EZ407	NA Harvard III	RN Historic Flight, Lee-on-Solent
	FE905	NA Harvard IIB (LN-BNM/12392)	RAF Museum Store, Cardington
	FE992	NA Harvard IIB (G-BDAM)	Privately owned, Lee-on-Solent
	FH153	NA Harvard IIB (G-BBHK) [GW-A]	Privately owned, Cardiff
	FR870	Curtiss Kittyhawk III (NL1009N) [GA-S]	Privately owned, Duxford
	FS728	NA Harvard IIB (G-BAFM)	Privately owned, Thruxton
	FT239	NA Harvard IV (G-BIWX)	Privately owned, White Waltham

Serial	*Type (alternative identity)*	*Owner, Operator or Location*	*Notes*
FT375	NA Harvard IIB	MoD(PE) A&AEE Boscombe Down	
FT391	NA Harvard IIB (G-AZBN)	Privately owned, Duxford	
FX301	NA Harvard III (G-JUDI) [FD-NQ]	Privately owned, Ipswich	
FX442	NA Harvard IIB	Privately owned, Bournemouth	
HB275	Be.C-45 Expeditor II (N5063N)	Privately owned, White Waltham	
HB751	Fairchild Argus III (G-BCBL)	Privately owned, Little Gransden	
HD368	NA B-25J Mitchell (N9089Z/ G-BKXW) [VO-A]	Aces High, Duxford	
HJ711	DH Mosquito NFII [VI-C]	Privately owned, York	
HM354	Percival Proctor III (G-ANPP)	Privately owned, Stansted	
HR792	HP Halifax II	Yorkshire Air Museum, Elvington	
HS503	Fairey Swordfish IV (BAPC 108)	RAF Museum store, Henlow	
HS649	VS Spitfire XVIII	Privately owned, Chichester	
HX922	DH Mosquito TT35 (G-AWJV) [EG-F] (really TA634)	Mosquito Aircraft Museum, London Colney	
JV482	Grumman Wildcat V	Ulster Aviation Society, Newtownards	
JV928	PBY-5A Catalina (G-BLSC) [Y]	Plane Sailing, Barkston Heath	
KB889	Avro Lancaster B10 (G-LANC)	Imperial War Museum, Duxford	
KB976	Avro Lancaster B10 (G-BCOH) [LQ-K]	Strathallan Aircraft Collection	
KD431	CV Corsair IV [E2-M]	FAA Museum, RNAS Yeovilton	
KE209	Grumman Hellcat II	FAA Museum, RNAS Yeovilton	
KE418	Hawker Tempest (rear fuselage)	RNEC, Manadon	
KF183	NA Harvard IIB	MoD(PE) A&AEE Boscombe Down	
KF388	NA Harvard IIB (nose only)	Wessex Aviation Society, Wimborne	
KF423	NA Harvard II	Booker Aviation Museum	
KF435	NA Harvard IIB	Privately owned, Camberley	
KF594	NA Harvard IIB (cockpit section)	Newark Air Museum, Winthorpe	
KG374	Douglas Dakota C-4 (really KN645/8355M)	RAF Cosford Aerospace Museum	
KG874	Douglas Dakota C-4 (really TS423/G-DAKS) [YS-L]	Aces High, North Weald	
KK995	Sikorsky Hoverfly I (KL110) [E]	RAF Museum, Hendon	
KN448	Douglas Dakota C4 (nose only)	Science Museum, South Kensington	
KN751	Consolidated Liberator VI [K]	RAF Cosford Aerospace Museum	
KP208	Douglas Dakota C-4 [YS]	Airborne Forces Museum, Aldershot	
KX829	Hawker Hurricane IV [JV-I]	Birmingham Museum of Science & Industry	
LA198	VS Spitfire F21 (7118M) [RAI-G]	RAF Leuchars, on display	
LA226	VS Spitfire F21 (7119M)	RAF Memorial Chapel, Biggin Hill	
LA255	VS Spitfire F21 (6490M) [JX-U]	RAF Wittering	
LA564	VS Seafire F46	Privately owned, Newport Pagnell	
LB294	Taylorcraft Plus D (G-AHWJ)	Museum of Army Flying, Middle Wallop	
LB312	Taylorcraft Plus D (G-AHXE)	Privately owned, Shoreham	
LB375	Taylorcraft Plus D (G-AHGW)	Privately owned, Coventry	
LF363	Hawker Hurricane IIC [VY-X]	RAF Battle of Britain Flight, Coningsby	
LF738	Hawker Hurricane IIC (5405M)	RAF, RAeS Medway Branch, Rochester	
LF751	Hawker Hurricane IIC (5466M)	RAF, RAeS Medway Branch, Rochester	
LF858	DH Queen Bee (G-BLUZ)	Privately owned, Meppershall	
LH208	Airspeed Horsa I (parts only)	Museum of Army Flying, Middle Wallop	
LS326	Fairey Swordfish II (G-AJVH) [5A]	RN Historic Flight, RNAS Yeovilton	
LZ551	DH Sea Vampire I [G]	FAA Museum, RNAS Yeovilton	
LZ766	Percival Proctor III (G-ALCK)	Skyfame Collection, Duxford	
MD497	WS Widgeon (G-ANLW) [NE-X]	Privately owned, Little Staughton	
MF628	Vickers Wellington T10	Bomber Command Museum, Hendon	
MH434	VS Spitfire IX (G-ASJV) [ZD-B]	Privately owned, Duxford	
MJ627	VS Spitfire TIX (G-ASOZ/ G-BMSB)	Privately owned, Kenilworth	
MJ730	VS Spitfire IX (G-BLAS)	Privately owned, East Midlands Airport	
MK356	VS Spitfire IX (5690M) [21-V]	RAF St Athan Historic Aircraft Collection	
ML407	VS Spitfire T9 (G-LFIX) [OU-V]	Privately owned, Middle Wallop	
ML417	VS Spitfire LFIXe (G-BJSG) [2I-T]	Privately owned, Duxford	
ML427	VS Spitfire IX (6457M) [I-ST]	Birmingham Museum of Science & Industry	
ML796	Short Sunderland V	Imperial War Museum, Duxford	
ML824	Short Sunderland V [NS-Z]	Battle of Britain Museum, Hendon	
MN235	Hawker Typhoon IB	RAF Museum, Hendon	
MP425	Airspeed Oxford (G-AITB)	RAF Museum Store, Cardington	

Notes	*Serial*	*Type (alternative identity)*	*Owner, Operator or Location*
	MT360	Auster 5 (G-AKWT)	Privately owned, Newark
	MT438	Auster III (G-AREI)	Privately owned, Chessington
	MT847	VS Spitfire XIV (6960M)	RAF Cosford Aerospace Museum
	MV154	VS Spitfire HF VIII (G-BKMI/ A58-671)	Privately owned, Huntingdon
	MV262	VS Spitfire XIV [42-G]	Privately owned, Winchester
	MV293	VS Spitfire XIV (G-SPIT/G-BGHB)	Privately owned, Duxford
	MV370	VS Spitfire XIV (G-FXIV) [AV-L]	Privately owned, North Weald
	MW100	Avro York C1 (G-AGNV/TS798)	RAF Cosford Aerospace Museum
	NF370	Fairey Swordfish II	Imperial War Museum, Duxford
	NF389	Fairey Swordfish III [5B]	FAA Museum, Lee-on-Solent
	NF875	DH Dragon Rapide 6 (G-AGTM) [603/CH]	Russavia Collection, Duxford
	NH238	VS Spitfire IX (N238V/ G-MKIX) [D-A]	Warbirds of GB, Bitteswell
	NH799	VS Spitfire XIV	Privately owned, Duxford
	NJ673	Auster 5D (G-AOCR)	Privately owned, Saltby
	NJ695	Auster 4 (G-AJXV)	Privately owned, Nottingham
	NJ703	Auster 5 (G-AKPI)	Privately owned, Doncaster
	NL985	DH Tiger Moth (7015M)	Vintage Aircraft Team, Cranfield
	NP181	Percival Proctor IV (G-AOAR)	Privately owned, Biggin Hill
	NP184	Percival Proctor IV (G-ANYP) [K]	Torbay Aircraft Museum, Paignton
	NP294	Percival Proctor IV [TS-M]	Lincolnshire Aviation Museum, East Kirkby
	NP303	Percival Proctor IV (G-ANZJ)	Privately owned, Byfleet, Surrey
	NR747	DH Dragon Rapide (G-AJHO)	Privately owned, near Bassingbourn
	NV778	Hawker Tempest V (8386M)	RAF Museum, Hendon
	NX611	Avro Lancaster VII (G-ASXX/ 8375M) [YF-C]	Privately owned, RAF Scampton
Staverton 8/87	PA474	Avro Lancaster I [SR-D]	RAF Battle of Britain Flight, Coningsby
	PG617	DH Tiger Moth (G-AYVY)	Privately owned, Ronaldsway
	PG651	DH Tiger Moth (G-AYUX)	Privately owned, Booker
	PG671	DH Tiger Moth (N82AM) [26]	Privately owned
	PK624	VS Spitfire F22 (8072M) [RAU-T]	RAF Abingdon, at main gate
	PK664	VS Spitfire F22 (7759M) (V6-B)	RAF Binbrook, at main gate
	PK683	VS Spitfire F24 (7150M)	Southampton Hall of Aviation
	PK724	VS Spitfire F24 (7288M)	RAF Museum, Hendon
	PL344	VS Spitfire IX	Privately owned, Winchester
	PL983	VS Spitfire XI (G-PRXI)	Privately owned, Duxford/Marseilles
	PM631	VS Spitfire XIX [DL-E]	RAF Battle of Britain Flight, Coningsby
	PM651	VS Spitfire XIX (7758M)	RAF Benson, at main gate
	PN323	HP Halifax VII (nose only)	Imperial War Museum, Duxford
	PS853	VS Spitfire XIX	RAF Battle of Britain Flight, Coningsby
	PS915	VS Spitfire XIX (7548M/7711M)	RAF Battle of Britain Flight, Coningsby
	PT462	VS Spitfire T9 (G-CTIX)	Privately owned, Micheldever, Hants
	PV202	VS Spitfire TIX (G-TRIX)	Privately owned, Battle, Sussex
	PV260	VS Spitfire IX (really BR601) [DB-P]	Privately owned (Sussex)
	PZ865	Hawker Hurricane II (G-AMAU)	RAF Battle of Britain Flight, Coningsby
	RA848	Slingsby Cadet TX1	Privately owned, Leeds
	RA854	Slingsby Cadet TX1	The Aeroplane Collection store, Wigan
	RA897	Slingsby Cadet TX1	Newark Air Museum store, Hucknall
	RD253	Bristol Beaufighter TF10 (7931M)	RAF Museum, Hendon
	RF342	Avro Lincoln B2 (G-29-1/ G-APRJ)	Aces High, North Weald
	RF398	Avro Lincoln B2 (8376M)	RAF Cosford Aerospace Museum
	RG333	Miles Messenger IIA (G-AIEK)	Privately owned, Filton, Bristol
	RG333	Miles Messenger IIA (G-AKEZ)	Torbay Aircraft Museum, Paignton
	RH377	Miles Messenger 4A (G-ALAH)	The Aeroplane Collection, RAF Henlow
	RH746	Bristol Brigand TF1	North East Aircraft Museum, Usworth
	RL962	DH Dragon Rapide (G-AHED)	RAF Museum Store, Cardington
	RM221	Percival Proctor IV (G-ANXR)	Privately owned, Biggin Hill
	RM689	VS Spitfire XIV (G-ALGT) [AP-D]	Rolls-Royce, Filton
	RR299	DH Mosquito T3 (G-ASKH) [HT-E]	British Aerospace, Hatfield
	RT520	Auster 4 (G-ALYB)	South Yorkshire Air Museum, Firbeck

Serial	Type (alternative identity)	Owner, Operator or Location	Notes
RW382	VS Spitfire XVIe (7245M/ 8075M)	RAF Uxbridge, London	
RW386	VS Spitfire XVIe (6944M/ G-BXVI) [RAK-A]	Warbirds of GB, Bitteswell	
RW388	VS Spitfire XVIe (6947M) [U4-U]	Stoke-on-Trent City Museum, Hanley	
RW393	VS Spitfire XVIe (7293M) [XT-A]	RAF Turnhouse, at main gate	
SL542	VS Spitfire XVIe (8390M) [4M-N]	RAF Coltishall, at main gate	
SL674	VS Spitfire XVIe (8392M)	RAF Memorial Chapel, Biggin Hill	
SM832	VS Spitfire XIV (G-WWII)	Privately owned, Micheldever, Hants	
SM969	VS Spitfire XVIII (G-BRAF)	Warbirds of GB, Bitteswell	
SX137	VS Seafire XVII	FAA Museum, RNAS Yeovilton	
SX300	VS Seafire XVII (A646/A2054)	Privately owned, Warwick	
SX336	VS Seafire XVII (A2055)	Privately owned, Twyford, Bucks	
TA122	DH Mosquito FBVI [UP-G]	Mosquito Aircraft Museum, London Colney	
TA634	DH Mosquito B35 (G-AWJV)	Mosquito Aircraft Museum, London Colney	
TA639	DH Mosquito TT35 (7806M)	RAF Cosford Aerospace Museum	
TA719	DH Mosquito TT35 (G-ASKC) [6T]	Skyfame Collection, Duxford	
TB252	VS Spitfire XVIe (7257M/7281M/ 8073M) [GW-H]	RAF Bentley Priory, on display	
TB382	VS Spitfire XVIe (7244M)	RAF Exhibition Flight, Abingdon	
TB752	VS Spitfire XVIe (7256M/ /7279M/8086M) [KH-Z]	RAF Manston, Memorial Hall	
TB863	VS Spitfire XVIe (G-CDAN)	Privately owned, Duxford	
TB885	VS Spitfire LFXVIE	Shoreham Aircraft Preservation Society	
TD248	VS Spitfire XVIe (7246M) [DW-A]	RAF Sealand, at main gate	
TE311	VS Spitfire XVIe (7241M)	RAF Exhibition Flight, Abingdon	
TE356	VS Spitfire XVIe (6709M/ 7001M)	Warbirds of GB, Bitteswell	
TE392	VS Spitfire XVIe (7000M)	Warbirds of GB, Bitteswell	
TE462	VS Spitfire XVIe (7243M)	Royal Scottish Museum of Flight, East Fortune	
TE476	VS Spitfire XVIe (7451M/ 8071M)	RAF Northolt at main gate	
TE517	VS Spitfire LFIX (2046/G-BIXP/ G-CCIX)	Privately owned, Micheldever, Hants	
TE566	VS Spitfire IX (G-BLCK)	Privately owned, Ludham	
TF956	Hawker Sea Fury FB11 [123/T]	RN Historic Flight, RNAS Yeovilton	
TG263	Saro SRA1 (G-12-1) [P]	Skyfame Collection, Duxford	
TG511	HP Hastings T5 (8554M)	RAF Cosford Aerospace Museum	
TG517	HP Hastings T5 [517]	Newark Air Museum, Winthorpe	
TG528	HP Hastings C1A	Skyfame Collection, Duxford	
TG568	HP Hastings C1A	RAE Bedford Fire Section	
TJ118	DH Mosquito TT35	Oxford Aircraft Collection	
TJ138	DH Mosquito B35 (7607M) [VO-L]	RAF St Athan Historic Aircraft Collection	
TJ343	Auster 5 (G-AJXC)	Privately owned, Popham	
TJ472	Auster AOP5 (BAPC 70)	Aircraft Preservation Society of Scotland, East Fortune	
TJ569	Auster 5 (G-AKOW)	Museum of Army Flying, Middle Wallop	
TJ672	Auster 5 (G-ANIJ)	Privately owned, Thruxton	
TK777	GAL Hamilcar I	Museum of Army Flying, Middle Wallop	
TL615	Airspeed Horsa II	Mosquito Aircraft Museum, London Colney	
TL659	Airspeed Horsa (BAPC 80) [74]	Museum of Army Flying, Middle Wallop	
TP298	VS Spitfire XIV (fuselage)	Privately owned, Ludham	
TV959	DH Mosquito T3 [AF-V]	Imperial War Museum, Lambeth	
TW117	DH Mosquito T3 (7805M)	Bomber Command Museum, Hendon	
TW439	Auster 5 (G-ANRP)	Warnham War Museum, Horsham	
TW467	Auster 5 (G-ANIE)	Privately owned, Cranfield	
TW511	Auster 5 (G-CMAL/G-APAF)	Privately owned, Leicester	
TW536	Auster AOP6 (7704M)	Museum of Army Flying, Middle Wallop	
TW591	Auster 6A (G-ARIH) [N]	Privately owned, Wigsley, Lincs	
TW641	Auster AOP6 (G-ATDN)	Privately owned, Biggin Hill	
TX183	Avro Anson C19	Privately owned, Arbroath	

Notes	*Serial*	*Type (alternative identity)*	*Owner, Operator or Location*
	TX192	Avro Anson C19	Guernsey Airport Fire Section
	TX213	Avro Anson C19 (G-AWRS)	NE Aircraft Museum, Usworth
	TX214	Avro Anson C19 (7817M)	RAF Cosford Aerospace Museum
	TX226	Avro Anson C19 (7865M)	Imperial War Museum, Duxford
	TX228	Avro Anson C19	City of Norwich Aviation Museum
	TX235	Avro Anson C19	Torbay Aircraft Museum, Paignton
	VF301	DH Vampire F1 (7060M) [RAL-B]	Midland Air Museum, Coventry
	VF516	Auster AOP6 (G-ASMZ) [T]	Museum of Army Flying, Middle Wallop
	VF548	Beagle Terrier I ((G-ASEG)	Privately owned, Woodvale
	VH127	Fairey Firefly TT4	FAA Museum, RNAS Yeovilton
	VL348	Avro Anson C19 (G-AVVO)	Newark Air Museum, Winthorpe
	VL349	Avro Anson C19 (G-AWSA)	Norfolk & Suffolk Aviation Museum, Flixton
	VM325	Avro Anson C19	Midland Air Museum, Coventry
	VM360	Avro Anson C19 (G-APHV)	Royal Scottish Museum of Flight, East Fortune
	VM791	Slingsby Cadet TX3 (really XA312) (8876M)	No 132 Redhill & Reigate Sqn ATC, RAF Kenley
	VN148	Grunau Baby IIb (BAPC 33)	Russavia Collection, Duxford
	VP293	Avro Shackleton T4	Strathallan Aircraft Collection
	VP519	Avro Anson C19 (nose only) (G-AVVR)	The Aeroplane Collection, Stockport
	VP952	DH Devon C2 (8820M)	RAF Cosford Aerospace Museum
	VP953	DH Devon C2	CTE, RAF Manston
Staverton 8/87	VP955	DH Devon C2 (G-DVON)	Privately owned, Staverton
	VP956	DH Devon C2	CTE, RAF Manston
	VP957	DH Devon C2 (8822M)	RAF Bishop's Court NI, BDRT
	VP958	DH Devon C2 [DC] (8795M)	RAF CTTS, St Athan
	VP959	DH Devon C2 [L]	MoD(PE) RAE West Freugh
	VP960	DH Devon C2	CTE, RAF Manston
	VP961	DH Devon C2 (G-ALFM)	Privately owned, Leavesden
	VP962	DH Devon C2 (G-BLRB)	Privately owned, RAF Kemble
	VP963	DH Devon C2	CTE, RAF Manston
	VP965	DH Devon C2 [DE] (8823M)	CTE, RAF Manston
	VP967	DH Devon C2 (G-KOOL)	East Surrey Technical College, Redhill
	VP968	DH Devon C2	MoD(PE) A&AEE Boscombe Down
	VP971	DH Devon C2 (8824M)	RAF FF&SS, Catterick
	VP975	DH Devon C2 [M]	Science Museum, Wroughton
	VP976	DH Devon C2 (8784M)	RAF Northolt Fire Section
	VP977	DH Devon C2 (G-ALTS)	RAE West Freugh Fire Section
Staverton 8/87	VP981	DH Devon C2	RAF Battle of Britain Flight, Coningsby
	VR137	Westland Wyvern TF1	FAA Museum, RNAS Yeovilton
	VR192	Pervical Prentice T1 (G-APIT)	Second World War Aircraft Preservation Society, Lasham
	VR249	Percival Prentice T1 (G-APIY) [FA-EL]	Newark Air Museum, Winthorpe
	VR930	Hawker Sea Fury FB11 (8382M)	FAA Museum store, Lee-on-Solent
	VS356	Percival Prentice T1 (G-AOLU)	Scottish Aircraft Collection Trust, Perth
	VS562	Avro Anson T21 (8012M)	Privately owned, Southampton
	VS610	Percival Prentice T1 (G-AOKL) [K-L]	Privately owned, Southend
	VS623	Percival Prentice T1 (G-AOKZ) [KQ-F]	Midland Air Museum, Coventry
	VT229	Gloster Meteor F4 (7151M) [60]	Newark Air Museum, Winthorpe
	VT260	Gloster Meteor F4 (8813M) [67]	Imperial War Museum, Duxford
	VT409	Fairey Firefly AS5 (really WD889)	NE Aircraft Museum, Usworth
	VT812	DH Vampire F3 (7200M) [N]	RAF Museum, Hendon
	VT921	Grunau Baby	Privately owned, Honington
	VT935	Boulton Paul P111A	Midland Air Museum, Coventry
	VV106	VS517 (7175M)	RAF Cosford Aerospace Museum
	VV119	Supermarine 535 (nose only) (7285M)	Lincolnshire Aviation Museum, East Kirkby
	VV217	DH Vampire FB5 (7323M)	No 301 Sqn ATC, Bury St Edmunds
	VV901	Avro Anson T21	Pennine Aviation Museum, Bacup
	VV950	Avro Anson T21	RAF Kinloss Fire Section
	VW453	Gloster Meteor T7 (8703M)	Cotswold Aircraft Restoration Group, RAF Innsworth
	VW985	Auster AOP6 (G-ASEF)	Privately owned, Upper Arncott, Oxon
	VX118	Auster 6A (G-ASNB)	Privately owned, Keevil
	VX185	EE Canberra B(I)8 (nose only)	Science Museum, South Kensington

Serial	Type (alternative identity)	Owner, Operator or Location	Notes
VX250	DH Sea Hornet 21 [48]	Mosquito Aircraft Museum, London Colney	
VX272	Hawker P1052 (7174M)	RAF Cosford Aerospace Museum	
VX275	Slingsby Sedbergh TX1 (8884M)	RAF Museum store, Cardington	
VX461	DH Vampire FB5 (7646M)	RAF Museum Store, Henlow	
VX573	Vickers Valetta C2 (8389M)	RAF Cosford Aerospace Museum	
VX577	Vickers Valetta C2	NE Aircraft Museum, Usworth	
VX580	Vickers Valetta C2	Norfolk & Suffolk Aviation Museum Flixton	
VX595	WS51 Dragonfly HR1 [29]	RAF Museum Store, Henlow	
VX653	Hawker Sea Fury FB11	RAF Museum, Hendon	
VZ304	DH Vampire FB5 (7630M) [S]	Vintage Aircraft Team, Cranfield	
VZ462	Gloster Meteor F8	Second World War Aircraft Preservation Society, store	
VZ467	Gloster Meteor F8 [01]	RAF Shawbury store	
VZ477	Gloster Meteor F8 (nose only)	Kimbolton School CCF, Cambs	
VZ608	Gloster Meteor FR9	Newark Air Museum, Winthorpe	
VZ634	Gloster Meteor T7 (8657M)	Newark Air Museum, Winthorpe	
VZ638	Gloster Meteor T7 (G-JETM)	Brencham Historic Collection, Bournemouth	
VZ728	RS4 Desford Trainer (G-AGOS)	Scottish Aircraft Collection Trust, Perth	
VZ962	WS51 Dragonfly HR1	Cornwall Aero Park, Helston	
VZ965	WS51 Dragonfly HR5	FAA Museum, at RNAS Culdrose	
WA473	VS Attacker F1 [102/J]	FAA Museum, RNAS Yeovilton	
WA576	Bristol Sycamore 3 (G-ALSS/ 7900M)	Privately owned, East Fortune	
WA577	Bristol Sycamore 3 (G-ALST/ 7718M)	NE Aircraft Museum, Usworth	
WA591	Gloster Meteor T7 (7917M) [W]	RAF Woodvale, on display	
WA634	Gloster Meteor T7/8	RAF Cosford Aerospace Museum	
WA638	Gloster Meteor T7	Martin Baker Aircraft, Chalgrove	
WA662	Gloster Meteor T7	MoD(PE) Marshalls, Cambridge	
WA984	Gloster Meteor F8 [A]	Wessex Aviation Society, Wimborne	
WB188	Hawker Hunter F3 (7154M)	RAF Cosford Aerospace Museum	
WB271	Fairey Firefly AS5 [204/R]	RN Historic Flight, RNAS Yeovilton	
WB440	Fairey Firefly AS6	Greater Manchester Museum of Science and Industry	
WB491	Avro Ashton 2 (nose only)	Wales Aircraft Museum, Cardiff	
WB530	DH Devon C2 (8825M)	RAF Swinderby Fire Section	
WB531	DH Devon C2 (G-BLRN)	Privately owned, Staverton	
WB533	DH Devon C2 (G-DEVN) [DA]	British Air Reserve, Lympne	
WB550	DH Chipmunk T10 [F]	RAF FSS, Swinderby	
WB556	DH Chipmunk T10	RAFGSA, Bicester	
WB560	DH Chipmunk T10	RAF No 4 AEF, Exeter	
WB565	DH Chipmunk T10 [X]	AAC BFWF, Middle Wallop	
WB567	DH Chipmunk T10	RAF No 12 AEF, Turnhouse	
WB569	DH Chipmunk T10 [2]	RAF No 1 AEF, Manston	
WB575	DH Chipmunk T10 [907]	RN Flying Grading Flt, Plymouth	
WB584	DH Chipmunk T10 PAX (7706M)	No 327 Sqn ATC, Kilmarnock	
WB586	DH Chipmunk T10 [A]	RAF No 6 AEF, Abingdon	
WB588	DH Chipmunk T10 (G-AOTD) [D]	Shuttleworth Collection, Old Warden	
WB615	DH Chipmunk T10 [E]	AAC BFWF, Middle Wallop	
WB624	DH Chipmunk T10 PAX	The Aeroplane Collection, Warmingham	
WB627	DH Chipmunk T10 [N]	RAF No 5 AEF, Cambridge	
WB647	DH Chipmunk T10 [R]	AAC BFWF, Middle Wallop	
WB652	DH Chipmunk T10 [V]	RAF No 5 AEF, Cambridge	
WB654	DH Chipmunk T10 [14]	RAF No 10 AEF, Woodvale	
WB657	DH Chipmunk T10 [908]	RN Flying Grading Flt, Plymouth	
WB660	DH Chipmunk T10 (G-ARMB)	Privately owned, Teesside	
WB670	DH Chipmunk T10 (8361M)	Newark Air Museum, Winthorpe	
WB671	DH Chipmunk T10 [910]	RN Flying Grading Flt, Plymouth	
WB685	DH Chipmunk T10 PAX	NE Aircraft Museum, Usworth	
WB693	DH Chipmunk T10 [S]	AAC BFWF, Middle Wallop	
WB697	DH Chipmunk T10 [O]	RAF No 3 AEF, Shawbury	
WB732	DH Chipmunk T10 (G-AOJZ/ 'G-ASTD')	Air Service Training, Perth	
WB739	DH Chipmunk T10 [8]	RAF No 8 AEF, Shawbury	
WB754	DH Chipmunk T10 [H]	AAC BFWF, Middle Wallop	
WB758	DH Chipmunk T10 (7729M) [P]	Torbay Aircraft Museum, Paignton	

Notes	Serial	Type (alternative identity)	Owner, Operator or Location
	WB763	DH Chipmunk T10 (G-BBMR) [14]	Southall Technical College
	WD289	DH Chipmunk T10	RAF Gatow Station Flight, Berlin
	WD293	DH Chipmunk T10 PAX (7645M)	No 2308 Sqn ATC, Cwmbran
	WD310	DH Chipmunk T10 [H]	RAF FSS, Swinderby
	WD318	DH Chipmunk T10 PAX (8207M)	No 145 Sqn ATC, Timperley
	WD325	DH Chipmunk T10 [N]	AAC BFWF, Middle Wallop
	WD331	DH Chipmunk T10 [A]	RAF FSS, Swinderby
	WD355	DH Chipmunk T10 PAX (8099M)	No 1955 Sqn ATC, Wells, Somerset
	WD356	DH Chipmunk T10 (7625M)	Privately owned, Huntingdon
	WD363	DH Chipmunk T10 (G-BCIH) [5]	Privately owned, Stansted
	WD373	DH Chipmunk T10 [12]	RAF No 2 AEF, Hurn
	WD374	DH Chipmunk T10 [903]	RN Flying Grading Flt, Plymouth
	WD379	DH Chipmunk T10 (really WB696/G-APLO) [K]	Privately owned, Jersey
	WD390	DH Chipmunk T10 [68]	RAF No 9 AEF, Finningley
	WD413	Avro Anson C 21 (G-BFIR/ 7881M)	Privately owned, Edinburgh
	WD496	HP Hastings C2	A&AEE Boscombe Down Fire Section
	WD646	Gloster Meteor TT20 (8189M) [R]	No 2030 Sqn ATC, Sheldon
	WD686	Gloster Meteor NF11	Imperial War Museum, Duxford
	WD790	Gloster Meteor NF11 (8743M) (nose only)	North East Aircraft Museum, Usworth
	WD889	Fairey Firefly AS6	North East Aircraft Museum, Usworth
	WD931	EE Canberra B2 (nose only)	No 425 Sqn ATC, Aldridge, W Midlands
	WD935	EE Canberra B2 (8440M)	RAF St Athan Historic Aircraft Collection
	WD954	EE Canberra B2 (nose only)	Lincolnshire Aviation Museum, East Kirkby
	WD955	EE Canberra T17 [EM]	RAF No 360 Sqn, Wyton
	WE113	EE Canberra B2 [BJ]	RAF No 231 OCU, Wyton
	WE122	EE Canberra TT18 [845]	RN FRADU, Yeovilton
	WE139	EE Canberra PR3 (8369M)	RAF Museum, Hendon
	WE146	EE Canberra PR3 (cockpit only)	MoD(PE) RAE Farnborough
	WE168	EE Canberra PR3 (8049M)	RAF Manston, on display
	WE173	EE Canberra PR3 (8740M)	RAF Coltishall, BDRT
	WE188	EE Canberra T4	BAe Samlesbury, stored
	WE192	EE Canberra T4 [92]	BAe Samlesbury, stored
	WE569	Auster T7 (G-ASAJ)	Privately owned, Oakington
	WE600	Auster T7 (mod) (7602M)	RAF St Athan Historic Aircraft Collection
	WE925	Gloster Meteor F8	Wales Aircraft Museum, Cardiff
	WE982	Slingsby Prefect TX1 (8781M)	RAF Museum, Hendon
	WF122	Sea Prince T1 (A2673) [575/CU]	Cornwall Aero Park, Helston
	WF125	Sea Prince T1 (A2674)	RN Predannack Fire School
	WF128	Sea Prince T1 (8611M) [CU]	Norfolk & Suffolk Aviation Museum, Flixton
	WF137	Sea Prince C1	Second World War Aircraft Preservation Society, Lasham
	WF219	Hawker Sea Hawk F1 (A2439)	FAA Museum, RNAS Yeovilton
	WF225	Hawker Sea Hawk F1 (A2645) [CU]	RNAS Culdrose, at main gate
	WF259	Hawker Sea Hawk F2 (A2483) [171/A]	Royal Scottish Museum of Flight, East Fortune
	WF299	Hawker Sea Hawk FB3 (A2662/A2509/8164M)	Cornwall Aero Park, Helston
	WF369	Vickers Varsity T1 [F]	Newark Air Museum, Winthorpe
	WF372	Vickers Varsity T1 [T]	Nene Valley Aviation Society, Sibson
	WF376	Vickers Varsity T1	Bristol Airport Fire Section
	WF408	Vickers Varsity T1 (8395M)	RAF Cosford Aerospace Museum
	WF410	Vickers Varsity T1 [F]	Bristol Airport Fire Section
	WF413	Vickers Varsity T1 [V]	CTE, RAF Manston
	WF425	Vickers Varsity T1	Imperial War Museum, Duxford
	WF643	Gloster Meteor F8 [X]	Norfolk & Suffolk Aviation Museum, Flixton
	WF714	Gloster Meteor F8 (Really WK914)	RAeS Medway Branch, Rochester

Serial	Type (alternative identity)	Owner, Operator or Location	Notes
WF784	Gloster Meteor T7 (7895M)	RAF Quedgeley, at main gate	
WF791	Gloster Meteor T7	RAF CFS, Scampton	
WF825	Gloster Meteor T7 (8359M) [Z]	No 2491 Sqn ATC, RAF Lyneham	
WF877	Gloster Meteor T7	Torbay Aircraft Museum, Paignton	
WF890	EE Canberra T17 [EJ]	RAF No 360 Sqn, Wyton	
WF911	EE Canberra B2 (nose only)	Pennine Aviation Museum, Bacup	
WF916	EE Canberra T17 [EL]	RAF No 360 Sqn, Wyton	
WF922	EE Canberra PR3	Midland Air Museum, Coventry	
WG300	DH Chipmunk T10 PAX	RAFGSA, Bicester	
WG303	DH Chipmunk T10 (8208M)	RAFGSA, Bicester	
WG307	DH Chipmunk T10 (G-BCYJ)	Privately owned, Lossiemouth	
WG308	DH Chipmunk T10	RAF No 7 AEF, Newton	
WG316	DH Chipmunk T10 (G-BCAH)	Privately owned, Wyberton	
WG321	DH Chipmunk T10 [G]	AAC BFWF, Middle Wallop	
WG323	DH Chipmunk T10 [F]	AAC BFWF, Middle Wallop	
WG348	DH Chipmunk T10 (G-BBMV)	Privately owned, Thruxton	
WG350	DH Chipmunk T10 (G-BPAL)	Privately owned, Denham	
WG362	DH Chipmunk T10 PAX (8437M/ 8630M)	RAF FSS, Swinderby	
WG403	DH Chipmunk T10 [O]	AAC BFWF, Middle Wallop	
WG407	DH Chipmunk T10 [67]	RAF No 9 AEF, Finningley	
WG418	DH Chipmunk T10 PAX (8209M/G-ATDY)	RAF No 10 AEF, Woodvale	
WG419	DH Chipmunk T10 PAX (8206M)	RAF Finningley	
WG422	DH Chipmunk T10 (G-BFAX/ 8394M) [16]	Privately owned, Breighton	
WG430	DH Chipmunk T10 [1]	RAF No 1 AEF, Manston	
WG432	DH Chipmunk T10 [L]	AAC BFWF, Middle Wallop	
WG458	DH Chipmunk T10	RAF Shawbury store	
WG463	DH Chipmunk T10 PAX (8363M)	No 188 Sqn ATC, Ipswich	
WG464	DH Chipmunk T10 PAX (8364M)	No 131 Sqn ATC, Newcastle	
WG465	DH Chipmunk T10 (G-BCEY)	Privately owned, Southend	
WG466	DH Chipmunk T10	RAF Shawbury store	
WG469	DH Chipmunk T10	RAF No 7 AEF, Newton	
WG471	DH Chipmunk T10 PAX (8210M)	RAF No 11 AEF, Leeming	
WG477	DH Chipmunk T10 PAX (8362M)	No 281 Sqn ATC, Birkdale	
WG478	DH Chipmunk T10 [J]	RAF Shawbury store	
WG479	DH Chipmunk T10 [K]	RAF FSS, Swinderby	
WG480	DH Chipmunk T10 [D]	RAF FSS, Swinderby	
WG486	DH Chipmunk T10	RAF Shawbury store	
WG511	Avro Shackleton T4 (nose only)	Cornwall Aero Park, Helston	
WG655	Hawker Sea Fury T20 [910/GN]	RN Historic Flight, RNAS Yeovilton	
WG677	EE Canberra B2 (nose only)	RNAS Yeovilton, Fire Section	
WG718	WS51 Dragonfly HR5 (A2531) [934/-]	Wales Aircraft Museum, Cardiff	
WG719	WS51 Dragonfly HR5 (G-BRMA) [902]	British Rotorcraft Museum, Weston-super-Mare	
WG724	WS51 Dragonfly HR5 [932]	NE Aircraft Museum, Usworth	
WG725	WS51 Dragonfly HR3 (7703M)	Cornwall Aero Park, Helston	
WG751	WS51 Dragonfly HR5	Privately owned, Ramsgreave, Lancs	
WG752	WS51 Dragonfly HR3	Imperial War Museum, Duxford	
WG760	English Electric P1A (7755M)	RAF Cosford Aerospace Museum	
WG763	English Electric P1A (7816M)	Greater Manchester Museum of Science and Industry	
WG768	Short SB5 (8005M)	RAF Cosford Aerospace Museum	
WG774	BAC 221	Science Museum, RNAS Yeovilton	
WG777	Fairey FD2 (7986M)	RAF Cosford Aerospace Museum	
WG789	EE Canberra B2	Privately owned, Burgess Hill	
WH132	Gloster Meteor T7 (7906M) [J]	No 276 Sqn ATC, Chelmsford	
WH166	Gloster Meteor T7 (8052M)	RAF Digby, at main gate	
WH291	Gloster Meteor F8	Second World War Aircraft Preservation Society, Lasham	
WH301	Gloster Meteor F8 (7930M) [T]	RAF Museum, Hendon	
WH364	Gloster Meteor F8 (8169M)	RAF Kemble, at main gate	
WH453	Gloster Meteor D16 [L]	MoD(PE) RAE Llanbedr	

Notes	Serial	Type (alternative identity)	Owner, Operator or Location
	WH646	EE Canberra T17 [EG]	RAF No 360 Sqn, Wyton
	WH657	EE Canberra B2	Brenzett Aeronautical Collection
	WH664	EE Canberra T17 [EH]	RAF No 360 Sqn, Wyton
	WH665	EE Canberra T17 (8763M) [J]	BAe Samlesbury
	WH670	EE Canberra B2 [CB]	RAF No 100 Sqn, Wyton
	WH699	EE Canberra B2T (8755M) (really WJ637)	RAFC Cranwell, Trenchard Hall on display
	WH703	EE Canberra B2 (8490M) [S]	RAF Abingdon BDRF
	WH718	EE Canberra TT18 [CW]	RAF No 100 Sqn, Wyton
	WH724	EE Canberra T19 (nose only)	RAF Shawbury Fire Section
	WH725	EE Canberra B2	Imperial War Museum, Duxford
	WH734	EE Canberra B(TT)2	Flight Refuelling Ltd, Llanbedr
	WH740	EE Canberra T17 (8762M) [K]	RAF No 2 SoTT, Cosford
	WH773	EE Canberra PR7 (8696M)	No 2331 Sqn ATC, RAF Wyton
	WH774	EE Canberra PR7	MoD(PE) RAE Bedford
	WH775	EE Canberra PR7 (8128M/8868M)	RAF No 2 SoTT, Cosford
	WH779	EE Canberra PR7 [CK]	RAF No 100 Sqn, Wyton
	WH780	EE Canberra T22 [853]	RN, St Athan store
	WH791	EE Canberra PR7 (8187M)	RAF Cottesmore, at main gate
	WH794	EE Canberra PR7 (8652M)	RAF FF&SS, Catterick
	WH796	EE Canberra PR7 (nose only)	Bomber County Aviation Museum, Cleethorpes
	WH797	EE Canberra T22 [851]	RN, St Athan store
	WH798	EE Canberra PR7	Wales Aircraft Museum, Cardiff
	WH801	EE Canberra T22 [850]	RN, St Athan store
	WH803	EE Canberra T22 [856]	RN, St Athan store
	WH840	EE Canberra T4 (8350M)	RAF Locking, at main gate
	WH844	EE Canberra T4	MoD(PE) RAE Farnborough, stored
	WH846	EE Canberra T4	BAe Samlesbury, stored
	WH848	EE Canberra T4 [BD]	RAF No 231 OCU, Wyton
	WH849	EE Canberra T4 [BE]	RAF No 231 OCU, Wyton
	WH850	EE Canberra T4	BAe Samlesbury, stored
	WH854	EE Canberra T4 (nose only)	Martin Baker Aircraft, Chalgrove
	WH863	EE Canberra T17 (8693M)	RAF Marham, BDRT
	WH869	EE Canberra B2 (8515M)	RAF Abingdon BDRF
	WH876	EE Canberra D14	MoD(PE) Boscombe Down, store
	WH887	EE Canberra TT18 [847]	RN FRADU, Yeovilton
	WH902	EE Canberra T17 [EK]	RAF No 360 Sqn, Wyton
	WH903	EE Canberra B2 (8584M) (nose only)	RAF Exhibition Flight, Abingdon
	WH904	EE Canberra T19 [04]	Newark Air Museum, Winthorpe
	WH911	EE Canberra B2	Wales Aircraft Museum, Cardiff
	WH914	EE Canberra B2 (G-27-373) [U]	BAe Samlesbury, stored
	WH919	EE Canberra B2	RAF St Athan, stored
	WH946	EE Canberra B6 (Mod) (8185M)	Bomber County Aviation Museum, Cleethorpes
	WH952	EE Canberra B6	Royal Artillery Museum, Woolwich
	WH953	EE Canberra B6	MoD(PE) RAE Bedford
	WH957	EE Canberra E15 (8869M) [CX]	RAF No 2 SoTT, Cosford
	WH960	EE Canberra B15 (8344M) [A]	RAF No 2 SoTT, Cosford
	WH964	EE Canberra E15 (8870M) [V]	RAF No 2 SoTT, Cosford
	WH972	EE Canberra E15 [CM]	RAF No 100 Sqn, Wyton
	WH981	EE Canberra E15 [CN]	RAF No 100 Sqn, Wyton
	WH983	EE Canberra E15 [CP]	RAF No 100 Sqn, Wyton
	WH984	EE Canberra B15 (8101M) [E]	RAF No 2 SoTT, Cosford
	WH991	WS51 Dragonfly HR5	Privately owned, Tattershall Thorpe
	WJ231	Hawker Sea Fury FB11 [115/0]	FAA Museum, RNAS Yeovilton
	WJ237	WAR Sea Fury replica (G-BLTG) [113/0]	Privately owned, Thruxton
	WJ288	Hawker Sea Fury FB11 (G-SALY) [029]	Privately owned, Duxford
	WJ329	HP Hastings C2	RAF Leeming Fire Section
	WJ350	Percival Sea Prince C2	Guernsey Airport Fire Section
	WJ358	Auster AOP6 (G-ARYD)	Museum of Army Flying, Middle Wallop
	WJ565	EE Canberra T17 (8871M) [C]	RAF No 2 SoTT, Cosford
	WJ567	EE Canberra B2 [CC]	RAF No 100 Sqn, Wyton
	WJ573	EE Canberra B2 (7656M)	RAF Museum Store, Henlow
	WJ574	EE Canberra TT18 [844]	RN, St Athan store

Serial	*Type (alternative identity)*	*Owner, Operator or Location*	*Notes*
WJ576	EE Canberra T17	Wales Aircraft Museum, Cardiff	
WJ581	EE Canberra T17	Wales Aircraft Museum, Cardiff	
WJ603	EE Canberra B2 (8664M) [G]	RAF Wattisham Fire Section	
WJ607	EE Canberra T17 [EB]	RAF No 360 Sqn, Wyton	
WJ614	EE Canberra TT18 [846]	RN FRADU, Yeovilton	
WJ629	EE Canberra TT18 (8747M) [845]	RAF Chivenor, BDRT	
WJ630	EE Canberra T17 [ED]	RAF No 360 Sqn, Wyton	
WJ633	EE Canberra T17 [EF]	RAF No 360 Sqn, Wyton	
WJ635	EE Canberra B2	RAF St Mawgan Fire Section	
WJ636	EE Canberra TT18 [842]	RN FRADU, Yeovilton	
WJ639	EE Canberra TT18 [39]	BAe Samlesbury, stored	
WJ640	EE Canberra B2 (8722M) [L]	RAF No 2 SoTT, Cosford	
WJ676	EE Canberra B2 (7796M)	Princess Alexandra RAF Hospital, Wroughton	
WJ677	EE Canberra B2 (nose only)	RNAS Yeovilton Fire Section	
WJ678	EE Canberra B2 (8864M) [CF]	RAF Abingdon, BDRF	
WJ680	EE Canberra TT18 [CT]	RAF No 100 Sqn, Wyton	
WJ681	EE Canberra B2T (8735M)	RAF Brawdy Fire Section	
WJ682	EE Canberra TT18 [CU]	RAF No 100 Sqn, Wyton	
WJ715	EE Canberra TT18 [CV]	RAF No 100 Sqn, Wyton	
WJ717	EE Canberra TT18 [841]	RN, St Athan store	
WJ721	EE Canberra TT18 [21]	BAe Samlesbury, stored	
WJ722	EE Canberra B2	Privately owned, Macclesfield	
WJ728	EE Canberra B2	RAE Farnborough, derelict	
WJ731	EE Canberra B2 [BK]	RAF No 231 OCU, Wyton	
WJ756	EE Canberra E15 [CL]	RAF No 100 Sqn, Wyton	
WJ775	EE Canberra B6 (8581M) [Z]	CSDE, RAF Swanton Morley	
WJ815	EE Canberra PR7 (8729M)	RAF Coningsby Fire Section	
WJ817	EE Canberra PR7 (8695M)	RAF Wyton, BDRT	
WJ821	EE Canberra PR7 (8668M)	Bassingbourn, on display	
WJ825	EE Canberra PR7 (8697M)	RAF FF&SS, Catterick	
WJ861	EE Canberra T4 [BF]	RAF No 231 OCU, Wyton	
WJ863	EE Canberra T4 (nose only)	Cambridge Airport Fire Section	
WJ865	EE Canberra T4	RAE Apprentice School, Farnborough	
WJ866	EE Canberra T4 [BL]	RAF No 231 OCU, Wyton	
WJ867	EE Canberra T4 (8643M)	RAF Abingdon, BDRF	
WJ870	EE Canberra T4 (8683M)	RAF St Mawgan, BDRT	
WJ872	EE Canberra T4 (8492M) (nose only)	No 327 Sqn ATC, Kilmarnock	
WJ874	EE Canberra T4 [BM]	RAF No 231 OCU, Wyton	
WJ876	EE Canberra T4 (nose only)	RAF Exhibition Flight, Abingdon	
WJ877	EE Canberra T4 [BG]	RAF No 231 OCU, Wyton	
WJ879	EE Canberra T4 [BH]	RAF No 231 OCU, Wyton	
WJ880	EE Canberra T4 (8491M) [39] (nose only)	Privately owned, North Weald ARF	
WJ893	Vickers Varsity T1	RAE Aberporth Fire Section	
WJ902	Vickers Varsity T1 [C]	RAF Wittering Fire Section	
WJ903	Vickers Varsity T1 [C]	Dumfries & Galloway Aviation Museum, Tinwald Downs	
WJ907	Vickers Varsity T1 [G]	Norwich Airport Fire Section	
WJ944	Vickers Varsity T1	Wales Aircraft Museum, Cardiff	
WJ945	Vickers Varsity T1 (G-BEDV) [21]	Duxford Aviation Society	
WJ975	EE Canberra T19 [S]	Bomber County Aviation Museum, Cleethorpes	
WJ977	EE Canberra T17 (8761M) [R]	RAF Wyton	
WJ981	EE Canberra T17 [EN]	RAF No 360 Sqn, Wyton	
WJ986	EE Canberra T17 [EP]	RAF No 360 Sqn, Wyton	
WJ992	EE Canberra T4	MoD(PE) RAE Bedford	
WK102	EE Canberra T17 [EQ] (8780M)	RAF No 2 SoTT, Cosford	
WK111	EE Canberra T17 [EA]	RAF No 360 Sqn, Wyton	
WK118	EE Canberra TT18 [CQ]	RAF No 100 Sqn, Wyton	
WK122	EE Canberra TT18 [22]	BAe Samlesbury, stored	
WK123	EE Canberra TT18 [840]	RN FRADU, Yeovilton	
WK124	EE Canberra TT18 [CR]	RAF No 100 Sqn, Wyton	
WK126	EE Canberra TT18 [843]	RN FRADU, Yeovilton	
WK127	EE Canberra TT18 [CS]	RAF No 100 Sqn, Wyton	
WK128	EE Canberra B2	Flight Refuelling Ltd, Llanbedr	
WK142	EE Canberra TT18 [848]	RN FRADU, Yeovilton	
WK143	EE Canberra B2	Flight Refuelling Ltd, Hurn	

Notes	*Serial*	*Type (alternative identity)*	*Owner, Operator or Location*
	WK145	EE Canberra B2	RAE Llanbedr, Fire Section
	WK146	EE Canberra B2 (nose only)	RAF Exhibition Flight, Abingdon
	WK162	EE Canberra B2 [A] (8887M)	RAF Marham
	WK163	EE Canberra B6	MoD(PE) RAE Bedford
	WK198	VS Swift F4 (7428M)	North East Aircraft Museum, Usworth
	WK275	VS Swift F4	Privately owned, Upper Hill, nr Leominster
	WK277	VS Swift FR5 (7719M) [N]	Newark Air Museum, Winthorpe
	WK281	VS Swift FR5 (7712M) [S]	RAF St Athan Historic Aircraft Collection
	WK511	DH Chipmunk T10 [905]	RN, Shawbury store
	WK512	DH Chipmunk T10 [A]	AAC BFWF, Middle Wallop
Teesside 4/87	WK517	DH Chipmunk T10 [84]	RAF No 11 AEF, Teesside
	WK518	DH Chipmunk T10	RAF Battle of Britain Flight, Coningsby
	WK522	DH Chipmunk T10 (G-BCOU)	Privately owned, Audley End
	WK549	DH Chipmunk T10 [Y]	Privately owned, Currock Hill
	WK550	DH Chipmunk T10 [J]	RAF FSS, Swinderby
	WK554	DH Chipmunk T10	RAF No 1 AEF, Manston
	WK559	DH Chipmunk T10 [M]	AAC BFWF, Middle Wallop
	WK562	DH Chipmunk T10 [T]	RAF No 3 AEF, Filton
	WK570	DH Chipmunk T10 PAX (8211M)	RAF No 2 AEF, Hurn
	WK572	DH Chipmunk T10 [X]	RAF No 3 AEF, Filton
	WK574	DH Chipmunk T10 [738/VL]	RNAS Yeovilton Station Flight
	WK575	DH Chipmunk T10 PAX [F]	No 301 Sqn ATC, Bury St Edmunds
	WK576	DH Chipmunk T10 PAX (8357M)	No 1206 Sqn ATC, Lichfield
	WK585	DH Chipmunk T10	RAF No 12 AEF, Turnhouse
	WK586	DH Chipmunk T10	RAF Shawbury store
	WK587	DH Chipmunk T10 PAX (8212M)	St Ignatius Coll, Enfield
	WK589	DH Chipmunk T10 [C]	RAF No 6 AEF, Abingdon
	WK590	DH Chipmunk T10 [69]	RAF No 9 AEF, Finningley
	WK608	DH Chipmunk T10 [906]	RN Flying Grading Flt, Plymouth
	WK609	DH Chipmunk T10 [L]	RAF No 3 AEF, Filton
	WK611	DH Chipmunk T10 (G-ARWB)	Privately owned, Shoreham
	WK613	DH Chipmunk T10 [P]	Pennine Aviation Museum, Bacup
	WK620	DH Chipmunk T10 [T]	AAC BFWF, Middle Wallop
	WK622	DH Chipmunk T10 (G-BCZH)	Privately owned, Norwich
	WK624	DH Chipmunk T10 [12]	RAF No 10 AEF, Woodvale
	WK626	DH Chipmunk T10 PAX (8213M)	No 358 Sqn ATC, Welling, Gtr London
	WK630	DH Chipmunk T10 [11]	RAF No 2 AEF, Hurn
	WK633	DH Chipmunk T10 [B]	RAF FSS, Swinderby
	WK634	DH Chipmunk T10 [902]	RN Flying Grading Flt, Plymouth
	WK635	DH Chipmunk T10	RAF
	WK638	DH Chipmunk T10 [83]	RAF No 11 AEF, Teesside
	WK639	DH Chipmunk T10 [10]	RAF No 10 AEF, Woodvale
	WK640	DH Chipmunk T10 [C]	RAF FSS, Swinderby
	WK642	DH Chipmunk T10	RAF No 4 AEF, Exeter
	WK643	DH Chipmunk T10 [G]	RAF FSS, Swinderby
	WK654	Gloster Meteor F8 (8092M) [X]	RAF Neatishead, at main gate
	WK800	Gloster Meteor D16 [Z]	MoD(PE) RAE Llanbedr
	WK935	Gloster Meteor Prone Pilot (7869M)	RAF Cosford Aerospace Museum
	WK968	Gloster Meteor F8 (8053M) [A]	RAF Odiham, at main gate
	WK991	Gloster Meteor F8 (7825M)	Imperial War Museum, Duxford
	WL131	Gloster Meteor F8 (nose only) (7751M)	Privately owned, Guernsey
	WL168	Gloster Meteor F8 (7750M) [A]	RAF St Athan Historic Aircraft Collection
	WL181	Gloster Meteor F8 [X]	North East Aircraft Museum, Usworth
	WL332	Gloster Meteor T7	Wales Aircraft Museum, Cardiff
	WL345	Gloster Meteor T7	Privately owned, Hastings
	WL349	Gloster Meteor T7 [Z]	Staverton Airport, on display
	WL360	Gloster Meteor T7 (7920M) [G]	RAF Locking, at main gate
	WL375	Gloster Meteor T7	Dumfries & Galloway Aviation Museum, Tinwald Downs
	WL405	Gloster Meteor T7	North East Aircraft Museum, Usworth

Serial	Type (alternative identity)	Owner, Operator or Location	Notes
WL419	Gloster Meteor T7	Martin Baker Aircraft, Chalgrove	
WL505	DH Vampire FB9 (7705M)	RAF St Athan Historic Aircraft Collection	
WL626	Vickers Varsity T1 (G-BHDD) [P]	East Midlands Aeropark	
WL627	Vickers Varsity T1 (8488M) [D]	RAF Police Dog Training School, Newton	
WL635	Vickers Varsity T1	RAF Machrihanish Police School	
WL679	Vickers Varsity T1	MoD(PE) RAE Farnborough	
WL732	BP Sea Balliol T21	RAF Cosford Aerospace Museum	
WL738	Avro Shackleton MR2C (8567M)	RAF Lossiemouth, at main gate	
WL741	Avro Shackleton AEW2 (8692M)	CTE, RAF Manston	
WL747	Avro Shackleton AEW2	RAF No 8 Sqn, Lossiemouth	
WL754	Avro Shackleton AEW2 (8665M) [54]	RAF Valley, Fire Section	
WL756	Avro Shackleton AEW2	RAF No 8 Sqn, Lossiemouth	
WL757	Avro Shackleton AEW2	RAF No 8 Sqn, Lossiemouth	
WL790	Avro Shackleton AEW2	RAF No 8 Sqn, Lossiemouth	
WL795	Avro Shackleton AEW2 (8753M)	RAF St Mawgan, on display	
WL798	Avro Shackleton MR2C (8114M) [Z]	RAF Lossiemouth	
WL925	Slingsby Cadet TX3 (really WV925)	Air Cadet Recruiting Team, Cosford	
WM145	AW Meteor NF11 (nose only)	N. Yorks Recovery Group, Chop Gate	
WM167	AW Meteor TT20 (G-LOSM) [M]	Brencham Historic Collection, Biggin Hill	
WM223	AW Meteor TT20	Second World War Aircraft Preservation Society, Lasham	
WM224	AW Meteor TT20 (8177M)	Privately owned, North Weald	
WM292	AW Meteor TT20 [841]	Wales Aircraft Museum, Cardiff	
WM366	AW Meteor NF13 (4X-FNA)	Second World War Aircraft Preservation Society, store	
WM367	AW Meteor NF13	Privately owned, Powick, Hereford & Worcs	
WM571	DH Sea Venom FAW 21 [742/VL]	Wessex Aviation Society, Wimborne	
WM729	DH Vampire NF10 (pod only) [A]	Privately owned, Ruislip	
WM913	Hawker Sea Hawk FB5 (A2510/8162M) [616]	Newark Air Museum, Winthorpe	
WM961	Hawker Sea Hawk FB5 [J] (A2517)	Torbay Aircraft Museum, Paignton	
WM969	Hawker Sea Hawk FB5 (A2530)	Imperial War Museum, Duxford	
WM983	Hawker Sea Hawk FGA6 (really XE489)	Chilton Cantelo House School, Somerset	
WM993	Hawker Sea Hawk FB5 (A2522) [034]	Privately owned, Peasedown St John, Avon	
WM994	Hawker Sea Hawk FB5 (A2503/G-SEAH)	Brencham Historic Collection, Hurn	
WN108	Hawker Sea Hawk FB5 [033]	Shorts Apprentice School, Belfast	
WN149	BP Balliol T2 (nose only)	Pennine Aviation Museum, Bacup	
WN464	Fairey Gannet AS6 (A2540)	Cornwall Aero Park, Helston	
WN493	WS51 Dragonfly HR5	FAA Museum, RNAS Yeovilton	
WN499	WS51 Dragonfly HR5 [Y]	Torbay Aircraft Museum, Paignton	
WN516	BP Balliol T2	NE Aircraft Museum, Usworth	
WN534	BP Balliol T2 (nose only)	Pennine Aviation Museum, Bacup	
WN901	Hawker Hunter F2 (7543M)	RAF Newton Fire Section	
WN904	Hawker Hunter F2 (7544M) [3]	Imperial War Museum, Duxford	
WN907	Hawker Hunter F2 (7416M)	Staravia, Ascot	
WP180	Hawker Hunter F5 (7582M/ 8473M) [K] (really WP190)	RAF Stanbridge, at main gate	
WP185	Hawker Hunter F5 (7583M)	RAF Museum, Hendon	
WP232	DH Vampire NF10 (nose only) [T]	Privately owned, Ecclesfield, S. Yorks	
WP250	DH Vampire NF10 (nose only)	Friends of Biggin Hill, Sevenoaks	

Notes	Serial	Type (alternative identity)	Owner, Operator or Location
	WP270	EoN Eton TX1 (8598M)	Greater Manchester Museum of Science and Industry
	WP271	EoN Eton TX1	Stored Keevil
	WP309	Percival Sea Prince T1 [570/CU]	RNAS Yeovilton Fire Section
	WP314	Percival Sea Prince T1 (8634M) [573/CU]	RAF Police Dog School, Syerston
	WP320	Percival Sea Prince T1 [573/CU]	RAF Leuchars Fire Section
	WP321	Percival Sea Prince T1 (G-BRFC) [750/CU]	Privately owned, Bourn
	WP503	WS51 Dragonfly HR3 [901]	Privately owned, Storwood, South Yorks
	WP515	EE Canberra B2 [CD]	RAF No 100 Sqn, Wyton
	WP772	DH Chipmunk T10 [Q]	AAC BFWF, Middle Wallop
	WP776	DH Chipmunk T10 [817]	RNAS Culdrose Station Flight
	WP778	DH Chipmunk T10 (G-BBNF)	Privately owned, Little Bursted, Essex
	WP786	DH Chipmunk T10 [D]	RAF Shawbury store
	WP788	DH Chipmunk T10 (G-BCHL)	Privately owned, Sleap
	WP790	DH Chipmunk T10 (G-BBNC) [T]	Mosquito Aircraft Museum, London Colney
	WP795	DH Chipmunk T10 [901]	RN Flying Grading Flt, Plymouth
	WP801	DH Chipmunk T10 [911]	RN Flying Grading Flt, Plymouth
	WP803	DH Chipmunk T10	RN, Shawbury store
	WP805	DH Chipmunk T10 [D]	RAF No 6 AEF, Abingdon
	WP808	DH Chipmunk T10 (G-BDEU)	Privately owned, Binham
	WP809	DH Chipmunk T10 [78]	RN Lee-on-Solent Station Flight
	WP833	DH Chipmunk T10	RAF No 4 AEF, Exeter
	WP837	DH Chipmunk T10 [L]	RAF No 5 AEF, Cambridge
	WP839	DH Chipmunk T10 [A]	RAF No 8 AEF, Shawbury
	WP840	DH Chipmunk T10 [9]	RAF No 2 AEF, Hurn
	WP843	DH Chipmunk T10 (G-BDBP)	Privately owned, Tollerton
	WP844	DH Chipmunk T10	RAF Shawbury store
	WP845	DH Chipmunk T10 PAX	No 1329 Sqn ATC, Stroud
	WP855	DH Chipmunk T10 [3]	RAF No 1 AEF, Manston
	WP856	DH Chipmunk T10 [904]	RN Flying Grading Flt, Plymouth
	WP857	DH Chipmunk T10 (G-BDRJ) [24]	Privately owned, Elstree
	WP859	DH Chipmunk T10 [E]	RAF No 8 AEF, Shawbury
	WP860	DH Chipmunk T10	RAF No 12 AEF, Turnhouse
	WP863	DH Chipmunk T10 PAX (8360M)	No 1304 Sqn ATC, Chippenham
	WP869	DH Chipmunk T10 PAX (8215M)	RAF
	WP871	DH Chipmunk T10	RAF Shawbury store
	WP872	DH Chipmunk T10	RAF Shawbury store
	WP896	DH Chipmunk T10 [11]	RAF No 10 AEF, Woodvale
	WP900	DH Chipmunk T10 [13]	RAF No 10 AEF, Woodvale
	WP901	DH Chipmunk T10 [B]	RAF No 6 AEF, Abingdon
	WP903	DH Chipmunk T10 (G-BCGC)	RN Gliding Club, Culdrose
	WP904	DH Chipmunk T10 [909]	RN Flying Grading Flt, Plymouth
	WP906	DH Chipmunk T10 [816]	RNAS Culdrose Station Flight
	WP907	DH Chipmunk T10 PAX (7970M)	Privately owned, Reading
	WP912	DH Chipmunk T10 (8467M)	RAF Cosford Aerospace Museum
	WP914	DH Chipmunk T10 [E]	RAF No 6 AEF, Abingdon
	WP920	DH Chipmunk T10 [10]	RAF No 2 AEF, Hurn
	WP925	DH Chipmunk T10 [C]	AAC BFWF, Middle Wallop
	WP927	DH Chipmunk T10 PAX (8216M/G-ATJK)	No 247 Sqn ATC, Ashton-under-Lyne
	WP928	DH Chipmunk T10 [D]	AAC BFWF, Middle Wallop
	WP929	DH Chipmunk T10 [F]	RAF No 8 AEF, Shawbury
	WP930	DH Chipmunk T10 [J]	AAC BFWF, Middle Wallop
	WP962	DH Chipmunk T10 [V]	RAF No 3 AEF, Filton
	WP964	DH Chipmunk T10	AAC BFWF, Middle Wallop
	WP967	DH Chipmunk T10	RAF No 12 AEF, Turnhouse
	WP970	DH Chipmunk T10 [T]	RAF No 5 AEF, Cambridge
	WP972	DH Chipmunk T10 PAX (8667M)	CSDE, RAF Swanton Morley
	WP974	DH Chipmunk T10 [N]	RAF No 3 AEF, Filton
	WP977	DH Chipmunk T10 (G-BHRD)	Privately owned, Leicester
	WP978	DH Chipmunk T10 PAX (7467M)	RAF No 2 AEF, Hurn
	WP979	DH Chipmunk T10 [J]	CSDE, RAF Swanton Morley
	WP980	DH Chipmunk T10 [E]	RAF FSS, Swinderby
	WP981	DH Chipmunk T10	AAC, Shawbury store
	WP983	DH Chipmunk T10 [B]	AAC BFWF, Middle Wallop

Serial	Type (alternative identity)	Owner, Operator or Location	Notes
WP984	DH Chipmunk T10	RAF No 7 AEF, Newton	
WR410	DH Venom FB54 (J1790/G-BLKA)	Privately owned, Cranfield	
WR539	DH Venom FB4 (8399M) [F]	Wales Aircraft Museum, Cardiff	
WR960	Avro Shackleton AEW2 (8772M)	Greater Manchester Museum of Science and Industry	
WR963	Avro Shackleton AEW2	RAF No 8 Sqn, Lossiemouth	
WR965	Avro Shackleton AEW2	RAF No 8 Sqn, Lossiemouth	
WR967	Avro Shackleton MR2C (8398M)	RAF Lossiemouth, as a simulator	
WR971	Avro Shackleton MR3 (8119M) [Q]	RAF No 2 SoTT, Cosford	
WR974	Avro Shackleton MR3 (8117M) [K]	RAF No 2 SoTT, Cosford	
WR977	Avro Shackleton MR3 (8186M) [B]	Newark Air Museum, Winthorpe	
WR982	Avro Shackleton MR3 (8106M) [J]	RAF No 2 SoTT, Cosford	
WR985	Avro Shackleton MR3 (8103M) [H]	RAF No 2 SoTT, Cosford	
WS103	Gloster Meteor T7 [709/VL]	FAA Museum store, Wroughton	
WS692	Gloster Meteor NF12 (7605M) [C]	Newark Air Museum, Winthorpe	
WS726	Gloster Meteor NF14 (7960M) [G]	No 1855 Sqn ATC, Royton	
WS739	Gloster Meteor NF14 (7961M)	Newark Air Museum, Winthorpe	
WS760	Gloster Meteor NF14 (7964M) [Z-14]	Privately owned, Cranfield	
WS774	Gloster Meteor NF14 (7959M)	RAF Hospital Ely, at main gate	
WS776	Gloster Meteor NF14 (7716M) [K]	RAF North Luffenham, at main gate	
WS792	Gloster Meteor NF14 (7965M) [K]	RAF Carlisle, at main gate	
WS807	Gloster Meteor NF14 (7973M) [N]	RAF Watton, at main gate	
WS832	Gloster Meteor NF14 [W]	Solway Aviation Society, Carlisle Airport	
WS838	Gloster Meteor NF14	Midland Air Museum, Coventry	
WS840	Gloster Meteor NF14 (7969M)	Aldergrove Fire Section	
WS843	Gloster Meteor NF14 (7937M) [Y]	RAF St Athan Historic Aircraft Collection	
WS844	Gloster Meteor NF14 (7967M) [JCF] (really WS788)	RAF Leeming, at main gate	
WT121	Douglas Skyraider AEW1 [415/CU]	FAA Museum, RNAS Yeovilton	
WT212	EE Canberra B2	Lovaux Ltd, Macclesfield	
WT301	EE Canberra B6 (Mod)	Defence School, Chattenden	
WT305	EE Canberra B6 (8511M) [X]	RAF Wyton, at main gate	
WT308	EE Canberra B(I)6	MoD(PE) RAE Farnborough, stored	
WT309	EE Canberra B(I)6	MoD(PE) A&AEE Boscombe Down	
WT327	EE Canberra B(I)8	MoD(PE) RAE Bedford	
WT333	EE Canberra B(I)8	RAE Farnborough	
WT339	EE Canberra B(I)8 (8198M)	RAFC Cranwell North Fire Section	
WT346	EE Canberra B(I)8 (8197M)	RAF Cosford Aerospace Museum	
WT478	EE Canberra T4 [BA]	RAF No 231 OCU, Wyton	
WT480	EE Canberra T4 [BC]	RAF No 231 OCU, Wyton	
WT483	EE Canberra T4 [83]	BAe Samlesbury, stored	
WT486	EE Canberra T4 (8102M) [C]	Aldergrove Fire Section	
WT488	EE Canberra T4	BAe Samlesbury, stored	
WT507	EE Canberra PR7 (8548M) [44] (nose only)	No 384 Sqn ATC, Mansfield	
WT509	EE Canberra PR7 [CG]	RAF No 100 Sqn, Wyton	
WT510	EE Canberra T22 [854]	RN, St Athan store	
WT518	EE Canberra PR7 (8691M)	Wales Aircraft Museum, Cardiff	
WT519	EE Canberra PR7 [CH]	RAF No 100 Sqn, Wyton	
WT520	EE Canberra PR7 (8094M/8184M) [20]	RAF Swinderby, on display	
WT525	EE Canberra T22 [855]	RN, St Athan store	
WT532	EE Canberra PR7 (8728M/ 8890M)	RAF No 2 SoTT, Cosford	
WT534	EE Canberra PR7 (8549M) [43] (nose only)	No 489 Sqn ATC, Solihull	

Notes	Serial	Type (alternative identity)	Owner, Operator or Location
	WT535	EE Canberra T22 [852]	RN, St Athan store
	WT536	EE Canberra PR7 (8063M) [F]	RAF No 2 SoTT, Cosford
	WT537	EE Canberra PR7	BAe Samlesbury, stored
	WT538	EE Canberra PR7 [CJ]	RAF No 100 Sqn, Wyton
	WT555	Hawker Hunter F1 (7499M)	RAF Cosford Aerospace Museum
	WT569	Hawker Hunter F1 (7491M)	No 2117 Sqn ATC, Kenfig Hill, Mid-Glamorgan
	WT612	Hawker Hunter F1 (7496M)	RAF Henlow on display
	WT619	Hawker Hunter F1 (7525M)	Greater Manchester Museum of Science and Industry
	WT648	Hawker Hunter F1 (7530M) (nose section)	RAF St Athan Fire Section
	WT651	Hawker Hunter F1 (7532M) [C]	RAF Lawford Heath, Warwicks, on display
	WT660	Hawker Hunter F1 (7421M) [C]	RAF Carlisle, at main gate
	WT680	Hawker Hunter F1 (7533M) [Z]	No 1429 Sqn ATC at RAE Aberporth
	WT684	Hawker Hunter F1 (7422M)	RAF Brize Norton Fire Section
	WT694	Hawker Hunter F1 (7510M)	RAF Newton, at main gate
	WT711	Hawker Hunter GA11 [833/DD]	RNAS Culdrose, SAH
	WT722	Hawker Hunter T8C [878/VL]	RN FRADU, Yeovilton
	WT723	Hawker Hunter PR11 [866/VL]	RN FRADU, Yeovilton
	WT744	Hawker Hunter GA11 [868/VL]	RN FRADU, Yeovilton
	WT745	Hawker Hunter T8C (8893M) [745]	RN, Shawbury store
	WT746	Hawker Hunter F4 (7770M) [A]	RAF No 1 SoTT, Halton
	WT799	Hawker Hunter T8C [879/-]	RN, Shawbury store
	WT804	Hawker Hunter GA11 [831/DD]	RNAS Culdrose, SAH
	WT806	Hawker Hunter GA11 [838/VL]	RN FRADU, Yeovilton
	WT809	Hawker Hunter GA11 [867/VL]	RN FRADU, Yeovilton
	WT933	Bristol Sycamore 3 (G-ALSW/7709M)	Newark Air Museum, Winthorpe
	WV106	Douglas Skyraider AEW1 [427/C]	Cornwall Aero Park, Helston
	WV198	S55 Sikorsky HAR21 (G-BJWY/A2576) [K]	Helicopter Museum of GB, Heysham, Lancs
	WV256	Hawker Hunter GA11 [862/VL]	RN FRADU, Yeovilton
	WV267	Hawker Hunter GA11 [836/VL]	RNAS Culdrose, SAH
	WV276	Hawker Hunter F4 (7847M) [D]	RAF No 1 SoTT, Halton
	WV318	Hawker Hunter T7B [M]	RAF No 208 Sqn, Lossiemouth
	WV322	Hawker Hunter T8C [U]	RAF No 237 OCU, Lossiemouth
	WV332	Hawker Hunter F4 (7673M) (nose only)	No 1254 Sqn ATC, Godalming
	WV363	Hawker Hunter T8C [872/VL]	RN FRADU, Yeovilton
	WV372	Hawker Hunter T7 [877/VL]	RN FRADU, Yeovilton
	WV381	Hawker Hunter GA11 [732]	UKAEA, Culham, Oxon
	WV382	Hawker Hunter GA11 [830]	RN BDRT, Lee-on-Solent
	WV383	Hawker Hunter T7	MoD(PE) RAE Farnborough
	WV396	Hawker Hunter T8C [879/VL]	RN FRADU, Yeovilton
	WV483	Percival Provost T1 (7693M) [N-E]	Privately owned
	WV486	Percival Provost T1 (7694M) [N-D]	Privately owned, Grazeley, Berks
	WV493	Percival Provost T1 (G-BDYG/7696M) [29]	Royal Scottish Museum of Flight, East Fortune
	WV495	Percival Provost T1 (7697M) [P-C]	Booker Air Museum
	WV499	Percival Provost T1 (7698M) [P-G]	RAF St Athan Historic Aircraft Collection
	WV544	Percival Provost T1 (7700M)	AAC Netheravon Fire Section
	WV562	Percival Provost T1 (7606M) [P-C]	RAF Cosford Aerospace Museum
	WV605	Percival Provost T1 [T-B]	Norfolk & Suffolk Aviation Museum, Flixton
	WV606	Percival Provost T1 (7622M) [P-B]	Newark Air Museum, Winthorpe
	WV679	Percival Provost T1 (7615M) [O-J]	Torbay Aircraft Museum, Paignton

Serial	Type (alternative identity)	Owner, Operator or Location	Notes
WV686	Percival Provost T1 (7621M) (G-BLFT) [O-P]	Privately owned, Camberley	
WV701	Percival Pembroke C1	RAF No 60 Sqn, Wildenrath	
WV703	Percival Pembroke C1 (8108M/ G-IIIM)	Privately owned, Tattershall Thorpe	
WV705	Percival Pembroke C1 (nose only)	Marine Aircraft Preservation Group, Wimborne	
WV740	Percival Pembroke C1	RAF No 60 Sqn, Wildenrath	
WV746	Percival Pembroke C1	RAF No 60 Sqn, Wildenrath	
WV753	Percival Pembroke C1 (8113M)	Wales Aircraft Museum, Cardiff	
WV781	Bristol Sycamore HR12 (G-ALTD/7839M)	Snowdon Mountain Aviation, Caernarfon	
WV783	Bristol Sycamore HR12 (G-ALSP/7841M)	RAF Museum Store, Henlow	
WV787	EE Canberra B2/8 (8799M)	Newark Air Museum, Winthorpe	
WV795	Hawker Sea Hawk FGA6 (A2661/8151M)	Privately owned, Peasedown St John, Avon	
WV797	Hawker Sea Hawk FGA6 (A2637/8155M)	Midland Air Museum, Coventry	
WV798	Hawker Sea Hawk FGA6 (A2557) [028/CU]	Second World War Aircraft Preservation Society, Lasham	
WV826	Hawker Sea Hawk FGA6 (A2532) [147/Z]	Wales Aircraft Museum, Cardiff	
WV843	Hawker Sea Hawk FGA4 (nose only)	Torbay Aircraft Museum, Paignton	
WV856	Hawker Sea Hawk FGA6 [163]	FAA Museum, RNAS Yeovilton	
WV903	Hawker Sea Hawk FGA6 (A2632/8153M) [128/C] [SAH-8]	RNAS Lee-on-Solent	
WV908	Hawker Sea Hawk FGA6 (A2660/8154M) [188/A]	RN Historic Flight, RNAS Yeovilton	
WV911	Hawker Sea Hawk FGA4 (A2526) [115/C]	RN AES, Lee-on-Solent	
WW138	DH Sea Venom FAW22 [229/0]	FAA Museum, RNAS Yeovilton	
WW145	DH Sea Venom FAW22 [680/LM]	Royal Scottish Museum of Flight, East Fortune	
WW217	DH Sea Venom FAW22 [736]	Newark Air Museum, Winthorpe	
WW388	Percival Provost T1 (7616M) [O-F]	Wales Aircraft Museum, Cardiff	
WW397	Percival Provost T1 (8060M/ G-BKHP) [N-E]	Privately owned, RAF Lyneham	
WW421	Percival Provost T1 (7688M) [O]	Lincolnshire Aviation Museum, East Kirkby	
WW442	Percival Provost T1 (7618M) [V-K]	Privately owned, Cranfield	
WW444	Percival Provost T1 [D]	Privately owned, Sibson	
WW447	Percival Provost T1	Privately owned, Grazeley, Berks	
WW453	Percival Provost T1 [B-P]	Air Service Training, Perth	
WW654	Hawker Hunter GA11 [833/VL]	RN FRADU, Yeovilton	
WX788	DH Venom NF3	Wales Aircraft Museum, Cardiff	
WX853	DH Venom NF3 (7443M)	Mosquito Aircraft Museum, London Colney	
WX905	DH Venom NF3 (7458M)	RAF Museum Store, Henlow	
WZ415	DH Vampire T11 [72]	No 2 Sqn ATC, Leavesden	
WZ425	DH Vampire T11	Wales Aircraft Museum, Cardiff	
WZ450	DH Vampire T11 (pod only) [23]	No 2371 Sqn ATC, Tile Cross, W. Mids	
WZ464	DH Vampire T11 (N62430) [40]	Vintage Aircraft Team, Cranfield	
WZ475	DH Vampire T11 [F] (really WZ549/8118M)	Lincolnshire Aviation Museum, RAF Coningsby	
WZ476	DH Vampire T11 (really XE985)	Mosquito Aircraft Museum, London Colney	
WZ507	DH Vampire T11 (G-VTII)	Privately owned, Cranfield	
WZ514	DH Vampire T11	Privately owned, Meols, Merseyside	
WZ515	DH Vampire T11 [60]	Skyfame Collection, stored	
WZ518	DH Vampire T11	North East Aircraft Museum, Usworth	
WZ550	DH Vampire T11 (7902M) [R]	Booker Aircraft Museum	
WZ553	DH Vampire T11 [40]	Wigston ATC, Leics	
WZ557	DH Vampire T11	N Yorks Recovery Group, Chop Gate	

Notes	Serial	Type (alternative identity)	Owner, Operator or Location
	WZ559	DH Vampire T11 (7736M) [45]	RAF Halton Fire Section
	WZ576	DH Vampire T11 (8174M)	No 2192 Sqn ATC, Appleby
	WZ581	DH Vampire T11 [77]	Privately owned, Ruislip
	WZ584	DH Vampire T11 [U]	St Albans College of FE
	WZ589	DH Vampire T11 [19]	Lashenden Air Warfare Museum, Headcorn
	WZ590	DH Vampire T11 [19]	Imperial War Museum, Duxford
	WZ608	DH Vampire T11 [56] (nose only)	Kibworth Aviation Group, Market Harborough
	WZ616	DH Vampire T11 [60]	Vintage Aircraft Team, Cranfield
	WZ662	Auster AOP9 (G-BKVK)	Privately owned, Swanton Morley
	WZ706	Auster AOP9 (7851M)	Royal Military College of Science, Shrivenham
	WZ711	Auster 9/Beagle E3 (G-AVHT)	Privately owned, Middle Wallop
	WZ721	Auster AOP9	Museum of Army Flying, Middle Wallop
	WZ724	Auster AOP9 (7432M)	AAC Middle Wallop, at main gate
	WZ736	Avro 707A (7868M)	Greater Manchester Museum of Science and Industry
	WZ744	Avro 707C (7932M)	RAF Cosford Aerospace Museum
	WZ753	Slingsby Grasshopper TX1	Emanuel School CCF, London SW11
	WZ754	Slingsby Grasshopper TX1	RAF No 4 MGSP, Dishforth
	WZ755	Slingsby Grasshopper TX1	RAF No 625 VGS, South Cerney
	WZ756	Slingsby Grasshopper TX1	RAF No 2 MGSP, Locking
	WZ757	Slingsby Grasshopper TX1	RAF No 2 MGSP, Locking
	WZ758	Slingsby Grasshopper TX1	RAF store, Syerston
	WZ760	Slingsby Grasshopper TX1	RAF No 2 MGSP, Locking
	WZ762	Slingsby Grasshopper TX1	RAF No 3 MGSP, Cosford
	WZ765	Slingsby Grasshopper TX1	Radley College CCF, Abingdon
	WZ767	Slingsby Grasshopper TX1	North East Aircraft Museum, Usworth
	WZ768	Slingsby Grasshopper TX1	RAF No 3 MGSP, Cosford
	WZ769	Slingsby Grasshopper TX1	RAF No 2 MGSP, Locking
	WZ772	Slingsby Grasshopper TX1	RAF No 1 MGSP, Halton
	WZ773	Slingsby Grasshopper TX1	Edinburgh Academy CCF, Lothian
	WZ778	Slingsby Grasshopper TX1	RAF No 4 MGSP, Dishforth
	WZ779	Slingsby Grasshopper TX1	RAF No 3 MGSP, Cosford
	WZ780	Slingsby Grasshopper TX1	Clifton College CCF, Bristol
	WZ781	Slingsby Grasshopper TX1	RAF No 4 MGSP, Dishforth
	WZ782	Slingsby Grasshopper TX1	Charterhouse School CCF, Godalming
	WZ784	Slingsby Grasshopper TX1	RAF No 4 MGSP, Dishforth
	WZ785	Slingsby Grasshopper TX1	RAF No 3 MGSP, Cosford
	WZ787	Slingsby Grasshopper TX1	RAF No 4 MGSP, Dishforth
	WZ789	Slingsby Grasshopper TX1	RAF No 3 MGSP, Cosford
	WZ791	Slingsby Grasshopper TX1	RAF store, Syerston
	WZ792	Slingsby Grasshopper TX1	RAF No 4 MGSP, Dishforth
	WZ793	Slingsby Grasshopper TX1	Lord Wandsworth College CCF, Basingstoke
	WZ794	Slingsby Grasshopper TX1	RAF store, Syerston
	WZ795	Slingsby Grasshopper TX1	RAF No 1 MGSP, Halton
	WZ796	Slingsby Grasshopper TX1	RAF No 1 MGSP, Halton
	WZ797	Slingsby Grasshopper TX1	Canford School CCF, Dorset
	WZ798	Slingsby Grasshopper TX1	RAF No 2 MGSP, Locking
	WZ816	Slingsby Grasshopper TX1	RAF No 2 MGSP, Locking
	WZ817	Slingsby Grasshopper TX1	RAF No 4 MGSP, Dishforth
	WZ818	Slingsby Grasshopper TX1	RAF No 3 MGSP, Cosford
	WZ819	Slingsby Grasshopper TX1	RAF No 1 MGSP, Halton
	WZ820	Slingsby Grasshopper TX1	Whitgift School CCF, Croydon
	WZ822	Slingsby Grasshopper TX1	Robertsbridge Aviation Society, E. Sussex
	WZ824	Slingsby Grasshopper TX1	RAF No 4 MGSP, Dishforth
	WZ825	Slingsby Grasshopper TX1	Bradfield College CCF, Reading, Berks
	WZ826	Slingsby Grasshopper TX1	Dulwich College CCF, London
	WZ827	Slingsby Grasshopper TX1	RAF ACCGS, Syerston
	WZ828	Slingsby Grasshopper TX1	Heles School CCF, Exeter, Devon
	WZ829	Slingsby Grasshopper TX1	Launceston College CCF, Cornwall
	WZ831	Slingsby Grasshopper TX1	RAF No 1 MGSP, Halton
	WZ845	DH Chipmunk T10	RAF No 1 AEF, Manston
	WZ846	DH Chipmunk T10 PAX (G-BCSC/8439M)	No 1404 Sqn ATC, Chatham
	WZ847	DH Chipmunk T10 [F]	RAF No 6 AEF, Abingdon
	WZ856	DH Chipmunk T10	RAF No 7 AEF, Newton
	WZ862	DH Chipmunk T10	RAF Gatow Station Flight, Berlin
	WZ866	DH Chipmunk T10 PAX (8217M) (G-ATEB)	No 2296 Sqn ATC, Dunoon, Strathclyde

Serial	Type (alternative identity)	Owner, Operator or Location	Notes
WZ868	DH Chipmunk T10 (G-BCIW) [H]	Privately owned, Duxford	
WZ869	DH Chipmunk T10 PAX (8019M) [R]	No 391 Sqn ATC, Handforth	
WZ872	DH Chipmunk T10 [E]	RAF No 5 AEF, Cambridge	
WZ877	DH Chipmunk T10 [G]	RAF No 6 AEF, Abingdon	
WZ878	DH Chipmunk T10 [85]	RAF No 11 AEF, Teesside	Teesside 4/87
WZ879	DH Chipmunk T10 [L]	RAF FSS, Swinderby	
WZ882	DH Chipmunk T10 [K]	AAC BFWF, Middle Wallop	
WZ884	DH Chipmunk T10 [P]	AAC BFWF, Middle Wallop	
XA109	DH Sea Vampire T22	Royal Scottish Museum of Flight, East Fortune	
XA129	DH Sea Vampire T22	FAA Museum store, Wroughton	
XA225	Slingsby Grasshopper TX1	Churchers College CCF, Petersfield	
XA228	Slingsby Grasshopper TX1	Glenalmond Trinity College CCF, Tayside	
XA229	Slingsby Grasshopper TX1	RAF No 3 MGSP, Cosford	
XA230	Slingsby Grasshopper TX1	Uppingham School CCF, Leics	
XA231	Slingsby Grasshopper TX1 (8888M)	Kimbolton School CCF, Cambs	
XA233	Slingsby Grasshopper TX1	RAF No 1 MGSP, Halton	
XA237	Slingsby Grasshopper TX1	Queen Victoria School CCF, Dunblane	
XA239	Slingsby Grasshopper TX1	Perse School CCF, Cambridge	
XA240	Slingsby Grasshopper TX1	Radley College CCF, Abingdon	
XA241	Slingsby Grasshopper TX1	Trinity School CCF, Croydon	
XA243	Slingsby Grasshopper TX1 (8886M)	RAF store, St Athan	
XA244	Slingsby Grasshopper TX1	RAF No 3 MGSP, Cosford	
XA282	Slingsby Cadet TX3	Snowdon Mountain Aviation Museum, Llandwrog	
XA454	Fairey Gannet COD4	RNAS Yeovilton Fire Section	
XA459	Fairey Gannet ECM6 (A2608) [E/-]	Wales Aircraft Museum, Cardiff	
XA460	Fairey Gannet ECM6 [768/BY]	Kelsterton College of Technology, Connah's Quay	
XA466	Fairey Gannet COD4 [777/LM]	FAA Museum, RNAS Yeovilton	
XA508	Fairey Gannet T2 (A2472) [627/GN]	Midland Air Museum, Coventry	
XA549	Gloster Javelin FAW1 (7717M) [E]	RAF Museum Store, Swinderby	
XA553	Gloster Javelin FAW1 (7470M)	RAF Stanmore Park, on display	
XA564	Gloster Javelin FAW1 (7464M)	RAF Cosford Aerospace Museum	
XA571	Gloster Javelin FAW1 (nose only) (7663M)	Booker Air Museum	
XA634	Gloster Javelin FAW4 (7641M) [L]	RAF Leeming, at main gate	
XA699	Gloster Javelin FAW5 (7809M)	Midland Air Museum, Coventry	
XA801	Gloster Javelin FAW2 (7739M)	RAF Stafford, at main gate	
XA847	English Electric P1B (8371M)	RAF Museum, Hendon	
XA862	WS55 Whirlwind HAR1 (A2542/G-AMJT) [9]	Midland Air Museum, Coventry	
XA864	WS55 Whirlwind HAR1	FAA Museum, RNAS Yeovilton	
XA870	WS55 Whirlwind HAR1 (A2543)	Cornwall Aero Park, Helston	
XA879	DH Devon C2	RAE Llanbedr, stored	
XA880	DH Devon C2	MoD(PE) RAE Llanbedr	
XA893	Avro Vulcan B1 (8591M) (nose only)	RAF Cosford Aerospace Museum	
XA900	Avro Vulcan B1 (7896M)	RAF Cosford Aerospace Museum	
XA903	Avro Vulcan B1 (nose only)	Wales Aircraft Museum, Cardiff	
XA917	HP Victor B1 (7827M) (nose only)	RAF Marham, ground instruction	
XA932	HP Victor K1 (8517M)	RAF Marham Fire Section	
XB259	Blackburn Beverley C1 (G-AOAI)	Museum of Army Transport, Beverley	
XB261	Blackburn Beverley C1	Southend Airport Hotel	
XB288	Blackburn Beverley C1	Privately owned, Worminghall, Bucks	
XB446	Grumman Avenger ECM6B [992/C]	FAA Museum, RNAS Yeovilton	
XB480	Hiller HT1 (A2577) [537]	FAA Museum, RNAS Yeovilton	
XB733	NA Sabre 4 (G-ATBF)	Privately owned, Much Hoole, Lancs	
XD145	SARO SR53	RAF Cosford Aerospace Museum	

Notes	Serial	Type (alternative identity)	Owner, Operator or Location
	XD163	WS55 Whirlwind HAR10 (8645M) [X]	British Rotorcraft Museum, Wroughton
	XD165	WS55 Whirlwind HAR10 (8673M) [B]	RAF No 1 SoTT, Halton
	XD182	WS55 Whirlwind HAR10 (8612M)	RAF FF&SS, Catterick
	XD186	WS55 Whirlwind HAR10 (8730M)	RAF Chivenor, on display
	XD234	VS Scimitar F1 [834]	RAE Farnborough derelict
	XD317	VS Scimitar F1 [112/R]	FAA Museum, RNAS Yeovilton
	XD332	VS Scimitar F1 (A2574) [612]	Cornwall Aero Park, Helston
	XD375	DH Vampire T11 (7887M)	City of Norwich Aviation Museum
	XD377	DH Vampire T11 (8203M) [A]	RAF Cosford
	XD382	DH Vampire T11 (8033M)	RAF Shawbury, at main gate
	XD425	DH Vampire T11 [16]	Dumfries & Galloway Aviation Museum, Tinwald Downs
	XD429	DH Vampire T11 (7604M) [28] (really XD542)	RAF Cranwell, at main gate
	XD434	DH Vampire T11 [25]	Manchester University, Barton
	XD435	DH Vampire T11 [26]	No 480 Sqn ATC, Kenilworth, Warwicks
	XD445	DH Vampire T11 [51]	Bomber County Aviation Museum, Cleethorpes
	XD447	DH Vampire T11 [50]	Lincolnshire Aviation Museum, East Kirkby
	XD452	DH Vampire T11 (7990M) [66]	Privately owned, Whitchurch, Salop
	XD453	DH Vampire T11 (7890M)	No 1010 Sqn ATC, Old Sarum
	XD459	DH Vampire T11 [63]	Vintage Aircraft Team, Cranfield
	XD463	DH Vampire T11 (8023M)	No 1360 Sqn ATC, Stapleford, Notts
	XD506	DH Vampire T11 (7983M) [E]	RAF Swinderby, on display
	XD515	DH Vampire T11 (7998M)	Newark Air Museum, Winthorpe
	XD528	DH Vampire T11 (8159M)	No 2415 Sqn ATC, Penkridge, Staffs
	XD534	DH Vampire T11 [41]	Military Aircraft Preservation Group, Hadfield, Derbys
	XD535	DH Vampire T11	Friends of Biggin Hill, Sevenoaks store
	XD536	DH Vampire T11 (7734M)	No 2287 Sqn ATC, Reading
	XD547	DH Vampire T11 [Z] (pod only)	Scotland West Aircraft Investigation Group, Strathallan
	XD593	DH Vampire T11 [50]	Newark Air Museum, Winthorpe
	XD596	DH Vampire T11 (7939M) [V2]	Ocean Village, Southampton Docks
	XD599	DH Vampire T11 [A]	Snowdon Mountain Aviation, Caernarfon
	XD602	DH Vampire T11 (7737M)	No 495 Sqn ATC, Wylde Green, W Midlands
	XD613	DH Vampire T11 (8122M) [M]	RAF Cosford, on parade ground
	XD616	DH Vampire T11 [56]	No 1239 Sqn ATC, Hoddesdon, Herts
	XD622	DH Vampire T11 (8160M)	No 2214 Sqn ATC, Usworth
	XD624	DH Vampire T11 [O]	Macclesfield Technical College
	XD626	DH Vampire T11 [Q]	Midland Air Museum, Coventry
	XD674	Hunting Jet Provost T1 (7570M) [T]	RAF Cosford Aerospace Museum
	XD818	Vickers Valiant B(K)1 (7894M)	Bomber Command Museum, Hendon
	XD826	Vickers Valiant B(K)1 (7872M) (nose only)	Wales Aircraft Museum, Cardiff
	XD875	Vickers Valiant B(K)1 (nose only)	No 163 Sqn ATC, Coventry
	XE317	Bristol Sycamore HR14 (G-AMWO) [S-N]	Newark Air Museum, Winthorpe
	XE327	Hawker Sea Hawk FGA6 (A2556) [644/LH]	RN Llangennech, Dyfed, on display
	XE339	Hawker Sea Hawk FGA6 (8156M/A2635) [149/E] [SAH-7]	RNAS Lee-on-Solent, stored
	XE340	Hawker Sea Hawk FGA6 [131/Z]	Strathallan Aircraft Collection
	XE364	Hawker Sea Hawk FB5 (really WM983/A2511) (G-JETH)	Bournemouth Flying Club, Hurn, on display
	XE368	Hawker Sea Hawk FGA6 (A2534) [200/J]	Cornwall Aero Park, Helston

Serial	Type (alternative identity)	Owner, Operator or Location	Notes
XE369	Hawker Sea Hawk FGA6 [5] (A2580/8158M/A2633)	RNAS Yeovilton Fire Section	
XE521	Fairey Rotodyne Y	British Rotorcraft Museum, Weston-super-Mare	
XE531	Hawker Hunter T12	RAE Farnborough Fire Section	
XE587	Hawker Hunter F6 [7]	MoD(PE) RAE Farnborough stored	
XE597	Hawker Hunter FGA9 (8874M) [F]	RAF Bentley Priory, on display	
XE601	Hawker Hunter FGA9	MoD(PE) ETPS Boscombe Down	
XE624	Hawker Hunter FGA9 (8875M) [G]	RAF Brawdy, on display	
XE627	Hawker Hunter F6A	Imperial War Museum, Duxford	
XE643	Hawker Hunter FGA9 (8586M) (nose only)	RAF Exhibition Flight, Abingdon	
XE650	Hawker Hunter FGA9 (G-9-449)	Lovaux Ltd, Macclesfield	
XE653	Hawker Hunter F6A (8829M) [D]	RAF TMTS, Scampton	
XE656	Hawker Hunter F6 (8678M)	RAF No 1 SoTT, Halton	
XE665	Hawker Hunter T8C [876/VL]	RN FRADU, Yeovilton	
XE668	Hawker Hunter GA11 [832/DD]	RN Culdrose, SAH	
XE670	Hawker Hunter F4 (7762M/8585M) (nose only)	RAF Exhibition Flight, Abingdon	
XE673	Hawker Hunter GA11 (8846M) (tail from XE689) [680/VL]	RAF Bawdsey, BDRT	
XE677	Hawker Hunter F4	Loughborough University of Technology	
XE682	Hawker Hunter GA11 [835]	RNAS Culdrose, SAH	
XE685	Hawker Hunter GA11 [861/VL]	RN FRADU, Yeovilton	
XE689	Hawker Hunter GA11 [869/VL]	RN FRADU, Yeovilton	
XE707	Hawker Hunter GA11 [865/VL]	RN FRADU, Yeovilton	
XE712	Hawker Hunter GA11 [708]	RN Lee-on-Solent, BDRT	
XE849	DH Vampire T11 (7928M) [V3]	No 936 Sqn ATC, Ware, Herts	
XE852	DH Vampire T11 [60]	BAe Apprentice School, Hawarden	
XE855	DH Vampire T11	Midland Air Museum, Coventry	
XE856	DH Vampire T11	Second World War Aircraft Preservation Society, Lasham	
XE864	DH Vampire T11	No 480 Sqn ATC, Studley, Warwicks	
XE872	DH Vampire T11 [62]	Midland Air Museum, Coventry	
XE874	DH Vampire T11 (8582M) [61]	RAF Valley	
XE897	DH Vampire T11 (really XD403)	Strathallan Aircraft Collection	
XE920	DH Vampire T11 (8196M) [D]	RAF Museum Store, Henlow	
XE921	DH Vampire T11 [64]	Privately owned, Keevil	
XE928	DH Vampire T11 [76]	Privately owned, Keevil	
XE935	DH Vampire T11 [30]	S Yorks Air Museum, Firbeck	
XE946	DH Vampire T11 (7473M) (nose only)	RAF Museum store, Cardington	
XE956	DH Vampire T11 [N]	St Albans College of FE	
XE979	DH Vampire T11 [54]	Privately owned, Stonehouse, Glos	
XE982	DH Vampire T11 (7564M)	No 124 Sqn ATC, Hereford	
XE993	DH Vampire T11 (8161M)	RAF Cosford Fire Section	
XE995	DH Vampire T11 [53]	Torbay Aircraft Museum, Paignton	
XE998	DH Vampire T11 [36]	The Aeroplane Collection, Warmingham	
XF113	VS Swift F7 (nose only) [19]	Privately owned, Peasedown St John, Avon	
XF114	VS Swift F7	Kelsterton College of Technology, Connah's Quay	
XF274	Gloster Meteor T7	RAE/AIU on display, Farnborough	
XF289	Hawker Hunter T8C [875/VL]	RN FRADU, Yeovilton	
XF300	Hawker Hunter GA11 [860/VL]	RN FRADU, Yeovilton	
XF301	Hawker Hunter GA11 [834/VL]	RN FRADU, Yeovilton	
XF310	Hawker Hunter T7 [869/VL]	RN FRADU, Yeovilton	
XF314	Hawker Hunter F51 [N] (really E-412)	Tangmere Military Aviation Museum	
XF319	Hawker Hunter F4 (7849M) [B]	RAF No 1 SoTT, Halton	
XF321	Hawker Hunter T7	RNEC Manadon	
XF357	Hawker Hunter T8C [871/VL]	RN FRADU, Yeovilton	
XF358	Hawker Hunter T8C [870/VL]	RN FRADU, Yeovilton	
XF368	Hawker Hunter GA11 [863/VL]	RN FRADU, Yeovilton	
XF375	Hawker Hunter F6 (8736M) [05]	RAFC Cranwell, Engineering Wing	
XF382	Hawker Hunter F6A [15]	Midland Air Museum, Coventry	

Notes	Serial	Type (alternative identity)	Owner, Operator or Location
	XF383	Hawker Hunter F6 (8706M) [V]	RAF Wittering, BDRT
	XF383	Hawker Hunter F51 (really E-409) [71]	Wales Aircraft Museum, Cardiff
	XF386	Hawker Hunter F6 (8707M) [75]	RAF
	XF419	Hawker Hunter FGA9 [C]	RAF store, Brawdy
	XF431	Hawker Hunter FGA9 [O]	RAF store, St Athan
	XF435	Hawker Hunter FGA9 (8880M) [52]	RAF Brawdy, BDRT
	XF445	Hawker Hunter FGA9 (8715M) [T] (really XG264)	RAF Brawdy Fire Section
	XF509	Hawker Hunter F6 (8708M) [73]	RAF Chivenor, at main gate
	XF515	Hawker Hunter F6A (8830M) [C]	RAF TMTS, Scampton
	XF516	Hawker Hunter F6A (8685M) [66]	RAFC Cranwell, Engineering Wing
	XF519	Hawker Hunter FGA9 (8677M/ 8738M) [J] (composite with XJ695)	CTE, RAF Manston
	XF526	Hawker Hunter F6 (8679M) [78/E]	RAF St Athan Fire Section
	XF527	Hawker Hunter F6 (8680M)	RAF Halton, on display
	XF545	Percival Provost T1 (7957M) [O-K]	RAF Linton-on-Ouse, at main gate
	XF597	Percival Provost T1 (G-BKFW) [G]	Privately owned, Oakington
	XF603	Percival Provost T1 [H]	Rolls-Royce Tech Coll, Filton
	XF690	Percival Provost T1 (G-BGKA/ 8041M)	Leicester Aircraft Preservation Group, RAF Newton
	XF708	Avro Shackleton MR3 [203/C]	Imperial War Museum, Duxford
	XF785	Bristol 173 (G-ALBN/7648M)	RAF Museum Store, Henlow
	XF799	Percival Pembroke C1	RAF No 60 Sqn, Wildenrath
	XF836	Percival Provost T1 (8043M/ G-AWRY) [JG]	Privately owned, Popham
	XF844	Percival Provost T1 [30]	RAE Farnborough Apprentice School
	XF877	Percival Provost T1 (G-AWVF) [JX]	Privately owned, Bourn
	XF898	Percival Provost T1 [Z]	Booker Fire Section
	XF914	Percival Provost T1	Vintage Aircraft Team, Cranfield
	XF926	Bristol 188 (8368M)	RAF Cosford Aerospace Museum
	XF967	Hawker Hunter T8C [V]	RAF No 237 OCU, Lossiemouth
	XF974	Hawker Hunter F4 (7949M) [C]	RAF No 1 SoTT, Halton
	XF979	Hawker Hunter F51 (really E-408 RDanAF) (8565M) [A]	RAFC Cranwell, on display
	XF985	Hawker Hunter T8C [873/VL]	RN FRADU, Yeovilton
	XF990	Hawker Hunter F6 (8007M) (nose only)	RAF FF&SS, Catterick
	XF994	Hawker Hunter T8C [874/VL]	RN FRADU, Yeovilton
	XF995	Hawker Hunter T8B [W]	RAF No 12 Sqn, Lossiemouth
	XG151	Hawker Hunter FGA9 (8798M) (nose only) [H]	RAF Lossiemouth Fire Section
	XG154	Hawker Hunter FGA9 (8863M) [54]	RAF Museum, Hendon
	XG158	Hawker Hunter F6A (8686M) [21]	RAE Farnborough Apprentice School
	XG160	Hawker Hunter F6A [B] (8831M)	RAF TMTS, Scampton
	XG164	Hawker Hunter F6 (8681M)	RAF No 1 SoTT, Halton
	XG172	Hawker Hunter F6A [A] (8832M)	RAF TMTS, Scampton
	XG194	Hawker Hunter FGA9 [55] (8839M)	RAF No 2 SoTT, Cosford
	XG195	Hawker Hunter FGA9 (composite with XG297)	Bomber County Aviation Museum, Cleethorpes
	XG196	Hawker Hunter F6A (8702M)	RAF Bracknell, on gate
	XG209	Hawker Hunter F6 (8709M)	RAF No 1 SoTT, Halton
	XG210	Hawker Hunter F6	RAE Apprentice School, Bedford
	XG225	Hawker Hunter F6A (8713M) [S]	RAF No 2 SoTT, Cosford
	XG226	Hawker Hunter F6A (8800M) (fuselage, etc)	RAF Abingdon BDRF

Serial	Type (alternative identity)	Owner, Operator or Location	Notes
XG226	Hawker Hunter F6A (8800M) [28] (nose only)	RAF FF&SS, Catterick	
XG228	Hawker Hunter FGA9 [56]	RAF store, St Athan	
XG252	Hawker Hunter FGA9 (8840M) [U]	RAF No 2 SoTT, Cosford	
XG254	Hawker Hunter FGA9 (8881M) [57]	RAF Coltishall, BDRT	
XG274	Hawker Hunter F6 (8710M) [71]	RAF No 1 SoTT, Halton	
XG290	Hawker Hunter F6 (8711M) [74]	RAF No 1 SoTT, Halton	
XG297	Hawker Hunter FGA9 (nose only)	Pennine Aviation Museum, Bacup	
XG325	EE Lightning F1 (nose only)	No 1476 Sqn ATC, Rayleigh, Essex	
XG327	EE Lightning F1 (8188M)	CTE, RAF Manston	
XG329	EE Lightning F1 (8050M)	RAF Swinderby	
XG331	EE Lightning F1 (nose only)	CARG store, RAF Innsworth	
XG337	EE Lightning F1 (8056M) [M]	RAF Cosford Aerospace Museum	
XG452	WS Belvedere HC1 (G-BRMB/7997M)	British Rotorcraft Museum, Weston-super-Mare	
XG454	WS Belvedere HC1 (8366M)	Greater Manchester Museum of Science and Industry	
XG474	WS Belvedere HC1 (8367M) [O]	RAF Museum, Hendon	
XG502	Bristol Sycamore HR14	Museum of Army Flying, Middle Wallop	
XG504	Bristol Sycamore HR14	Privately owned, Causewayhead, Stirling	
XG506	Bristol Sycamore HR14 (7852M)	Bomber County Aviation Museum, Cleethorpes	
XG518	Bristol Sycamore HR14 (8009M) [S-E]	North East Aircraft Museum, Usworth	
XG540	Bristol Sycamore HR14 (7899M/8345M) [Y-S]	RAF Shawbury at main gate	
XG544	Bristol Sycamore HR14	Torbay Aircraft Museum, Paignton	
XG547	Bristol Sycamore HR14 (G-HAPR/8010M) [S-T]	British Rotorcraft Museum, Weston-super-Mare	
XG573	WS55 Whirlwind HAR3	CDE, Porton Down, Wilts	
XG574	WS55 Whirlwind HAR3 (A2575) [752/PO]	FAA Museum store, Wroughton	
XG577	WS55 Whirlwind HAR3 (A2571)	RE 39 Regt, Waterbeach, on display	
XG592	WS55 Whirlwind HAS7 [54]	Wales Aircraft Museum, Cardiff	
XG594	WS55 Whirlwind HAS7 [517/PO]	Strathallan Aircraft Collection	
XG596	WS55 Whirlwind HAS7 (A2651) [66]	British Rotorcraft Museum, Weston-super-Mare	
XG613	DH Sea Venom FAW21	Imperial War Museum, Duxford	
XG629	DH Sea Venom FAW22	Torbay Aircraft Museum, Paignton	
XG680	DH Sea Venom FAW22 [735/VL]	North East Aircraft Museum, Usworth	
XG691	DH Sea Venom FAW22 [493]	Cornwall Aero Park, Helston	
XG692	DH Sea Venom FAW22 [668/LM]	Privately owned, Alcester	
XG730	DH Sea Venom FAW22 [499/A]	Mosquito Aircraft Museum, London Colney	
XG734	DH Sea Venom FAW22	Ulster Aviation Society, Newtownards	
XG736	DH Sea Venom FAW22	Ulster Aviation Society, Newtownards	
XG737	DH Sea Venom FAW22 [220/Z]	Wales Aircraft Museum, Cardiff	
XG743	DH Sea Vampire T22 [597/LM]	Imperial War Museum, Duxford	
XG797	Fairey Gannet ECM6 [766/BY]	Imperial War Museum, Duxford	
XG831	Fairey Gannet ECM6 (A2539) [396]	Cornwall Aero Park, Helston	
XG882	Fairey Gannet T5 (8754M) [771/LM]	RAF Lossiemouth on display	
XG883	Fairey Gannet T5 [773/BY]	Wales Aircraft Museum, Cardiff	
XG888	Fairey Gannet T5 [-/LM]	RNAS Lee-on-Solent, stored	
XG900	Short SC1	Science Museum store, Hayes	
XG905	Short SC1	Ulster Folk & Transport Museum, County Down	
XH124	Blackburn Beverley C1 (8025M)	RAF Museum, Hendon	
XH131	EE Canberra PR9 [AF]	RAF No 1 PRU, Wyton	
XH132	Short SC9 Canberra	RAF St Mawgan BDRT	

Notes	Serial	Type (alternative identity)	Owner, Operator or Location
	XH133	EE Canberra PR9	RAF No 1 PRU, Wyton
	XH134	EE Canberra PR9	RAF No 1 PRU, Wyton
	XH135	EE Canberra PR9	RAF No 1 PRU, Wyton
	XH136	EE Canberra PR9 (8782M) [W]	RAF No 2 SoTT, Cosford
	XH165	EE Canberra PR9 [AK]	RAF No 1 PRU, Wyton
	XH169	EE Canberra PR9 [AQ]	RAF No 1 PRU, Wyton
	XH170	EE Canberra PR9 (8739M)	RAF Wyton, on gate
	XH171	EE Canberra PR9 (8746M) [U]	RAF No 2 SoTT, Cosford
	XH174	EE Canberra PR9	RAF No 1 PRU, Wyton
	XH175	EE Canberra PR9 [AP]	RAF No 1 PRU, Wyton
	XH274	DH Vampire T11	RAF Ternhill Fire Section
	XH278	DH Vampire T11 (8595M/ 7866M)	No 2482 Sqn ATC, RAF Henlow
	XH312	DH Vampire T11 [18]	Privately owned, Chester
	XH313	DH Vampire T11 [E]	St Albans College of FE
	XH318	DH Vampire T11 (7761M) [64]	No 424 Sqn ATC, Hants
	XH328	DH Vampire T11 [66]	Privately owned, Croxley Green
	XH329	DH Vampire T11 [70]	Privately owned, Keevil
	XH330	DH Vampire T11 [73]	Privately owned, Bushey
	XH537	Avro Vulcan B2 MRR (8749M)	RAF Abingdon, on display
	XH539	Avro Vulcan B2	RAF Waddington, rescue training
	XH558	Avro Vulcan B2	RAF Vulcan Memorial Flight, Waddington
	XH560	Avro Vulcan K2	RAF Marham Fire Section
	XH567	EE Canberra B6(mod)	MoD(PE) RAE Bedford
	XH568	EE Canberra B6(mod)	MoD(PE) RAE Bedford
	XH583	EE Canberra T4 (G-27-374)	BAe Samlesbury, stored
	XH590	HP Victor K1A	CTE, RAF Manston
	XH592	HP Victor K1A (8429M) [L]	RAF Cosford Aerospace Museum
	XH593	HP Victor K1A (8428M) [T]	RAF No 2 SoTT, Cosford
	XH616	HP Victor K1A	CTE, RAF Manston
	XH648	HP Victor K1A	Imperial War Museum, Duxford
	XH669	HP Victor K2	RAF No 55 Sqn, Marham
	XH670	HP Victor SR2 (nose only)	Lincolnshire Aviation Museum, East Kirkby
	XH671	HP Victor K2	RAF No 55 Sqn, Marham
	XH672	HP Victor K2	RAF No 55 Sqn, Marham
	XH673	HP Victor K2 (8911M)	RAF Marham, on display
	XH675	HP Victor K2	RAF No 55 Sqn, Marham
	XH764	Gloster Javelin FAW9 (7972M)	RAF Manston, on display
	XH767	Gloster Javelin FAW9 (7955M) [K]	No 187 Sqn ATC, Perdiswell, Worcester
	XH837	Gloster Javelin FAW7 (8032M) (nose only)	RAF Northolt Fire Section
	XH892	Gloster Javelin FAW9 (7982M) [B]	Norfolk & Suffolk Aviation Museum, Flixton
	XH897	Gloster Javelin FAW9	Imperial War Museum, Duxford
	XH903	Gloster Javelin FAW9 (7938M)	RAF Innsworth, at main gate
	XH980	Gloster Javelin FAW8 (7867M) [A]	RAF West Raynham, at main gate
	XH992	Gloster Javelin FAW8 (7829M) [P]	Newark Air Museum, Winthorpe
	XJ314	RR Thrust Measuring Rig	Science Museum, Strathallan
	XJ319	DH Sea Devon C20 (G-AMXP)	RNAS Culdrose Station Flight
	XJ324	DH Sea Devon C20 (G-AMXZ)	RNAS Culdrose Station Flight
	XJ348	DH Sea Devon C20 (G-AMXX/ G-NAVY)	Privately owned, Shoreham
	XJ380	Bristol Sycamore HR14 (8628M)	RAF Finningley, for display
	XJ389	Fairey Jet Gyrodyne (XD759/ G-AJJP)	RAF Cosford Aerospace Museum
	XJ393	WS55 Whirlwind HAR3 (A2538)	Torbay Aircraft Museum, Paignton
	XJ396	WS55 Whirlwind HAR10	RAE Farnborough Fire Section
	XJ402	WS55 Whirlwind HAR3 (A2572) [61]	FAA Museum Store, RNAS Yeovilton
	XJ407	WS55 Whirlwind HAR10 (G-BKHB)	Privately owned, Tattershall Thorpe
	XJ409	WS55 Whirlwind HAR10	Wales Aircraft Museum, Cardiff
	XJ411	WS55 Whirlwind HAR10 [Z]	RAE Farnborough Fire Section

Serial	Type (alternative identity)	Owner, Operator or Location	Notes
XJ430	WS55 Whirlwind HAR10	CTE, RAF Manston	
XJ435	WS55 Whirlwind HAR10 (8671M) [V]	RAF No 1 SoTT, Halton	
XJ445	WS55 Whirlwind HAR5	CDE, Porton Down, Wilts	
XJ476	DH Sea Vixen FAW1 (nose section)	No 424 Sqn ATC, Southampton Hall of Aviation	
XJ481	DH Sea Vixen FAW1 [VL]	Ocean Village, Southampton Docks	
XJ482	DH Sea Vixen FAW1 (A2598) [713/VL]	Norfolk & Suffolk Aviation Museum, Flixton	
XJ494	DH Sea Vixen FAW2	Privately owned, Kings Langley, Herts	
XJ560	DH Sea Vixen FAW2 (8142M) [243]	Newark Air Museum, Winthorpe	
XJ565	DH Sea Vixen FAW2 [127/E]	Mosquito Aircraft Museum, London Colney	
XJ571	DH Sea Vixen FAW2 (8140M) [242/H]	RAF No 2 SoTT, Cosford	
XJ575	DH Sea Vixen FAW2 (A2611) [-/VL] [SAH-13]	Cornwall Aero Park, Helston	
XJ580	DH Sea Vixen FAW2 [131/E]	Christchurch Memorial Group	
XJ582	DH Sea Vixen FAW2 (8139M) [702]	RAF Cottesmore Fire Section	
XJ584	DH Sea Vixen FAW2 (A2621) [SAH-16]	Cornwald Aero Park, Helston	
XJ604	DH Sea Vixen FAW2 (8222M) [755]	Cranfield Institute of Technology	
XJ607	DH Sea Vixen FAW2 (8171M) [701/VL]	RAF No 2 SoTT, Cosford	
XJ608	DH Sea Vixen FAW2 (8802M)	RAF North Luffenham Fire Section	
XJ609	DH Sea Vixen FAW2 (8172M) painted 8171M [702/VL]	RAF Abingdon Fire Section	
XJ634	Hawker Hunter F6A (8684M) [29]	RAFC Cranwell, Engineering Wing	
XJ639	Hawker Hunter F6A (8687M) [31]	RAFC Cranwell, Engineering Wing	
XJ676	Hawker Hunter F6A [32] (8844M)	RAF Lyneham Fire Section	
XJ683	Hawker Hunter FGA9 [X]	RAF store, Brawdy	
XJ690	Hawker Hunter FGA9 (composite with XG195)	Lovaux Ltd, Hurn	
XJ723	WS55 Whirlwind HAR10	OPITB, Montrose	
XJ726	WS55 Whirlwind HAR10 [F]	Snowdon Mountain Aviation Collection, Caernarfon	
XJ727	WS55 Whirlwind HAR10 (8661M) [L]	RAF No 1 SoTT, Halton	
XJ729	WS55 Whirlwind HAR10 (8732M)	RAF Finningley, for display	
XJ763	WS55 Whirlwind HAR10 (G-BKHA)	Privately owned, Biggin Hill	
XJ772	DH Vampire T11 [H]	Brooklands Technical College	
XJ782	Avro Vulcan B2 MRR (8766M)	RAF Finningley on display	
XJ823	Avro Vulcan B2A	Privately owned, Carlisle Airport	
XJ824	Avro Vulcan B2A	Imperial War Museum, Duxford	
XJ825	Avro Vulcan K2 (8810M)	RAF Waddington, BDRT	
XJ917	Bristol Sycamore HR14 [S-H]	Cornwall Aero Park, Helston	
XJ918	Bristol Sycamore HR14 (8190M)	RAF Cosford Aerospace Museum	
XK149	Hawker Hunter F6A (8714M) [34]	RAFC Cranwell, Engineering Wing	
XK412	Auster AOP9	Privately owned, Wootton Bassett	
XK416	Auster AOP9 (G-AYUA/ 7855M)	Vintage Aircraft Team, Cranfield	
XK417	Auster AOP9 (G-AVXY)	Privately owned, Leicester	
XK418	Auster AOP9 (7976M)	Second World War Aircraft Preservation Society, Lasham	
XK421	Auster AOP9 (8365M)	Cotswold Aircraft Restoration Group, RAF Innsworth	
XK482	Saro Skeeter AOP12 (7840M/ G-BJWC) [C]	Privately owned, Tattershall Thorpe	
XK488	Blackburn Buccaneer S1	FAA Museum, RNAS Yeovilton	
XK526	Blackburn Buccaneer S2 (8648M)	RAF Honington, at main gate	
XK530	Blackburn Buccaneer S1	RAE Bedford Fire Section	

Notes	Serial	Type (alternative identity)	Owner, Operator or Location
	XK531	Blackburn Buccaneer S1 (8403M)	Defence School, Winterbourne Gunner
	XK532	Blackburn Buccaneer S1 (8867M/A2581) [632/LM]	RAF Lossiemouth, on display
	XK533	Blackburn Buccaneer S1 (nose only)	Museum of Flight, East Fortune
	XK590	DH Vampire T11 [V]	Wellesbourne Aviation Group
	XK623	DH Vampire T11 [56]	Snowdon Mountain Aviation, Caernarfon
	XK624	DH Vampire T11 [32]	Norfolk & Suffolk Aviation Museum, Flixton
	XK625	DH Vampire T11 [12]	Privately owned, North Weald
	XK627	DH Vampire T11	Pennine Aviation Museum, Bacup
	XK632	DH Vampire T11 [67]	Privately owned, Croxley Green
	XK637	DH Vampire T11 [56]	No 1855 Sqn ATC, Royton, Greater Manchester
	XK655	DH Comet 2R (G-AMXA)	Strathallan Aircraft Collection
	XK659	DH Comet 2 (nose only)	Privately owned, Elland, W. Yorks
	XK695	DH Comet 2R (G-AMXH)	Imperial War Museum, Duxford
	XK697	DH Comet 2R (G-AMXJ) [D]	Air Scouts, RAF Wyton
	XK699	DH Comet C2 (G-AMXM/ 7971M)	RAF Lyneham for display
	XK724	Folland Gnat F1 (7715M)	RAF Cosford Aerospace Museum
	XK740	Folland Gnat F1 (8396M)	RAF Cosford Aerospace Museum
	XK741	Folland Gnat F1	Midland Air Mûseum, Coventry
	XK776	ML Utility 1	Museum of Army Flying, Middle Wallop
	XK788	Slingsby Grasshopper TX1	RAF No 1 MGSP, Halton
	XK789	Slingsby Grasshopper TX1	RAF No 3 MGSP, Cosford
	XK819	Slingsby Grasshopper TX1	RAF No 3 MGSP, Cosford
	XK820	Slingsby Grasshopper TX1	RAF No 2 MGSP, Locking
	XK822	Slingsby Grasshopper TX1	Kings College School CCF, Wimbledon
	XK824	Slingsby Grasshopper TX1	Wycliffe School CCF, Stonehouse, Glos
	XK884	Percival Pembroke C1	RAF No 60 Sqn, Wildenrath
	XK895	DH Sea Devon C20	RN store, Kemble
	XK906	WS55 Whirlwind HAS7	AAC Netheravon Fire Section
	XK907	WS55 Whirlwind HAS7 [U]	Midland Air Museum, Coventry
	XK911	WS55 Whirlwind HAS7 (A2603) [519/PO]	RN store, Wroughton
	XK912	WS55 Whirlwind HAS7 [60/CU]	Privately owned, Crudwell, Wilts
	XK936	WS55 Whirlwind HAS7 [62]	Imperial War Museum, Duxford
	XK943	WS55 Whirlwind HAS7 (A2653/8796M) [57]	RAF Abingdon, BDRF
	XK944	WS55 Whirlwind HAS7 (A2607)	Brunel Technical College, Bristol
	XK968	WS55 Whirlwind HAR10 (8445M) [E]	RAF Manston, on display
	XK969	WS55 Whirlwind HAR10 (8646M)	CTE, RAF Manston
	XK987	WS55 Whirlwind HAR10 (8393M)	MoD Swynnerton, Staffs
	XK988	WS55 Whirlwind HAR10 (A2646) [N]	Museum of Army Flying, Middle Wallop
	XL149	Blackburn Beverley C1 (nose only) (7988M)	Newark Air Museum, Winthorpe
	XL158	HP Victor K2	RAF No 55 Sqn, Marham
	XL160	HP Victor K2 (8910M)	RAF Marham, for display
	XL161	HP Victor K2	RAF No 55 Sqn, Marham
	XL162	HP Victor K2	RAF No 55 Sqn, Marham
	XL163	HP Victor K2	RAF St Athan store
	XL164	HP Victor K2	RAF No 55 Sqn, Marham
	XL188	HP Victor K2	RAF No 55 Sqn, Marham
	XL189	HP Victor K2 (8912M)	RAF Marham
	XL190	HP Victor K2	RAF No 55 Sqn, Marham
	XL191	HP Victor K2	RAF No 55 Sqn, Marham
	XL192	HP Victor K2	RAF Marham
	XL231	HP Victor K2	RAF No 55 Sqn, Marham
	XL233	HP Victor K2	RAF Marham
	XL318	Avro Vulcan B2 (8733M)	Bomber Command Museum, Hendon
	XL319	Avro Vulcan B2	North East Aircraft Museum, Usworth
	XL360	Avro Vulcan B2	Midland Air Museum, Coventry
	XL384	Avro Vulcan B2 (8505M/ 8670M)	RAF Scampton Fire Section

Serial	Type (alternative identity)	Owner, Operator or Location	Notes
XL386	Avro Vulcan B2 (8760M)	CTE, RAF Manston	
XL391	Avro Vulcan B2	Privately owned, Blackpool	
XL392	Avro Vulcan B2 (8745M)	RAF Valley Fire Section	
XL426	Avro Vulcan B2	Vulcan Memorial Flight, RAF Waddington	
XL427	Avro Vulcan B2 (8756M)	RAF Machrihanish Fire Section	
XL445	Avro Vulcan K2 (8811M)	RAF Lyneham Fire Section	
XL449	Fairey Gannet AEW3	Wales Aircraft Museum, Cardiff	
XL471	Fairey Gannet AEW3 [043/R]	Privately owned, Carlisle	
XL472	Fairey Gannet AEW3 [044/R]	A&AEE Boscombe Down, derelict	
XL497	Fairey Gannet AEW3 [041/R]	HMS *Gannet*, Prestwick, at gate	
XL500	Fairey Gannet AEW3 (A2701)	RNAS Lee-on-Solent, stored	
XL502	Fairey Gannet AEW3 (8610M) [G-BMYP]	Privately owned, Leuchars	
XL503	Fairey Gannet AEW3 [070/E]	FAA Museum, RNAS Yeovilton	
XL511	HP Victor K2	CTE, RAF Manston	
XL512	HP Victor K2	RAF No 55 Sqn, Marham	
XL563	Hawker Hunter T7	MoD(PE) RAE/IAM Farnborough	
XL564	Hawker Hunter T7 [4]	MoD(PE) ETPS Boscombe Down	
XL565	Hawker Hunter T7	MoD(PE) IAM/RAE Farnborough	
XL567	Hawker Hunter T7 (8723M) [84]	RAF Chivenor Fire Section	
XL568	Hawker Hunter T7A [N]	RAF No 12 Sqn, Lossiemouth	
XL569	Hawker Hunter T7 (8833M) [80]	RAF No 2 SoTT, Cosford	
XL572	Hawker Hunter T7 (8834M) [83]	RAF No 2 SoTT, Cosford	
XL573	Hawker Hunter T7 [F]	RAF No 12 Sqn, Lossiemouth	
XL576	Hawker Hunter T7 (8835M) [81]	RAF No 2 SoTT, Cosford	
XL577	Hawker Hunter T7 (8676M) [01]	RAFC Cranwell, Engineering Wing	
XL578	Hawker Hunter T7 [77]	RAF store, St Athan	
XL580	Hawker Hunter T8M [719/VL]	RN No 899 Sqn, Yeovilton	
XL586	Hawker Hunter T7 [85]	MoD(PE) BAe Warton	
XL587	Hawker Hunter T7 (8807M) [Z]	RAF TMTS, Scampton	
XL591	Hawker Hunter T7 [G]	RAF No 237 OCU, Lossiemouth	
XL592	Hawker Hunter T7 (8836M) [Y]	RAF TMTS, Scampton	
XL595	Hawker Hunter T7 [78]	RAF store, St Athan	
XL598	Hawker Hunter T8C [880/VL]	RN FRADU, Yeovilton	
XL600	Hawker Hunter T7 [FL]	RNAY Fleetlands Apprentice School	
XL601	Hawker Hunter T7	RN store, Yeovilton	
XL602	Hawker Hunter T8M	MoD(PE) BAe Dunsfold	
XL603	Hawker Hunter T8M [720]	RN No 899 Sqn, Yeovilton	
XL609	Hawker Hunter T7 (8866M) [YF]	RAF Lossiemouth, BDRT	
XL612	Hawker Hunter T7 [2]	MoD(PE) ETPS Boscombe Down	
XL613	Hawker Hunter T7A [H]	RAF No 237 OCU, Lossiemouth	
XL614	Hawker Hunter T7 [O]	RAF No 237 OCU, Lossiemouth	
XL616	Hawker Hunter T7 [P]	RAF No 208 Sqn, Lossiemouth	
XL617	Hawker Hunter T7 (8837M) [89]	RAF No 2 SoTT, Cosford	
XL618	Hawker Hunter T7 (8892M) [05]	RAF Cottesmore BDRT	
XL621	Hawker Hunter T7 (G-BN..)	Lovaux Ltd, Hurn	
XL623	Hawker Hunter T7 (8770M) [90]	RAF No 2 SoTT, Cosford	
XL629	EE Lightning T4	A&AEE Boscombe Down, at main gate	
XL703	SAL Pioneer CC1 (8034M)	Greater Manchester Museum of Science and Industry	
XL717	DH Tiger Moth (G-AOXG/T7291) [LM]	FAA Museum, RNAS Yeovilton	
XL728	WS58 Wessex HAS1	MoD(PE) RAE Pendine	
XL738	Saro Skeeter AOP12 (7860M)	Southampton Hall of Aviation	
XL762	Saro Skeeter AOP12 (8017M)	Royal Scottish Museum of Flight, East Fortune	
XL763	Saro Skeeter AOP12	Southall Technical College	
XL764	Saro Skeeter AOP12 (7940M)	Newark Air Museum, Winthorpe	
XL765	Saro Skeeter AOP12	Privately owned, Leamington Spa	
XL770	Saro Skeeter AOP12 (8046M)	Southampton Hall of Aviation	
XL809	Saro Skeeter AOP12 (G-BLIX/PH-HOF)	Privately owned, Clapham, Beds	
XL811	Saro Skeeter AOP12 [157]	The Aircraft Collection, Warmingham	
XL812	Saro Skeeter AOP12 (G-SARO)	Privately owned, Dalcross	
XL813	Saro Skeeter AOP12	Museum of Army Flying, Middle Wallop	
XL814	Saro Skeeter AOP12	AAC Historic Aircraft Flight, Middle Wallop	
XL824	Bristol Sycamore HR14 (8021M)	Greater Manchester Museum of Science and Industry	
XL829	Bristol Sycamore HR14	Bristol Industrial Museum	

Notes	Serial	Type (alternative identity)	Owner, Operator or Location
	XL836	WS55 Whirlwind HAS7 (A2642) [65/FL]	RN Predannack Fire School
	XL840	WS55 Whirlwind HAS7 [56]	City of Norwich Aviation Museum
	XL846	WS55 Whirlwind HAS7 (A2625) [85]	RN Predannack Fire School
	XL847	WS55 Whirlwind HAS7 (A2626) [83]	AAC Middle Wallop, Fire Section
	XL853	WS55 Whirlwind HAS7 (A2630)	Southampton Hall of Aviation
	XL875	WS55 Whirlwind HAR9	Air Service Training, Perth
	XL880	WS55 Whirlwind HAR9 (A2714) [433/ED]	RN Lee-on-Solent, BDRT
	XL898	WS55 Whirlwind HAR9 (8654M) [30/ED]	Boscombe Down Fire Section
	XL899	WS55 Whirlwind HAR9 [587/CU]	RN Predannack Fire School
	XL929	Percival Pembroke C1	RAF No 60 Sqn, Wildenrath
	XL954	Percival Pembroke C1	RAF No 60 Sqn, Wildenrath
	XL993	SAL Twin Pioneer CC1 (8388M)	RAF Cosford Aerospace Museum
	XM135	BAC Lightning F1 [135]	Imperial War Museum, Duxford
	XM139	BAC Lightning F1 (8411M) [F]	RAF
	XM144	BAC Lightning F1 (8417M) [J]	RAF Leuchars, at main gate
	XM147	BAC Lightning F1 (8412M) [J]	RAF
	XM169	BAC Lightning F1A (8422M) [W]	RAF Leuchars Fire Section
	XM172	BAC Lightning F1A (8427M) [B]	RAF Coltishall, at main gate
	XM173	BAC Lightning F1A (8414M) [A]	RAF Bentley Priory, at main gate
	XM178	BAC Lightning F1A (8418M) [Y]	RAF Leuchars Fire Section
	XM181	BAC Lightning F1A (8415M)	RAF Binbrook
	XM183	BAC Lightning F1A (8416M)	RAF Binbrook
	XM191	BAC Lightning F1A (7854M/ 8590M) (nose only)	RAF Exhibition Flight, Abingdon
	XM192	BAC Lightning F1A (8413M) [K]	RAF Wattisham, at main gate
	XM223	DH Devon C2 [J]	MoD(PE) RAE West Freugh
	XM279	EE Canberra B(I)8 (nose only)	S Yorks Air Museum, Firbeck
	XM296	DH Heron C4	RN FONAC, RNAS Yeovilton
	XM300	WS58 Wessex HAS1	Wales Aircraft Museum, Cardiff
	XM326	WS58 Wessex HAS1 [515]	RNAS Portland Fire Section
	XM327	WS58 Wessex HAS3 [401/KE]	College of Nautical Studies, Warsash
	XM328	WS58 Wessex HAS3 [06/AN]	RNAS Culdrose, SAH
	XM329	WS58 Wessex HAS1 (A2609) [437]	RNAS Lee-on-Solent Fire Section
	XM330	WS58 Wessex HAS1	MoD(PE) RAE Farnborough
	XM331	WS58 Wessex HAS3 [653/PO]	RN Predannack Fire School
	XM349	Hunting Jet Provost T3A [H]	RAF CFS, Scampton
	XM350	Hunting Jet Provost T3A [89]	RAF No 7 FTS, Church Fenton
	XM351	Hunting Jet Provost T3 (8078M) [05]	RAF No 2 SoTT, Cosford
	XM352	Hunting Jet Provost T3A [92]	RAF No 7 FTS, Church Fenton
	XM355	Hunting Jet Provost T3 (8229M) [D]	RAF No 1 SoTT, Halton
	XM357	Hunting Jet Provost T3A [45]	RAF No 1 FTS, Linton-on-Ouse
	XM358	Hunting Jet Provost T3A [53]	RAF No 1 FTS, Linton-on-Ouse
	XM362	Hunting Jet Provost T3 (8230M)	RAF No 1 SoTT, Halton
	XM365	Hunting Jet Provost T3A [37]	RAF No 1 FTS, Linton-on-Ouse
	XM367	Hunting Jet Provost T3 (8083M) [04]	RAF No 2 SoTT, Cosford
	XM369	Hunting Jet Provost T3 (8084M) [07]	RAF No 1 SoTT, Halton
	XM370	Hunting Jet Provost T3A [93]	RAF No 7 FTS, Church Fenton
	XM371	Hunting Jet Provost T3A [K]	RAF CFS, Scampton

Serial	Type (alternative identity)	Owner, Operator or Location	Notes
XM372	Hunting Jet Provost T3A [55]	RAF Linton-on-Ouse Fire Section	
XM374	Hunting Jet Provost T3A [83]	RAF No 7 FTS, Church Fenton	
XM375	Hunting Jet Provost T3 (8231M) [B]	RAF No 1 SoTT, Halton	
XM376	Hunting Jet Provost T3A [97]	RAF No 7 FTS, Church Fenton	
XM378	Hunting Jet Provost T3A	RAF St Athan, hack	
XM379	Hunting Jet Provost T3	Army Apprentice College, Arborfield	
XM381	Hunting Jet Provost T3 (8232M) [O]	RAF No 1 SoTT, Halton	
XM383	Hunting Jet Provost T3A [90]	RAF No 7 FTS, Church Fenton	
XM386	Hunting Jet Provost T3 (8076M) [08]	RAF No 1 SoTT, Halton	
XM387	Hunting Jet Provost T3A [I]	RAF CFS, Scampton	
XM401	Hunting Jet Provost T3A [17]	RAF No 1 FTS, Linton-on-Ouse	
XM402	Hunting Jet Provost T3 (8055AM) [J]	RAF No 1 SoTT, Halton	
XM403	Hunting Jet Provost T3A [A]	RAF CFS, Scampton	
XM404	Hunting Jet Provost T3 (8055BM) [24]	RAF No 1 SoTT, Halton	
XM405	Hunting Jet Provost T3A [42]	RAF No 1 FTS, Linton-on-Ouse	
XM408	Hunting Jet Provost T3 (8233M) [P]	RAF No 1 SoTT, Halton	
XM409	Hunting Jet Provost T3 (8082M) [A]	RAF No 1 SoTT, Halton	
XM410	Hunting Jet Provost T3 (8054AM) [C]	RAF No 1 SoTT, Halton	
XM411	Hunting Jet Provost T3 (8434M) [L]	RAF No 1 SoTT, Halton	
XM412	Hunting Jet Provost T3A [41]	RAF No 1 FTS, Linton-on-Ouse	
XM413	Hunting Jet Provost T3	Army Apprentice College, Arborfield	
XM414	Hunting Jet Provost T3A [101]	RAF No 7 FTS, Church Fenton	
XM415	Hunting Jet Provost T3 (nose only)	No 424 Sqn ATC, Southampton Hall of Aviation	
XM417	Hunting Jet Provost T3 (8054BM) [D]	RAF No 1 SoTT, Halton	
XM419	Hunting Jet Provost T3A [102]	RAF No 7 FTS, Church Fenton	
XM424	Hunting Jet Provost T3A [30]	RAF No 1 FTS, Linton-on-Ouse	
XM425	Hunting Jet Provost T3A [88]	RAF No 7 FTS, Church Fenton	
XM426	Hunting Jet Provost T3 (nose only)	No 1151 Sqn ATC, Wallsend-on-Tyne	
XM455	Hunting Jet Provost T3A [F]	RAF CFS, Scampton	
XM458	Hunting Jet Provost T3A [B]	RAF CFS, Scampton	
XM459	Hunting Jet Provost T3A [104]	RAF No 7 FTS, Church Fenton	
XM461	Hunting Jet Provost T3A [11]	RAF No 1 FTS, Linton-on-Ouse	
XM463	Hunting Jet Provost T3A [38]	RAF No 1 FTS, Linton-on-Ouse	
XM464	Hunting Jet Provost T3A [23]	RAF No 1 FTS, Linton-on-Ouse	
XM465	Hunting Jet Provost T3A [85]	RAF No 7 FTS, Church Fenton	
XM466	Hunting Jet Provost T3A [31]	RAF No 1 FTS, Linton-on-Ouse	
XM467	Hunting Jet Provost T3 (8085M) [06] [69]	RAF No 1 SoTT, Halton	
XM468	Hunting Jet Provost T3 (8081M) [B]	RAF No 1 SoTT, Halton	
XM470	Hunting Jet Provost T3A [M]	RAF CFS, Scampton	
XM471	Hunting Jet Provost T3A [10]	RAF No 1 FTS, Linton-on-Ouse	
XM472	Hunting Jet Provost T3A [22]	RAF No 1 FTS, Linton-on-Ouse	
XM473	Hunting Jet Provost T3A [19]	RAF No 1 FTS, Linton-on-Ouse	
XM475	Hunting Jet Provost T3A [96]	RAF No 7 FTS, Church Fenton	
XM478	Hunting Jet Provost T3A [33]	RAF No 1 FTS, Linton-on-Ouse	
XM479	Hunting Jet Provost T3A [54]	RAF No 1 FTS, Linton-on-Ouse	
XM480	Hunting Jet Provost T3 (8080M)	RAF No 1 SoTT, Halton	
XM529	Saro Skeeter AOP12 (7979M/ G-BDNS)	Privately owned, Handforth	
XM553	Saro Skeeter AOP12 (G-AWSV)	Privately owned, Middle Wallop	
XM555	Saro Skeeter AOP12 (8027M)	RAF Cosford Aerospace Museum	
XM556	Saro Skeeter AOP12 (G-HELI/7870M) [V]	British Rotorcraft Museum, Weston-super-Mare	
XM561	Saro Skeeter AOP12 (7980M)	Lincolnshire Aviation Museum, East Kirkby	
XM564	Saro Skeeter AOP12	Royal Armoured Corps, Bovington	
XM569	Avro Vulcan B2	Wales Aircraft Museum, Cardiff	
XM594	Avro Vulcan B2	Newark Air Museum, Winthorpe	

Notes	*Serial*	*Type (alternative identity)*	*Owner, Operator or Location*
	XM597	Avro Vulcan B2	Royal Scottish Museum of Flight, East Fortune
	XM598	Avro Vulcan B2 (8778M)	RAF Cosford Aerospace Museum
	XM602	Avro Vulcan B2 (8771M)	RAF St Athan Historic Aircraft Collection
	XM603	Avro Vulcan B2	BAe Woodford
	XM607	Avro Vulcan B2 (8779M)	RAF Waddington, on display
	XM612	Avro Vulcan B2	City of Norwich Aviation Museum
	XM652	Avro Vulcan B2 (nose only)	Privately owned, Burntwood, Staffs
	XM655	Avro Vulcan B2 (G-VULC/ N655AV)	Privately owned, Wellesbourne Mountford
	XM656	Avro Vulcan B2 (8757M) (nose only)	RAF Cottesmore Fire Section
	XM657	Avro Vulcan B2 (8734M)	CTE, RAF Manston
	XM660	WS55 Whirlwind HAS7 [78]	North East Aircraft Museum, Usworth
	XM665	WS55 Whirlwind HAS7	Booker Aircraft Museum
	XM667	WS58 Westland HAS7 (A2629) [56/CU]	RN Predannack Fire School
	XM685	WS55 Whirlwind HAS7 (G-AYZJ) [518/PO]	Newark Air Museum, Winthorpe
	XM693	HS Gnat T1 (7891M)	BAe Hamble on display
	XM694	HS Gnat T1	RAE Bedford Apprentice School
	XM697	HS Gnat T1	No 1349 Sqn ATC, Woking
	XM698	HS Gnat T1 (8090M/8497M)	RAF Cosford Aerospace Museum
	XM705	HS Gnat T1 (8574M)	RAF St Athan
	XM706	HS Gnat T1 (8572M) [12]	RAF No 1 SoTT, Halton
	XM708	HS Gnat T1 (8573M)	RAF Locking, on display
	XM709	HS Gnat T1 (8617M) [67]	RAF No 1 SoTT, Halton
	XM715	HP Victor K2	RAF No 55 Sqn, Marham
	XM717	HP Victor K2	RAF No 55 Sqn, Marham
	XM832	WS58 Wessex HAS1	RN NASU, Yeovilton
	XM833	WS58 Wessex HAS3	Second World War Aircraft Preservation Society, Lasham
	XM836	WS58 Wessex HAS3 [651/PO]	RNAY Fleetlands, instructional use
	XM838	WS58 Wessex HAS3 [405/LN]	RN AES Lee-on-Solent
	XM841	WS58 Wessex HAS1	RN Predannack Fire School
	XM843	WS58 Wessex HAS1 (A2693) [527/LS]	RNAS Lee-on-Solent Fire Section
	XM845	WS58 Wessex HAS1 (A2682) [530/PO]	RNAS Yeovilton Fire Section
	XM868	WS58 Wessex HAS1 (A2706) [517/PO]	RN AES Lee-on-Solent
	XM870	WS58 Wessex HAS3 [652/PO]	RN AES Lee-on-Solent
	XM874	WS58 Wessex HAS1 (A2689) [521/CU]	RNAS Culdrose, SAH
	XM916	WS58 Wessex HAS3 [666/PO]	Fire Section, Wroughton
	XM917	WS58 Wessex HAS1 (A2692) [528/CU]	RN AES Lee-on-Solent
	XM919	WS58 Wessex HAS3 [55]	RNAS Yeovilton Fire Section
	XM923	WS58 Wessex HAS3	RNAY Fleetlands Fire Section
	XM926	WS58 Wessex HAS1	MoD(PE) RAE Farnborough
	XM927	WS58 Wessex HAS3 (8814M) [660/PO]	RAF Shawbury, BDRT
	XM969	BAC Lightning T4 (8592M)	RAF Binbrook Fire Section
	XM987	BAC Lightning T4	RAF Coningsby, BDRT
	XM997	BAC Lightning T4	RAF FF&SS, Catterick
	XN126	WS55 Whirlwind HAR10 (8655M) [S]	RAF No 1 SoTT, Halton
	XN132	Sud Alouette AH2	AAC UNFICYP, Nicosia
	XN137	Hunting Jet Provost T3 [95] (nose only)	RAF Exhibition Flight, Abingdon
	XN239	Slingsby Cadet TX3 [G] (8889M)	Imperial War Museum, Duxford
	XN258	WS55 Whirlwind HAR9 [589/CU]	Cornwall Aero Park, Helston
	XN263	WS55 Whirlwind HAS7	Royal Military College of Science, stored, Shrivenham
	XN264	WS55 Whirlwind HAS7 [53]	Privately owned, Grovesend, Avon
	XN297	WS55 Whirlwind HAR9 (really XN311/A2643)	RN HMS *Phoenix* Fire School, Portsmouth

Serial	Type (alternative identity)	Owner, Operator or Location	Notes
XN298	WS55 Whirlwind HAR9 [810/LS]	Privately owned, Stoke-on-Trent	
XN299	WS55 Whirlwind HAS7 [758]	Torbay Aircraft Museum, Paignton	
XN302	WS55 Whirlwind HAS7 (A2654) [LS]	RNAS Lee-on-Solent Fire Section	
XN304	WS55 Whirlwind HAS7 [64]	Norfolk & Suffolk Aviation Museum, Flixton	
XN306	WS55 Whirlwind HAR9 [434/ED]	RNAS Portland Fire Section	
XN308	WS55 Whirlwind HAS7 (A2605) [510/PO]	RNAS Lee-on-Solent Fire Section	
XN309	WS55 Whirlwind HAR9 (A2663) [590/CU]	Second World War Aircraft Preservation Society, Lasham	
XN314	WS55 Whirlwind HAS7 (A2614)	RN Predannack Fire School	
XN332	Saro P531 (G-APNV/A2579) [759]	FAA Museum, RNAS Yeovilton	
XN334	Saro P531 (A2525)	British Rotorcraft Museum, Weston-super-Mare	
XN341	Saro Skeeter AOP12 (8022M)	RAF St Athan Historic Aircraft Collection	
XN344	Saro Skeeter AOP12 (8018M)	Science Museum, South Kensington	
XN351	Saro Skeeter AOP12 (G-BKSC)	Privately owned, Lossiemouth	
XN359	WS55 Whirlwind HAR9 (A2712) [434/ED]	RNAS Lee-on-Solent, BDRT	
XN380	WS55 Whirlwind HAS7 [67]	Lashenden Air Warfare Museum, Headcorn	
XN382	WS55 Whirlwind HAS7 [17]	Privately owned, Thruxton	
XN385	WS55 Whirlwind HAS7	RN Historic Flight, stored Wroughton	
XN386	WS55 Whirlwind HAR9 [435/ED] (A2713)	RN AES Lee-on-Solent	
XN387	WS55 Whirlwind HAR9 (8564M)	RAF Odiham, BDRT	
XN412	Auster AOP9	Cotswold Aircraft Restoration Group, RAF Innsworth	
XN435	Auster AOP9 (G-BGBU)	Privately owned, Egham	
XN437	Auster AOP9 (G-AXWA)	Privately owned, Welling, Kent	
XN441	Auster AOP9 (G-BGKT)	Privately owned, Reymerston Hall	
XN453	DH Comet 2e	RAE Farnborough Fire Section	
XN458	Hunting Jet Provost T3 (8234M) [H]	RAF CTTS, St Athan	
XN459	Hunting Jet Provost T3A [20]	MoD(PE) BAe Warton	
XN461	Hunting Jet Provost T3A [28]	RAF No 1 FTS, Linton-on-Ouse	
XN462	Hunting Jet Provost T3A [87]	RAF No 7 FTS, Church Fenton	
XN466	Hunting Jet Provost T3A [29]	RAF No 1 FTS, Linton-on-Ouse	
XN467	Hunting Jet Provost T4 (8559M) [F]	RAF No 1 SoTT, Halton	
XN470	Hunting Jet Provost T3A [84]	RAF No 7 FTS, Church Fenton	
XN471	Hunting Jet Provost T3A [24]	RAF No 1 FTS, Linton-on-Ouse	
XN472	Hunting Jet Provost T3A [32]	RAF No 1 FTS, Linton-on-Ouse	
XN473	Hunting Jet Provost T3A (8862M) [98]	RAF Church Fenton Fire Section	
XN492	Hunting Jet Provost T3 (8079M) [08]	RAF No 2 SoTT, Cosford	
XN493	Hunting Jet Provost T3 (nose only)	RAF Exhibition Flight, Abingdon	
XN494	Hunting Jet Provost T3A [43]	RAF No 1 FTS, Linton-on-Ouse	
XN495	Hunting Jet Provost T3A [102] (8786M)	RAF Abingdon, BDRF	
XN497	Hunting Jet Provost T3A [52]	RAF No 1 FTS, Linton-on-Ouse	
XN498	Hunting Jet Provost T3A [16]	RAF No 1 FTS, Linton-on-Ouse	
XN499	Hunting Jet Provost T3A [L]	RAF CFS, Scampton	
XN500	Hunting Jet Provost T3A [80]	RAF No 7 FTS, Church Fenton	
XN501	Hunting Jet Provost T3A [G]	RAF CFS, Scampton	
XN502	Hunting Jet Provost T3A [D]	RAF CFS, Scampton	
XN503	Hunting Jet Provost T3 (nose only)	RAF Exhibition Flight, Abingdon	
XN505	Hunting Jet Provost T3A [25]	RAF No 1 FTS, Linton-on-Ouse	
XN506	Hunting Jet Provost T3A [81]	RAF No 7 FTS, Church Fenton	
XN508	Hunting Jet Provost T3A [98]	RAF No 7 FTS, Church Fenton	
XN509	Hunting Jet Provost T3A [50]	RAF No 1 FTS, Linton-on-Ouse	
XN510	Hunting Jet Provost T3A [40]	RAF No 1 FTS, Linton-on-Ouse	

Notes	Serial	Type (alternative identity)	Owner, Operator or Location
	XN511	Hunting Jet Provost T3 [21] (nose only)	No 177 Sqn ATC, Blackpool Airport
	XN512	Hunting Jet Provost T3 (8435M)	RAF No 1 SoTT, Halton
	XN547	Hunting Jet Provost T3A [48]	RAF No 1 FTS, Linton-on-Ouse
	XN548	Hunting Jet Provost T3A [103]	RAF No 7 FTS, Church Fenton
	XN549	Hunting Jet Provost T3 (8235M) [R]	RAF No 1 SoTT, Halton
	XN551	Hunting Jet Provost T3A [100]	RAF No 7 FTS, Church Fenton
	XN552	Hunting Jet Provost T3A [86]	RAF No 7 FTS, Church Fenton
	XN553	Hunting Jet Provost T3A [34]	MoD(PE) BAe Warton
	XN554	Hunting Jet Provost T3 (8436M) [K]	RAF No 1 SoTT, Halton
	XN574	Hunting Jet Provost T3A [21]	RAF No 1 FTS, Linton-on-Ouse
	XN577	Hunting Jet Provost T3A [18]	RAF No 1 FTS, Linton-on-Ouse
	XN579	Hunting Jet Provost T3A [14]	RAF No 1 FTS, Linton-on-Ouse
	XN581	Hunting Jet Provost T3A [C]	RAF CFS, Scampton
	XN582	Hunting Jet Provost T3A [95]	RAF No 7 FTS, Church Fenton
	XN584	Hunting Jet Provost T3A [E]	RAF CFS, Scampton
	XN585	Hunting Jet Provost T3A [12]	RAF Linton-on-Ouse Fire Section
	XN586	Hunting Jet Provost T3A [91]	RAF No 7 FTS, Church Fenton
	XN589	Hunting Jet Provost T3A [46]	RAF No 1 FTS, Linton-on-Ouse
	XN592	Hunting Jet Provost T3 (nose only)	No 1105 Sqn ATC, Winchester
	XN593	Hunting Jet Provost T3A [27]	RAF No 1 FTS, Linton-on-Ouse
	XN594	Hunting Jet Provost T3 (8077M) [09]	RAF No 2 SoTT, Cosford
	XN595	Hunting Jet Provost T3A [82]	RAF No 7 FTS, Church Fenton
	XN597	Hunting Jet Provost T3 (7984M) [11] (nose only)	Brencham Historic Aircraft, Biggin Hill
	XN602	Hunting Jet Provost T3 (8088M)	CTE, RAF Manston
	XN605	Hunting Jet Provost T3A [J]	RAF CFS, Scampton
	XN606	Hunting Jet Provost T3A [36]	RAF No 1 FTS, Linton-on-Ouse
	XN629	Hunting Jet Provost T3A [39]	RAF No 1 FTS, Linton-on-Ouse
	XN632	Hunting Jet Provost T3 (8352M)	RAF St Athan, CTTS
	XN634	Hunting Jet Provost T3A [94]	RAF No 7 FTS, Church Fenton
	XN635	Hunting Jet Provost T3 [575]	RN Predannack Fire School
	XN636	Hunting Jet Provost T3A [15]	RAF No 1 FTS, Linton-on-Ouse
	XN637	Hunting Jet Provost T3 (G-BKOU)	Vintage Aircraft Team, Cranfield
	XN640	Hunting Jet Provost T3A [99]	RAF No 7 FTS, Church Fenton
	XN641	Hunting Jet Provost T3A (8865M) [47]	RAF Newton Fire Section
	XN643	Hunting Jet Provost T3A (8704M) [26]	RAF Abingdon, BDRF
	XN647	DH Sea Vixen FAW2 (A2610)	Cornwall Aero Park, Helston
	XN649	DH Sea Vixen FAW2 [126]	MoD(PE) RAE Farnborough store
	XN650	DH Sea Vixen FAW2 (A2612/ A2620/A2639) [VL]	Wales Aircraft Museum, Cardiff
	XN651	DH Sea Vixen FAW2 (A2616) (nose only)	Privately owned, Pucklechurch, Avon
	XN657	DH Sea Vixen D3 [TR-1]	MoD(PE) RAE Llanbedr Fire Section
	XN685	DH Sea Vixen FAW2 (8173M)	RAF No 2 SoTT, Cosford
	XN688	DH Sea Vixen FAW2 (8141M)	RAE Farnborough Fire Section
	XN691	DH Sea Vixen FAW2 (8143M) [247/H]	RAF No 2 SoTT, Cosford
	XN692	DH Sea Vixen FAW2 (A2624) [SAH-17] [254/H]	RNAS Yeovilton for display
	XN694	DH Sea Vixen FAW2	Flight Refuelling Ltd, Hurn
	XN696	DH Sea Vixen FAW2 [751]	Privately owned, Suffolk
	XN699	DH Sea Vixen FAW2 (8224M)	RAF Hereford
	XN714	Hunting H126	RAF Cosford Aerospace Museum
	XN724	BAC Lightning F2A [F] (8513M)	Privately owned, Newcastle-on-Tyne
	XN728	BAC Lightning F2A (8546M) [V]	Privately owned, Balderton, Notts
	XN734	BAC Lightning F2/3A (8346M/ G-27-239/G-BNCA)	Aces High, North Weald
	XN769	BAC Lightning F2 (8402M) [Z]	London ATCC, West Drayton
	XN774	BAC Lightning F2A (8551M) [F]	RAF Coningsby

Serial	Type (alternative identity)	Owner, Operator or Location	Notes
XN776	BAC Lightning F2A [B] (8535M)	Royal Scottish Museum of Flight, East Fortune	
XN781	BAC Lightning F2A (8538M) [B]	RAF Leuchars Fire Section	
XN816	AW Argosy E1 (8489M) [G]	RAF No 2 SoTT, Cosford	
XN817	AW Argosy C1	MoD(PE) RAE West Freugh Fire Section	
XN819	AW Argosy C1 (8205M) (nose only)	Newark Air Museum, Winthorpe	
XN855	AW Argosy E1 (8556M)	CTE, RAF Manston	
XN923	HS Buccaneer S1	MoD(PE) A&AEE Boscombe Down	
XN925	HS Buccaneer S1 (8087M/ A2602)	RAF FF&SS, Catterick	
XN928	HS Buccaneer S1 (8179M)	Wales Aircraft Museum, Cardiff	
XN929	HS Buccaneer S1 (8051M) (nose only)	RAF Lossiemouth procedures trainer	
XN930	HS Buccaneer S1 (8180M) [632/LM]	RAF Honington, BDRT	
XN934	HS Buccaneer S1 (A2600) [631/LS]	RN Predannack Fire School	
XN953	HS Buccaneer S1 (A2655/ 8182M) [SAH-23]	RNAS Culdrose Fire Section	
XN957	HS Buccaneer S1 [630/LM]	FAA Museum, RNAS Yeovilton	
XN962	HS Buccaneer S1 (8183M) (nose only)	RAF Exhibition Flight, Abingdon	
XN964	HS Buccaneer S1 [613/LM]	Phoenix Aviation Museum, Bruntingthorpe	
XN967	HS Buccaneer S1 (A2627) [103/E]	Cornwall Aero Park, Helston	
XN973	HS Buccaneer S1 (nose only)	BAe Samlesbury	
XN974	HS Buccaneer S2A	MoD(PE) BAe Warton	
XN976	HS Buccaneer S2B	RAF No 12 Sqn, Lossiemouth	
XN977	HS Buccaneer S2B [G]	RAF Shawbury store	
XN979	HS Buccaneer S2 (nose only)	Cranfield Institute of Technology	
XN981	HS Buccaneer S2B [981]	RAF No 12 Sqn, Lossiemouth	
XN982	HS Buccaneer S2A	MoD(PE) BAe Brough	
XN983	HS Buccaneer S2B	RAF No 12 Sqn, Lossiemouth	
XP107	WS58 Wessex HAS1 (A2527)	RN Predannack Fire School	
XP110	WS58 Wessex HAS3 [55/FL]	RNAY Fleetlands Apprentice School	
XP116	WS58 Wessex HAS3 (A2618) [520]	RN AES Lee-on-Solent	
XP117	WS58 Wessex HAS1 (A2681) [521/PO]	RNAS Culdrose Fire Section	
XP137	WS58 Wessex HAS3 [665/PO]	RN AES Lee-on-Solent	
XP139	WS58 Wessex HAS3	RN Predannack Fire School	
XP140	WS58 Wessex HAS3 (8806M) [653/PO]	RAF Chilmark, BDRT	
XP142	WS58 Wessex HAS3	FAA Museum, RNAS Yeovilton	
XP149	WS58 Wessex HAS1 (A2669) [574/CU]	RN Predannack Fire School	
XP150	WS58 Wessex HAS3 [406/AN]	RN AES Lee-on-Solent	
XP151	WS58 Wessex HAS1 (A2684) [047/R]	RN AES Lee-on-Solent	
XP155	WS58 Wessex HAS1 (A2640)	RNAS Culdrose Fire Section	
XP157	WS58 Wessex HAS1 (A2680)	RN AES Lee-on-Solent	
XP158	WS58 Wessex HAS1 (A2688) [522/CU]	RNAS Culdrose, SAH MT School	
XP159	WS58 Wessex HAS1 (8877M) [047/R]	RAF Odiham, BDRT	
XP160	WS58 Wessex HAS1 (A2650) [521/CU] [SAH-24]	RNAS Culdrose, SAH MT School	
XP165	WS Scout AH1	British Rotorcraft Museum, Weston-super-Mare	
XP166	WS Scout AH1 (G-APVL)	MoD(PE) RAE Farnborough, in store	
XP167	WS Scout AH1	RAE Farnborough Fire Section	
XP190	WS Scout AH1	Army Apprentice College, Arborfield	
XP191	WS Scout AH1	AAC Middle Wallop, BDRT	

Notes	Serial	Type (alternative identity)	Owner, Operator or Location
	XP226	Fairey Gannet AEW3 (A2667) [073/E]	Newark Air Museum, Winthorpe
	XP241	Auster AOP9	Tagmore Nurseries, Rabley Heath, Herts
	XP242	Auster AOP9	Museum of Army Flying store, Middle Wallop
	XP244	Auster AOP9 (7864M) [M7922]	Army Apprentice College, Arborfield
	XP248	Auster AOP9 (7822M)	No 2293 Sqn ATC, Marlborough
	XP279	Auster AOP9 (G-BWKK)	Privately owned, Ripley, Derbys
	XP280	Auster AOP9	Leicester Museum of Technology store
	XP281	Auster AOP9	Imperial War Museum, Duxford
	XP282	Auster AOP9 (G-BGTC)	Privately owned, Swanton Morley
	XP283	Auster AOP9 (7859M)	Privately owned, Middle Wallop
	XP299	WS55 Whirlwind HAR10 (8726M)	RAF Cosford Aerospace Museum
	XP328	WS55 Whirlwind HAR10 (G-BKHC)	Privately owned, Tattershall Thorpe
	XP329	WS55 Whirlwind HAR10 [V] (8791M)	RAF Shawbury
	XP330	WS55 Whirlwind HAR10	CAA Fire School, Teesside Airport
	XP333	WS55 Whirlwind HAR10 (8650M) [G]	CTE, RAF Manston
	XP338	WS55 Whirlwind HAR10 (8647M) [N]	RAF No 2 SoTT, Cosford
	XP339	WS55 Whirlwind HAR10	Bomber County Aviation Museum, Cleethorpes
	XP344	WS55 Whirlwind HAR10 (8764M) [X]	RAFC Cranwell, Engineering Wing
	XP345	WS55 Whirlwind HAR10 (8792M) [UN]	RAF Shawbury
	XP346	WS55 Whirlwind HAR10 (8793M)	RAF Shawbury
	XP350	WS55 Whirlwind HAR10	Cornwall Aero Park, Helston
	XP351	WS55 Whirlwind HAR10 (8672M) [Z]	RAF Shawbury, BDRT
	XP352	WS55 Whirlwind HAR10 (8701M)	RAF Abingdon, BDRF
	XP354	WS55 Whirlwind HAR10 (8721M)	RAF No 1 SoTT, Halton
	XP355	WS55 Whirlwind HAR10 (8463M/G-BEBC) [A]	City of Norwich Aviation Museum
	XP356	WS55 Whirlwind HAR10	RAE Farnborough Fire Section
	XP357	WS55 Whirlwind HAR10 (8499M)	CTE, RAF Manston
	XP359	WS55 Whirlwind HAR10 (8447M)	RAF Exhibition Flight, Abingdon
	XP360	WS55 Whirlwind HAR10 [V]	Second World War Aircraft Preservation Society, Lasham
	XP361	WS55 Whirlwind HAR10 (8731M)	RAF Valley, preserved at gate
	XP393	WS55 Whirlwind HAR10 [U]	RAE Farnborough Fire Section
	XP394	WS55 Whirlwind HAR10 [C]	CTE, RAF Manston
	XP395	WS55 Whirlwind HAR10 (8674M) [A]	RAF No 1 SoTT, Halton
	XP398	WS55 Whirlwind HAR10 (8794M)	RAF Shawbury
	XP399	WS55 Whirlwind HAR10	Privately owned, Tor View Garage, Glastonbury, Som
	XP400	WS55 Whirlwind HAR10 (8444M) [N]	CTE, RAF Manston
	XP404	WS55 Whirlwind HAR10 (8682M)	RAF SAREW, Finningley
	XP405	WS55 Whirlwind HAR10 (8656M) [Y]	RAF No 1 SoTT, Halton
	XP411	AW Argosy C1 (8442M) [Y]	RAF No 2 SoTT, Cosford
	XP439	AW Argosy E1 (8558M)	RAF Lossiemouth Fire Section
	XP442	AW Argosy T2 (8454M) [442]	RAF No 1 SoTT, Halton
	XP444	AW Argosy C1 (8455M) [D]	RAF No 2 SoTT, Cosford
	XP454	Slingsby Grasshopper TX1	Kimbolton School CCF, Cambs
	XP459	Slingsby Grasshopper TX1	Woodbridge School CCF, Suffolk
	XP462	Slingsby Grasshopper TX1	RAF No 1 MGSP, Halton
	XP463	Slingsby Grasshopper TX1	William Parker School CCF, East Sussex
	XP464	Slingsby Grasshopper TX1	Sherborne School CCF, Dorset
	XP487	Slingsby Grasshopper TX1	RAF store, Syerston

Serial	*Type (alternative identity)*	*Owner, Operator or Location*	*Notes*
XP490	Slingsby Grasshopper TX1	RAF ACCGS, Syerston	
XP492	Slingsby Grasshopper TX1	King's College CCF, Taunton	
XP493	Slingsby Grasshopper TX1	RAF ACCGS, Syerston	
XP494	Slingsby Grasshopper TX1	Stamford School, Lincs	
XP502	HS Gnat T1 (8576M) [02]	RAF St Athan Fire Section	
XP503	HS Gnat T1 (8568M) [73]	RAF No 1 SoTT, Halton	
XP504	HS Gnat T1 (8618M) [68] [04]	RAF No 1 SoTT, Halton	
XP505	HS Gnat T1 [05]	Science Museum, South Kensington	
XP511	HS Gnat T1 (8619M) [65]	RAF No 1 SoTT, Halton	
XP514	HS Gnat T1 (8635M)	RAF No 2 SoTT, Cosford	
XP515	HS Gnat T1 (8614M) [59]	RAF Wattisham, BDRT	
XP516	HS Gnat T1 (8580M) [16]	MoD(PE) RAE Farnborough	
XP530	HS Gnat T1 (8606M) [60]	RAF No 1 soTT, Halton	
XP532	HS Gnat T1 (8577M/8615M) [32]	MoD(PE) RAE Farnborough	
XP533	HS Gnat T1 (8632M) [74]	RAF No 1 SoTT, Halton	
XP534	HS Gnat T1 (8620M) [64]	RAF No 1 SoTT, Halton	
XP535	HS Gnat T1 (A2679) [SAH-1]	RNAS Culdrose, SAH	
XP538	HS Gnat T1 (8607M) [61]	RAF No 1 SoTT, Halton	
XP540	HS Gnat T1 (8608M) [62]	RAF No 1 SoTT, Halton	
XP541	HS Gnat T1 (8616M) [41]	RAF Abingdon, BDRF	
XP542	HS Gnat T1 (8575M) [42]	RAF St Athan, CTTS	
XP547	Hunting Jet Provost T4 [03]	RAF No 1 TWU/79 Sqn, Brawdy	
XP556	Hunting Jet Provost T4 [B]	RAF CATCS, Shawbury	
XP557	Hunting Jet Provost T4 (8494M)	RAF No 1 SoTT, Halton	
XP558	Hunting Jet Provost T4 (8627M/A2628) [20]	RAF St Athan, CTTS	
XP563	Hunting Jet Provost T4 [C]	RAF CATCS, Shawbury	
XP567	Hunting Jet Provost T4 (8510M) [23]	RAF No 1 SoTT, Halton	
XP573	Hunting Jet Provost T4 (8236M) [19]	RAF No 1 SoTT, Halton	
XP585	Hunting Jet Provost T4 (8407M) [24]	RAF No 1 SoTT, Halton	
XP627	Hunting Jet Provost T4	North East Aircraft Museum, Usworth	
XP629	Hunting Jet Provost T4 [P]	RAF CATCS, Shawbury	
XP638	Hunting Jet Provost T4 [A]	RAF CATCS, Shawbury	
XP640	Hunting Jet Provost T4 (8501M) [E]	RAF No 1 SoTT, Halton	
XP672	Hunting Jet Provost T4 (8458M) [27]	RAF No 1 SoTT, Halton	
XP677	Hunting Jet Provost T4 (8587M) (nose only)	No 2530 Sqn ATC, Headley Court, Uckfield, East Sussex	
XP680	Hunting Jet Provost T4 (8460M)	RAF St Athan	
XP686	Hunting Jet Provost T4 (8401M/8502M) [G]	RAF No 1 SoTT, Halton	
XP688	Hunting Jet Provost T4 [E]	RAF CATCS, Shawbury	
XP693	BAC Lightning F6 [M]	MoD(PE) BAe Warton	
XP694	BAC Lightning F3	RAF Binbrook, store	
XP695	BAC Lightning F3 (8808M) [6]	RAF Binbrook, BDRT	
XP701	BAC Lightning F3	RAF No 11 Sqn, Binbrook	
XP702	BAC Lightning F3	RAF Binbrook, store	
XP706	BAC Lightning F3	RAF Binbrook, store	
XP707	BAC Lightning F3 [DB]	RAF LTF, Binbrook	
XP741	BAC Lightning F3	RAF Binbrook	
XP745	BAC Lightning F3 (8453M) [H]	RAF Boulmer, at main gate	
XP748	BAC Lightning F3 (8446M) [M]	RAF Binbrook, at main gate	
XP749	BAC Lightning F3 [DA]	RAF LTF, Binbrook	
XP750	BAC Lightning F3	RAF No 11 Sqn, Binbrook	
XP751	BAC Lightning F3	RAF Binbrook, store	
XP761	BAC Lightning F3 (8438M) [N]	RAF Binbrook Fire Section	
XP764	BAC Lightning F3 [DC]	RAF LTF, Binbrook	
XP769	DHC Beaver AL1	AAC, Aldergrove	
XP771	DHC Beaver AL1	AAC, Aldergrove	
XP772	DHC Beaver AL1	Museum of Army Transport, Beverley	
XP774	DHC Beaver AL1	AAC, Shawbury store	
XP775	DHC Beaver AL1	AAC, Shawbury store	
XP778	DHC Beaver AL1	AAC Beaver Training Flt, Middle Wallop	
XP779	DHC Beaver AL1	AAC Beaver Training Flt, Middle Wallop	

Notes	Serial	Type (alternative identity)	Owner, Operator or Location
	XP780	DHC Beaver AL1	AAC, Shawbury store
	XP804	DHC Beaver AL1	AAC, Shawbury store
	XP806	DHC Beaver AL1	Army Apprentice College, Arborfield
	XP808	DHC Beaver AL1	AAC, Shawbury store
	XP810	DHC Beaver AL1	AAC, Shawbury store
	XP814	DHC Beaver AL1	AAC, Shawbury store
	XP816	DHC Beaver AL1	AAC, Shawbury store
	XP817	DHC Beaver AL1	AAC, Shawbury store
	XP818	DHC Beaver AL1	AAC, Shawbury store
	XP820	DHC Beaver AL1	AAC Beaver Training Flt, Middle Wallop
	XP821	DHC Beaver AL1	Museum of Army Flying, Middle Wallop
	XP822	DHC Beaver AL1	AAC, Shawbury store
	XP823	DHC Beaver AL1	AAC, Shawbury store
	XP825	DHC Beaver AL1	AAC, Aldergrove
	XP827	DHC Beaver AL1	AAC, Shawbury store
	XP831	Hawker P1127 (8406M)	RAF Museum, Hendon
	XP841	Handley Page HP115	FAA Museum, RNAS Yeovilton
	XP846	WS Scout AH1 [B]	AAC store, Wrougthon
	XP847	WS Scout AH1	Museum of Army Flying, Middle Wallop
	XP848	WS Scout AH1	AAC AETW, Middle Wallop
	XP849	WS Scout AH1	MoD(PE) ETPS Boscombe Down
	XP850	WS Scout AH1	AAC store, Wroughton
	XP852	WS Scout AH1	AAC store, Wroughton
	XP853	WS Scout AH1	AAC AETW, Middle Wallop
	XP854	WS Scout AH1 (7898M/ TAD043)	AAC AETW, Middle Wallop
	XP855	WS Scout AH1	AAC store, Wroughton
	XP856	WS Scout AH1	AAC AETW, Middle Wallop
	XP857	WS Scout AH1	Museum of Army Flying store, Middle Wallop
	XP883	WS Scout AH1	AAC, store Wroughton
	XP884	WS Scout AH1	AAC AETW, Middle Wallop
	XP885	WS Scout AH1 [Y]	AAC No 666 (TA) Sqn, Netheravon
	XP886	WS Scout AH1	AAC store, Wroughton
	XP887	WS Scout AH1 [C]	AAC No 660 Sqn, Sek Kong
	XP888	WS Scout AH1	AAC AETW, Middle Wallop
	XP890	WS Scout AH1 [G]	AAC store, Wroughton
	XP891	WS Scout AH1 [S]	AAC No 666 (TA) Sqn, Netheravon
	XP893	WS Scout AH1	AAC Garrison Air Sqn, Falklands
	XP894	WS Scout AH1 [D]	AAC No 660 Sqn, Sek Kong
	XP897	WS Scout AH1	AAC store, Wroughton
	XP898	WS Scout AH1	AAC store, Wroughton
	XP899	WS Scout AH1 [D]	Army Apprentice College, Arborfield
	XP900	WS Scout AH1 [Z]	AAC ATS, Middle Wallop
	XP901	WS Scout AH1 [E]	AAC No 660 Sqn, Sek Kong
	XP902	WS Scout AH1	AAC Garrison Air Sqn, Falklands
	XP903	WS Scout AH1	AAC store, Wroughton
	XP905	WS Scout AH1	AAC AETW, Middle Wallop
	XP907	WS Scout AH1	AAC store, Wroughton
	XP909	WS Scout AH1	AAC AETW, Middle Wallop
	XP910	WS Scout AH1	AAC store, Wroughton
	XP915	DH Comet 3B (G-ANLO)	BAe Woodford
	XP919	DH Sea Vixen FAW2 (8163M) [706/VL]	City of Norwich Aviation Museum
	XP921	DH Sea Vixen FAW2 (8226M)	RAF No 1 SoTT, Halton
	XP924	DH Sea Vixen D3	Flight Refuelling Ltd, Hurn
	XP967	Sud Alouette AH2	AAC No 16 Flt, Dhekelia
	XP976	Hawker Kestrel FGA1	RAF Wittering Fire Section
	XP980	Hawker Kestrel FGA1 (A2700)	RNAS Culdrose, SAH
	XP984	Hawker Kestrel FGA1 (A2658)	RNEC Manadon, for instruction
	XR107	AW Argosy T2 (8441M) [B]	RAF No 2 SoTT, Cosford
	XR137	AW Argosy E1	RAF Northolt Fire Section
	XR140	AW Argosy E1 (8579M) [140]	RAF No 1 SoTT, Halton
	XR220	BAC TSR2 (7933M)	RAF Cosford Aerospace Museum
	XR222	BAC TSR2	Imperial War Museum, Duxford
	XR232	Sud Alouette AH2 (F-WEIP)	AAC UNFICYP, Nicosia
	XR240	Auster AOP9 (G-BDFH)	Privately owned, Booker
	XR241	Auster AOP9 (G-AXRR)	Privately owned, Duxford
	XR243	Auster AOP9 (8057M)	RAF St Athan Historic Aircraft Collection
	XR244	Auster AOP9	AAC Historic Aircraft Flight, Middle Wallop
	XR246	Auster AOP9 (7862M/ G-AZBU)	Privately owned, Reymerston Hall

Serial	Type (alternative identity)	Owner, Operator or Location	Notes
XR267	Auster AOP9 (G-BJXR)	Cotswold Aircraft Restoration Group, RAF Innsworth	
XR269	Auster AOP9 (G-BDXY)	Privately owned, Eaglescott, Devon	
XR271	Auster AOP9	Museum of Artillery, Woolwich	
XR363	SC5 Belfast (G-OHCA)	Privately owned, Southend	
XR371	SC5 Belfast C1	RAF Cosford Aerospace Museum	
XR376	Sud Alouette AH2	AAC UNFICYP, Nicosia	
XR378	Sud Alouette AH2	AAC No 16 Flt, Dhekelia	
XR379	Sud Alouette AH2	AAC No 16 Flt, Dhekelia	
XR382	Sud Alouette AH2	AAC UNFICYP, Nicosia	
XR385	Sud Alouette AH2	AAC No 16 Flt, Dhekelia	
XR386	Sud Alouette AH2	AAC UNFICYP, Nicosia	
XR396	DH Comet 4C (8882M) (G-BDIU)	RAF Kinloss BDRT	
XR436	Saro Scout AH1	AAC Middle Wallop, BDRT	
XR441	DH Sea Heron C1 (G-AORG)	RNAS Yeovilton, Station Flight	
XR442	DH Sea Heron C1 (G-AORH)	RNAS Yeovilton, Station Flight	
XR443	DH Sea Heron C1 (G-ARKU)	RN FONAC, Yeovilton	
XR445	DH Sea Heron C1 (G-ARKW)	RN NATIU, Lee-on-Solent	
XR453	WS55 Whirlwind HAR10 (8873M) [A]	RAF Odiham, on display	
XR458	WS55 Whirlwind HAR10 (8662M) [H]	RAF No 1 SoTT, Halton	
XR478	WS55 Whirlwind HAR10 [P]	Defence School, Winterbourne Gunner	
XR479	WS55 Whirlwind HAR10 [A]	RAE Farnborough Fire Section	
XR481	WS55 Whirlwind HAR10	RAF store, Wroughton	
XR482	WS55 Whirlwind HAR10 [G]	Defence School, Winterbourne Gunner	
XR483	WS55 Whirlwind HAR10	RAF store, Wroughton	
XR485	WS55 Whirlwind HAR10 [Q]	Norfolk & Suffolk Aviation Museum, Flixton	
XR486	WS55 Whirlwind HCC12 (8727M)	RAF St Athan Historic Aircraft Collection	
XR493	Saro Scout AH1 (G-APVM/8040M)	MoD(PE) RAE Farnborough	
XR497	WS58 Wessex HC2	RAF No 22 Sqn SAR*	

Note: * No 22 Sqn SAR and the SAREW are based at RAF Finningley with detached Flights at: A Flt — RAF Chivenor; B Flt — RAF Leuchars; C Flt and SARTF — RAF Valley; D Flt — RAF Leconfield; E Flt — RAF Manston.

Serial	Type (alternative identity)	Owner, Operator or Location	Notes
XR498	WS58 Wessex HC2 [X]	RAF No 72 Sqn, Aldergrove	
XR499	WS58 Wessex HC2 [W]	RAF No 72 Sqn, Aldergrove	
XR501	WS58 Wessex HC2	RAF No 22 Sqn SAR*	
XR502	WS58 Wessex HC2 [Z]	RAF No 72 Sqn, Aldergrove	
XR503	WS58 Wessex HC2	MoD(PE) RAE Bedford	
XR504	WS58 Wessex HC2	RAF No 22 Sqn SAR*	
XR505	WS58 Wessex HC2 [WA]	RAF No 2 FTS, Shawbury	
XR506	WS58 Wessex HC2 [V]	RAF No 72 Sqn, Aldergrove	
XR507	WS58 Wessex HC2	RAF No 22 Sqn SAR*	
XR508	WS58 Wessex HC2 [D]	RAF No 28 Sqn, Sek Kong	
XR509	WS58 Wessex HC2 (8752M)	RAF WSF, Benson	
XR511	WS58 Wessex HC2 [L]	RAF No 72 Sqn, Aldergrove	
XR515	WS58 Wessex HC2 [B]	RAF No 28 Sqn, Sek Kong	
XR516	WS58 Wessex HC2 [WB]	RAF No 2 FTS, Shawbury	
XR517	WS58 Wessex HC2 [N]	RAF No 72 Sqn, Aldergrove	
XR518	WS58 Wessex HC2	RAF No 22 Sqn SAR*	
XR519	WS58 Wessex HC2 [WC]	RAF No 2 FTS, Shawbury	
XR520	WS58 Wessex HC2	RAF No 22 Sqn SAR*	
XR521	WS58 Wessex HC2 [WD]	RAF No 2 FTS, Shawbury	
XR522	WS58 Wessex HC2 [I]	RAF No 28 Sqn, Sek Kong	
XR523	WS58 Wessex HC2 [M]	RAF No 72 Sqn, Aldergrove	
XR524	WS58 Wessex HC2	RAF No 22 Sqn SAR*	
XR525	WS58 Wessex HC2 [G]	RAF No 72 Sqn, Aldergrove	
XR526	WS58 Wessex HC2 (8147M)	Westlands, Sherborne	
XR527	WS58 Wessex HC2 [C]	RAF No 28 Sqn, Sek Kong	
XR528	WS58 Wessex HC2 [A]	RAF No 28 Sqn, Sek Kong	
XR529	WS58 Wessex HC2 [E]	RAF No 72 Sqn, Aldergrove	
XR534	HS Gnat T1 (8578M) [65]	RAF Valley	
XR535	HS Gnat T1 (8569M) [05]	RAF No 1 SoTT, Halton	
XR537	HS Gnat T1 (8642M)	RAF No 2 SoTT, Cosford	
XR538	HS Gnat T1 (8621M) [69]	RAF No 1 SoTT, Halton	
XR540	HS Gnat T1 (8636M/A2708) [SAH-5]	RNAS Culdrose	

Notes	Serial	Type (alternative identity)	Owner, Operator or Location
	XR541	HS Gnat T1 (8602M)	RAF St Athan, CTTS
	XR544	HS Gnat T1	RAE Farnborough Fire Section
	XR569	HS Gnat T1 (8560M) [08]	RAF No 1 SoTT, Halton
	XR571	HS Gnat T1 (8493M) [23]	RAF *Red Arrows* Scampton on display
	XR572	HS Gnat T1 (A2676) [SAH-3]	RNAS Culdrose, SAH
	XR574	HS Gnat T1 (8631M) [72]	RAF No 1 SoTT, Halton
	XR588	WS58 Wessex HC2	RAF No 22 Sqn SAR*
	XR595	WS Scout AH1 [M]	AAC No 666 (TA) Sqn, Netheravon
	XR597	WS Scout AH1	AAC AETW, Middle Wallop
	XR600	WS Scout AH1 [B]	AAC store, Wroughton
	XR601	WS Scout AH1	Army Apprentice College, Arborfield
	XR602	WS Scout AH1	AAC store, Wroughton
	XR603	WS Scout AH1 [A]	AAC store, Wroughton
	XR604	WS Scout AH1	AAC Middle Wallop, BDRT
	XR627	WS Scout AH1	AAC Garrison Air Sqn, Falklands
	XR629	WS Scout AH1	AAC store, Wroughton
	XR630	WS Scout AH1 [U]	AAC Middle Wallop, BDRT
	XR632	WS Scout AH1 [Q]	AAC No 666 (TA) Sqn, Netheravon
	XR635	WS Scout AH1	AAC AETW, Middle Wallop
	XR637	WS Scout AH1	AAC store, Wroughton
	XR639	WS Scout AH1 [X]	AAC store, Wroughton
	XR643	Hunting Jet Provost T4 (8516M) [26]	RAF No 1 SoTT, Halton
	XR650	Hunting Jet Provost T4 (8459M) [28]	RAF No 1 SoTT, Halton
	XR651	Hunting Jet Provost T4 (8431M) [A]	RAF No 1 SoTT, Halton
	XR653	Hunting Jet Provost T4 [H]	RAF CATCS, Shawbury
	XR654	Hunting Jet Provost T4 [34]	Lovaux Ltd, Hurn
	XR658	Hunting Jet Provost T4 (8192M)	RAF Exhibition Flight, Abingdon
	XR662	Hunting Jet Provost T4 (8410M) [25]	RAF No 1 SoTT, Halton
	XR669	Hunting Jet Provost T4 (8062M) [02] (nose only)	RAF No 1 SoTT, Halton
	XR670	Hunting Jet Provost T4 (8498M)	RAF No 1 SoTT, Halton
	XR672	Hunting Jet Provost T4 (8495M) [C] [73]	RAF No 1 SoTT, Halton
	XR673	Hunting Jet Provost T4 [L]	RAF CATCS, Shawbury
	XR674	Hunting Jet Provost T4 [D]	RAF CATCS, Shawbury
	XR679	Hunting Jet Provost T4 [04]	RAF No 1 TWU/79 Sqn Brawdy
	XR681	Hunting Jet Provost T4 (8588M) (nose only)	No 1349 Sqn ATC, Odiham
	XR700	Hunting Jet Provost T4 (8589M) (nose only)	RAF Exhibition Flight, Aldergrove
	XR701	Hunting Jet Provost T4 [K]	RAF CATCS, Shawbury
	XR704	Hunting Jet Provost T4 (8506M) [30]	RAF No 1 SoTT, Halton
	XR713	EE Lightning F3 [DD]	RAF LTF, Binbrook
	XR716	EE Lightning F3 [AS]	RAF Binbrook store
	XR717	EE Lightning F3	A&AEE Boscombe Down Fire Section
	XR718	EE Lightning F3 [DE]	RAF LTF, Binbrook
	XR720	EE Lightning F3	RAF Binbrook store
	XR724	EE Lightning F6 [AE]	RAF No 5 Sqn, Binbrook
	XR725	EE Lightning F6 [BA]	RAF No 11 Sqn, Binbrook
	XR726	EE Lightning F6 [DF]	RAF LTF, Binbrook
	XR727	EE Lightning F6 [AB]	RAF No 5 Sqn, Binbrook
	XR728	EE Lightning F6 [BF]	RAF No 11 Sqn, Binbrook
	XR747	EE Lightning F6 [AL]	RAF No 5 Sqn, Binbrook
	XR749	EE Lightning F3 [DA]	RAF Binbrook store
	XR751	EE Lightning F3	RAF Binbrook store
	XR752	EE Lightning F6 [BL]	RAF No 11 Sqn, Binbrook
	XR753	EE Lightning F6	RAF No 5 Sqn, Binbrook
	XR754	EE Lightning F6	RAF No 5 Sqn, Binbrook
	XR755	EE Lightning F6 [BN]	RAF No 11 Sqn, Binbrook
	XR756	EE Lightning F6 [BH]	RAF No 11 Sqn, Binbrook
	XR757	EE Lightning F6 [BL]	RAF No 11 Sqn, Binbrook
	XR758	EE Lightning F6 [BF]	RAF No 11 Sqn, Binbrook
	XR759	EE Lightning F6 [BJ]	RAF No 11 Sqn, Binbrook
	XR763	EE Lightning F6	RAF No 5 Sqn, Binbrook
	XR769	EE Lightning F6 [BE]	RAF No 11 Sqn, Binbrook
	XR770	EE Lightning F6 [AA]	RAF No 5 Sqn, Binbrook
	XR771	EE Lightning F6 [AN]	RAF No 5 Sqn, Binbrook

Serial	Type (alternative identity)	Owner, Operator or Location	Notes
XR772	EE Lightning F6	RAF Binbrook store	
XR773	EE Lightning F6 [AB]	RAF No 5 Sqn, Binbrook	
XR777	WS Scout AH1 (really XT625)	St George's Barracks, Sutton Coldfield	
XR806	BAC VC10 C1	RAF No 10 Sqn, Brize Norton	
XR807	BAC VC10 C1	RAF No 10 Sqn, Brize Norton	
XR808	BAC VC10 C1	RAF No 10 Sqn, Brize Norton	
XR810	BAC VC10 C1	RAF No 10 Sqn, Brize Norton	
XR951	HS Gnat T1 (8603M) [26]	RAF No 1 SoTT, Halton	
XR953	HS Gnat T1 (8609M) [63]	RAF No 1 SoTT, Halton	
XR954	HS Gnat T1 (8570M) [30]	RAF No 1 SoTT, Halton	
XR955	HS Gnat T1 (A2678) [SAH-2]	RNAS Culdrose, SAH	
XR977	HS Gnat T1 (8640M)	RAF Cosford Aerospace Museum	
XR980	HS Gnat T1 (8622M) [70]	RAF No 1 SoTT, Halton	
XR984	HS Gnat T1 (8571M)	RAF No 1 SoTT, Halton	
XR987	HS Gnat T1 (8641M) [10]	RAF No 2 SoTT, Cosford	
XR991	HS Gnat T1 (8637M/ A2709) [SAH-6]	RNAS Culdrose, SAH	
XR993	HS Gnat T1 (A2677/8878M) [SAH-4]	RAF Museum, Hendon	
XR998	HS Gnat T1 (8623M) [71]	RAF No 1 SoTT, Halton	
XS100	HS Gnat T1 (8561M) [57]	RAF No 1 SoTT, Halton	
XS101	HS Gnat T1 (8638M) (G-GNAT)	Privately owned, Cranfield	
XS102	HS Gnat T1 (8624M) [66]	RAF No 1 SoTT, Halton	
XS104	HS Gnat T1 (8604M) [44]	RAF No 2 SoTT, Cosford	
XS105	HS Gnat T1 (8625M) [35]	RAF No 2 SoTT, Cosford	
XS107	HS Gnat T1 (8639M)	RAF No 2 SoTT, Cosford	
XS109	HS Gnat T1 (8626M) [75]	RAF No 1 SoTT, Halton	
XS110	HS Gnat T1 (8562M) [20]	RAF No 1 SoTT, Halton	
XS119	WS58 Wessex HAS3 [655/PO]	RN Predannack Fire School	
XS120	WS58 Wessex HAS1 (8653M) [520/CU]	RAF Abingdon Fire Section	
XS122	WS58 Wessex HAS3 (A2707) [655/PO]	RNEC Manadon, for instruction	
XS125	WS58 Wessex HAS1 (A2648) [517]	RN Predannack Fire School	
XS127	WS58 Wessex HAS3	RN Predannack Fire School	
XS128	WS58 Wessex HAS1 (A2670)	RNAS Yeovilton BDRT	
XS149	WS58 Wessex HAS3 [661/GL]	RN store, Wroughton	
XS153	WS58 Wessex HAS3 [662/PO]	RN AES Lee-on-Solent	
XS176	Hunting Jet Provost T4 (8514M) [N]	RAF No 1 SoTT, Halton	
XS177	Hunting Jet Provost T4 [N]	RAF CATCS, Shawbury	
XS178	Hunting Jet Provost T4 [05]	RAF No 1 TWU/79 Sqn, Brawdy	
XS179	Hunting Jet Provost T4 (8237M) [20]	RAF No 1 SoTT, Halton	
XS180	Hunting Jet Provost T4 (8238M) [21]	RAF No 1 SoTT, Halton	
XS181	Hunting Jet Provost T4 [F]	RAF CATCS, Shawbury	
XS186	Hunting Jet Provost T4 (8408M) [M]	RAF No 1 SoTT, Halton	
XS209	Hunting Jet Provost T4 (8409M) [29]	RAF No 1 SoTT, Halton	
XS210	Hunting Jet Provost T4 (8239M) [22]	RAF No 1 SoTT, Halton	
XS215	Hunting Jet Provost T4 (8507M) [17]	RAF No 1 SoTT, Halton	
XS216	Hunting Jet Provost T4 [Q]	RAF Finningley, for rescue training	
XS217	Hunting Jet Provost T4 [O]	RAF CATCS, Shawbury	
XS218	Hunting Jet Provost T4 (8508M) [18]	RAF No 1 SoTT, Halton	
XS219	Hunting Jet Provost T4 [06]	RAF No 1 TWU/79 Sqn, Brawdy	
XS230	BAC Jet Provost T5P	MoD(PE) ETPS Boscombe Down	
XS231	BAC Jet Provost T5 (G-ATAJ)	RAF Shawbury store	
XS235	HS Comet 4C	MoD(PE) A&AEE Boscombe Down	
XS241	WS58 Wessex HU5	MoD(PE) RAE Farnborough	
XS416	EE Lightning T5 [AZ]	RAF No 5 Sqn, Binbrook	
XS417	EE Lightning T5 [DZ]	RAF LTF, Binbrook	

Notes	Serial	Type (alternative identity)	Owner, Operator or Location
	XS418	EE Lightning T5 (8531M)	RAF Binbrook
	XS419	EE Lightning T5 [DV]	RAF LTF, Binbrook
	XS420	EE Lightning T5 [DU]	RAF Binbrook store
	XS422	EE Lightning T5	MoD(PE) ETPS Boscombe Down
	XS423	EE Lightning T5 (8532M)	RAF Binbrook
	XS449	EE Lightning T5 (8533M) [5]	RAF Binbrook
	XS450	EE Lightning T5 (8534M) [X]	RAF Binbrook Fire Section
	XS451	EE Lightning T5 (8503M)	RAF Newton, for ground instruction
	XS452	EE Lightning T5 [BT]	RAF No 11 Sqn, Binbrook
	XS454	EE Lightning T5 (8535M) [4]	RAF Binbrook
	XS456	EE Lightning T5 [DX]	RAF LTF, Binbrook
	XS457	EE Lightning T5 [AT]	RAF Binbrook store
	XS458	EE Lightning T5	RAF Binbrook
	XS459	EE Lightning T5 [DW]	RAF LTF, Binbrook
	XS463	WS Wasp HAS1 (A2647)	RN Predannack Fire School
	XS463	WS Wasp HAS1 (really XT431)	British Rotorcraft Museum, Weston-super-Mare
	XS479	WS58 Wessex HU5 [XF] (8819M)	RAF JATE, Brize Norton
	XS481	WS58 Wessex HU5	RN store, Wroughton
	XS482	WS58 Wessex HU5 [A-D]	RAE Farnborough Apprentice School
	XS483	WS58 Wessex HU5 [T]	RN store, Wroughton
	XS484	WS58 Wessex HU5 [821/CU]	RN No 771 Sqn, Culdrose
	XS485	WS58 Wessex HC5C (*Hearts*)	RAF No 84 Sqn, Akrotiri
	XS486	WS58 Wessex HU5 [825/CU]	RN No 771 Sqn, Culdrose
	XS488	WS58 Wessex HU5 [XK]	RN store, Wroughton
	XS489	WS58 Wessex HU5 [R]	RN store, Wroughton
	XS491	WS58 Wessex HU5 [XM]	RN store, Wroughton
	XS492	WS58 Wessex HU5 [623/PO]	RN No 772 Sqn, Portland
	XS493	WS58 Wessex HU5 (*Clubs*)	RN Exhibition Unit (846 Sqn), Fleetlands
	XS496	WS58 Wessex HU5 [625/PO]	RN No 772 Sqn, Portland
	XS498	WS58 Wessex HC5C (*Diamonds*)	RAF No 84 Sqn, Akrotiri
	XS506	WS58 Wessex HU5 [XE]	RN store, Wroughton
	XS507	WS58 Wessex HU5 [627/PO]	RN No 772 Sqn, Portland
	XS508	WS58 Wessex HU5	RN No 707 Sqn, Yeovilton
	XS509	WS58 Wessex HU5 (A2597)	MoD(PE) ETPS Boscombe Down
	XS510	WS58 Wessex HU5 [626/PO]	RN No 772 Sqn, Portland
	XS511	WS58 Wessex HU5 [M]	RN AES, Lee-on-Solent
	XS513	WS58 Wessex HU5 [419/PO]	RN No 772 Sqn, Portland
	XS514	WS58 Wessex HU5 [L]	RN AES, Lee-on-Solent
	XS515	WS58 Wessex HU5 [N]	RN AES, Lee-on-Solent
	XS516	WS58 Wessex HU5 [Q]	RN AES, Lee-on-Solent
	XS517	WS58 Wessex HC5C (*Spades*)	RAF No 84 Sqn, Akrotiri
	XS518	WS58 Wessex HC5C (*Joker*)	RAF No 84 Sqn, Akrotiri
	XS520	WS58 Wessex HU5 [F]	RN AES, Lee-on-Solent
	XS521	WS58 Wessex HU5 [YB]	RN store, Wroughton
	XS522	WS58 Wessex HU5 [ZL]	RN store, Wroughton
	XS523	WS58 Wessex HU5 [824/CU]	RN No 771 Sqn, Culdrose
	XS527	WS Wasp HAS1	FAA Museum, RNAS Yeovilton
	XS529	WS Wasp HAS1 [461]	AES, Lee-on-Solent
	XS535	WS Wasp HAS1 [500]	RAOC, West Moors, Dorset
	XS537	WS Wasp HAS1 (A2672) [582]	RNAS Portland Fire Section
	XS538	WS Wasp HAS1 [451/FIR2]	RN Lee-on-Solent, BDRT
	XS539	WS Wasp HAS1 [435/E]	RN AES, Lee-on-Solent
	XS541	WS Wasp HAS1 [602]	RN store, Wroughton
	XS545	WS Wasp HAS1 (A2702) [635]	RN AES, Lee-on-Solent
	XS562	WS Wasp HAS1 [609]	RN No 829 Sqn, Portland
	XS565	WS Wasp HAS1 [445]	MoD(PE) RAE Farnborough
	XS566	WS Wasp HAS1 [607]	RN No 829 Sqn, Portland
	XS567	WS Wasp HAS1 [434/E]	RN AES Lee-on-Solent
	XS568	WS Wasp HAS1 [441]	RNAY Fleetlands Apprentice School
	XS569	WS Wasp HAS1	RNAY Fleetlands Apprentice School
	XS570	WS Wasp HAS1 (A2699) [AP]	RN AES Lee-on-Solent
	XS572	WS Wasp HAS1 (8845M) [414]	RAF Stafford Fire Section (No 16 MU)
	XS576	DH Sea Vixen FAW2 [125/E]	Imperial War Museum, Duxford

Serial	Type (alternative identity)	Owner, Operator or Location	Notes
XS577	DH Sea Vixen D3	Flight Refuelling Ltd, Hurn	
XS587	DH Sea Vixen FAW(TT)2 (G-VIXN/8828M)	Privately owned, Hurn	
XS590	DH Sea Vixen FAW2 [131/E]	FAA Museum, RNAS Yeovilton	
XS595	HS Andover C1 [A]	RAF Brize Norton Fire Section	
XS596	HS Andover C1	RAF No 115 Sqn, Benson	
XS597	HS Andover C1	RAF No 32 Sqn, Northolt	
XS598	HS Andover C1 [E]	RAF AMS, Brize Norton	
XS603	HS Andover E3	RAF No 115 Sqn, Benson	
XS605	HS Andover E3	RAF No 115 Sqn, Benson	
XS606	HS Andover C1	MoD(PE) ETPS Boscombe Down	
XS607	HS Andover C1	MoD(PE) RAE Bedford	
XS610	HS Andover E3	RAF No 115 Sqn, Benson	
XS637	HS Andover C1	RAF No 32 Sqn, Northolt	
XS639	HS Andover E3A	RAF No 115 Sqn, Benson	
XS640	HS Andover E3	RAF No 115 Sqn, Benson	
XS641	HS Andover E3A	RAF No 115 Sqn, Benson	
XS642	HS Andover C1 [C] (8785M)	RAF Benson Fire Section	
XS643	HS Andover E3A	RAF No 115 Sqn, Benson	
XS644	HS Andover C1	RAF No 115 Sqn, Benson	
XS646	HS Andover C1	MoD(PE) RAE Farnborough	
XS647	HS Andover C1	British Aerospace, Woodford	
XS650	Slingsby Swallow TX1 (8801M)	RAF St Athan Historic Aircraft Collection	
XS674	WS58 Wessex HC2 [R]	RAF No 72 Sqn, Aldergrove	
XS675	WS58 Wessex HC2	RAF No 22 Sqn SAR*	
XS676	WS58 Wessex HC2 [WJ]	RAF No 2 FTS, Shawbury	
XS677	WS58 Wessex HC2 [WK]	RAF No 2 FTS, Shawbury	
XS679	WS58 Wessex HC2 [WG]	RAF No 2 FTS, Shawbury	
XS695	HS Kestrel FGA1 (A2619) [SAH-6]	RNAS Culdrose, SAH	
XS709	HS Dominie T1 [M]	RAF No 6 FTS, Finningley	
XS710	HS Dominie T1 [O]	RAF No 6 FTS, Finningley	
XS711	HS Dominie T1 [L]	RAF No 6 FTS, Finningley	
XS712	HS Dominie T1 [A]	RAF No 6 FTS, Finningley	
XS713	HS Dominie T1 [C]	RAF No 6 FTS, Finningley	
XS714	HS Dominie T1 [P]	RAF No 6 FTS, Finningley	
XS726	HS Dominie T1 [T]	RAF No 6 FTS, Finningley	
XS727	HS Dominie T1 [D]	RAF No 6 FTS, Finningley	
XS728	HS Dominie T1 [E]	RAF No 6 FTS, Finningley	
XS729	HS Dominie T1 [G]	RAF No 6 FTS, Finningley	
XS730	HS Dominie T1 [H]	RAF No 6 FTS, Finningley	
XS731	HS Dominie T1 [J]	RAF No 6 FTS, Finningley	
XS732	HS Dominie T1 [B]	RAF No 6 FTS, Finningley	
XS733	HS Dominie T1 [Q]	RAF No 6 FTS, Finningley	
XS734	HS Dominie T1 [N]	RAF No 6 FTS, Finningley	
XS735	HS Dominie T1 [R]	RAF No 6 FTS, Finningley	
XS736	HS Dominie T1 [S]	RAF No 6 FTS, Finningley	
XS737	HS Dominie T1 [K]	RAF No 6 FTS, Finningley	
XS738	HS Dominie T1 [U]	RAF No 6 FTS, Finningley	
XS739	HS Dominie T1 [F]	RAF No 6 FTS, Finningley	
XS743	Beagle Basset CC1	MoD(PE) ETPS Boscombe Down	
XS765	Beagle Basset CC1 (G-BSET)	Privately owned, Shoreham	
XS770	Beagle Basset CC1	RAF Aerospace Museum, Cosford	
XS789	HS Andover CC2	RAF No 32 Sqn, Northolt	
XS790	HS Andover CC2	RAF Queen's Flight, Benson	
XS791	HS Andover CC2	RAF No 32 Sqn, Northolt	
XS792	HS Andover CC2	RAF No 32 Sqn, Northolt	
XS793	HS Andover CC2	RAF No 32 Sqn, Northolt	
XS794	HS Andover CC2	RAF No 32 Sqn, Northolt	
XS862	WS58 Wessex HAS3 [650/PO]	RNAS Lee-on-Solent, at gate	
XS863	WS58 Wessex HAS1	Imperial War Museum, Duxford	
XS865	WS58 Wessex HAS1 (A2694) [529/CU]	RN AES Lee-on-Solent	
XS866	WS58 Wessex HAS1 (A2705) [520/CU]	RN AES Lee-on-Solent	
XS867	WS58 Wessex HAS1 (A2671)	RNAS Lee-on-Solent Fire Section	
XS868	WS58 Wessex HAS1 (A2691)	RNAY Fleetlands, on gate	
XS869	WS58 Wessex HAS1 (A2649) [508/PO]	FAA Air Medical School, Seafield Park, rescue training	

Notes	Serial	Type (alternative identity)	Owner, Operator or Location
	XS870	WS58 Wessex HAS1 (A2697) [-/PO]	RN AES Lee-on-Solent
	XS871	WS58 Wessex HAS1 (8457M) [AI]	RAF Odiham Fire Section
	XS872	WS58 Wessex HAS1 (A2666) [572/CU]	RNAY Fleetlands Apprentice School
	XS873	WS58 Wessex HAS1 (A2686) [525/CU]	RN AES Lee-on-Solent
	XS876	WS58 Wessex HAS1 (A2695) [523]	RN AES Lee-on-Solent
	XS877	WS58 Wessex HAS1 (A2687) [516/PO]	RNAS Culdrose, SAH
	XS878	WS58 Wessex HAS1 (A2683)	RN AES Lee-on-Solent
	XS881	WS58 Wessex HAS1 (A2675) [046/CU]	FAA Museum, RNAS Yeovilton
	XS882	WS58 Wessex HAS1 (A2696) [524]	RN AES Lee-on-Solent
	XS885	WS58 Wessex HAS1 (A2668) [512/PO]	RNAS Culdrose, SAH
	XS886	WS58 Wessex HAS1 (A2685) [527/CU]	RN AES Lee-on-Solent
	XS887	WS58 Wessex HAS1 (A2690) [514/PO]	RNAS Culdrose, SAH
	XS888	WS58 Wessex HAS1 [521]	RN Exhibition Unit, Fleetlands
	XS895	EE Lightning F6 [BC]	RAF No 11 Sqn, Binbrook
	XS897	EE Lightning F6 [AC]	RAF No 5 Sqn, Binbrook
	XS898	EE Lightning F6 [BM]	RAF No 11 Sqn, Binbrook
	XS899	EE Lightning F6 [AJ]	RAF No 5 Sqn, Binbrook
	XS901	EE Lightning F6 [AH]	RAF No 5 Sqn, Binbrook
	XS903	EE Lightning F6 [AM]	RAF No 5 Sqn, Binbrook
	XS904	EE Lightning F6 [BM]	RAF No 11 Sqn, Binbrook
	XS919	EE Lightning F6	RAF No 11 Sqn, Binbrook
	XS922	EE Lightning F6 [AG]	RAF No 5 Sqn, Binbrook
	XS923	EE Lightning F6 [BG]	RAF No 11 Sqn, Binbrook
	XS925	EE Lightning F6 [BD]	RAF No 11 Sqn, Binbrook
	XS927	EE Lightning F6 [BB]	RAF No 11 Sqn, Binbrook
	XS928	EE Lightning F6 [AH]	RAF No 5 Sqn, Binbrook
	XS929	EE Lightning F6 [BG]	RAF No 11 Sqn, Binbrook
	XS932	EE Lightning F6 [AG]	RAF No 5 Sqn, Binbrook
	XS933	EE Lightning F6 [AJ]	RAF No 5 Sqn, Binbrook
	XS935	EE Lightning F6 [AK]	RAF No 5 Sqn, Binbrook
	XS936	EE Lightning F6 [AS]	RAF No 5 Sqn, Binbrook
	XT108	Agusta-Bell Sioux AH1 [U]	Museum of Army Flying, Middle Wallop
	XT131	Agusta-Bell Sioux AH1 [B]	AAC Historic Aircraft Flight, Middle Wallop
	XT133	Agusta-Bell Sioux AH1 (7923M)	Royal Engineers' Museum, Chatham
	XT140	Agusta-Bell Sioux AH1	Air Service Training, Perth
	XT141	Agusta-Bell Sioux AH1 (8509M)	RAF AMS, Brize Norton
	XT148	Agusta-Bell Sioux AH1	Privately owned, Panshanger
	XT150	Agusta-Bell Sioux AH1 (7883M) [R]	Museum of Army Flying, Middle Wallop
	XT151	WS Sioux AH1	Museum of Army Flying store, Middle Wallop
	XT175	WS Sioux AH1 (TAD175)	CSE Oxford for ground instruction
	XT176	WS Sioux AH1 [C]	FAA Museum, RNAS Yeovilton
	XT190	WS Sioux AH1	Museum of Army Flying, Middle Wallop
	XT200	WS Sioux AH1 [F]	Newark Air Museum, Winthorpe
	XT236	WS Sioux AH1 (frame only)	Museum of Army Flying, Middle Wallop
	XT255	WS58 Wessex HAS3 (8751M)	RAF No 14 MU, Carlisle, BDRT
	XT256	WS58 Wessex HAS3 (A2615)	RN AES Lee-on-Solent
	XT257	WS58 Wessex HAS3 (8719M)	RAF No 1 SoTT, Halton
	XT270	HS Buccaneer S2B	RAF Shawbury store
	XT271	HS Buccaneer S2A [C]	RAF store, St Athan
	XT272	HS Buccaneer S2	MoD(PE) RAE Farnborough
	XT273	HS Buccaneer S2A [D]	RAF store, St Athan
	XT274	HS Buccaneer S2A (8856M) [E]	RAF Abingdon, BDRF

Serial	Type (alternative identity)	Owner, Operator or Location	Notes
XT275	HS Buccaneer S2B [A]	RAF Shawbury store	
XT276	HS Buccaneer S2B [S]	RAF Shawbury store	
XT277	HS Buccaneer S2A (8853M) [F]	RAF No 2 SoTT, Cosford	
XT279	HS Buccaneer S2B	RAF St Athan	
XT280	HS Buccaneer S2B [NS]	RAF No 208 Sqn, Lossiemouth	
XT281	HS Buccaneer S2B (8705M) [ET]	RAF Lossiemouth, ground instruction	
XT283	HS Buccaneer S2A [283]	RAF No 237 OCU, Lossiemouth	
XT284	HS Buccaneer S2A (8855M) [H]	RAF Abingdon, BDRF	
XT286	HS Buccaneer S2B [W]	RAF store, St Athan	
XT287	HS Buccaneer S2B	RAF No 208 Sqn, Lossiemouth	
XT288	HS Buccaneer S2B	MoD(PE) A&AEE Boscombe Down	
XT415	WS Wasp HAS1 [FIR3]	RN store, Wroughton	
XT416	WS Wasp HAS1 [442]	RNAY Fleetlands	
XT420	WS Wasp HAS1 [606]	RN No 829 Sqn, Portland	
XT421	WS Wasp HAS1 [FIR4]	RN store, Wroughton	
XT422	WS Wasp HAS1 [326]	Privately owned, Burgess Hill	
XT423	WS Wasp HAS1 [434/E]	RN Falklands, ground instruction	
XT426	WS Wasp HAS1 [455]	RN No 829 Sqn, Portland	
XT427	WS Wasp HAS1 [606]	Cornwall Aero Park, Helston	
XT429	WS Wasp HAS1 [445]	RN No 829 Sqn, Portland	
XT430	WS Wasp HAS1 [444]	Defence School, Winterbourne Gunner	
XT432	WS Wasp HAS1 [605]	RN No 829 Sqn, Portland	
XT434	WS Wasp HAS1 [FIR2]	RN No 829 Sqn, Portland	
XT437	WS Wasp HAS1 [FIR1]	RN No 829 Sqn, Portland	
XT439	WS Wasp HAS1	RN No 829 Sqn, Portland	
XT441	WS Wasp HAS1 (A2703) [337]	RNAS Culdrose Fire Section	
XT443	WS Wasp HAS1 [422/AU]	RN No 829 Sqn, Portland	
XT449	WS58 Wessex HU5 [C]	RN store, Wroughton	
XT450	WS58 Wessex HU5 [V]	RN Predannack Fire School	
XT451	WS58 Wessex HU5 [XN]	RN store, Wroughton	
XT453	WS58 Wessex HU5 [A]	RN AES, Lee-on-Solent	
XT455	WS58 Wessex HU5 [U]	RN AES, Lee-on-Solent	
XT456	WS58 Wessex HU5 [XZ]	RN store, Wroughton	
XT458	WS58 Wessex HU5 [622/PO]	RN No 772 Sqn, Portland	
XT459	WS58 Wessex HU5 [D]	RNAS Lee-on-Solent Fire Section	
XT460	WS58 Wessex HU5 [K]	RN AES, Lee-on-Solent	
XT461	WS58 Wessex HU5 [825/CU]	RN NATIU, Lee-on-Solent	
XT463	WS58 Wessex HC5C (*Clubs*)	RAF No 84 Sqn, Akrotiri	
XT466	WS58 Wessex HU5 [XV]	RN store, Wroughton	
XT467	WS58 Wessex HU5	RN store, Wroughton	
XT468	WS58 Wessex HU5 [628/PO]	RN No 772 Sqn, Portland	
XT469	WS58 Wessex HU5 [XN]	RN store, Wroughton	
XT470	WS58 Wessex HU5 [A]	AAC Netheravon Fire Section	
XT471	WS58 Wessex HU5	RN No 771 Sqn, Culdrose	
XT472	WS58 Wessex HU5 [X-C]	RAF Hullavington for instruction	
XT474	WS58 Wessex HU5 [820/CU]	RN No 771 Sqn, Culdrose	
XT475	WS58 Wessex HU5 [624/PO]	RN No 772 Sqn, Portland	
XT479	WS58 Wessex HC5C	MoD(PE) A&AEE Boscombe Down	
XT480	WS58 Wessex HU5 [XQ]	RN store, Wroughton	
XT481	WS58 Wessex HU5 [XF]	RN store, Wroughton	
XT482	WS58 Wessex HU5 [ZM/VL]	RN store, Wroughton	
XT484	WS58 Wessex HU5 [H]	RNAS Lee-on-Solent BDRT	
XT485	WS58 Wessex HU5 [621/PO]	RN No 772 Sqn, Portland	
XT486	WS58 Wessex HU5 [XR]	RN store, Wroughton	
XT487	WS58 Wessex HU5 (A2723) [815/LS]	RNAS Lee-on-Solent Fire Section	
XT548	WS Sioux AH1 [D]	Museum of Army Flying store, Middle Wallop	
XT550	WS Sioux AH1 [D]	Museum of Army Flying, Middle Wallop	
XT567	WS Sioux AH1	Privately owned, Fairoaks	
XT575	Vickers Viscount (OE-LAG)	MoD(PE) RS&RE Bedford	
XT595	McD Phantom FG1 (fuselage etc) (8851M)	RAF Wattisham, BDRT	
XT595	McD Phantom FG1 (nose only) (8550M)	RAF Exhibition Flight, Abingdon	
XT596	McD Phantom FG1	MoD(PE) BAe Scampton	

Notes	Serial	Type (alternative identity)	Owner, Operator or Location
	XT597	McD Phantom FG1	MoD(PE) A&AEE Boscombe Down
	XT601	WS58 Wessex HC2	RAF No 22 Sqn SAR*
	XT602	WS58 Wessex HC2	RAF No 22 Sqn SAR*
	XT603	WS58 Wessex HC2 [WF]	RAF No 2 FTS, Shawbury
	XT604	WS58 Wessex HC2	RAF No 22 Sqn SAR*
	XT605	WS58 Wessex HC2 [E]	RAF No 28 Sqn, Sek Kong
	XT606	WS58 Wessex HC2	RAF No 22 Sqn SAR*
	XT607	WS58 Wessex HC2 [P]	RAF No 72 Sqn, Aldergrove
	XT614	WS Scout AH1 [G]	AAC No 660 Sqn, Sek Kong
	XT616	WS Scout AH1 [W]	AAC AETW, Middle Wallop
	XT617	WS Scout AH1	AAC store, Wroughton
	XT618	WS Scout AH1 [V]	AAC No 660 Sqn, Brunei
	XT620	WS Scout AH1 [B]	AAC store, Wroughton
	XT621	WS Scout AH1	Royal Military College of Science, Shrivenham
	XT623	WS Scout AH1	AAC store, Wroughton
	XT624	WS Scout AH1 [W]	AAC store, Wroughton
	XT626	WS Scout AH1	AAC store, Wroughton
	XT627	WS Scout AH1 [H]	AAC No 660 Sqn, Sek Kong
	XT628	WS Scout AH1 [J]	AAC No 660 Sqn, Sek Kong
	XT630	WS Scout AH1 [F]	AAC store, Wroughton
	XT631	WS Scout AH1	MoD(PE) A&AEE Boscombe Down
	XT632	WS Scout AH1	AAC store, Wroughton
	XT633	WS Scout AH1	AAC store, Wroughton
	XT634	WS Scout AH1 [T]	AAC No 666 (TA) Sqn, Netheravon
	XT636	WS Scout AH1 [X]	AAC store, Wroughton
	XT637	WS Scout AH1	AAC store, Wroughton
	XT638	WS Scout AH1 [N]	AAC No 666 (TA) Sqn, Netheravon
	XT639	WS Scout AH1 [Y]	AAC store, Wroughton
	XT640	WS Scout AH1	AAC AETW, Middle Wallop
	XT642	WS Scout AH1	AAC store, Wroughton
	XT643	WS Scout AH1 [B]	AAC No 660 Sqn, Sek Kong
	XT644	WS Scout AH1	AAC store, Wroughton
	XT645	WS Scout AH1	AAC store, Wroughton
	XT646	WS Scout AH1 [Z]	AAC No 666 (TA) Sqn, Netheravon
	XT648	WS Scout AH1	AAC store, Wroughton
	XT649	WS Scout AH1	AAC No 658 Sqn, Netheravon
	XT657	BHC SR.N6 Winchester 5	British Hovercraft Corpn
	XT661	Vickers Viscount (9G-AAV)	MoD(PE) RS&RE Bedford
	XT667	WS58 Wessex HC2 [F]	RAF No 28 Sqn, Sek Kong
	XT668	WS58 Wessex HC2 [S]	RAF No 72 Sqn, Aldergrove
	XT669	WS58 Wessex HC2 (8894M) [T]	RAF Aldergrove Fire Section
	XT670	WS58 Wessex HC2	RAF No 22 Sqn SAR*
	XT671	WS58 Wessex HC2 [D]	RAF No 72 Sqn, Aldergrove
	XT672	WS58 Wessex HC2 [WE]	RAF No 2 FTS, Shawbury
	XT673	WS58 Wessex HC2 [G]	RAF No 28 Sqn, Sek Kong
	XT674	WS58 Wessex HC2	RAF No 22 Sqn SAR*
	XT675	WS58 Wessex HC2 [J]	RAF No 28 Sqn, Sek Kong
	XT676	WS58 Wessex HC2 [I]	RAF No 72 Sqn, Aldergrove
	XT678	WS58 Wessex HC2 [H]	RAF No 28 Sqn, Sek Kong
	XT680	WS58 Wessex HC2	RAF No 22 Sqn SAR*
	XT681	WS58 Wessex HC2 [U]	RAF No 72 Sqn, Aldergrove
	XT752	Fairey Gannet T5 [-/LM] (G-APYO/WN365)	RNAS Lee-on-Solent, stored
	XT755	WS58 Wessex HU5 [V]	RN store, Wroughton
	XT756	WS58 Wessex HU5 [ZJ/VL]	RN store, Wroughton
	XT757	WS58 Wessex HU5 [XH] (A2722)	RN AES Lee-on-Solent
	XT759	WS58 Wessex HU5 [XY]	RN store, Wroughton
	XT760	WS58 Wessex HU5 [420/PO]	RN No 772 Sqn, Portland
	XT761	WS58 Wessex HU5	RN NASU, Yeovilton
	XT762	WS58 Wessex HU5	RN store, Wroughton
	XT764	WS58 Wessex HU5 [G]	RN store, Wroughton
	XT765	WS58 Wessex HU5 [J]	RN AES, Lee-on-Solent
	XT766	WS58 Wessex HU5 [822/CU]	RN No 771 Sqn, Culdrose
	XT768	WS58 Wessex HU5	RN store, Wroughton
	XT769	WS58 Wessex HU5 [823/CU]	RN No 771 Sqn, Culdrose
	XT770	WS58 Wessex HU5 [P]	RN store, Wroughton
	XT771	WS58 Wessex HU5 [620/PO]	RN No 772 Sqn, Portland
	XT772	WS58 Wessex HU5 (8805M)	RAF SARTU, Valley

Serial	Type (alternative identity)	Owner, Operator or Location	Notes
XT773	WS58 Wessex HU5	RN No 771 Sqn, Culdrose'	
XT778	WS Wasp HAS1 [430]	RN No 829 Sqn, Portland	
XT779	WS Wasp HAS1 [456]	RN store, Wroughton	
XT780	WS Wasp HAS1 [636]	RNAY Fleetlands Apprentice School	
XT782	WS Wasp HAS1	RN No 829 Sqn, Portland	
XT783	WS Wasp HAS1 [470]	RN AES, Lee-on-Solent	
XT784	WS Wasp HAS1 [FIR1]	RN store, Wroughton	
XT785	WS Wasp HAS1 [462]	RN No 829 Sqn, Portland	
XT786	WS Wasp HAS1 [441]	RN Portland, ground instruction	
XT788	WS Wasp HAS1 [442] (G-BMIR)	Privately owned, Tattershall Thorpe	
XT790	WS Wasp HAS1 [608]	RN No 829 Sqn, Portland	
XT791	WS Wasp HAS1 [433]	RN No 829 Sqn, Portland	
XT793	WS Wasp HAS1 [456]	RN No 829 Sqn, Portland	
XT795	WS Wasp HAS1 [476/LE]	RN AES, Lee-on-Solent	
XT803	WS Sioux AH1 [Y]	Privately owned, Panshanger	
XT827	WS Sioux AH1 [D]	Army Apprentice College, Arborfield	
XT847	WS Sioux AH1 [F]	Privately owned, Fairoaks	
XT852	McD Phantom FGR2	MoD(PE) BAe Scampton	
XT853	McD Phantom FGR2	MoD(PE) BAe Scampton	
XT857	McD Phantom FG1 [C]	RAF ASF, Leuchars	
XT858	McD Phantom FG1	MoD(PE) BAe Brough (structures test)	
XT859	McD Phantom FG1 [BK]	RAF No 111 Sqn, Leuchars	
XT860	McD Phantom FG1 [AL]	RAF No 43 Sqn, Leuchars	
XT861	McD Phantom FG1 [AC]	RAF No 43 Sqn, Leuchars	
XT863	McD Phantom FG1 [BG]	RAF No 111 Sqn, Leuchars	
XT864	McD Phantom FG1 [BJ]	RAF No 111 Sqn, Leuchars	
XT865	McD Phantom FG1 [BU]	RAF No 111 Sqn, Leuchars	
XT867	McD Phantom FG1 [BH]	RAF No 111 Sqn, Leuchars	
XT870	McD Phantom FG1 [BS]	RAF No 111 Sqn, Leuchars	
XT872	McD Phantom FG1 [BT]	RAF No 111 Sqn, Leuchars	
XT873	McD Phantom FG1 [BA]	RAF No 111 Sqn, Leuchars	
XT874	McD Phantom FG1 [BE]	RAF No 111 Sqn, Leuchars	
XT875	McD Phantom FG1 [AK]	RAF No 43 Sqn, Leuchars	
XT891	McD Phantom FGR2 [Z]	RAF No 228 OCU, Coningsby	
XT892	McD Phantom FGR2 [V]	RAF No 228 OCU, Coningsby	
XT893	McD Phantom FGR2 [Q]	RAF No 228 OCU, Coningsby	
XT894	McD Phantom FGR2 [P]	RAF No 228 OCU, Coningsby	
XT895	McD Phantom FGR2 [H]	RAF No 228 OCU, Coningsby	
XT896	McD Phantom FGR2 [Y]	RAF No 228 OCU, Coningsby	
XT897	McD Phantom FGR2 [M]	RAF No 228 OCU, Coningsby	
XT898	McD Phantom FGR2 [E]	RAF No 228 OCU, Coningsby	
XT899	McD Phantom FGR2 [K]	RAF No 19 Sqn, Wildenrath	
XT900	McD Phantom FGR2 [O]	RAF No 228 OCU, Coningsby	
XT901	McD Phantom FGR2 [Y]	RAF No 56 Sqn, Wattisham	
XT902	McD Phantom FGR2 [M]	RAF No 29 Sqn, Coningsby	
XT903	McD Phantom FGR2 [R]	RAF No 228 OCU, Coningbsy	
XT905	McD Phantom FGR2 [U]	RAF No 228 OCU, Coningsby	
XT906	McD Phantom FGR2 [X]	RAF No 56 Sqn, Wattisham	
XT907	McD Phantom FGR2 [T]	RAF No 228 OCU, Coningsby	
XT908	McD Phantom FGR2 [W]	RAF No 228 OCU, Coningsby	
XT909	McD Phantom FGR2 [W]	RAF No 19 Sqn, Wildenrath	
XT910	McD Phantom FGR2 [J]	RAF No 228 OCU, Coningsby	
XT911	McD Phantom FGR2 [T]	RAF No 92 Sqn, Wildenrath	
XT914	McD Phantom FGR2 [N]	RAF No 228 OCU, Coningsby	
XV101	BAC VC10 C1	RAF No 10 Sqn, Brize Norton	
XV102	BAC VC10 C1	RAF No 10 Sqn, Brize Norton	
XV103	BAC VC10 C1	RAF No 10 Sqn, Brize Norton	
XV104	BAC VC10 C1	RAF No 10 Sqn, Brize Norton	
XV105	BAC VC10 C1	RAF No 10 Sqn, Brize Norton	
XV106	BAC VC10 C1	RAF No 10 Sqn, Brize Norton	
XV107	BAC VC10 C1	RAF No 10 Sqn, Brize Norton	
XV108	BAC VC10 C1	RAF No 10 Sqn, Brize Norton	
XV109	BAC VC10 C1	RAF No 10 Sqn, Brize Norton	
XV118	WS Scout AH1	AAC store, Wroughton	
XV119	WS Scout AH1	AAC store, Wroughton	
XV121	WS Scout AH1 [V]	AAC No 658 Sqn, Netheravon	
XV122	WS Scout AH1 [A]	AAC No 660 Sqn, Sek Kong	
XV123	WS Scout AH1	AAC store, Wroughton	
XV124	WS Scout AH1	AAC store, Wroughton	
XV126	WS Scout AH1	AAC store, Wroughton	
XV127	WS Scout AH1	AAC D&TS, Middle Wallop	
XV128	WS Scout AH1	AAC D&TS, Middle Wallop	
XV129	WS Scout AH1 [V]	AAC No 666 (TA) Sqn, Netheravon	

Notes	Serial	Type (alternative identity)	Owner, Operator or Location
	XV130	WS Scout AH1 [R]	AAC No 666 (TA) Sqn, Netheravon
	XV131	WS Scout AH1 [X]	AAC No 660 Sqn, Brunei
	XV134	WS Scout AH1	AAC No 658 Sqn, Netheravon
	XV135	WS Scout AH1	AAC store, Wroughton
	XV136	WS Scout AH1 [X]	AAC No 666 (TA) Sqn, Netheravon
	XV137	WS Scout AH1 [Z]	AAC No 658 Sqn, Netheravon
	XV138	WS Scout AH1	AAC No 658 Sqn, Netheravon
	XV139	WS Scout AH1	AAC store, Wroughton
	XV140	WS Scout AH1 [K]	AAC No 666 (TA) Sqn, Netheravon
	XV141	WS Scout AH1	Army Apprentice College, Arborfield
	XV147	HS Nimrod MR1 (Mod)	MoD(PE) RAE Farnborough, stored
	XV148	HS Nimrod MR1 (Mod)	MoD(PE) BAe Woodford
	XV152	HS Buccaneer S2A (8776M) [A]	RAF CSDE, Swanton Morley
	XV154	HS Buccaneer S2A (8854M) [A]	RAF Lossiemouth, ground instruction
	XV155	HS Buccaneer S2B (8716M)	BAe Brough Apprentice School
	XV156	HS Buccaneer S2A (8773M)	RAF St Athan Fire Section
	XV157	HS Buccaneer S2B	RAF Shawbury store
	XV161	HS Buccaneer S2A	RAF No 12 Sqn, Lossiemouth
	XV163	HS Buccaneer S2A	RAF store, St Athan
	XV165	HS Buccaneer S2B	RAF No 12 Sqn, Lossiemouth
	XV168	HS Buccaneer S2B	RAF No 208 Sqn, Lossiemouth
	XV176	Lockheed Hercules C3	RAF Lyneham Transport Wing
	XV177	Lockheed Hercules C3	RAF Lyneham Transport Wing
	XV178	Lockheed Hercules C1P	RAF Lyneham Transport Wing
	XV179	Lockheed Hercules C1P	RAF Lyneham Transport Wing
	XV181	Lockheed Hercules C1	RAF Lyneham Transport Wing
	XV182	Lockheed Hercules C1	RAF Lyneham Transport Wing
	XV183	Lockheed Hercules C3	RAF Lyneham Transport Wing
	XV184	Lockheed Hercules C3	RAF Lyneham Transport Wing
	XV185	Lockheed Hercules C1P	RAF Lyneham Transport Wing
	XV186	Lockheed Hercules C1	RAF Lyneham Transport Wing
	XV187	Lockheed Hercules C1P	RAF Lyneham Transport Wing
	XV188	Lockheed Hercules C3	RAF Lyneham Transport Wing
	XV189	Lockheed Hercules C3	RAF Lyneham Transport Wing
	XV190	Lockheed Hercules C3	RAF Lyneham Transport Wing
	XV191	Lockheed Hercules C1P	RAF Lyneham Transport Wing
	XV192	Lockheed Hercules C1K	RAF Lyneham Transport Wing
	XV193	Lockheed Hercules C3	RAF Lyneham Transport Wing
	XV195	Lockheed Hercules C1P	RAF Lyneham Transport Wing
	XV196	Lockheed Hercules C1P	RAF Lyneham Transport Wing
	XV197	Lockheed Hercules C3	RAF Lyneham Transport Wing
	XV199	Lockheed Hercules C3	RAF Lyneham Transport Wing
	XV200	Lockheed Hercules C1P	RAF Lyneham Transport Wing
	XV201	Lockheed Hercules C1K	RAF Lyneham Transport Wing/ 1312 Flt, Stanley
	XV202	Lockheed Hercules C3	RAF Lyneham Transport Wing
	XV203	Lockheed Hercules C1K	RAF Lyneham Transport Wing
	XV204	Lockheed Hercules C1K	RAF Lyneham Transport Wing/ 1312 Flt, Stanley
	XV205	Lockheed Hercules C1P	RAF Lyneham Transport Wing/ 1312 Flt, Stanley
	XV206	Lockheed Hercules C1P	RAF Lyneham Transport Wing
	XV207	Lockheed Hercules C3	RAF Lyneham Transport Wing
	XV208	Lockheed Hercules W2	MoD(PE) RAE Farnborough
	XV209	Lockheed Hercules C3	RAF Lyneham Transport Wing
	XV210	Lockheed Hercules C1P	MoD(PE) A&AEE Boscombe Down
	XV211	Lockheed Hercules C1P	RAF Lyneham Transport Wing
	XV212	Lockheed Hercules C3	RAF Lyneham Transport Wing
	XV213	Lockheed Hercules C1K	RAF Lyneham Transport Wing
	XV214	Lockheed Hercules C3P	RAF Lyneham Transport Wing
	XV215	Lockheed Hercules C1	RAF Lyneham Transport Wing
	XV217	Lockheed Hercules C3	RAF Lyneham Transport Wing
	XV218	Lockheed Hercules C1P	RAF Lyneham Transport Wing
	XV219	Lockheed Hercules C3	RAF Lyneham Transport Wing
	XV220	Lockheed Hercules C3	RAF Lyneham Transport Wing
	XV221	Lockheed Hercules C3	RAF Lyneham Transport Wing
	XV222	Lockheed Hercules C3	RAF Lyneham Transport Wing
	XV223	Lockheed Hercules C3	RAF Lyneham Transport Wing
	XV226	HS Nimrod MR2	RAF No 42 Sqn, St Mawgan
	XV227	HS Nimrod MR2P	RAF Kinloss MR Wing
	XV228	HS Nimrod MR2P	RAF Kinloss MR Wing
	XV229	HS Nimrod MR2	RAF No 42 Sqn, St Mawgan
	XV230	HS Nimrod MR2P	RAF Kinloss MR Wing
	XV231	HS Nimrod MR2	RAF No 42 Sqn, St Mawgan

Serial	Type (alternative identity)	Owner, Operator or Location	Notes
XV232	HS Nimrod MR2P	RAF Kinloss MR Wing	
XV233	HS Nimrod MR2	RAF No 42 Sqn, St Mawgan	
XV234	HS Nimrod MR2P	RAF Kinloss MR Wing	
XV235	HS Nimrod MR2	RAF Kinloss MR Wing	
XV236	HS Nimrod MR2P	RAF No 42 Sqn, St Mawgan	
XV237	HS Nimrod MR2P	RAF Kinloss MR Wing	
XV238	HS Nimrod MR2P	RAF Kinloss MR Wing	
XV239	HS Nimrod MR2P	RAF Kinloss MR Wing	
XV240	HS Nimrod MR2	RAF Kinloss MR Wing	
XV241	HS Nimrod MR2	MoD(PE) A&AEE Boscombe Down	
XV242	HS Nimrod MR2	RAF No 42 Sqn, St Mawgan	
XV243	HS Nimrod MR2P	RAF No 42 Sqn, St Mawgan	
XV244	HS Nimrod MR2	RAF Kinloss MR Wing	
XV245	HS Nimrod MR2	RAF Kinloss MR Wing	
XV246	HS Nimrod MR2	RAF Kinloss MR Wing	
XV247	HS Nimrod MR2P	RAF Kinloss MR Wing	
XV248	HS Nimrod MR2P	RAF Kinloss MR Wing	
XV249	HS Nimrod MR2	RAF Kinloss MR Wing	
XV250	HS Nimrod MR2P	RAF Kinloss MR Wing	
XV251	HS Nimrod MR2	MoD(PE) BAe Woodford	
XV252	HS Nimrod MR2	RAF Kinloss MR Wing	
XV253	HS Nimrod MR2P	RAF Kinloss MR Wing	
XV254	HS Nimrod MR2P	RAF Kinloss MR Wing	
XV255	HS Nimrod MR2P	RAF Kinloss MR Wing	
XV257	HS Nimrod MR2	RAF St Mawgan on rebuild	
XV258	HS Nimrod MR2	RAF Kinloss MR Wing	
XV259	BAe Nimrod AEW3	MoD(PE) BAe Woodford	
XV260	HS Nimrod MR2P	RAF Kinloss MR Wing	
XV261	BAe Nimrod AEW3	MoD(PE) BAe Woodford	
XV262	BAe Nimrod AEW3	MoD(PE) BAe Woodford	
XV263	BAe Nimrod AEW3P	MoD(PE) RAF Waddington	
XV268	DHC Beaver AL1	AAC 7 Regt, Aldergrove	
XV269	DHC Beaver AL1 (8011M)	AAC AETW, Middle Wallop	
XV270	DHC Beaver AL1	AAC, Aldergrove	
XV271	DHC Beaver AL1	AAC, Aldergrove	
XV272	DHC Beaver AL1	AAC Middle Wallop, BDRT	
XV277	HS Harrier GR1	MoD(PE) Rolls-Royce, Filton	
XV281	HS Harrier GR1	MoD(PE) BAe Dunsfold	
XV290	Lockheed Hercules C3	RAF Lyneham Transport Wing	
XV291	Lockheed Hercules C1P	RAF Lyneham Transport Wing	
XV292	Lockheed Hercules C1P	RAF Lyneham Transport Wing	
XV293	Lockheed Hercules C1	RAF Lyneham Transport Wing	
XV294	Lockheed Hercules C3	RAF Lyneham Transport Wing	
XV295	Lockheed Hercules C1	RAF Lyneham Transport Wing	
XV296	Lockheed Hercules C1K	RAF Lyneham Transport Wing	
XV297	Lockheed Hercules C1	RAF Lyneham Transport Wing	
XV298	Lockheed Hercules C1P	RAF Lyneham Transport Wing	
XV299	Lockheed Hercules C3	RAF Lyneham Transport Wing	
XV300	Lockheed Hercules C1P	RAF Lyneham Transport Wing	
XV301	Lockheed Hercules C3	RAF Lyneham Transport Wing	
XV302	Lockheed Hercules C3	RAF Lyneham Transport Wing	
XV303	Lockheed Hercules C3	RAF Lyneham Transport Wing	
XV304	Lockheed Hercules C3	RAF Lyneham Transport Wing	
XV305	Lockheed Hercules C3	RAF Lyneham Transport Wing	
XV306	Lockheed Hercules C1	RAF Lyneham Transport Wing	
XV307	Lockheed Hercules C3	RAF Lyneham Transport Wing	
XV328	EE Lightning T5 [DU]	RAF LTF, Binbrook	
XV332	HS Buccaneer S2B	RAF No 237 OCU, Lossiemouth	
XV333	HS Buccaneer S2B	RAF No 208 Sqn, Lossiemouth	
XV334	HS Buccaneer S2B [D]	RAF Shawbury store	
XV336	HS Buccaneer S2A	RAF Shawbury store	
XV337	HS Buccaneer S2C (8852M)	RAF Abingdon, BDRF	
XV338	HS Buccaneer S2A (fuselage etc) (8774M)	RAF St Athan (for RAF Honington ground instruction)	
XV338	HS Buccaneer S2A (nose only)	RAF Exhibition Flight, Abingdon	
XV342	HS Buccaneer S2B [T]	RAF ASF, Lossiemouth	
XV344	HS Buccaneer S2C	MoD(PE) RAE Farnborough	
XV349	HS Buccaneer S2B	RAF Shawbury store	
XV350	HS Buccaneer S2B	MoD(PE) BAe Woodford	
XV352	HS Buccaneer S2B	RAF No 237 OCU, Lossiemouth	
XV353	HS Buccaneer S2B [353]	RAF No 208 Sqn, Lossiemouth	
XV355	HS Buccaneer S2B	RAF No 237 OCU, Lossiemouth	
XV356	HS Buccaneer S2A [B]	RAF Shawbury store	
XV359	HS Buccaneer S2B	RAF No 237 OCU, Lossiemouth	

Notes	Serial	Type (alternative identity)	Owner, Operator or Location
	XV361	HS Buccaneer S2B	RAF No 208 Sqn, Lossiemouth
	XV370	Sikorsky SH-3D (G-ATYU)	MoD(PE) ETPS Boscombe Down
	XV371	WS67 Sea King HAS1	MoD(PE) RAE Farnborough
	XV372	WS67 Sea King HAS1	Westland Helicopters, Yeovil
	XV373	WS67 Sea King HAS1	MoD(PE) A&AEE Boscombe Down
	XV393	McD Phantom FGR2 [A]	RAF No 228 OCU, Coningsby
	XV394	McD Phantom FGR2 [C]	RAF No 228 OCU, Coningsby
	XV396	McD Phantom FGR2 [D]	RAF No 228 OCU, Coningsby
	XV398	McD Phantom FGR2 [I]	RAF No 228 OCU, Coningsby
	XV399	McD Phantom FGR2 [L]	RAF No 56 Sqn, Wattisham
	XV400	McD Phantom FGR2 [D]	RAF No 56 Sqn, Wattisham
	XV401	McD Phantom FGR2 [A]	RAF No 23 Sqn, Mount Pleasant, Fl
	XV402	McD Phantom FGR2 [A]	RAF No 29 Sqn, Coningsby
	XV404	McD Phantom FGR2	RAF No 29 Sqn, Coningsby
	XV406	McD Phantom FGR2 [K]	RAF No 228 OCU, Coningsby
	XV407	McD Phantom FGR2 [X]	RAF No 29 Sqn, Coningbsy
	XV408	McD Phantom FGR2 [P]	RAF No 29 Sqn, Coningsby
	XV409	McD Phantom FGR2 [A]	RAF No 29 Sqn, Coningsby
	XV410	McD Phantom FGR2 [E]	RAF No 56 Sqn, Wattisham
	XV411	McD Phantom FGR2 [O]	RAF No 29 Sqn, Coningsby
	XV412	McD Phantom FGR2 [S]	RAF No 29 Sqn, Coningsby
	XV414	McD Phantom FGR2 [R]	RAF Wattisham, BDRT
	XV415	McD Phantom FGR2 [O]	RAF No 23 Sqn, Mount Pleasant, Fl
	XV419	McD Phantom FGR2	RAF St Athan
	XV420	McD Phantom FGR2 [B]	RAF No 23 Sqn, Mount Pleasant, Fl
	XV421	McD Phantom FGR2 [B]	RAF No 228 OCU, Coningsby
	XV422	McD Phantom FGR2 [J]	RAF No 19 Sqn, Wildenrath
	XV423	McD Phantom FGR2 [D]	RAF Coningsby
	XV424	McD Phantom FGR2 [W]	RAF No 92 Sqn, Wildenrath
	XV425	McD Phantom FGR2 [A]	RAF No 56 Sqn, Wattisham
	XV426	McD Phantom FGR2 [F]	RAF No 29 Sqn, Coningsby
	XV428	McD Phantom FGR2 [I]	RAF No 56 Sqn, Wattisham
	XV429	McD Phantom FGR2 [K]	RAF No 56 Sqn, Wattisham
	XV430	McD Phantom FGR2 [A]	RAF No 19 Sqn, Wildenrath
	XV432	McD Phantom FGR2 [C]	RAF Coningsby
	XV433	McD Phantom FGR2 [I]	RAF No 29 Sqn, Coningsby
	XV435	McD Phantom FGR2 [R]	RAF No 92 Sqn, Wildenrath
	XV436	McD Phantom FGR2 [E] (8850M)	RAF Abingdon, BDRF
	XV437	McD Phantom FGR2 [D]	RAF No — Sqn, Wildenrath
	XV438	McD Phantom FGR2 [Y]	RAF No 29 Sqn, Coningsby
	XV439	McD Phantom FGR2 [D]	RAF No 19 Sqn, Wildenrath
	XV442	McD Phantom FGR2 [E]	RAF No — Sqn, Wildenrath
	XV460	McD Phantom FGR2 [G]	RAF No 228 OCU, Coningsby
	XV461	McD Phantom FGR2 [G]	RAF No 56 Sqn, Wattisham
	XV462	McD Phantom FGR2 [B]	RAF No 19 Sqn, Wildenrath
	XV464	McD Phantom FGR2 [N]	RAF No 29 Sqn, Coningsby
	XV465	McD Phantom FGR2 [F]	RAF No 19 Sqn, Wildenrath
	XV466	McD Phantom FGR2	RAF
	XV467	McD Phantom FGR2 [Q]	RAF No 92 Sqn, Wildenrath
	XV468	McD Phantom FGR2 [P]	RAF No 92 Sqn, Wildenrath
	XV469	McD Phantom FGR2 [T]	RAF No 56 Sqn, Wattisham
	XV470	McD Phantom FGR2 [X]	RAF No 228 OCU, Coningsby
	XV472	McD Phantom FGR2 [E]	RAF No 19 Sqn, Wildenrath
	XV473	McD Phantom FGR2 [E]	RAF No 29 Sqn, Coningsby
	XV474	McD Phantom FGR2 [M]	RAF No 56 Sqn, Wattisham
	XV475	McD Phantom FGR2 [Z]	RAF No 92 Sqn, Wildenrath
	XV476	McD Phantom FGR2 [G]	RAF No 19 Sqn, Wildenrath
	XV478	McD Phantom FGR2 [C]	RAF No 19 Sqn, Wildenrath
	XV480	McD Phantom FGR2 [X]	RAF No 92 Sqn, Wildenrath
	XV481	McD Phantom FGR2	RAF No 23 Sqn, Mount Pleasant, Fl
	XV482	McD Phantom FGR2 [C]	RAF No 56 Sqn, Wattisham
	XV485	McD Phantom FGR2 [M]	RAF No 19 Sqn, Wildenrath
	XV486	McD Phantom FGR2 [N]	RAF No 29 Sqn, Coningsby
	XV487	McD Phantom FGR2 [Q]	RAF No 29 Sqn, Coningsby
	XV488	McD Phantom FGR2 [O]	RAF No 92 Sqn, Wildenrath
	XV489	McD Phantom FGR2	RAF No 23 Sqn, Mount Plesant, Fl
	XV490	McD Phantom FGR2 [S]	RAF No 92 Sqn, Wildenrath
	XV492	McD Phantom FGR2 [U]	RAF No 56 Sqn, Wattisham
	XV494	McD Phantom FGR2 [T]	RAF No 29 Sqn, Coningsby
	XV495	McD Phantom FGR2 [C]	RAF
	XV496	McD Phantom FGR2 [L]	RAF No 92 Sqn, Wildenrath
	XV497	McD Phantom FGR2 [V]	RAF No — Sqn, Wildenrath
	XV498	McD Phantom FGR2 [U]	RAF No 92 Sqn, Wildenrath
	XV499	McD Phantom FGR2 [F]	RAF No 228 OCU, Coningsby

Serial	Type (alternative identity)	Owner, Operator or Location	Notes
XV500	McD Phantom FGR2 [J]	RAF No 56 Sqn, Wattisham	
XV501	McD Phantom FGR2 [B]	RAF No 56 Sqn, Wattisham	
XV555	HS Harrier GR1 (8566M) (really XV279)	RAF Wittering, for instructional use	
XV567	McD Phantom FG1 [AI]	RAF No 43 Sqn, Leuchars	
XV568	McD Phantom FG1 [AT]	RAF No 43 Sqn, Leuchars	
XV569	McD Phantom FG1 [BQ]	RAF No 111 Sqn, Leuchars	
XV570	McD Phantom FG1 [BN]	RAF No 111 Sqn, Leuchars	
XV571	McD Phantom FG1 [AA]	RAF No 43 Sqn, Leuchars	
XV572	McD Phantom FG1 [AN]	RAF No 43 Sqn, Leuchars	
XV573	McD Phantom FG1 [BD]	RAF No 111 Sqn, Leuchars	
XV574	McD Phantom FG1 [BZ]	RAF No 111 Sqn, Leuchars	
XV575	McD Phantom FG1 [AS]	RAF No 43 Sqn, Leuchars	
XV576	McD Phantom FG1 [AD]	RAF No 43 Sqn, Leuchars	
XV577	McD Phantom FG1 [AM]	RAF No 43 Sqn, Leuchars	
XV579	McD Phantom FG1 [AR]	RAF No 43 Sqn, Leuchars	
XV581	McD Phantom FG1 [AE]	RAF No 43 Sqn, Leuchars	
XV582	McD Phantom FG1 [AF]	RAF No 43 Sqn, Leuchars	
XV583	McD Phantom FG1 [BB]	RAF No 111 Sqn, Leuchars	
XV584	McD Phantom FG1 [BF]	RAF No 111 Sqn, Leuchars	
XV585	McD Phantom FG1 [AP]	RAF No 43 Sqn, Leuchars	
XV586	McD Phantom FG1 [AJ]	RAF No 43 Sqn, Leuchars	
XV587	McD Phantom FG1 [AG]	RAF No 43 Sqn, Leuchars	
XV590	McD Phantom FG1 [AX]	RAF No 43 Sqn, Leuchars	
XV591	McD Phantom FG1 [BM]	RAF No 111 Sqn, Leuchars	
XV592	McD Phantom FG1 [BL]	RAF No 111 Sqn, Leuchars	
XV615	BHC SR.N6 Winchester 2	RN Hong Kong	
XV623	WS Wasp HAS1 [601]	RN No 829 Sqn, Portland	
XV624	WS Wasp HAS1 [FIR4]	RN store Wroughton	
XV625	WS Wasp HAS1 [471/PB]	RNEC Manadon, for instruction	
XV626	WS Wasp HAS1 [325/HR]	RN No 829 Sqn, Portland	
XV629	WS Wasp HAS1	AAC Middle Wallop, BDRT	
XV631	WS Wasp HAS1	MoD(PE) RAE Farnborough	
XV632	WS Wasp HAS1 [610]	RN No 829 Sqn, Portland	
XV634	WS Wasp HAS1 [423]	RN No 829 Sqn, Portland	
XV636	WS Wasp HAS1 [606]	RN No 829 Sqn, Portland	
XV638	WS Wasp HAS1 (8826M) [A/430]	RAF AMS, Brize Norton	
XV639	WS Wasp HAS1 [612]	RN store, Wroughton	
XV642	WS61 Sea King AEW2	MoD(PE) Westlands, Yeovil	
XV643	WS61 Sea King HAS5 [015/R]	RN No 820 Sqn, Culdrose	
XV644	WS61 Sea King HAS1 (A2664) [64]	RN AES Lee-on-Solent	
XV647	WS61 Sea King HAS5 [265]	RN No 814 Sqn, Culdrose	
XV648	WS61 Sea King HAS5	RNAY Fleetlands	
XV649	WS61 Sea King AEW2 [183]	RN No 849 Sqn, Culdrose	
XV650	WS61 Sea King AEW2 [180]	RN No 849 Sqn, Culdrose	
XV651	WS61 Sea King HAS5 [131]	RN No 826 Sqn, Culdrose	
XV652	WS61 Sea King HAS5 [132]	RN No 826 Sqn, Culdrose	
XV653	WS61 Sea King HAS5 [015/R]	RN No 820 Sqn, Culdrose	
XV654	WS61 Sea King HAS5 [018/R]	RN No 820 Sqn, Culdrose	
XV655	WS61 Sea King HAS5 [134]	RN No 826 Sqn, Culdrose	
XV656	WS61 Sea King AEW2 [186]	RN No 849 Sqn, Culdrose	
XV657	WS61 Sea King HAS5	RNAY Fleetlands	
XV659	WS61 Sea King HAS5 [584]	RNAY Fleetlands	
XV660	WS61 Sea King HAS5 [507]	RN No 810 Sqn, Culdrose	
XV661	WS61 Sea King HAS5	RN NATIU, Lee-on-Solent	
XV663	WS61 Sea King HAS5 [703]	RN No 819 Sqn, Prestwick	
XV664	WS61 Sea King HAS2A	MoD(PE) A&AEE Boscombe Down	
XV665	WS61 Sea King HAS5 [508]	RN No 810 Sqn, Culdrose	
XV666	WS61 Sea King HAS5 [598]	RNAY Fleetlands	
XV668	WS61 Sea King HAS5 [586]	RN No 706 Sqn, Culdrose	
XV669	WS61 Sea King HAS1 (A2659) [410/BL]	RNAS Culdrose, Engineering Training School	
XV670	WS61 Sea King HAS5 [592]	RN No 706 Sqn, Culdrose	
XV671	WS61 Sea King AEW2 [185]	RN No 849 Sqn, Culdrose	
XV672	WS61 Sea King AEW2 [182]	RN No 849 Sqn, Culdrose	
XV673	WS61 Sea King HAS5 [588]	RN No 706 Sqn, Culdrose	
XV674	WS61 Sea King HAS5 [274]	RN No 814 Sqn, Culdrose	
XV675	WS61 Sea King HAS5	RN No — Sqn, Culdrose	

Notes	Serial	Type (alternative identity)	Owner, Operator or Location
	XV676	WS61 Sea King HAS5 [266/L]	RN No 814 Sqn, Culdrose
	XV677	WS61 Sea King HAS5 [705]	RN No 819 Sqn, Prestwick
	XV696	WS61 Sea King HAS5 [503]	RN No 810 Sqn, Culdrose
	XV697	WS61 Sea King AEW2 [184]	RN No 849 Sqn, Culdrose
	XV699	WS61 Sea King HAS5 [272/L]	RN No 814 Sqn, Culdrose
	XV700	WS61 Sea King HAS5 [011/R]	RN No 820 Sqn, Culdrose
	XV701	WS61 Sea King HAS5 [706]	RN No 819 Sqn, Prestwick
	XV703	WS61 Sea King HAS5 [271/L]	RN No 814 Sqn, Culdrose
	XV704	WS61 Sea King AEW2	RN No 849 Sqn, Culdrose
	XV705	WS61 Sea King HAS5 [596]	RNAY Fleetlands
	XV706	WS61 Sea King HAS5 [597]	RN No 706 Sqn, Culdrose
	XV707	WS61 Sea King AEW2 [181]	RNAY Fleetlands
	XV708	WS61 Sea King HAS5 [596/CU]	RN No 706 Sqn, Culdrose
	XV709	WS61 Sea King HAS5 [585]	RN No 706 Sqn, Culdrose
	XV710	WS61 Sea King HAS5 [701/PW]	RNAY Fleetlands
	XV711	WS61 Sea King HAS5	RN NASU, Culdrose
	XV712	WS61 Sea King HAS5 [270/L]	RN No 814 Sqn, Culdrose
	XV713	WS61 Sea King HAS5 [594]	RN No 706 Sqn, Culdrose
	XV714	WS61 Sea King AEW2 [180]	RN No 849 Sqn, Culdrose
	XV719	WS58 Wessex HC2 [B]	RAF No 72 Sqn, Aldergrove
	XV720	WS58 Wessex HC2	RAF No 22 Sqn SAR*
	XV721	WS58 Wessex HC2 [H]	RAF No 72 Sqn Aldergrove
	XV722	WS58 Wessex HC2 [WH]	RAF No 2 FTS, Shawbury
	XV723	WS58 Wessex HC2 [Q]	RAF No 72 Sqn, Aldergrove
	XV724	WS58 Wessex HC2	RAF No 22 Sqn SAR*
	XV725	WS58 Wessex HC2 [C]	RAF No 72 Sqn, Aldergrove
	XV726	WS58 Wessex HC2 [J]	RAF No 72 Sqn, Aldergrove
	XV728	WS58 Wessex HC2 [A]	RAF No 72 Sqn, Aldergrove
	XV729	WS58 Wessex HC2	RAF No 22 Sqn SAR*
	XV730	WS58 Wessex HC2	RAF No 22 Sqn SAR*
	XV731	WS58 Wessex HC2 [Y]	RAF No 72 Sqn, Aldergrove
	XV732	WS58 Wessex HCC4	RAF Queen's Flight, Benson
	XV733	WS58 Wessex HCC4	RAF Queen's Flight, Benson
	XV738	HS Harrier GR3 [B]	RAF No 4 Sqn, Gutersloh
	XV740	HS Harrier GR3 [05]	RAF No 1 Sqn, Wittering
	XV741	HS Harrier GR3 [A]	RAF No 233 OCU, Wittering
	XV744	HS Harrier GR3 [D]	RAF No 233 OCU, Wittering
	XV747	HS Harrier GR3 [G]	RAF No 233 OCU, Wittering
	XV748	HS Harrier GR3 [11]	RAF No 1 Sqn, Wittering
	XV751	HS Harrier GR3 [AU]	RAF No 3 Sqn, Gutersloh
	XV752	HS Harrier GR3 [AG]	RAF No 3 Sqn, Gutersloh
	XV753	HS Harrier GR3 [06]	RAF No 1 Sqn, Wittering
	XV755	HS Harrier GR3 [AK]	RAF No 3 Sqn, Gutersloh
	XV758	HS Harrier GR3 [AV]	RAF No 3 Sqn, Gutersloh
	XV759	HS Harrier GR3 [H]	RAF No 233 OCU, Wittering
	XV760	HS Harrier GR3 [C]	RAF No 4 Sqn, Gutersloh
	XV762	HS Harrier GR3 [09]	RAF SSF, Wittering
	XV778	HS Harrier GR3 [08]	RAF No 1 Sqn, Wittering
	XV779	HS Harrier GR3 [AA]	RAF No 3 Sqn, Gutersloh
	XV782	HS Harrier GR3 [F]	RAF No 4 Sqn, Gutersloh
	XV783	HS Harrier GR3 [I]	RAF No 4 Sqn, Gutersloh
	XV784	HS Harrier GR3 (8909M) [C]	RAF Wittering
	XV786	HS Harrier GR3 [E]	RAF No 4 Sqn, Gutersloh
	XV789	HS Harrier GR3 [07]	RAF No 1 Sqn, Wittering
	XV790	HS Harrier GR3 [AP]	RAF No 3 Sqn, Gutersloh
	XV793	HS Harrier GR3 [L]	RAF No 4 Sqn, Gutersloh
	XV804	HS Harrier GR3 [AD]	RAF No 3 Sqn, Gutersloh
	XV806	HS Harrier GR3 [AN]	RAF No 3 Sqn, Gutersloh
	XV808	HS Harrier GR3 [L]	RAF No 233 OCU, Wittering
	XV809	HS Harrier GR3 [AF]	RAF No 3 Sqn, Gutersloh
	XV810	HS Harrier GR3 [X]	RAF No 4 Sqn, Gutersloh
	XV814	HS Comet 4C (G-APDF)	MoD(PE) RAE Farnborough
	XV859	BHC SR.N6 Winchester 6	RN NHTU Lee-on-Solent
	XV863	HS Buccaneer S2B	RAF No 208 Sqn, Lossiemouth
	XV864	HS Buccaneer S2B	RAF No 12 Sqn, Lossiemouth
	XV865	HS Buccaneer S2B [BS]	RAF No 208 Sqn, Lossiemouth
	XV866	HS Buccaneer S2B [Y]	RAF Shawbury store
	XV867	HS Buccaneer S2B [EF]	RAF No 12 Sqn, Lossiemouth
	XV868	HS Buccaneer S2B [FS]	RAF No 208 Sqn, Lossiemouth
	XV869	HS Buccaneer S2B [MF]	RAF No 12 Sqn, Lossiemouth
	XW174	HS Harrier T2 (forward fuselage)	CARG store, RAF Innsworth
	XW175	HS Harrier T4A	MoD(PE) RAE Bedford

Serial	*Type (alternative identity)*	*Owner, Operator or Location*	*Notes*
XW198	WS Puma HC1 [DL]	RAF No 230 Sqn, Gutersloh	
XW199	WS Puma HC1 [DU]	RAF No 230 Sqn, Gutersloh	
XW200	WS Puma HC1 [FA]	RAF No 240 OCU, Odiham	
XW201	WS Puma HC1 [FB]	RAF No 240 OCU, Odiham	
XW202	WS Puma HC1	RAF No 240 OCU, Odiham	
XW204	WS Puma HC1 [CA]	RAF No 33 Sqn, Odiham	
XW206	WS Puma HC1 [CC]	RAF No 1563 Flt, Belize	
XW207	WS Puma HC1 [CD]	RAF No 33 Sqn, Odiham	
XW208	WS Puma HC1 [DP]	RAF No 230 Sqn, Gutersloh	
XW209	WS Puma HC1 [CF]	RAF No 33 Sqn, Odiham	
XW210	WS Puma HC1 [CG]	RAF No 33 Sqn, Odiham	
XW211	WS Puma HC1 [CH]	RAF No 33 Sqn, Odiham	
XW212	WS Puma HC1 [FD]	RAF No 240 OCU, Odiham	
XW213	WS Puma HC1 [CJ]	RAF No 1563 Flt, Belize	
XW214	WS Puma HC1 [CK]	RAF No 33 Sqn, Odiham	
XW215	WS Puma HC1 [DM]	RAF No 230 Sqn, Gutersloh	
XW216	WS Puma HC1 [CL]	RAF No 33 Sqn, Odiham	
XW217	WS Puma HC1 [DA]	RAF No 230 Sqn, Gutersloh	
XW218	WS Puma HC1 [DT]	RAF No 230 Sqn, Gutersloh	
XW219	WS Puma HC1 [DC]	RAF No 230 Sqn, Gutersloh	
XW220	WS Puma HC1 [DD]	RAF No 230 Sqn, Gutersloh	
XW221	WS Puma HC1 [DE]	RAF No 230 Sqn, Gutersloh	
XW222	WS Puma HC1 [DF]	RAF No 230 Sqn, Gutersloh	
XW223	WS Puma HC1 [DG]	RAF No 230 Sqn, Gutersloh	
XW224	WS Puma HC1 [DH]	RAF No 230 Sqn, Gutersloh	
XW225	WS Puma HC1 [FE]	RAF No 240 OCU, Odiham	
XW226	WS Puma HC1 [DK]	RAF No 230 Sqn, Gutersloh	
XW227	WS Puma HC1 [DN]	RAF No 230 Sqn, Gutersloh	
XW229	WS Puma HC1 [DB]	RAF No 230 Sqn, Gutersloh	
XW231	WS Puma HC1 [CM]	RAF No 33 Sqn, Odiham	
XW232	WS Puma HC1 [DJ]	RAF No 230 Sqn, Gutersloh	
XW233	WS Puma HC1 [CN]	RAF No 33 Sqn, Odiham	
XW234	WS Puma HC1 [CO]	RAF No 33 Sqn, Odiham	
XW235	WS Puma HC1 [CP]	RAF No 33 Sqn, Odiham	
XW236	WS Puma HC1 [CQ]	RAF No 33 Sqn, Odiham	
XW237	WS Puma HC1 [CR]	RAF No 33 Sqn, Odiham	
XW241	Sud SA330E Puma (F-ZJUX)	MoD(PE) RAE Bedford	
XW249	Cushioncraft CC7	Cornwall Aero Park, Helston	
XW255	BHC BH-7 Wellington	RN NHTU Lee-on-Solent	
XW265	HS Harrier T4A [V]	RAF No 233 OCU, Wittering	
XW266	HS Harrier T4A [S]	RAF No 233 OCU, Wittering	
XW267	HS Harrier T4	MoD(PE) RAE Farnborough	
XW268	HS Harrier T4A [U]	RAF No 233 OCU, Wittering	
XW269	HS Harrier T4 [AY]	RAF No 3 Sqn, Gutersloh	
XW270	HS Harrier T4 [T]	RAF No 4 Sqn, Gutersloh	
XW271	HS Harrier T4 [12]	RAF No 1 Sqn, Wittering	
XW272	HS Harrier T4 (8783M) (nose only)	Cranfield Institute of Technology	
XW276	Aerospatiale SA341 (F-ZWRI)	Science Museum, Wroughton	
XW280	WS Scout AH1	AAC No 666 (TA) Sqn, Netheravon	
XW281	WS Scout AH1 [U]	AAC No 666 (TA) Sqn, Netheravon	
XW282	WS Scout AH1 [W]	AAC No 666 (TA) Sqn, Netheravon	
XW283	WS Scout AH1 [W]	AAC No 658 Sqn, Netheravon	
XW284	WS Scout AH1 [A]	AAC store, Wroughton	
XW287	BAC Jet Provost T5 [P]	RAF No 6 FTS, Finningley	
XW289	BAC Jet Provost T5A [61]	RAF No 1 FTS, Linton-on-Ouse	
XW290	BAC Jet Provost T5A [41]	RAF College, Cranwell	
XW291	BAC Jet Provost T5 [N]	RAF No 6 FTS, Finningley	
XW292	BAC Jet Provost T5A [32]	RAF College, Cranwell	
XW293	BAC Jet Provost T5 [Z]	RAF No 6 FTS, Finningley	
XW294	BAC Jet Provost T5A [45]	RAF College, Cranwell	
XW295	BAC Jet Provost T5A [29]	RAF College, Cranwell	
XW296	BAC Jet Provost T5	RAF No 6 FTS, Finningley	
XW298	BAC Jet Provost T5 [O]	RAF No 6 FTS, Finningley	
XW299	BAC Jet Provost T5A [60]	RAF No 1 FTS, Linton-on-Ouse	
XW301	BAC Jet Provost T5A [63]	RAF No 1 FTS, Linton-on-Ouse	
XW302	BAC Jet Provost T5 [T]	RAF No 6 FTS, Finningley	
XW303	BAC Jet Provost T5A [127]	RAF No 7 FTS, Church Fenton	
XW304	BAC Jet Provost T5 [X]	RAF No 6 FTS, Finningley	
XW305	BAC Jet Provost T5A [42]	RAF College, Cranwell	
XW306	BAC Jet Provost T5 [Y]	RAF No 6 FTS, Finningley	
XW307	BAC Jet Provost T5 [S]	RAF No 6 FTS, Finningley	
XW309	BAC Jet Provost T5 [V]	RAF No 6 FTS, Finningley	
XW310	BAC Jet Provost T5A [37]	RAF College, Cranwell	

Notes	*Serial*	*Type (alternative identity)*	*Owner, Operator or Location*
	XW311	BAC Jet Provost T5 [W]	RAF No 6 FTS, Finningley
	XW312	BAC Jet Provost T5A [64]	RAF No 1 FTS, Linton-on-Ouse
	XW313	BAC Jet Provost T5A [30]	RAF College, Cranwell
	XW315	BAC Jet Provost T5A [50]	RAF No 3 FTS, Scampton
	XW316	BAC Jet Provost T5A [28]	RAF College, Cranwell
	XW317	BAC Jet Provost T5A [25]	RAF College, Cranwell
	XW318	BAC Jet Provost T5A [12]	RAF College, Cranwell
	XW319	BAC Jet Provost T5A [57]	RAF No 3 FTS, Scampton
	XW320	BAC Jet Provost T5A [71]	RAF No 1 FTS, Linton-on-Ouse
	XW321	BAC Jet Provost T5A [132]	RAF No 7 FTS, Church Fenton
	XW322	BAC Jet Provost T5A [43]	RAF College, Cranwell
Staverton 8/87	XW323	BAC Jet Provost T5A [44]	RAF College, Cranwell
	XW324	BAC Jet Provost T5 [U]	RAF No 6 FTS, Finningley
	XW325	BAC Jet Provost T5A [33]	RAF College, Cranwell
	XW326	BAC Jet Provost T5A [62]	RAF No 1 FTS, Linton-on-Ouse
	XW327	BAC Jet Provost T5A [134]	RAF No 7 FTS, Church Fenton
	XW328	BAC Jet Provost T5A [22]	RAF College, Cranwell
	XW329	BAC Jet Provost T5A [48] (8741M)	RAF Church Fenton Fire Section
	XW330	BAC Jet Provost T5A [130]	RAF No 7 FTS, Church Fenton
	XW332	BAC Jet Provost T5A [34]	RAF College, Cranwell
	XW333	BAC Jet Provost T5A [61]	RAF No 3 FTS, Scampton
	XW334	BAC Jet Provost T5A [131]	RAF No 7 FTS, Church Fenton
	XW335	BAC Jet Provost T5A	RAF No 1 FTS, Linton-on-Ouse
	XW336	BAC Jet Provost T5A [6]	RAF College, Cranwell
	XW351	BAC Jet Provost T5A [31]	RAF College, Cranwell
	XW352	BAC Jet Provost T5 [R]	RAF No 6 FTS, Finningley
	XW353	BAC Jet Provost T5A [51]	RAF No 3 FTS, Scampton
	XW354	BAC Jet Provost T5A [7]	RAF College, Cranwell
	XW355	BAC Jet Provost T5A [20]	RAF College, Cranwell
	XW357	BAC Jet Provost T5A [5]	RAF College, Cranwell
	XW358	BAC Jet Provost T5A	RAF No 6 FTS, Finningley
	XW359	BAC Jet Provost T5A [65]	RAF No 1 FTS, Linton-on-Ouse
	XW360	BAC Jet Provost T5A [129]	RAF No 7 FTS, Church Fenton
	XW361	BAC Jet Provost T5A [128]	RAF No 7 FTS, Church Fenton
	XW362	BAC Jet Provost T5A [17]	RAF College, Cranwell
	XW363	BAC Jet Provost T5A [36]	RAF College, Cranwell
	XW364	BAC Jet Provost T5A [35]	RAF College, Cranwell
	XW365	BAC Jet Provost T5A [73]	RAF No 1 FTS, Linton-on-Ouse
	XW366	BAC Jet Provost T5A [75]	RAF No 1 FTS, Linton-on-Ouse
	XW367	BAC Jet Provost T5A [26]	RAF College, Cranwell
	XW368	BAC Jet Provost T5A [L]	RAF No 6 FTS, Finningley
	XW369	BAC Jet Provost T5A [9]	RAF College, Cranwell
	XW370	BAC Jet Provost T5A [72]	RAF No 1 FTS, Linton-on-Ouse
	XW372	BAC Jet Provost T5A [M]	RAF No 6 FTS, Finningley
	XW373	BAC Jet Provost T5A [11]	RAF College, Cranwell
Staverton 8/87	XW374	BAC Jet Provost T5A [38]	RAF College, Cranwell
	XW375	BAC Jet Provost T5A [52]	RAF No 3 FTS, Scampton
	XW404	BAC Jet Provost T5A [77]	RAF No 1 FTS, Linton-on-Ouse
	XW405	BAC Jet Provost T5A [J]	RAF No 6 FTS, Finningley
	XW406	BAC Jet Provost T5A [23]	RAF College, Cranwell
	XW408	BAC Jet Provost T5A [24]	RAF College, Cranwell
	XW409	BAC Jet Provost T5A [123]	RAF No 7 FTS, Church Fenton
	XW410	BAC Jet Provost T5A [80]	RAF No 1 FTS, Linton-on-Ouse
	XW412	BAC Jet Provost T5A [15]	RAF College, Cranwell
	XW413	BAC Jet Provost T5A [69]	RAF No 1 FTS, Linton-on-Ouse
	XW415	BAC Jet Provost T5A [53]	RAF No 3 FTS, Scampton
	XW416	BAC Jet Provost T5A [19]	RAF College, Cranwell
	XW418	BAC Jet Provost T5A [126]	RAF No 7 FTS, Church Fenton
	XW419	BAC Jet Provost T5A [125]	RAF No 7 FTS, Church Fenton
	XW420	BAC Jet Provost T5A [8]	RAF College, Cranwell
	XW421	BAC Jet Provost T5A [60]	RAF No 3 FTS, Scampton
	XW422	BAC Jet Provost T5A [3]	RAF College, Cranwell
	XW423	BAC Jet Provost T5A [14]	RAF College, Cranwell
	XW424	BAC Jet Provost T5A [62]	Privately owned, Misson, Notts
	XW425	BAC Jet Provost T5A [H]	RAF No 6 FTS, Finningley
	XW427	BAC Jet Provost T5A [56]	RAF No 3 FTS, Scampton
	XW428	BAC Jet Provost T5A [39]	RAF College, Cranwell
	XW429	BAC Jet Provost T5A [66]	RAF No 1 FTS, Linton-on-Ouse
	XW430	BAC Jet Provost T5A [58]	RAF No 3 FTS, Scampton
	XW431	BAC Jet Provost T5A [59]	RAF No 3 FTS, Scampton
	XW432	BAC Jet Provost T5A [76]	RAF No 1 FTS, Linton-on-Ouse
	XW433	BAC Jet Provost T5A [124]	RAF No 7 FTS, Church Fenton
	XW434	BAC Jet Provost T5A [78]	RAF No 1 FTS, Linton-on-Ouse

Serial	Type (alternative identity)	Owner, Operator or Location	Notes
XW435	BAC Jet Provost T5A [4]	RAF College, Cranwell	
XW436	BAC Jet Provost T5A [62]	RAF No 3 FTS, Scampton	
XW437	BAC Jet Provost T5A [1]	RAF College, Cranwell	
XW438	BAC Jet Provost T5A [2]	RAF College, Cranwell	
XW527	HS Buccaneer S2B [527]	RAF No 12 Sqn, Lossiemouth	
XW528	HS Buccaneer S2B (8861M) [C]	RAF Coningsby, BDRT	
XW529	HS Buccaneer S2B	MoD(PE) BAe Woodford	
XW530	HS Buccaneer S2B	RAF No 12 Sqn, Lossiemouth	
XW533	HS Buccaneer S2B	RAF No 208 Sqn, Lossiemouth	
XW534	HS Buccaneer S2B	MoD(PE) BAe Woodford	
XW538	HS Buccaneer S2B (8660M) [T]	RAF Lossiemouth Fire Section	
XW540	HS Buccaneer S2B	RAF No 237 OCU, Lossiemouth	
XW541	HS Buccaneer S2B (8858M)	RAF Honington Fire Section	
XW542	HS Buccaneer S2B	RAF No 208 Sqn, Lossiemouth	
XW543	HS Buccaneer S2B [E]	RAF store, St Athan	
XW544	HS Buccaneer S2B (8857M) [O]	RAF No 2 SoTT, Cosford	
XW545	HS Buccaneer S2B (8859M)	RAF St Athan, BDRT	
XW546	HS Buccaneer S2B	MoD(PE) BAe Woodford	
XW547	HS Buccaneer S2B	RAF No 12 Sqn, Lossiemouth	
XW549	HS Buccaneer S2B (8860M)	RAF Kinloss, BDRT	
XW550	HS Buccaneer S2B [X]	RAF store, St Athan	
XW566	SEPECAT Jaguar T2	MoD(PE) RAE Farnborough store	
XW612	WS Scout AH1 [X]	AAC No 658 Sqn, Netheravon	
XW613	WS Scout AH1 [V]	AAC store, Wroughton	
XW614	WS Scout AH1	AAC store, Wroughton	
XW615	WS Scout AH1	AAC store, Wroughton	
XW616	WS Scout AH1	AAC Garrison Air Sqn, Falkland Islands	
XW626	HS Comet 4AEW (G-APDS)	MoD(PE) RAE Bedford	
XW630	HS Harrier GR3 [M]	RAF No 4 Sqn, Gutersloh	
XW635	Beagle D5/180 (G-AWSW)	RAF No 5 AEF, Teversham	
XW664	HS Nimrod R1P	RAF No 51 Sqn, Wyton	
XW665	HS Nimrod R1	RAF No 51 Sqn, Wyton	
XW666	HS Nimrod R1	RAF No 51 Sqn, Wyton	
XW750	HS748 Series 107 (G-ASJT)	MoD(PE) RAE Bedford	
XW763	HS Harrier GR3 [02]	RAF No 1 Sqn, Wittering	
XW764	HS Harrier GR3 [AC]	RAF No 3 Sqn, Gutersloh	
XW768	HS Harrier GR3 [01]	RAF No 1 Sqn, Wittering	
XW788	HS125 CC1	RAF No 32 Sqn, Northolt	
XW789	HS125 CC1	RAF No 32 Sqn, Northolt	
XW790	HS125 CC1	RAF No 32 Sqn, Northolt	
XW791	HS125 CC1	RAF No 32 Sqn, Northolt	
XW795	WS Scout AH1	AAC No 658 Sqn, Netheravon	
XW796	WS Scout AH1 [H]	AAC No 660 Sqn, Sek Kong	
XW797	WS Scout AH1 [T]	AAC store, Wroughton	
XW798	WS Scout AH1 [U]	AAC store, Wroughton	
XW799	WS Scout AH1 [Z]	AAC No 658 Sqn, Netheravon	
XW836	WS Lynx	AAC Middle Wallop, BDRT	
XW838	WS Lynx [TAD 009]	AAC AETW, Middle Wallop	
XW839	WS Lynx	Rolls-Royce, Filton	
XW843	WS Gazelle AH1	AAC No 2 Flt, Netheravon	
XW844	WS Gazelle AH1	AAC No 661 Sqn, Hildesheim	
XW845	WS Gazelle HT2	RN store, Wroughton	
XW846	WS Gazelle AH1	AAC store, Wroughton	
XW847	WS Gazelle AH1	AAC D&TS, Middle Wallop	
XW848	WS Gazelle AH1 [D]	AAC ARWS, Middle Wallop	
XW849	WS Gazelle AH1 [13C]	RM 3 CBAS, Yeovilton	
XW851	WS Gazelle AH1 [33A]	RM 3 CBAS, Yeovilton	
XW852	WS Gazelle HT3	RAF No 32 Sqn, Northolt	
XW853	WS Gazelle HT2 [53/CU]	RN No 705 Sqn, Culdrose	
XW854	WS Gazelle HT2 [46/CU]	RN No 705 Sqn, Culdrose	
XW855	WS Gazelle HT3	RAF No 32 Sqn, Northolt	
XW856	WS Gazelle HT2 [47/CU]	RN No 705 Sqn, Culdrose	
XW857	WS Gazelle HT2 [55/CU]	RN No 705 Sqn, Culdrose	
XW858	WS Gazelle HT3 [C]	RAF No 2 FTS, Shawbury	
XW860	WS Gazelle HT2	RN store, Wroughton	
XW861	WS Gazelle HT2 [59/CU]	RN No 705 Sqn, Culdrose	
XW862	WS Gazelle HT3 [D]	RAF No 2 FTS, Shawbury	
XW863	WS Gazelle HT2 [42/CU]	RN No 705 Sqn, Culdrose	
XW864	WS Gazelle HT2 [54/CU]	RN No 705 Sqn, Culdrose	
XW865	WS Gazelle AH1	AAC AETW, Middle Wallop	
XW866	WS Gazelle HT3 [E]	RAF No 2 FTS, Shawbury	
XW868	WS Gazelle HT2 [50/CU]	RN No 705 Sqn, Culdrose	
XW870	WS Gazelle HT3 [F]	RAF No 2 FTS, Shawbury	

Notes	Serial	Type (alternative identity)	Owner, Operator or Location
	XW871	WS Gazelle HT2 [44/CU]	RN No 705 Sqn, Culdrose
	XW884	WS Gazelle HT2 [41/CU]	RN No 705 Sqn, Culdrose
	XW885	WS Gazelle AH1 [B]	AAC ARWS, Middle Wallop
	XW886	WS Gazelle HT2 [48/CU]	RN No 705 Sqn, Culdrose
	XW887	WS Gazelle HT2 [57/CU]	RN store, Wroughton
	XW888	WS Gazelle AH1	AAC AETW, Middle Wallop
	XW889	WS Gazelle AH1	AAC AETW, Middle Wallop
	XW890	WS Gazelle HT2 [–/CU]	RN store, Wroughton
	XW891	WS Gazelle HT2 [49/CU]	RN No 705 Sqn, Culdrose
	XW892	WS Gazelle AH1	AAC No 662 Sqn, Soest
	XW893	WS Gazelle AH1	AAC Garrison Air Sqn, FI
	XW894	WS Gazelle HT2 [52/CU]	RN No 705 Sqn, Culdrose
	XW895	WS Gazelle HT2 [51/CU]	RN No 705 Sqn, Culdrose
	XW897	WS Gazelle AH1	AAC No 664 Sqn, Minden
	XW898	WS Gazelle HT3 [G]	RAF No 2 FTS, Shawbury
	XW899	WS Gazelle AH1	AAC No 655 Sqn, Aldergrove
	XW900	WS Gazelle AH1 (TAD-900)	AAC AETW, Middle Wallop
	XW902	WS Gazelle HT3 [H]	RAF No 2 FTS, Shawbury
	XW903	WS Gazelle AH1 [E]	AAC ARWS, Middle Wallop
	XW904	WS Gazelle AH1	AAC No 664 Sqn, Minden
	XW906	WS Gazelle HT3 [J]	RAF No 2 FTS, Shawbury
	XW907	WS Gazelle HT2 [40/CU]	RN No 705 Sqn, Culdrose
	XW908	WS Gazelle AH1	AAC store, Wroughton
	XW909	WS Gazelle AH1	AAC No 664 Sqn, Detmold
	XW910	WS Gazelle HT3 [K]	RAF No 2 FTS, Shawbury
	XW911	WS Gazelle AH1 [I]	AAC ARWS, Middle Wallop
	XW912	WS Gazelle AH1	AAC AETW, Middle Wallop
	XW913	WS Gazelle AH1	AAC No 664 Sqn, Minden
	XW917	HS Harrier GR3 [AL]	RAF No 3 Sqn, Gutersloh
	XW919	HS Harrier GR3 [03]	RAF No 1 Sqn, Wittering
	XW921	HS Harrier GR3 [V]	RAF No 4 Sqn, Gutersloh
	XW922	HS Harrier GR3 (8885M) [B]	RAF Wittering
	XW923	HS Harrier GR3 (cockpit) (8724M)	RAF Wittering for rescue training
	XW924	HS Harrier GR3 [G]	RAF No 4 Sqn, Gutersloh
	XW925	HS Harrier T4 [Y]	RAF No 4 Sqn, Gutersloh
	XW927	HS Harrier T4 [S]	RAF No 4 Sqn, Gutersloh
	XW930	HS125 (G-ATPC)	MoD(PE) RAE Bedford
	XW934	HS Harrier T4 [12]	RAF No 1 Sqn, Wittering
	XW986	HS Buccaneer S2B	MoD(PE) RAE Farnborough
	XW987	HS Buccaneer S2B	MoD(PE) RAE West Freugh
	XW988	HS Buccaneer S2B	MoD(PE) RAE West Freugh
	XX101	Cushioncraft CC7	British Rotorcraft Museum, Weston-super-Mare
	XX102	Cushioncraft CC7	Museum of Army Transport, Beverley
	XX105	BAC 1-11/201 (G-ASJD)	MoD(PE) RAE Bedford
	XX108	SEPECAT Jaguar GR1 (G27-313)	MoD(PE) BAe Warton
	XX109	SEPECAT Jaguar GR1 (8898M)	RAF Coltishall, ground instruction
	XX110	SEPECAT Jaguar GR1 [EP]	RAF store, Shawbury
	XX110	SEPECAT Jaguar Replica (BAPC 169)	RAF No 1 SoTT, Halton
	XX112	SEPECAT Jaguar GR1A [EA]	RAF No 6 Sqn, Coltishall
	XX115	SEPECAT Jaguar GR1 (JI005) (8821M)	RAF No 1 SoTT, Halton
	XX116	SEPECAT Jaguar GR1A (JI008) [EE]	RAF No 6 Sqn, Coltishall
	XX117	SEPECAT Jaguar GR1A (JI004) [05]	RAF No 226 OCU, Lossiemouth
	XX118	SEPECAT Jaguar GR1 (JI018) (8815M)	RAF Abingdon, BDRF
	XX119	SEPECAT Jaguar GR1 [01]	RAF No 226 OCU, Lossiemouth
	XX121	SEPECAT Jaguar GR1 [EQ]	RAF store, Shawbury
	XX139	SEPECAT Jaguar T2A	RAF No 6 Sqn, Coltishall
	XX140	SEPECAT Jaguar T2 [D]	RAF store, Shawbury
	XX141	SEPECAT Jaguar T2A [ET]	RAF No 6 Sqn, Coltishall
	XX143	SEPECAT Jaguar T2A (JI002) [B]	RAF No 226 OCU, Lossiemouth
	XX144	SEPECAT Jaguar T2A [I]	RAF No 226 OCU, Lossiemouth
	XX145	SEPECAT Jaguar T2	MoD(PE) A&AEE, Boscombe Down
	XX146	SEPECAT Jaguar T2A [GS]	RAF No 54 Sqn, Coltishall
	XX150	SEPECAT Jaguar T2 [AX]	RAF store, Shawbury
	XX154	HS Hawk T1 [1]	MoD(PE) RAE Llanbedr
	XX156	HS Hawk T1 [1]	MoD(PE) RAE Bedford

Serial	Type (alternative identity)	Owner, Operator or Location	Notes
XX157	HS Hawk T1 [A]	RAF No 2 TWU/63 Sqn, Chivenor	
XX158	HS Hawk T1A	RAF No 2 TWU/63 Sqn, Chivenor	
XX159	HS Hawk T1A	RAF No 1 TWU/234 Sqn Brawdy	
XX160	HS Hawk T1	MoD(PE) RAE Llanbedr	
XX161	HS Hawk T1	RAF No 4 FTS, Valley	
XX162	HS Hawk T1 replica (BAPC 152)	RAF Exhibition Flight, Abingdon	
XX162	HS Hawk T1	RAF No 4 FTS, Valley	
XX163	HS Hawk T1	RAF No 4 FTS, Valley	
XX164	HS Hawk T1	RAF No 4 FTS, Valley	
XX165	HS Hawk T1	RAF No 4 FTS, Valley	
XX167	HS Hawk T1	RAF No 4 FTS, Valley	
XX168	HS Hawk T1	RAF No 4 FTS, Valley	
XX169	HS Hawk T1	RAF No 4 FTS, Valley	
XX170	HS Hawk T1	RAF No 4 FTS, Valley	
XX171	HS Hawk T1	RAF No 4 FTS, Valley	
XX172	HS Hawk T1	RAF No 4 FTS, Valley	
XX173	HS Hawk T1	RAF No 4 FTS, Valley	
XX174	HS Hawk T1	RAF No 4 FTS, Valley	
XX175	HS Hawk T1	RAF No 4 FTS, Valley	
XX176	HS Hawk T1	RAF No 4 FTS, Valley	
XX177	HS Hawk T1	RAF No 4 FTS, Valley	
XX178	HS Hawk T1	RAF No 4 FTS, Valley	
XX179	HS Hawk T1	RAF No 4 FTS, Valley	
XX181	HS Hawk T1	RAF CFS, Valley	
XX182	HS Hawk T1	RAF No 4 FTS, Valley	
XX183	HS Hawk T1	RAF No 4 FTS, Valley	
XX184	HS Hawk T1	RAF No 4 FTS, Valley	
XX185	HS Hawk T1	RAF No 4 FTS, Valley	
XX186	HS Hawk T1A	RAF No 2 TWU/63 Sqn, Chivenor	
XX187	HS Hawk T1A	RAF No 1 TWU/79 Sqn, Brawdy	
XX188	HS Hawk T1A	RAF No 1 TWU/234 Sqn, Brawdy	
XX189	HS Hawk T1A [J]	RAF No 2 TWU/151 Sqn, Chivenor	
XX190	HS Hawk T1A	RAF No 1 TWU/234 Sqn, Brawdy	
XX191	HS Hawk T1A	RAF No 1 TWU/79 Sqn, Brawdy	
XX192	HS Hawk T1A	RAF No 1 TWU/79 Sqn, Brawdy	
XX193	HS Hawk T1A	RAF No 1 TWU/234 Sqn, Brawdy	
XX194	HS Hawk T1A	RAF No 1 TWU/234 Sqn, Brawdy	
XX195	HS Hawk T1A	RAF No 2 TWU/63 Sqn, Chivenor	
XX196	HS Hawk T1A	RAF No 1 TWU/234 Sqn, Brawdy	
XX197	HS Hawk T1A	RAF No 1 TWU/79 Sqn, Brawdy	
XX198	HS Hawk T1A	RAF No 1 TWU/79 Sqn, Brawdy	
XX199	HS Hawk T1A	RAF No 1 TWU, Brawdy	
XX200	HS Hawk T1A	RAF No 1 TWU, Brawdy	
XX201	HS Hawk T1A [N]	RAF No 2 TWU/151 Sqn, Chivenor	
XX202	HS Hawk T1A [P]	RAF No 2 TWU/151 Sqn, Chivenor	
XX203	HS Hawk T1A	RAF No 2 TWU/63 Sqn, Chivenor	
XX204	HS Hawk T1A	RAF No 2 TWU/63 Sqn, Chivenor	
XX205	HS Hawk T1A	RAF No 2 TWU/63 Sqn, Chivenor	
XX217	HS Hawk T1A	RAF No 2 TWU/63 Sqn, Chivenor	
XX218	HS Hawk T1A	RAF No 1 TWU/234 Sqn, Brawdy	
XX219	HS Hawk T1A	RAF No 2 TWU/63 Sqn, Chivenor	
XX220	HS Hawk T1A	RAF No 1 TWU/234 Sqn, Brawdy	
XX221	HS Hawk T1A	RAF No 1 TWU/79 Sqn, Brawdy	
XX222	HS Hawk T1A	RAF No 1 TWU/79 Sqn, Brawdy	
XX223	HS Hawk T1	RAF CFS, Valley	
XX224	HS Hawk T1	RAF CFS, Valley	
XX225	HS Hawk T1	RAF No 4 FTS, Valley	
XX226	HS Hawk T1	RAF No 4 FTS, Valley	
XX227	HS Hawk T1A	RAF Red Arrows, Scampton	
XX228	HS Hawk T1A [Q]	RAF No 2 TWU/151 Sqn, Chivenor	
XX230	HS Hawk T1A [M]	RAF No 2 TWU/151 Sqn, Chivenor	
XX231	HS Hawk T1	RAF No 4 FTS, Valley	
XX232	HS Hawk T1	RAF No 4 FTS, Valley	
XX233	HS Hawk T1	RAF No 4 FTS, Valley	
XX234	HS Hawk T1	RAF CFS, Valley	
XX235	HS Hawk T1	RAF No 4 FTS, Valley	
XX236	HS Hawk T1	RAF No 4 FTS, Valley	
XX237	HS Hawk T1A	RAF Red Arrows, Scampton	
XX238	HS Hawk T1	RAF No 4 FTS, Valley	
XX239	HS Hawk T1	RAF No 4 FTS, Valley	
XX240	HS Hawk T1	RAF No 4 FTS, Valley	
XX241	HS Hawk T1	RAF No 4 FTS, Valley	
XX242	HS Hawk T1	RAF No 4 FTS, Valley	

Notes	Serial	Type (alternative identity)	Owner, Operator or Location
	XX243	HS Hawk T1A	RAF Red Arrows, Scampton
	XX244	HS Hawk T1	RAF No 4 FTS, Valley
	XX245	HS Hawk T1	RAF No 4 FTS, Valley
	XX246	HS Hawk T1A	RAF No 2 TWU/63 Sqn, Chivenor
	XX247	HS Hawk T1A	RAF No 1 TWU/234 Sqn, Brawdy
	XX248	HS Hawk T1A [E]	RAF No 2 TWU/151 Sqn, Chivenor
	XX249	HS Hawk T1	RAF No 4 FTS, Valley
	XX250	HS Hawk T1	RAF No 4 FTS, Valley
	XX252	HS Hawk T1A	RAF Red Arrows, Scampton
	XX253	HS Hawk T1A	RAF Red Arrows, Scampton
	XX254	HS Hawk T1A	RAF No 2 TWU/63 Sqn, Chivenor
	XX255	HS Hawk T1A	RAF No 2 TWU/63 Sqn, Chivenor
	XX256	HS Hawk T1A	RAF No 2 TWU/63 Sqn, Chivenor
	XX257	HS Hawk T1	RAF No 1 SoTT, Halton
	XX258	HS Hawk T1A	RAF No 1 TWU/79 Sqn, Brawdy
	XX259	HS Hawk T1A	RAF Red Arrows, Scampton
	XX260	HS Hawk T1A	RAF Red Arrows, Scampton
	XX261	HS Hawk T1A	RAF No 1 TWU/234 Sqn, Brawdy
	XX263	HS Hawk T1A	RAF No 2 TWU/63 Sqn, Chivenor
	XX264	HS Hawk T1A	RAF Red Arrows, Scampton
	XX265	HS Hawk T1A [U]	RAF No 2 TWU/151 Sqn, Chivenor
	XX266	HS Hawk T1A	RAF Red Arrows, Scampton
	XX278	HS Hawk T1A	RAF No 2 TWU/63 Sqn, Chivenor
	XX280	HS Hawk T1A	RAF No 1 TWU/79 Sqn, Brawdy
	XX281	HS Hawk T1A [O]	RAF No 2 TWU/151 Sqn, Chivenor
	XX282	HS Hawk T1A	RAF No 2 TWU/63 Sqn, Chivenor
	XX283	HS Hawk T1A	RAF No 2 TWU/63 Sqn, Chivenor
	XX284	HS Hawk T1A	RAF No 2 TWU/63 Sqn, Chivenor
	XX285	HS Hawk T1A [R]	RAF No 2 TWU/151 Sqn, Chivenor
	XX286	HS Hawk T1A	RAF No 1 TWU/79 Sqn, Brawdy
	XX287	HS Hawk T1A	RAF No 2 TWU/63 Sqn, Chivenor
	XX288	HS Hawk T1A	RAF No 2 TWU/63 Sqn, Chivenor
	XX289	HS Hawk T1A	RAF No 2 TWU/63 Sqn, Chivenor
	XX290	HS Hawk T1	RAF No 4 FTS, Valley
	XX291	HS Hawk T1	RAF No 4 FTS, Valley
	XX292	HS Hawk T1	RAF No 4 FTS, Valley
	XX293	HS Hawk T1	RAF Wattisham Fire Section
	XX294	HS Hawk T1	RAF No 4 FTS, Valley
	XX295	HS Hawk T1	RAF No 4 FTS, Valley
	XX296	HS Hawk T1	RAF No 4 FTS, Valley
	XX297	HS Hawk T1A	RAF Red Arrows, Scampton
	XX297	HS Hawk T1 replica (BAPC171)	RAF Exhibition Flight, Abingdon
	XX299	HS Hawk T1	RAF No 4 FTS, Valley
	XX300	HS Hawk T1 [S] (8827M)	RAF Abingdon, BDRF
	XX301	HS Hawk T1A [L]	RAF No 2 TWU/151 Sqn, Chivenor
	XX302	HS Hawk T1A	RAF No 1 TWU/234 Sqn, Brawdy
	XX303	HS Hawk T1A	RAF No 1 TWU/234 Sqn, Brawdy
	XX304	HS Hawk T1A	RAF Red Arrows, Scampton
	XX306	HS Hawk T1A	RAF Red Arrows, Scampton
	XX307	HS Hawk T1	RAF No 4 FTS, Valley
	XX308	HS Hawk T1A	RAF Red Arrows, Scampton
	XX309	HS Hawk T1	RAF No 4 FTS, Valley
	XX310	HS Hawk T1	RAF CFS, Valley
	XX311	HS Hawk T1	RAF No 4 FTS, Valley
	XX312	HS Hawk T1	RAF CFS, Valley
	XX313	HS Hawk T1	RAF No 4 FTS, Valley
	XX314	HS Hawk T1	RAF No 4 FTS, Valley
	XX315	HS Hawk T1A	RAF No 1 TWU/234 Sqn, Brawdy
	XX316	HS Hawk T1A	RAF No 1 TWU/79 Sqn, Brawdy
	XX317	HS Hawk T1A	RAF No 1 TWU/234 Sqn, Brawdy
	XX318	HS Hawk T1A	RAF No 1 TWU/79 Sqn, Brawdy
	XX319	HS Hawk T1A	RAF No 1 TWU/79 Sqn, Brawdy
	XX320	HS Hawk T1A [V]	RAF No 2 TWU/151 Sqn, Chivenor
	XX321	HS Hawk T1A	RAF No 2 TWU/63 Sqn, Chivenor
	XX322	HS Hawk T1A [W]	RAF No 2 TWU/151 Sqn, Chivenor
	XX323	HS Hawk T1A	RAF No 1 TWU/234 Sqn, Brawdy
	XX324	HS Hawk T1A	RAF No 1 TWU/234 Sqn, Brawdy
	XX325	HS Hawk T1A [X]	RAF No 2 TWU/151 Sqn, Chivenor
	XX326	HS Hawk T1A [A]	RAF No 2 TWU/151 Sqn, Chivenor
	XX327	HS Hawk T1A [B]	RAF No 2 TWU/151 Sqn, Chivenor
	XX329	HS Hawk T1A [C]	RAF No 2 TWU/151 Sqn, Chivenor
	XX330	HS Hawk T1A [D]	RAF No 2 TWU/151 Sqn, Chivenor
	XX331	HS Hawk T1A	RAF No 2 TWU/63 Sqn, Chivenor

Serial	*Type (alternative identity)*	*Owner, Operator or Location*	*Notes*
XX332	HS Hawk T1A [F]	RAF No 2 TWU/151 Sqn, Chivenor	
XX334	HS Hawk T1A [H]	RAF No 2 TWU/151 Sqn, Chivenor	
XX335	HS Hawk T1A [I]	RAF No 2 TWU/151 Sqn, Chivenor	
XX337	HS Hawk T1A [K]	RAF No 2 TWU/151 Sqn, Chivenor	
XX338	HS Hawk T1	RAF No 4 FTS, Valley	
XX339	HS Hawk T1A	RAF No 1 TWU/234 Sqn, Brawdy	
XX341	HS Hawk T1 ASTRA [1]	MoD(PE) Institute of Technology, Cranfield	
XX342	HS Hawk T1 [2]	MoD(PE) ETPS Boscombe Down	
XX343	HS Hawk T1 [3]	MoD(PE) ETPS Boscombe Down	
XX344	HS Hawk T1 (8847M)	RAF Abingdon, BDRF	
XX345	HS Hawk T1A [Y]	RAF No 2 TWU/151 Sqn, Chivenor	
XX346	HS Hawk T1A [T]	RAF No 2 TWU/151 Sqn, Chivenor	
XX347	HS Hawk T1	RAF No 4 FTS, Valley	
XX348	HS Hawk T1A	RAF No 2 TWU/63 Sqn, Chivenor	
XX349	HS Hawk T1	RAF No 4 FTS, Valley	
XX350	HS Hawk T1A	RAF No 1 TWU/234 Sqn, Brawdy	
XX351	HS Hawk T1A	RAF No 1 TWU/234 Sqn, Brawdy	
XX352	HS Hawk T1A	RAF No 2 TWU/63 Sqn, Chivenor	
XX370	WS Gazelle AH1 [A]	AAC No 658 Sqn, Netheravon	
XX371	WS Gazelle AH1	AAC No 12 Flt, Wildenrath	
XX372	WS Gazelle AH1 [B]	AAC No 658 Sqn, Netheravon	
XX373	WS Gazelle AH1	AAC No 663 Sqn, Soest	
XX375	WS Gazelle AH1 [C]	AAC No 658 Sqn, Netheravon	
XX376	WS Gazelle AH1 [D]	RM 3 CBAS, Yeovilton	
XX377	WS Gazelle AH1 [L]	RM 3 CBAS, Yeovilton	
XX378	WS Gazelle AH1	AAC store, Wroughton	
XX379	WS Gazelle AH1 [D]	AAC No 658 Sqn, Netheravon	
XX380	WS Gazelle AH1	RM 3 CBAS, Yeovilton	
XX381	WS Gazelle AH1	AAC No 2 Flt, Netheravon	
XX382	WS Gazelle HT3 [M]	RAF No 2 FTS, Shawbury	
XX383	WS Gazelle AH1 [E]	AAC No 658 Sqn, Netheravon	
XX384	WS Gazelle AH1	AAC No 2 Flt, Netheravon	
XX385	WS Gazelle AH1 [W]	AAC No 663 Sqn, Soest	
XX386	WS Gazelle AH1	AAC No 12 Flt, Wildenrath	
XX387	WS Gazelle AH1	AAC No 661 Sqn, Hildesheim	
XX388	WS Gazelle AH1	AAC No 652 Sqn, Hildesheim	
XX389	WS Gazelle AH1	AAC No 652 Sqn, Hildesheim	
XX391	WS Gazelle HT2 [56/CU]	RN No 705 Sqn, Culdrose	
XX392	WS Gazelle AH1 [W]	AAC ARWS, Middle Wallop	
XX393	WS Gazelle AH1	AAC No 2 Flt, Netheravon	
XX394	WS Gazelle AH1	AAC No 2 Flt, Netheravon	
XX395	WS Gazelle AH1	AAC No 633 Sqn, Soest	
XX396	WS Gazelle HT3 (8718M) [N]	RAF Exhibition Flight, Henlow	
XX398	WS Gazelle AH1	AAC No 661 Sqn, Hildesheim	
XX399	WS Gazelle AH1	RM store, Wroughton	
XX403	WS Gazelle AH1 [Y]	AAC ARWS, Middle Wallop	
XX405	WS Gazelle AH1	AAC No 669 Sqn, Detmold	
XX406	WS Gazelle HT3 [P]	RAF No 2 FTS, Shawbury	
XX407	WS Gazelle AH1	AAC No 661 Sqn, Hildesheim	
XX408	WS Gazelle AH1	AAC Garrison Air Sqn, Falklands	
XX409	WS Gazelle AH1	AAC No 656 Sqn, Netheravon	
XX410	WS Gazelle HT2 [58/CU]	RN AES Lee-on-Solent	
XX411	WS Gazelle AH1 [X]	AAC Middle Wallop	
XX411	WS Gazelle AH1 (tail only)	FAA Museum, RNAS Yeovilton	
XX412	WS Gazelle AH1 [33C]	RM 3 CBAS, Yeovilton	
XX413	WS Gazelle AH1 [13A]	RM 3 CBAS, Yeovilton	
XX414	WS Gazelle AH1	AAC No 663 Sqn, Soest	
XX416	WS Gazelle AH1	AAC No 664 Sqn, Minden	
XX417	WS Gazelle AH1 [C]	AAC No 665 Sqn, Aldergrove	
XX418	WS Gazelle AH1	AAC No 664 Sqn, Minden	
XX419	WS Gazelle AH1	AAC No 664 Sqn, Minden	
XX431	WS Gazelle HT2 [43/CU]	RN No 705 Sqn, Culdrose	
XX432	WS Gazelle AH1	AAC No 664 Sqn, Minden	
XX433	WS Gazelle AH1 [B]	AAC, RNAY Fleetlands	
XX434	WS Gazelle AH1	RAF Abingdon, BDRF	
XX435	WS Gazelle AH1	AAC No 663 Sqn, Soest	
XX436	WS Gazelle HT2 [39/CU]	RN No 705 Sqn, Culdrose	
XX437	WS Gazelle AH1	AAC No 663 Sqn, Soest	
XX438	WS Gazelle AH1	AAC No 664 Sqn, Minden	
XX439	WS Gazelle AH1	AAC No 651 Sqn, Hildesheim	
XX440	WS Gazelle AH1 (G-BCHN) [E]	AAC No 655 Sqn, Aldergrove	
XX441	WS Gazelle HT2 [38/CU]	RN No 705 Sqn, Culdrose	
XX442	WS Gazelle AH1	AAC No 664 Sqn, Detmold	

Notes	*Serial*	*Type (alternative identity)*	*Owner, Operator or Location*
	XX443	WS Gazelle AH1 [X]	AAC No 663 Sqn, Soest
	XX444	WS Gazelle AH1	AAC No 658 Sqn, Netheravon
	XX445	WS Gazelle AH1	AAC No 659 Sqn, Detmold
	XX446	WS Gazelle HT2 [57/CU]	RN No 705 Sqn, Culdrose
	XX447	WS Gazelle AH1 [Y]	AAC No 663 Sqn, Soest
	XX448	WS Gazelle AH1	AAC No 659 Sqn, Detmold
	XX449	WS Gazelle AH1	AAC No 669 Sqn, Detmold
	XX450	WS Gazelle AH1 [13B]	RM 3 CBAS, Yeovilton
	XX451	WS Gazelle HT2 [58/CU]	RN No 705 Sqn, Culdrose
	XX452	WS Gazelle AH1	AAC Middle Wallop Fire Section
	XX453	WS Gazelle AH1	AAC No 661 Sqn, Detmold
	XX454	WS Gazelle AH1	AAC No 664 Sqn, Detmold
	XX455	WS Gazelle AH1	AAC No 663 Sqn, Soest
	XX456	WS Gazelle AH1	AAC No 664 Sqn, Detmold
	XX457	WS Gazelle AH1 [H]	AAC ARWS, Middle Wallop
	XX460	WS Gazelle AH1	AAC No 652 Sqn, Hildesheim
	XX462	WS Gazelle AH1	AAC No 661 Sqn, Hildesheim
	XX466	HS Hunter T66B/T7 [830/DD]	RNAS Culdrose, SAH
	XX467	HS Hunter T66B/T7 [86]	Air Service Training, Perth
	XX469	WS Lynx HAS2	Helicopter Museum of GB, Heysham
	XX475	SA Jetstream T2 [572/CU] (G-AWVJ/N1036S)	RN No 750 Sqn, Culdrose
	XX476	SA Jetstream T2 [561/CU] (G-AXGL/N1037S)	RN No 750 Sqn, Culdrose
	XX477	SA Jetstream T1 (8462M) (G-AXXS)	RAF Finningley — ground instruction
	XX478	SA Jetstream T2 [564/CU] (G-AXXT)	RN No 750 Sqn, Culdrose
	XX479	SA Jetstream T2 [563/CU] (G-AXUR)	RN No 750 Sqn, Culdrose
	XX480	SA Jetstream T2 [565/CU] (G-AXXU)	RN No 750 Sqn, Culdrose
	XX481	SA Jetstream T2 [560/CU] (G-AXUP)	RN No 750 Sqn, Culdrose
	XX482	SA Jetstream T1 [J]	RAF No 6 FTS, Finningley
	XX483	SA Jetstream T2 [562/CU]	RN No 750 Sqn, Culdrose
	XX484	SA Jetstream T2 [566/CU]	RN No 750 Sqn, Culdrose
	XX485	SA Jetstream T2 [567/CU]	RN No 750 Sqn, Culdrose
	XX486	SA Jetstream T2 [569/CU]	RN No 750 Sqn, Culdrose
	XX487	SA Jetstream T2 [568/CU]	RN No 750 Sqn, Culdrose
	XX488	SA Jetstream T2 [571/CU]	RN No 750 Sqn, Culdrose
	XX489	SA Jetstream T2 [575/CU]	RN No 750 Sqn, Culdrose
	XX490	SA Jetstream T2 [570/CU]	RN No 750 Sqn, Culdrose
	XX491	SA Jetstream T1 [K]	RAF No 6 FTS, Finningley
	XX492	SA Jetstream T1 [A]	RAF No 6 FTS, Finningley
	XX493	SA Jetstream T1 [L]	RAF No 6 FTS, Finningley
	XX494	SA Jetstream T1 [B]	RAF No 6 FTS, Finningley
	XX495	SA Jetstream T1 [C]	RAF No 6 FTS, Finningley
	XX496	SA Jetstream T1 [D]	RAF No 6 FTS, Finningley
	XX497	SA Jetstream T1 [E]	RAF No 6 FTS, Finningley
	XX498	SA Jetstream T1 [F]	RAF No 6 FTS, Finningley
	XX499	SA Jetstream T1 [G]	RAF No 6 FTS, Finningley
	XX500	SA Jetstream T1 [H]	RAF No 6 FTS, Finningley
	XX507	HS125 CC2	RAF No 32 Sqn, Northolt
	XX508	HS125 CC2	RAF No 32 Sqn, Northolt
	XX513	SA Bulldog T1 [A]	RAF No 1 FTS/RNEFTS, Topcliffe
	XX515	SA Bulldog T1 [7]	RAF CFS, Scampton
	XX516	SA Bulldog T1 [C]	RAF No 1 FTS/RNEFTS, Topcliffe
	XX517	SA Bulldog T1 [8]	RAF
	XX518	SA Bulldog T1 [24]	RAF Shawbury store
	XX519	SA Bulldog T1 [I]	RAF No 1 FTS/RNEFTS, Topcliffe
	XX520	SA Bulldog T1 [2]	RAF CFS, Scampton
	XX521	SA Bulldog T1 [01]	RAF, East Lowlands UAS, Turnhouse
	XX522	SA Bulldog T1 [E]	RAF No 1 FTS/RNEFTS, Topcliffe
	XX523	SA Bulldog T1 [F]	RAF No 1 FTS/RNEFTS, Topcliffe
	XX524	SA Bulldog T1 [04]	RAF, London UAS, Abingdon
	XX525	SA Bulldog T1 [03]	RAF, East Lowlands UAS, Turnhouse
	XX526	SA Bulldog T1 [C]	RAF, Oxford UAS, Abingdon
	XX527	SA Bulldog T1 [G]	RAF No 1 FTS/RNEFTS, Topcliffe
	XX528	SA Bulldog T1 [D]	RAF, Oxford UAS, Abingdon
	XX529	SA Bulldog T1 [H]	RAF No 1 FTS/RNEFTS, Topcliffe
	XX530	SA Bulldog T1 [12]	CTE, RAF Manston
	XX531	SA Bulldog T1 [4]	RAF CFS, Scampton
	XX532	SA Bulldog T1 [J]	RAF, Yorkshire UAS, Finningley

Serial	Type (alternative identity)	Owner, Operator or Location	Notes
XX533	SA Bulldog T1 [J]	RAF No 1 FTS/RNEFTS, Topcliffe	
XX534	SA Bulldog T1 [04]	RAF, East Lowlands UAS, Turnhouse	
XX535	SA Bulldog T1 [10]	RAF, London UAS, Abingdon	
XX536	SA Bulldog T1	RAF	
XX537	SA Bulldog T1 [02]	RAF, East Lowlands UAS, Turnhouse	
XX538	SA Bulldog T1 [E]	RAF Shawbury store	
XX539	SA Bulldog T1 [1]	RAF CFS, Scampton	
XX540	SA Bulldog T1 [K]	RAF No 1 FTS/RNEFTS, Topcliffe	
XX541	SA Bulldog T1 [L]	RAF No 1 FTS/RNEFTS, Topcliffe	
XX543	SA Bulldog T1 [F]	RAF, Yorkshire UAS, Finningley	
XX544	SA Bulldog T1 [01]	RAF, London UAS, Abingdon	
XX545	SA Bulldog T1 PAX [02]	RAF, East Lowlands UAS, Turnhouse	
XX546	SA Bulldog T1 [03]	RAF, London UAS, Abingdon	
XX547	SA Bulldog T1 [05]	RAF, London UAS, Abingdon	
XX548	SA Bulldog T1 [06]	RAF, London UAS, Abingdon	
XX549	SA Bulldog T1 [5]	RAF, Manchester UAS, Woodvale	
XX550	SA Bulldog T1 [8]	RAF, Northumbria UAS, Teesside	
XX551	SA Bulldog T1 [M]	RAF No 1 FTS/RNEFTS, Topcliffe	
XX552	SA Bulldog T1 [08]	RAF, London UAS, Abingdon	
XX553	SA Bulldog T1 [07]	RAF, London UAS, Abingdon	
XX554	SA Bulldog T1 [09]	RAF, London UAS, Abingdon	
XX555	SA Bulldog T1 [10]	RAF CFS, Scampton	
XX556	SA Bulldog T1	RAF, East Midlands UAS, Newton	
XX557	SA Bulldog T1 PAX	RAF Topcliffe, ground instruction	
XX558	SA Bulldog T1 [A]	RAF, Birmingham UAS, Cosford	
XX559	SA Bulldog T1 [bk]	RAF, Glasgow & Strathclyde UAS, Glasgow	
XX560	SA Bulldog T1 [r]	RAF, Glasgow & Strathclyde UAS, Glasgow	
XX561	SA Bulldog T1 [A]	RAF, Aberdeen, Dundee & St Andrews UAS, Leuchars	
XX562	SA Bulldog T1 [E]	RAF No 13 AEF, Sydenham	
XX611	SA Bulldog T1 [y]	RAF, Glasgow & Strathclyde UAS, Glasgow	
XX612	SA Bulldog T1 [05]	RAF, Wales UAS, St Athan	
XX613	SA Bulldog T1 [A]	RAF, Queen's UAS, Sydenham	
XX614	SA Bulldog T1 [1]	RAF Shawbury store	
XX615	SA Bulldog T1 [2]	RAF, Manchester UAS, Woodvale	
XX616	SA Bulldog T1 [3]	RAF, Manchester UAS, Woodvale	
XX617	SA Bulldog T1 [4]	RAF, Manchester UAS, Woodvale	
XX619	SA Bulldog T1 [B]	RAF, Yorkshire UAS, Finningley	
XX620	SA Bulldog T1 [C]	RAF, Yorkshire UAS, Finningley	
XX621	SA Bulldog T1 [D]	RAF, Yorkshire UAS, Finningley	
XX622	SA Bulldog T1 [E]	RAF, Yorkshire UAS, Finningley	
XX623	SA Bulldog T1 [M]	RAF, East Midlands UAS, Newton	
XX624	SA Bulldog T1 [G]	RAF, Yorkshire UAS, Finningley	
XX625	SA Bulldog T1 [01]	RAF, Wales UAS, St Athan	
XX626	SA Bulldog T1 [02]	RAF, Wales UAS, St Athan	
XX627	SA Bulldog T1 [03]	RAF, Wales UAS, St Athan	
XX628	SA Bulldog T1 [04]	RAF, Wales UAS, St Athan	
XX629	SA Bulldog T1 [V]	RAF, Northumbria UAS, Teesside	
XX630	SA Bulldog T1 [A]	RAF, Liverpool UAS, Woodvale	
XX631	SA Bulldog T1 [W]	RAF, Northumbria UAS, Teesside	
XX632	SA Bulldog T1 [D]	RAF, Bristol UAS, Filton	
XX633	SA Bulldog T1 [X]	RAF, Northumbria UAS, Teesside	
XX634	SA Bulldog T1 [C]	RAF, Cambridge UAS, Teversham	
XX635	SA Bulldog T1 (8767M) [S]	RAF St Athan, CTTS	
XX636	SA Bulldog T1 [Y]	RAF, Northumbria UAS, Teesside	
XX637	SA Bulldog T1 [Z]	RAF, Northumbria UAS, Teesside	
XX638	SA Bulldog T1 [N]	RAF No 1 FTS/RNEFTS, Topcliffe	
XX639	SA Bulldog T1 [02]	RAF, London UAS, Abingdon	
XX640	SA Bulldog T1 [U]	RAF, Queen's UAS, Sydenham	
XX653	SA Bulldog T1 [E]	RAF, Bristol UAS, Filton	
XX654	SA Bulldog T1 [A]	RAF, Bristol UAS, Filton	
XX655	SA Bulldog T1 [B]	RAF, Bristol UAS, Filton	
XX656	SA Bulldog T1 [C]	RAF, Bristol UAS, Filton	
XX657	SA Bulldog T1 [U]	RAF, Cambridge UAS, Teversham	
XX658	SA Bulldog T1 [A]	RAF, Cambridge UAS, Teversham	
XX659	SA Bulldog T1 [S]	RAF, Cambridge UAS, Teversham	
XX661	SA Bulldog T1 [B]	RAF, Oxford UAS, Abingdon	
XX663	SA Bulldog T1 [B]	RAF, Aberdeen, Dundee & St Andrews UAS, Leuchars	
XX664	SA Bulldog T1 [05]	RAF, East Lowlands UAS, Turnhouse	

Notes	Serial	Type (alternative identity)	Owner, Operator or Location
	XX665	SA Bulldog T1 [E]	RAF, Aberdeen, Dundee & St Andrews UAS, Leuchars
	XX666	SA Bulldog T1 [C]	RAF, Aberdeen, Dundee & St Andrews UAS, Leuchars
	XX667	SA Bulldog T1 [D]	RAF, Aberdeen, Dundee & St Andrews UAS, Leuchars
	XX668	SA Bulldog T1 [P]	RAF No 1 FTS/RNEFTS, Topcliffe
	XX669	SA Bulldog T1 [B]	RAF, Birmingham UAS, Cosford
	XX670	SA Bulldog T1 [C]	RAF, Birmingham UAS, Cosford
	XX671	SA Bulldog T1 [D]	RAF, Birmingham UAS, Cosford
	XX672	SA Bulldog T1 [E]	RAF, Birmingham UAS, Cosford
	XX685	SA Bulldog T1 [L]	RAF, Liverpool UAS, Woodvale
	XX686	SA Bulldog T1 [U]	RAF, Liverpool UAS, Woodvale
	XX687	SA Bulldog T1 [A]	RAF, East Midlands UAS, Newton
	XX688	SA Bulldog T1 [S]	RAF, Liverpool UAS, Woodvale
	XX689	SA Bulldog T1 [3]	RAF CFS, Scampton
	XX690	SA Bulldog T1 [A]	RAF, Yorkshire UAS, Finningley
	XX691	SA Bulldog T1 [H]	RAF, Yorkshire UAS, Finningley
	XX692	SA Bulldog T1 [5]	RAF CFS, Scampton
	XX693	SA Bulldog T1 [11]	RAF CFS, Scampton
	XX694	SA Bulldog T1 [E]	RAF, East Midlands UAS, Newton
	XX695	SA Bulldog T1 [A]	RAF, Oxford UAS, Abingdon
	XX696	SA Bulldog T1 [8]	RAF CFS, Scampton
	XX697	SA Bulldog T1 [Q]	RAF, Queen's UAS, Sydenham
	XX698	SA Bulldog T1 [9]	RAF CFS, Scampton
	XX699	SA Bulldog T1 [Q]	RAF No 1 FTS/RNEFTS, Topcliffe
	XX700	SA Bulldog T1 [R]	RAF No 1 FTS/RNEFTS, Topcliffe
	XX701	SA Bulldog T1 [02]	RAF, Southampton UAS, Hurn
	XX702	SA Bulldog T1 [bl]	RAF, Glasgow & Strathclyde UAS, Glasgow
	XX704	SA Bulldog T1 [U]	RAF, East Midlands UAS, Newton
	XX705	SA Bulldog T1 [05]	RAF, Southampton UAS, Hurn
	XX706	SA Bulldog T1 [01]	RAF, Southampton UAS, Hurn
	XX707	SA Bulldog T1 [04]	RAF, Southampton UAS, Hurn
	XX708	SA Bulldog T1 [03]	RAF, Southampton UAS, Hurn
	XX709	SA Bulldog T1 [33]	RAF Shawbury store
	XX710	SA Bulldog T1 [34]	RAF Shawbury store
	XX711	SA Bulldog T1 [S]	RAF, Queen's UAS, Sydenham
	XX712	SA Bulldog T1 [1]	RAF, Manchester UAS, Woodvale
	XX713	SA Bulldog T1 [6]	RAF CFS, Scampton
	XX714	SA Bulldog T1	MoD(PE) BAe Prestwick
	XX718	SEPECAT Jaguar replica (BAPC150)	RAF Exhibition Flight, Abingdon
	XX719	SEPECAT Jaguar GR1A [EQ]	RAF No 6 Sqn, Coltishall
	XX720	SEPECAT Jaguar GR1A (JI003) [GQ]	RAF No 54 Sqn, Coltishall
	XX722	SEPECAT Jaguar GR1 [EF]	RAF store, Shawbury
	XX723	SEPECAT Jaguar GR1A [07]	RAF No 226 OCU, Lossiemouth
	XX724	SEPECAT Jaguar GR1A [GA]	RAF No 54 Sqn, Coltishall
	XX725	SEPECAT Jaguar GR1A (JI010) [EL]	RAF No 6 Sqn, Coltishall
	XX726	SEPECAT Jaguar GR1 [EB]	RAF store, Shawbury
	XX727	SEPECAT Jaguar GR1 [ER]	RAF store, Shawbury
	XX729	SEPECAT Jaguar GR1 (JI012) [EJ]	RAF store, Shawbury
	XX730	SEPECAT Jaguar GR1 [EC]	RAF store, Shawbury
	XX732	SEPECAT Jaguar GR1A [03]	RAF No 226 OCU, Lossiemouth
	XX733	SEPECAT Jaguar GR1A [GL]	RAF No 54 Sqn, Coltishall
	XX734	SEPECAT Jaguar GR1 (JI014) (8816M)	RAF Coltishall, BDRT
	XX736	SEPECAT Jaguar GR1 (JI013)	BAe Warton
	XX737	SEPECAT Jaguar GR1A [GG] (JI015)	RAF No 54 Sqn, Coltishall
	XX738	SEPECAT Jaguar GR1A (JI016) [GJ]	RAF No 54 Sqn, Coltishall
	XX739	SEPECAT Jaguar GR1 (8902M) [I]	RAF No 1 SoTT, Halton
	XX741	SEPECAT Jaguar GR1A [EJ]	RAF No 6 Sqn, Coltishall
	XX743	SEPECAT Jaguar GR1 [EG]	RAF store, Shawbury
	XX744	SEPECAT Jaguar GR1 [DJ]	RAF store, Shawbury
	XX745	SEPECAT Jaguar GR1A [GN]	RAF No 54 Sqn, Coltishall
	XX746	SEPECAT Jaguar GR1A [09] (8895M)	RAF No 1 SoTT, Halton
	XX747	SEPECAT Jaguar GR1 [B] (8903M)	RAF store, Shawbury
	XX748	SEPECAT Jaguar GR1 [GK]	RAF No 54 Sqn, Coltishall

Serial	Type (alternative identity)	Owner, Operator or Location	Notes
XX751	SEPECAT Jaguar GR1 [10]	RAF No 226 OCU, Lossiemouth	
XX752	SEPECAT Jaguar GR1A [GF]	RAF No 54 Sqn, Coltishall	
XX753	SEPECAT Jaguar GR1 [05]	RAF store, Shawbury	
XX754	SEPECAT Jaguar GR1 [23]	RAF No 226 OCU, Lossiemouth	
XX756	SEPECAT Jaguar GR1 [AM] (8899M)	RAF No 1 SoTT, Halton	
XX757	SEPECAT Jaguar GR1 [CU]	RAF store, Shawbury	
XX763	SEPECAT Jaguar GR1 [24]	RAF store, Shawbury	
XX764	SEPECAT Jaguar GR1 [13]	RAF store, Shawbury	
XX765	SEPECAT Jaguar ACT	MoD(PE) BAe Warton	
XX766	SEPECAT Jaguar GR1A [GP]	RAF No 54 Sqn, Coltishall	
XX767	SEPECAT Jaguar GR1 [GE]	RAF No 54 Sqn, Coltishall	
XX818	SEPECAT Jaguar GR1 [DE]	RAF store, Shawbury	
XX819	SEPECAT Jaguar GR1 [CE]	RAF store, Shawbury	
XX821	SEPECAT Jaguar GR1 [P] (8896M)	RAFC Cranwell Engineering School	
XX824	SEPECAT Jaguar GR1 [AD]	RAF store, Shawbury	
XX825	SEPECAT Jaguar GR1 [BN]	RAF store, Shawbury	
XX826	SEPECAT Jaguar GR1 [34]	RAF store, Shawbury	
XX829	SEPECAT Jaguar T2 [D]	RAF No 226 OCU, Lossiemouth	
XX830	SEPECAT Jaguar T2	MoD(PE) ETPS, Boscombe Down	
XX832	SEPECAT Jaguar T2 [S]	RAF No 226 OCU, Lossiemouth	
XX833	SEPECAT Jaguar T2A [Z]	RAF No 41 Sqn, Coltishall	
XX834	SEPECAT Jaguar T2A [U]	RAF No 226 OCU, Lossiemouth	
XX835	SEPECAT Jaguar T2	MoD(PE) RAE Farnborough	
XX836	SEPECAT Jaguar T2A [GR]	RAF No 6 Sqn, Coltishall	
XX837	SEPECAT Jaguar T2A [Z]	RAF No 226 OCU, Lossiemouth	
XX838	SEPECAT Jaguar T2A [X]	RAF No 226 OCU, Lossiemouth	
XX839	SEPECAT Jaguar T2 [Y]	RAF No 226 OCU, Lossiemouth	
XX840	SEPECAT Jaguar T2 [T]	RAF No 226 OCU, Lossiemouth	
XX841	SEPECAT Jaguar T2 [S]	RAF No 41 Sqn, Coltishall	
XX842	SEPECAT Jaguar T2 [T]	RAF No 41 Sqn, Coltishall	
XX843	SEPECAT Jaguar T2A [36]	RAF No 2 Sqn, Laarbruch	
XX844	SEPECAT Jaguar T2 [F]	RAF No 226 OCU, Lossiemouth	
XX845	SEPECAT Jaguar T2 [AZ]	RAF Coltishall	
XX846	SEPECAT Jaguar T2A [A]	RAF No 226 OCU, Lossiemouth	
XX847	SEPECAT Jaguar T2 [G]	RAF No 226 OCU, Lossiemouth	
XX885	HS Buccaneer S2B	RAF No 208 Sqn, Lossiemouth	
XX886	HS Buccaneer S2B	RAF Honington, ASF	
XX887	HS Buccaneer S2B [N]	RAF Shawbury store	
XX888	HS Buccaneer S2B [Z]	RAF Shawbury store	
XX889	HS Buccaneer S2B	RAF No 208 Sqn, Lossiemouth	
XX892	HS Buccaneer S2B	RAF No 208 Sqn, Lossiemouth	
XX893	HS Buccaneer S2B	RAF No 237 OCU, Lossiemouth	
XX894	HS Buccaneer S2B	RAF No 208 Sqn, Lossiemouth	
XX895	HS Buccaneer S2B	RAF No 237 OCU, Lossiemouth	
XX896	HS Buccaneer S2B	RAF Shawbury store	
XX897	HS Buccaneer S2B	MoD(PE) RS&RE Bedford	
XX899	HS Buccaneer S2B	RAF No 237 OCU, Lossiemouth	
XX900	HS Buccaneer S2B	RAF No 208 Sqn, Lossiemouth	
XX901	HS Buccaneer S2B	RAF No 208 Sqn, Lossiemouth	
XX907	WS Lynx AH1	RAE Farnborough, stored	
XX910	WS Lynx HAS2	RAE Farnborough, stored	
XX914	BAC VC10 srs 1103 (G-ATDJ/ 8777M)	RAF AMS, Brize Norton	
XX919	BAC 1-11/402 (PI-C 1121)	MoD(PE) RAE Farnborough	
XX946	Panavia Tornado (P02) (8883M)	RAF Honington for ground instruction/ Saudi Support Unit	
XX947	Panavia Tornado (P03) (8797M)	RAF Marham for ground instruction	
XX948	Panavia Tornado (P06) (8879M)	RAF No 2 SoTT, Cosford	
XX955	SEPECAT Jaguar GR1 [GK]	MoD(PE) A&AEE, Boscombe Down	
XX956	SEPECAT Jaguar GR1 [BE]	RAF store, Shawbury	
XX958	SEPECAT Jaguar GR1 [BK]	RAF store, Shawbury	
XX959	SEPECAT Jaguar GR1 [CJ]	RAF store, Shawbury	
XX962	SEPECAT Jaguar GR1 [EK]	RAF No 6 Sqn, Coltishall	
XX965	SEPECAT Jaguar GR1A [04]	RAF No 226 OCU, Lossiemouth	
XX966	SEPECAT Jaguar GR1A (8904M) [EL]	RAF No 1 SoTT, Halton	
XX967	SEPECAT Jaguar GR1 [AC]	RAF store, Shawbury	
XX968	SEPECAT Jaguar GR1 [AJ]	RAF store, Shawbury	
XX969	SEPECAT Jaguar GR1A (8897M) [01]	RAF No 2 SoTT, Cosford	
XX970	SEPECAT Jaguar GR1 [EH]	RAF No 6 Sqn, Coltishall	

Notes	Serial	Type (alternative identity)	Owner, Operator or Location
	XX974	SEPECAT Jaguar GR1A [EG]	RAF No 6 Sqn, Coltishall
	XX975	SEPECAT Jaguar GR1 (8905M) [EL]	RAF No 6 Sqn, Coltishall
	XX976	SEPECAT Jaguar GR1 (8906M) [BD]	RAF No 1 SoTT, Halton
	XX977	SEPECAT Jaguar GR1 [DL]	RAF store, Shawbury
	XX979	SEPECAT Jaguar GR1A	MoD(PE) A&AEE Boscombe Down
	XZ101	SEPECAT Jaguar GR1A [Q]	RAF No 41 Sqn, Coltishall
	XZ103	SEPECAT Jaguar GR1A [23]	RAF No 2 Sqn, Laarbruch
	XZ104	SEPECAT Jaguar GR1A [24]	RAF No 2 Sqn, Laarbruch
	XZ106	SEPECAT Jaguar GR1A [26]	RAF No 2 Sqn, Laarbruch
	XZ107	SEPECAT Jaguar GR1 [H]	RAF No 41 Sqn, Coltishall
	XZ108	SEPECAT Jaguar GR1A [28]	RAF No 2 Sqn, Laarbruch
	XZ109	SEPECAT Jaguar GR1A [29]	RAF No 2 Sqn, Laarbruch
	XZ111	SEPECAT Jaguar GR1A [31]	RAF No 2 Sqn, Laarbruch
	XZ112	SEPECAT Jaguar GR1A [32]	RAF No 2 Sqn, Laarbruch
	XZ113	SEPECAT Jaguar GR1A [30]	RAF No 2 Sqn, Laarbruch
	XZ114	SEPECAT Jaguar GR1 [B]	RAF No 41 Sqn, Coltishall
	XZ115	SEPECAT Jaguar GR1A [C]	RAF No 41 Sqn, Coltishall
	XZ116	SEPECAT Jaguar GR1A [D]	RAF No 41 Sqn, Coltishall
	XZ117	SEPECAT Jaguar GR1 [E]	RAF No 41 Sqn, Coltishall
	XZ118	SEPECAT Jaguar GR1 [F]	RAF No 41 Sqn, Coltishall
	XZ119	SEPECAT Jaguar GR1 [G]	RAF No 41 Sqn, Coltishall
	XZ129	HS Harrier GR3 [09]	RAF No 1 Sqn, Wittering
	XZ130	HS Harrier GR3 [AH]	RAF No 3 Sqn, Gutersloh
	XZ131	HS Harrier GR3 [N]	RAF No 1417 Flt, Belize
	XZ132	HS Harrier GR3 [04]	RAF No 1 Sqn, Wittering
	XZ133	HS Harrier GR3 [10]	RAF No 1 Sqn, Wittering
	XZ135	HS Harrier GR3 [P] (8848M) (nose only)	RAF Exhibition Flight, Abingdon
	XZ136	HS Harrier GR3	MoD(PE) A&AEE Boscombe Down
	XZ138	HS Harrier GR3 [K]	RAF No 233 OCU, Wittering
	XZ145	HS Harrier T4 [T]	RAF No 233 OCU, Wittering
	XZ146	HS Harrier T4 [W]	RAF No 233 OCU, Wittering
	XZ147	HS Harrier T4A [Z]	RAF No 233 OCU, Wittering
	XZ170	WS Lynx AH1	MoD(PE) Westlands, Yeovil
	XZ171	WS Lynx AH1	MoD(PE) Rolls-Royce, Filton
	XZ172	WS Lynx AH1 [K]	AAC ARW/LCF, Middle Wallop
	XZ173	WS Lynx AH1	AAC No 651 Sqn, Hildesheim
	XZ174	WS Lynx AH1	AAC No 651 Sqn, Hildesheim
	XZ175	WS Lynx AH1 [A]	AAC OTS/LCF, Middle Wallop
	XZ176	WS Lynx AH1 [A]	AAC ARW/LCF, Middle Wallop
	XZ177	WS Lynx AH1	AAC No 652 Sqn, Hildesheim
	XZ178	WS Lynx AH1	AAC No 654 Sqn, Detmold
	XZ179	WS Lynx AH1/5	MoD(PE) ETPS Boscombe Down
	XZ180	WS Lynx AH1	MoD(PE) Westlands, Yeovil
	XZ181	WS Lynx AH1	AAC Soest
	XZ182	WS Lynx AH1 [23A]	RM 3 CBAS, Yeovilton
	XZ183	WS Lynx AH1	AAC No 669 Sqn, Detmold
	XZ184	WS Lynx AH1	AAC No 654 Sqn, Detmold
	XZ185	WS Lynx AH1	AAC No 662 Sqn, Soest
	XZ186	WS Lynx AH1	AAC No 662 Sqn, Soest
	XZ187	WS Lynx AH1	AAC No 655 Sqn, Aldergrove
	XZ188	WS Lynx AH1	AAC No 655 Sqn, Aldergrove
	XZ190	WS Lynx AH1	AAC No 651 Sqn, Hildesheim
	XZ191	WS Lynx AH1	AAC No 651 Sqn, Hildesheim
	XZ192	WS Lynx AH1	AAC No 651 Sqn, Hildesheim
	XZ193	WS Lynx AH1 [A]	AAC No 665 Sqn, Aldergrove
	XZ194	WS Lynx AH1	AAC No 663 Sqn, Soest
	XZ195	WS Lynx AH1 [X]	AAC No 665 Sqn, Aldergrove
	XZ196	WS Lynx AH1 [B]	AAC No 663 Sqn, Soest
	XZ197	WS Lynx AH1 [Y]	AAC No 665 Sqn, Aldergrove
	XZ198	WS Lynx AH1	AAC No 653 Sqn, Soest
	XZ199	WS Lynx AH1 [C]	AAC No 663 Sqn, Soest
	XZ203	WS Lynx AH1 [B]	AAC ARW/LCF, Middle Wallop
	XZ204	WS Lynx AH1	AAC No 662 Sqn, Soest
	XZ205	WS Lynx AH1	AAC AETW, Middle Wallop
	XZ206	WS Lynx AH1	AAC No 655 Sqn, Aldergrove
	XZ207	WS Lynx AH1	AAC No 655 Sqn, Aldergrove
	XZ208	WS Lynx AH1	AAC No 659 Sqn, Detmold
	XZ209	WS Lynx AH1	AAC No 662 Sqn, Soest
	XZ210	WS Lynx AH1	AAC No — Sqn, Soest
	XZ211	WS Lynx AH1	AAC No — Sqn, Soest

Serial	Type (alternative identity)	Owner, Operator or Location	Notes
XZ212	WS Lynx AH1	AAC No 663 Sqn, Soest	
XZ213	WS Lynx AH1	AAC No 659 Sqn, Detmold	
XZ214	WS Lynx AH1	AAC store, Wroughton	
XZ215	WS Lynx AH1	AAC AETW, Middle Wallop	
XZ216	WS Lynx AH1	AAC No 662 Sqn, Soest	
XZ217	WS Lynx AH1	AAC No 663 Sqn, Soest	
XZ218	WS Lynx AH1 [Y]	AAC No 653 Sqn, Soest	
XZ219	WS Lynx AH1	AAC No 662 Sqn, Soest	
XZ220	WS Lynx AH1	AAC No 654 Sqn, Detmold	
XZ221	WS Lynx AH1	AAC No 657 Sqn, Oakington	
XZ222	WS Lynx AH1	AAC D&TS, Middle Wallop	
XZ227	WS Lynx HAS3 [303/PO]	RN No 815 Sqn, Portland	
XZ228	WS Lynx HAS3	RNAY Fleetlands	
XZ229	WS Lynx HAS3	RN No 829 Sqn, Portland	
XZ230	WS Lynx HAS3 [301/PO]	RN No 815 Sqn, Portland	
XZ231	WS Lynx HAS2 [645/PO]	RN No 702 Sqn, Portland	
XZ232	WS Lynx HAS2 [647/PO]	RN No 702 Sqn, Portland	
XZ233	WS Lynx HAS2	RN No 815 Sqn, Portland	
XZ234	WS Lynx HAS2 [335/CF]	RN No 815 Sqn, Portland	
XZ235	WS Lynx HAS2 [403/BX]	RN No 829 Sqn, Portland	
XZ236	WS Lynx HAS2	MoD(PE) Westlands, Yeovil	
XZ237	WS Lynx HAS2 [302/PO]	RN No 815 Sqn, Portland	
XZ238	WS Lynx HAS2	RNAY Fleetlands	
XZ239	WS Lynx HAS2 [375]	RN No 829 Sqn, Portland	
XZ240	WS Lynx HAS2 [308]	RN No 815 Sqn, Portland	
XZ241	WS Lynx HAS2 [417/NM]	RN No 815 Sqn, Portland	
XZ243	WS Lynx HAS3 [635/PO]	RN No 702 Sqn, Portland	
XZ244	WS Lynx HAS3 [472/AM]	RN No 815 Sqn, Portland	
XZ245	WS Lynx HAS3 [600/PO]	RN No 829 Sqn, Portland	
XZ246	WS Lynx HAS2 [306/PO]	RN No 815 Sqn, Portland	
XZ248	WS Lynx HAS2 [404/FF]	RN No 815 Sqn, Portland	
XZ249	WS Lynx HAS2	RNEC Manadon for instruction	
XZ250	WS Lynx HAS2 [648/PO]	RN No 702 Sqn, Portland	
XZ252	WS Lynx HAS3 [644/PO]	RN No 702 Sqn, Portland	
XZ254	WS Lynx HAS2 [407/YK]	RN No 815 Sqn, Portland	
XZ255	WS Lynx HAS3 [450/SS]	RN No 815 Sqn, Portland	
XZ256	WS Lynx HAS2	RN No 815 Sqn, Portland	
XZ257	WS Lynx HAS3 [634/PO]	RN No 702 Sqn, Portland	
XZ280	BAe Nimrod AEW3	MoD(PE) BAe Woodford	
XZ281	BAe Nimrod AEW3	MoD(PE) BAe Woodford	
XZ282	BAe Nimrod AEW3	MoD(PE) BAe Woodford	
XZ283	BAe Nimrod AEW3	RAF JTU, Waddington	
XZ284	HS Nimrod MR2	RAF No 42 Sqn, St Mawgan	
XZ285	BAe Nimrod AEW3	RAF JTU, Waddington	
XZ286	BAe Nimrod AEW3	RAF JTU, Waddington	
XZ287	BAe Nimrod AEW3	RAF JTU, Waddington	
XZ290	WS Gazelle AH1	AAC store, Wroughton	
XZ291	WS Gazelle AH1	AAC No 12 Flt, Wildenrath	
XZ292	WS Gazelle AH1	AAC No 664 Sqn, Detmold	
XZ294	WS Gazelle AH1	AAC No 664 Sqn, Minden	
XZ295	WS Gazelle AH1	AAC No 12 Flt, Wildenrath	
XZ296	WS Gazelle AH1	AAC No 663 Sqn, Soest	
XZ297	WS Gazelle AH1	AAC No 661 Sqn, Hildesheim	
XZ298	WS Gazelle AH1	AAC No 664 Sqn, Detmold	
XZ299	WS Gazelle AH1	AAC No 657 Sqn, Oakington	
XZ300	WS Gazelle AH1	AAC No 664 Sqn, Minden	
XZ301	WS Gazelle AH1	AAC No 664 Sqn, Minden	
XZ302	WS Gazelle AH1	AAC No 655 Sqn, Aldergrove	
XZ303	WS Gazelle AH1	AAC No 663 Sqn, Soest	
XZ304	WS Gazelle AH1	AAC No 664 Sqn, Minden	
XZ305	WS Gazelle AH1	AAC No 655 Sqn, Aldergrove	
XZ307	WS Gazelle AH1 [B]	AAC No 665 Sqn, Aldergrove	
XZ308	WS Gazelle AH1 [L]	AAC ARWS, Middle Wallop	
XZ309	WS Gazelle AH1	AAC No 664 Sqn, Minden	
XZ310	WS Gazelle AH1	AAC No 661 Sqn, Hildesheim	
XZ311	WS Gazelle AH1	AAC No 664 Sqn, Minden	
XZ312	WS Gazelle AH1	AAC No 2 Flt, Netheravon	
XZ313	WS Gazelle AH1	AAC store, Wroughton	
XZ314	WS Gazelle AH1	AAC No 656 Sqn, Netheravon	
XZ315	WS Gazelle AH1	AAC ARWS, Middle Wallop	
XZ316	WS Gazelle AH1 [R]	AAC ARWS, Middle Wallop	
XZ317	WS Gazelle AH1 [Q]	AAC ARWS, Middle Wallop	
XZ318	WS Gazelle AH1 [U]	AAC ARWS, Middle Wallop	
XZ319	WS Gazelle AH1 [S]	AAC ARWS, Middle Wallop	

Notes	Serial	Type (alternative identity)	Owner, Operator or Location
	XZ320	WS Gazelle AH1	RM store, Wroughton
	XZ321	WS Gazelle AH1	AAC store, Wroughton
	XZ322	WS Gazelle AH1 [N]	AAC ARWS, Middle Wallop
	XZ323	WS Gazelle AH1	AAC No 655 Sqn, Aldergrove
	XZ324	WS Gazelle AH1	AAC Garrison Air Sqn, Falklands
	XZ325	WS Gazelle AH1	AAC No 655 Sqn, Aldergrove
	XZ326	WS Gazelle AH1 [C]	RM store, Wroughton
	XZ327	WS Gazelle AH1	AAC store, Wroughton
	XZ328	WS Gazelle AH1	AAC No 657 Sqn, Oakington
	XZ329	WS Gazelle AH1 [J]	AAC ARWS, Middle Wallop
	XZ330	WS Gazelle AH1	AAC No 657 Sqn, Oakington
	XZ331	WS Gazelle AH1	AAC, RNAY Fleetlands
	XZ332	WS Gazelle AH1 [O]	AAC ARWS, Middle Wallop
	XZ333	WS Gazelle AH1 [A]	AAC ARWS, Middle Wallop
	XZ334	WS Gazelle AH1	AAC No 657 Sqn, Oakington
	XZ335	WS Gazelle AH1	AAC No 3 Flt, Topcliffe
	XZ336	WS Gazelle AH1	AAC No 3 Flt, Topcliffe
	XZ337	WS Gazelle AH1	AAC No 664 Sqn, Detmold
	XZ338	WS Gazelle AH1 [X]	AAC ARWS, Middle Wallop
	XZ339	WS Gazelle AH1	MoD(PE) Westlands, Weston-super-Mare
	XZ340	WS Gazelle AH1 [T]	AAC ARWS, Middle Wallop
	XZ341	WS Gazelle AH1	AAC D&TS, Middle Wallop
	XZ342	WS Gazelle AH1 [Z]	AAC No 663 Sqn, Soest
	XZ343	WS Gazelle AH1	AAC No 12 Flt, Wildenrath
	XZ344	WS Gazelle AH1	AAC No 656 Sqn, Netheravon
	XZ345	WS Gazelle AH1	AAC No 3 Flt, Topcliffe
	XZ346	WS Gazelle AH1	AAC store, Wroughton
	XZ347	WS Gazelle AH1	AAC No 3 Flt, Topcliffe
	XZ348	WS Gazelle AH1	AAC No 2 Flt, Netheravon
	XZ349	WS Gazelle AH1 [M]	AAC ARWS, Middle Wallop
	XZ355	SEPECAT Jaguar GR1 [J]	RAF No 41 Sqn, Coltishall
	XZ356	SEPECAT Jaguar GR1 [R]	RAF No 41 Sqn, Coltishall
	XZ357	SEPECAT Jaguar GR1 [K]	RAF No 41 Sqn, Coltishall
	XZ358	SEPECAT Jaguar GR1 [L]	RAF No 41 Sqn, Coltishall
	XZ359	SEPECAT Jaguar GR1 [M]	RAF No 41 Sqn, Coltishall
	XZ360	SEPECAT Jaguar GR1A [N]	RAF No 41 Sqn, Coltishall
	XZ361	SEPECAT Jaguar GR1A [25]	RAF No 2 Sqn, Laarbruch
	XZ362	SEPECAT Jaguar GR1A [27]	RAF No 2 Sqn, Laarbruch
	XZ363	SEPECAT Jaguar GR1 [A]	RAF No 41 Sqn, Coltishall
	XZ363	SEPECAT Jaguar replica [A] (BAPC 151)	RAF Exhibition Flight, Abingdon
	XZ364	SEPECAT Jaguar GR1A [21]	RAF No 2 Sqn, Laarbruch
	XZ366	SEPECAT Jaguar GR1A [22]	RAF No 2 Sqn, Laarbruch
	XZ367	SEPECAT Jaguar GR1A [20]	RAF No 2 Sqn, Laarbruch
	XZ368	SEPECAT Jaguar GR1 [8900M] [AG]	RAF No 41 Sqn, Coltishall
	XZ369	SEPECAT Jaguar GR1 [BF]	RAF store, Shawbury
	XZ370	SEPECAT Jaguar GR1 [BN]	RAF store, Shawbury
	XZ371	SEPECAT Jaguar GR1 (8907M) [AP]	RAF store, Shawbury
	XZ372	SEPECAT Jaguar GR1A [ED]	RAF No 6 Sqn, Coltishall
	XZ373	SEPECAT Jaguar GR1A [EC]	RAF No 6 Sqn, Coltishall
	XZ374	SEPECAT Jaguar GR1 [AD]	RAF Shawbury store
	XZ375	SEPECAT Jaguar GR1 [GB]	RAF No 54 Sqn, Coltishall
	XZ377	SEPECAT Jaguar GR1A [02]	RAF No 226 OCU, Lossiemouth
	XZ378	SEPECAT Jaguar GR1A [EP]	RAF No 6 Sqn, Coltishall
	XZ381	SEPECAT Jaguar GR1 [BL]	RAF store, Shawbury
	XZ382	SEPECAT Jaguar GR1 (8908M) [AE]	RAF No 1 SoTT, Halton
	XZ383	SEPECAT Jaguar GR1 (8901M) [AF]	RAF No 41 Sqn, Coltishall
	XZ384	SEPECAT Jaguar GR1 [BC]	RAF store, Shawbury
	XZ385	SEPECAT Jaguar GR1A [GM]	RAF No 54 Sqn, Coltishall
	XZ386	SEPECAT Jaguar GR1 [05]	RAF No 226 OCU, Lossiemouth
	XZ387	SEPECAT Jaguar GR1A [EB]	RAF No 6 Sqn, Coltishall
	XZ389	SEPECAT Jaguar GR1 [BL]	RAF store, Shawbury
	XZ390	SEPECAT Jaguar GR1A [35]	RAF store, Shawbury
	XZ391	SEPECAT Jaguar GR1A [GE]	RAF No 54 Sqn, Coltishall
	XZ392	SEPECAT Jaguar GR1A [GR]	RAF No 54 Sqn, Coltishall
	XZ394	SEPECAT Jaguar GR1 [BJ]	RAF store, Shawbury
	XZ395	SEPECAT Jaguar GR1A [GJ]	RAF AST, Coltishall
	XZ396	SEPECAT Jaguar GR1A [EM]	RAF No 6 Sqn, Coltishall

Serial	Type (alternative identity)	Owner, Operator or Location	Notes
XZ398	SEPECAT Jaguar GR1A (JI007) [EF]	RAF No 6 Sqn, Coltishall	
XZ399	SEPECAT Jaguar GR1A [EN]	RAF No 6 Sqn, Coltishall	
XZ400	SEPECAT Jaguar GR1A [GH]	RAF No 54 Sqn, Coltishall	
XZ431	HS Buccaneer S2B	RAF No 208 Sqn, Lossiemouth	
XZ432	HS Buccaneer S2B	RAF No 12 Sqn, Lossiemouth	
XZ439	BAe Sea Harrier FRS1 [2]	MoD(PE) BAe Dunsfold	
XZ440	BAe Sea Harrier FRS1 [40]	MoD(PE) A&AEE Boscombe Down	
XZ445	BAe Harrier T4A [Q]	RAF No 233 OCU, Wittering	
XZ451	BAe Sea Harrier FRS1 [000/R]	RN No 801 Sqn, Yeovilton	
XZ455	BAe Sea Harrier FRS1	RN No 800 Sqn, Yeovilton	
XZ457	BAe Sea Harrier FRS1 [715]	RN No 899 Sqn, Yeovilton	
XZ459	BAe Sea Harrier FRS1 [127/L]	RN No 800 Sqn, Yeovilton	
XZ460	BAe Sea Harrier FRS1	RN No 899 Sqn, Yeovilton	
XZ492	BAe Sea Harrier FRS1 [125/L]	RN No 800 Sqn, Yeovilton	
XZ493	BAe Sea Harrier FRS1 [713]	RN No 899 Sqn, Yeovilton	
XZ494	BAe Sea Harrier FRS1 [721]	RN No 899 Sqn, Yeovilton	
XZ495	BAe Sea Harrier FRS1 [714]	RN No 899 Sqn, Yeovilton	
XZ497	BAe Sea Harrier FRS1 [4]	MoD(PE) BAe Dunsfold	
XZ498	BAe Sea Harrier FRS1 [002/R]	RN No 801 Sqn, Yeovilton	
XZ499	BAe Sea Harrier FRS1 [126/L]	RN No 800 Sqn, Yeovilton	
XZ550	Slingsby Venture T2	RAF No 642 VGS, Linton-on-Ouse	
XZ551	Slingsby Venture T2	RAF No 624 VGS, Chivenor	
XZ552	Slingsby Venture T2 [A]	RAF No 632 VGS, Ternhill	
XZ553	Slingsby Venture T2 [Q]	RAF No 616 VGS, Henlow	
XZ554	Slingsby Venture T2 [4]	RAF No 633 VGS, Cosford	
XZ555	Slingsby Venture T2	RAF ACCGS, Syerston	
XZ556	Slingsby Venture T2 [56]	RAF No 611 VGS, Swanton Morley	
XZ557	Slingsby Venture T2 [7]	RAF No 633 VGS, Cosford	
XZ558	Slingsby Venture T2 [8]	RAF No 613 VGS, Halton	
XZ559	Slingsby Venture T2 [3]	RAF No 613 VGS, Halton	
XZ560	Slingsby Venture T2 [60]	RAF No 611 VGS, Swanton Morley	
XZ561	Slingsby Venture T2 [B]	RAF No 632 VGS, Ternhill	
XZ562	Slingsby Venture T2 [2]	RAF No 635 VGS, Samlesbury	
XZ563	Slingsby Venture T2	RAF No 635 VGS, Samlesbury	
XZ564	Slingsby Venture T2 [4]	RAF No 635 VGS, Samlesbury	
XZ570	WS61 Sea King HAS5	MoD(PE) A&AEE Boscombe Down/ Westlands, Yeovil	
XZ571	WS61 Sea King HAS5 [136]	RN No 826 Sqn, Culdrose	
XZ574	WS61 Sea King HAS5 [506]	RN No 810 Sqn, Culdrose	
XZ575	WS61 Sea King HAS5 [135]	RN No 826 Sqn, Culdrose	
XZ576	WS61 Sea King Mk 6 [11]	MoD(PE) Westlands, Yeovil	
XZ577	WS61 Sea King HAS5 [138]	RN No 826 Sqn, Culdrose	
XZ578	WS61 Sea King HAS5 [501]	RN No 810 Sqn, Culdrose	
XZ579	WS61 Sea King HAS5 [017/R]	RN No 820 Sqn, Culdrose	
XZ580	WS61 Sea King Mk 6	MoD(PE) Westlands, Yeovil	
XZ581	WS61 Sea King HAS5	RN No 826 Sqn, Culdrose	
XZ582	WS61 Sea King HAS5	RNAY Fleetlands	
XZ585	WS61 Sea King HAR3	RAF No 202 Sqn SAR*	
XZ586	WS61 Sea King HAR3 [S]	RAF No 202 Sqn SAR*	
XZ587	WS61 Sea King HAR3	RAF No 202 Sqn SAR*	
XZ588	WS61 Sea King HAR3	RAF No 202 Sqn SAR*	
XZ589	WS61 Sea King HAR3	RAF No 202 Sqn SAR*	
XZ590	WS61 Sea King HAR3	RAF No 202 Sqn SAR*	
XZ591	WS61 Sea King HAR3	RAF No 78 Sqn, Mount Pleasant, FI	
XZ592	WS61 Sea King HAR3	RAF No 78 Sqn, Mount Pleasant, FI	
XZ593	WS61 Sea King HAR3	RAF No 202 Sqn SAR*	
XZ594	WS61 Sea King HAR3	RAF No 202 Sqn SAR*	
XZ595	WS61 Sea King HAR3	RAF No 202 Sqn SAR*	
XZ596	WS61 Sea King HAR3	RAF No 202 Sqn SAR*	
XZ597	WS61 Sea King HAR3 [S]	RAF No 78 Sqn, Mount Pleasant, FI	
XZ598	WS61 Sea King HAR3	RAF No 202 Sqn SAR*	
XZ599	WS61 Sea King HAR3 [S]	RAF No 202 Sqn SAR*	

Note: *No 202 Sqn SAR and the SAREW are based at RAF Finningley with detached Flights at: A Flt — RAF Boulmer; B Flt — RAF Brawdy; C Flt — RAF Coltishall; D Flt — RAF Lossiemouth; SKTF — RNAS Culdrose.

Serial	Type (alternative identity)	Owner, Operator or Location	Notes
XZ605	WS Lynx AH1 [23B]	RM 3 CBAS, Yeovilton	
XZ606	WS Lynx AH1	RNAY Fleetlands	
XZ607	WS Lynx AH1	AAC No 654 Sqn, Detmold	
XZ608	WS Lynx AH1	AAC No 654 Sqn, Detmold	
XZ609	WS Lynx AH1	AAC store, Wroughton	
XZ610	WS Lynx AH1	AAC No 654 Sqn, Detmold	

Notes	*Serial*	*Type (alternative identity)*	*Owner, Operator or Location*
	XZ611	WS Lynx AH1 [H]	AAC ARW/LCF, Middle Wallop
	XZ612	WS Lynx AH1 [23C]	RM 3 CBAS, Yeovilton
	XZ613	WS Lynx AH1	MoD(PE) A&AEE, Boscombe Down
	XZ614	WS Lynx AH1 [23D]	RM 3 CBAS, Yeovilton
	XZ615	WS Lynx AH1	AAC No 651 Sqn, Hildesheim
	XZ616	WS Lynx AH1	AAC store, Wroughton
	XZ617	WS Lynx AH1	AAC store, Wroughton
	XZ630	Panavia Tornado	MoD(PE) A&AEE/BAe Warton
	XZ631	Panavia Tornado	MoD(PE) A&AEE, Boscombe Down
	XZ641	WS Lynx AH1	AAC store, Wroughton
	XZ642	WS Lynx AH1	AAC No 653 Sqn, Soest
	XZ643	WS Lynx AH1	AAC No 653 Sqn, Soest
	XZ644	WS Lynx AH1	AAC No 657 Sqn, Oakington
	XZ645	WS Lynx AH1	AAC No 669 Sqn, Detmold
	XZ646	WS Lynx AH1	AAC No 654 Sqn, Detmold
	XZ647	WS Lynx AH1	AAC No 669 Sqn, Detmold
	XZ648	WS Lynx AH1 [D]	AAC ARW/LCF, Middle Wallop
	XZ649	WS Lynx AH1 [E]	AAC ARW/LCF, Middle Wallop
	XZ650	WS Lynx AH1	AAC No 659 Sqn, Detmold
	XZ651	WS Lynx AH1	AAC No 659 Sqn, Detmold
	XZ652	WS Lynx AH1	AAC No 659 Sqn, Detmold
	XZ653	WS Lynx AH1	AAC No 654 Sqn, Detmold
	XZ654	WS Lynx AH1	AAC No 654 Sqn, Detmold
	XZ655	WS Lynx AH1	AAC No 652 Sqn, Hildesheim
	XZ661	WS Lynx AH1	AAC No 652 Sqn, Hildesheim
	XZ662	WS Lynx AH1	AAC No 652 Sqn, Hildesheim
	XZ663	WS Lynx AH1	AAC No — Sqn
	XZ664	WS Lynx AH1	AAC No 655 Sqn, Aldergrove
	XZ665	WS Lynx AH1	AAC No 655 Sqn, Aldergrove
	XZ666	WS Lynx AH1	AAC No 655 Sqn, Aldergrove
	XZ667	WS Lynx AH1 [D]	AAC No 663 Sqn, Soest
	XZ668	WS Lynx AH1 [E]	AAC No 663 Sqn, Soest
	XZ669	WS Lynx AH1 [F]	AAC No 663 Sqn, Soest
	XZ670	WS Lynx AH1 [G]	AAC No 663 Sqn, Soest
	XZ671	WS Lynx AH1	AAC No 652 Sqn, Hildesheim
	XZ672	WS Lynx AH1	AAC No 659 Sqn, Detmold
	XZ673	WS Lynx AH1	AAC No 652 Sqn, Hildesheim
	XZ674	WS Lynx AH1	AAC No 652 Sqn, Hildesheim
	XZ675	WS Lynx AH1	AAC No 663 Sqn, Detmold
	XZ676	WS Lynx AH1	AAC No 656 Sqn, Netheravon
	XZ677	WS Lynx AH1	AAC No 651 Sqn, Hildesheim
	XZ678	WS Lynx AH1	AAC No 651 Sqn, Hildesheim
	XZ679	WS Lynx AH1	AAC No 651 Sqn, Hildesheim
	XZ680	WS Lynx AH1 [F]	AAC ARW/LCF, Middle Wallop
	XZ681	WS Lynx AH1	AAC Middle Wallop, BDRT
	XZ689	WS Lynx HAS2	RN No 815 Sqn, Portland
	XZ690	WS Lynx HAS2 [330/BZ]	RN No 829 Sqn, Portland
	XZ691	WS Lynx HAS2 [374]	RN No 829 Sqn, Portland
	XZ692	WS Lynx HAS3 [643/PO]	RN No 702 Sqn, Portland
	XZ693	WS Lynx HAS3 [424/MV]	RN No 815 Sqn, Portland
	XZ694	WS Lynx HAS2	RNAY Fleetlands
	XZ695	WS Lynx HAS2 [466/AT]	RN No 815 Sqn, Portland
	XZ696	WS Lynx HAS3 [642/PO]	RN No 702 Sqn, Portland
	XZ697	WS Lynx HAS3 [307/PO]	RN No 815 Sqn, Portland
	XZ698	WS Lynx HAS2 [424/MV]	RN No 815 Sqn, Portland
	XZ699	WS Lynx HAS2 [300/PO]	RN No 815 Sqn, Portland
	XZ719	WS Lynx HAS2 [443/JP]	RN No 815 Sqn, Portland
	XZ720	WS Lynx HAS2 [475/HM]	RN No 815 Sqn, Portland
	XZ721	WS Lynx HAS2 [603]	RN No 829 Sqn, Portland
	XZ722	WS Lynx HAS2 [410/GC]	RN No 815 Sqn, Portland
	XZ723	WS Lynx HAS3 [454/PN]	RN No 815 Sqn, Portland
	XZ724	WS Lynx HAS3 [347]	RN No 829 Sqn, Portland
	XZ725	WS Lynx HAS2 [320/AZ]	RN No 815 Sqn, Portland
	XZ726	WS Lynx HAS3 [464/DN]	RN No 815 Sqn, Portland
	XZ727	WS Lynx HAS2 [305/PO]	RN No 815 Sqn, Portland
	XZ728	WS Lynx HAS2 [332/LP]	RN No 815 Sqn, Portland
	XZ729	WS Lynx HAS2 [471/PB]	RN No 815 Sqn, Portland
	XZ730	WS Lynx HAS2 [326/AW]	RN No 815 Sqn, Portland
	XZ731	WS Lynx HAS2 [341/AG]	RN No 815 Sqn, Portland
	XZ732	WS Lynx HAS3 [641/PO]	RN No 702 Sqn, Portland
	XZ733	WS Lynx HAS2 [420/EX]	RN No 815 Sqn, Portland
	XZ734	WS Lynx HAS2 [405]	RN No 829 Sqn, Portland
	XZ735	WS Lynx HAS3 [341/AG]	RN No 815 Sqn, Portland
	XZ736	WS Lynx HAS2 [360/MC]	RN No 815 Sqn, Portland

Serial	Type (alternative identity)	Owner, Operator or Location	Notes
XZ916	WS61 Sea King HAS5 [130]	RN No 826 Sqn, Culdrose	
XZ918	WS61 Sea King HAS5 [016]	RNAY Fleetlands	
XZ920	WS61 Sea King HAS5 [510]	RN No 810 Sqn, Culdrose	
XZ921	WS61 Sea King HAS5 [593/R]	RN No 706 Sqn, Culdrose	
XZ922	WS61 Sea King HAS5 [500]	RN No 810 Sqn, Culdrose	
XZ930	WS Gazelle HT3 [Q]	RAF No 2 FTS, Shawbury	
XZ931	WS Gazelle HT3 [R]	RAF No 2 FTS, Shawbury	
XZ932	WS Gazelle HT3 [S]	RAF No 2 FTS, Shawbury	
XZ933	WS Gazelle HT3 [T]	RAF No 2 FTS, Shawbury	
XZ934	WS Gazelle HT3 [U]	RAF No 2 FTS, Shawbury	
XZ935	WS Gazelle HT3	RAF No 32 Sqn, Northolt	
XZ936	WS Gazelle HT3	MoD(PE) ETPS Boscombe Down	
XZ937	WS Gazelle HT3 [Y]	RAF No 2 FTS, Shawbury	
XZ938	WS Gazelle HT2 [45/CU]	RN No 705 Sqn, Culdrose	
XZ939	WS Gazelle HT3 [Z]	RAF No 2 FTS, Shawbury	
XZ940	WS Gazelle HT3 [O]	RAF No 2 FTS, Shawbury	
XZ941	WS Gazelle HT3 [B]	RAF No 2 FTS, Shawbury	
XZ942	WS Gazelle HT2	RNAY Fleetlands	
XZ964	BAe Harrier GR3	RAF No 1417 Flt, Belize	
XZ965	BAe Harrier GR3 [AM]	RAF No 3 Sqn, Gutersloh	
XZ966	BAe Harrier GR3 [K]	RAF No 4 Sqn, Gutersloh	
XZ967	BAe Harrier GR3 [AB]	RAF No 3 Sqn, Gutersloh	
XZ968	BAe Harrier GR3 [01]	RAF No 1 Sqn, Wittering	
XZ969	BAe Harrier GR3 [D]	RAF No 4 Sqn, Gutersloh	
XZ970	BAe Harrier GR3 [AR]	RAF No 3 Sqn, Gutersloh	
XZ971	BAe Harrier GR3	RAF Wittering	
XZ987	BAe Harrier GR3 [O]	RAF No 4 Sqn, Gutersloh	
XZ990	BAe Harrier GR3 [H]	RAF No 4 Sqn, Gutersloh	
XZ991	BAe Harrier GR3	RAF St Athan	
XZ992	BAe Harrier GR3 [T]	RAF St Athan	
XZ993	BAe Harrier GR3 [04]	RAF No 1 Sqn, Wittering	
XZ994	BAe Harrier GR3 [F]	RAF No 233 OCU, Wittering	
XZ995	BAe Harrier GR3 [B]	RAF No 233 OCU, Wittering	
XZ996	BAe Harrier GR3 [K]	RAF No 1417 Flt, Belize	
XZ997	BAe Harrier GR3 [03]	RAF No 1 Sqn, Wittering	
XZ998	BAe Harrier GR3 [G]	RAF Wittering	
XZ999	BAe Harrier GR3 [M]	RAF No 233 OCU, Wittering	
ZA101	BAe Hawk T50 (G-HAWK)	BAe Dunsfold	
ZA105	WS61 Sea King HAR3 [S]	RAF No 202 Sqn SAR*	
ZA110	BAe Jetstream T2 [573/CU] (G-AXUO)	RN No 750 Sqn, Culdrose	
ZA111	BAe Jetstream T2 [574/CU] (G-AXFV)	RN No 750 Sqn, Culdrose	
ZA126	WS61 Sea King HAS5	RN No 820 Sqn, Culdrose	
ZA127	WS61 Sea King HAS5 [591]	RN No 810 Sqn, Culdrose	
ZA128	WS61 Sea King HAS5 [504]	RN No 706 Sqn, Culdrose	
ZA129	WS61 Sea King HAS5 [139]	RN No 826 Sqn, Culdrose	
ZA130	WS61 Sea King HAS5 [253]	RN No 824 Sqn, Culdrose	
ZA131	WS61 Sea King HAS5 [133]	RN No 826 Sqn, Culdrose	
ZA133	WS61 Sea King HAS5 [252]	RN No 824 Sqn, Culdrose	
ZA134	WS61 Sea King HAS5	RNAY Fleetlands	
ZA135	WS61 Sea King HAS5 [505]	RN No 810 Sqn, Culdrose	
ZA136	WS61 Sea King HAS5 [264]	RN No 814 Sqn, Culdrose	
ZA137	WS61 Sea King HAS5 [589]	RN No 706 Sqn, Culdrose	
ZA140	BAe VC10 K2 (G-ARVL) [A]	RAF No 101 Sqn, Brize Norton	
ZA141	BAe VC10 K2 (G-ARVG) [B]	RAF No 101 Sqn, Brize Norton	
ZA142	BAe VC10 K2 (G-ARVI) [C]	RAF No 101 Sqn, Brize Norton	
ZA143	BAe VC10 K2 (G-ARVK) [D]	RAF No 101 Sqn, Brize Norton	
ZA144	BAe VC10 K2 (G-ARVC) [E]	RAF No 101 Sqn, Brize Norton	
ZA147	BAe VC10 K3 (5H-MMT) [F]	RAF No 101 Sqn, Brize Norton	
ZA148	BAe VC10 K3 (5Y-ADA) [G]	RAF No 101 Sqn, Brize Norton	
ZA149	BAe VC10 K3 (5X-UVJ) [H]	RAF No 101 Sqn, Brize Norton	
ZA150	BAe VC10 K3 (5H-MOG) [J]	RAF No 101 Sqn, Brize Norton	
ZA166	WS61 Sea King HAS5 [590/R]	RN No 706 Sqn, Culdrose	
ZA167	WS61 Sea King HAS5 [273/L]	RN No 814 Sqn, Culdrose	
ZA168	WS61 Sea King HAS5 [267/L]	RN No 814 Sqn, Culdrose	
ZA169	WS61 Sea King HAS5	RN No 706 Sqn, Culdrose	
ZA170	WS61 Sea King HAS5 [584]	RN No 706 Sqn, Culdrose	
ZA175	BAe Sea Harrier FRS1 [003]	RN No 801 Sqn, Yeovilton	
ZA176	BAe Sea Harrier FRS1 [716]	RN No 899 Sqn, Yeovilton	
ZA190	BAe Sea Harrier FRS1 [001/R]	RN No 801 Sqn, Yeovilton	
ZA191	BAe Sea Harrier FRS1 [123/L]	RN No 800 Sqn, Yeovilton	

Notes	Serial	Type (alternative identity)	Owner, Operator or Location
	ZA193	BAe Sea Harrier FRS1	RN NASU, Yeovilton
	ZA195	BAe Sea Harrier FRS1	MoD(PE) BAe Dunsfold
	ZA250	BAe Harrier T52 (G-VTOL)	BAe Dunsfold
	ZA254	Panavia Tornado F2	MoD(PE) BAe Warton
	ZA267	Panavia Tornado F2T	MoD(PE) BAe Warton
	ZA283	Panavia Tornado F2	MoD(PE) BAe Warton
	ZA291	WS61 Sea King HC4 [VB]	RN No 846 Sqn, Yeovilton
	ZA292	WS61 Sea King HC4 [E]	RN No 845 Sqn, Yeovilton
	ZA293	WS61 Sea King HC4 [VK]	RN No 846 Sqn, Yeovilton
	ZA295	WS61 Sea King HC4 [ZC]	RN No 707 Sqn, Yeovilton
	ZA296	WS61 Sea King HC4 [VF]	RN No 846 Sqn, Yeovilton
	ZA297	WS61 Sea King HC4 [F]	RN No 845 Sqn, Yeovilton
	ZA298	WS61 Sea King HC4 (G-BJNM) [G]	RN No 845 Sqn, Yeovilton
	ZA299	WS61 Sea King HC4 [ZD]	RN No 707 Sqn, Yeovilton
	ZA310	WS61 Sea King HC4 [VS]	RN No 846 Sqn, Yeovilton
	ZA312	WS61 Sea King HC4 [ZB]	RN No 707 Sqn, Yeovilton
	ZA313	WS61 Sea King HC4 [VZ]	RN No 846 Sqn, Yeovilton
	ZA314	WS61 Sea King HC4	RN NASU, Culdrose
	ZA319	Panavia Tornado GR1T [B-11]	RAF TTTE, Cottesmore
	ZA320	Panavia Tornado GR1T [B-01]	RAF TTTE, Cottesmore
	ZA321	Panavia Tornado GR1 [B-58]	RAF TTTE, Cottesmore
	ZA322	Panavia Tornado GR1 [B-50]	RAF TTTE, Cottesmore
	ZA322	Panavia Tornado GR1 replica (BAPC 155) [B-50]	RAF Exhibition Flight, Abingdon
	ZA323	Panavia Tornado GR1T [B-14]	RAF TTTE, Cottesmore
	ZA324	Panavia Tornado GR1T [B-02]	RAF TTTE, Cottesmore
	ZA325	Panavia Tornado GR1T [B-03]	RAF TTTE, Cottesmore
	ZA326	Panavia Tornado GR1T	MoD(PE) RAE Bedford
	ZA327	Panavia Tornado GR1 [B-51]	RAF TTTE, Cottesmore
	ZA328	Panavia Tornado GR1	MoD(PE) A&AEE Boscombe Down
	ZA329	Panavia Tornado GR1 [B-52)	RAF TTTE, Cottesmore
	ZA330	Panavia Tornado GR1T [B-08]	RAF TTTE, Cottesmore
	ZA352	Panavia Tornado GR1T [B-04)	RAF TTTE, Cottesmore
	ZA353	Panavia Tornado GR1 [B-53)	RAF TTTE, Cottesmore
	ZA354	Panavia Tornado GR1	MoD(PE) BAe Warton
	ZA355	Panavia Tornado GR1 [B-54]	RAF TTTE, Cottesmore
	ZA356	Panavia Tornado GR1T [B-07]	RAF TTTE, Cottesmore
	ZA357	Panavia Tornado GR1T [B-05]	RAF TTTE, Cottesmore
	ZA358	Panavia Tornado GR1T [B-06]	RAF TTTE, Cottesmore
	ZA359	Panavia Tornado GR1 [B-55]	RAF TTTE, Cottesmore
	ZA360	Panavia Tornado GR1 [B-56]	RAF TTTE, Cottesmore
	ZA361	Panavia Tornado GR1 [B-57]	RAF TTTE, Cottesmore
	ZA362	Panavia Tornado GR1T [B-09]	RAF TTTE, Cottesmore
	ZA365	Panavia Tornado GR1T	RAF TWCU/45 Sqn, Honington
	ZA366	Panavia Tornado GR1T	RAF TWCU/45 Sqn, Honington
	ZA367	Panavia Tornado GR1T	RAF TWCU/45 Sqn, Honington
	ZA368	Panavia Tornado GR1T [Y]	RAF No 9 Sqn, Honington
	ZA369	Panavia Tornado GR1	RAF TWCU/45 Sqn, Honington
	ZA370	Panavia Tornado GR1	RAF TWCU/45 Sqn, Honington
	ZA371	Panavia Tornado GR1 [GF]	RAF No 20 Sqn, Laarbruch
	ZA372	Panavia Tornado GR1	RAF TWCU/45 Sqn, Honington
	ZA373	Panavia Tornado GR1	RAF TWCU/45 Sqn, Honington
	ZA374	Panavia Tornado GR1	RAF TWCU/45 Sqn, Honington
	ZA375	Panavia Tornado GR1	RAF TWCU/45 Sqn, Honington
	ZA376	Panavia Tornado GR1 [E]	MoD(PE) TOEU Boscombe Down
	ZA392	Panavia Tornado GR1 [EK]	RAF No 15 Sqn, Laarbruch
	ZA393	Panavia Tornado GR1	RAF TWCU/45 Sqn, Honington
	ZA394	Panavia Tornado GR1 [K]	MoD(PE) BAe Warton
	ZA395	Panavia Tornado GR1	RAF
	ZA396	Panavia Tornado GR1 [GE]	RAF No 20 Sqn, Laarbruch
	ZA397	Panavia Tornado GR1 [EN]	RAF No 15 Sqn, Laarbruch
	ZA398	Panavia Tornado GR1	RAF TWCU/45 Sqn, Honington
	ZA399	Panavia Tornado GR1 [GA]	RAF No 20 Sqn, Laarbruch
	ZA400	Panavia Tornado GR1	RAF TWCU/45 Sqn, Honington
	ZA401	Panavia Tornado GR1 [BM]	RAF No 145 Sqn, Bruggen
	ZA402	Panavia Tornado GR1	MoD(PE) BAe Warton
	ZA403	Panavia Tornado GR1	BAe Warton, Saudi Support Unit
	ZA404	Panavia Tornado GR1	RAF TWCU/45 Sqn, Honington
	ZA405	Panavia Tornado GR1	RAF TWCU/45 Sqn, Honington
	ZA406	Panavia Tornado GR1	RAF TWCU/45 Sqn, Honington
	ZA407	Panavia Tornado GR1	RAF TWCU/45 Sqn, Honington
	ZA409	Panavia Tornado GR1T [EW]	RAF No 15 Sqn, Laarbruch
	ZA410	Panavia Tornado GR1T [EX]	RAF No 15 Sqn, Laarbruch

Serial	Type (alternative identity)	Owner, Operator or Location	Notes
ZA411	Panavia Tornado GR1T [GY]	RAF No 20 Sqn, Laarbruch	
ZA412	Panavia Tornado GR1T [FZ]	RAF No 16 Sqn, Laarbruch	
ZA446	Panavia Tornado GR1 [F]	RAF No 15 Sqn, Laarbruch	
ZA447	Panavia Tornado GR1 [EA]	RAF No 15 Sqn, Laarbruch	
ZA448	Panavia Tornado GR1 [EB]	RAF No 15 Sqn, Laarbruch	
ZA449	Panavia Tornado GR1	MoD(PE) BAe Warton	
ZA450	Panavia Tornado GR1 [EC]	RAF No 15 Sqn, Laarbruch	
ZA452	Panavia Tornado GR1 [GK]	RAF No 20 Sqn, Laarbruch	
ZA453	Panavia Tornado GR1 [EG]	RAF No 15 Sqn, Laarbruch	
ZA454	Panavia Tornado GR1 [EH]	RAF No 15 Sqn, Laarbruch	
ZA455	Panavia Tornado GR1 [EJ]	RAF No 15 Sqn, Laarbruch	
ZA456	Panavia Tornado GR1 [GB]	RAF No 20 Sqn, Laarbruch	
ZA457	Panavia Tornado GR1 [AJ]	RAF No 9 Sqn, Bruggen	
ZA458	Panavia Tornado GR1 [FB]	RAF No 16 Sqn, Laarbruch	
ZA459	Panavia Tornado GR1 [EL]	RAF No 15 Sqn, Laarbruch	
ZA460	Panavia Tornado GR1 [FD]	RAF No 16 Sqn, Laarbruch	
ZA461	Panavia Tornado GR1	RAF St Athan	
ZA462	Panavia Tornado GR1 [EM]	RAF No 15 Sqn, Laarbruch	
ZA463	Panavia Tornado GR1 [GL]	RAF No 20 Sqn, Laarbruch	
ZA464	Panavia Tornado GR1 [GM]	RAF No 20 Sqn, Laarbruch	
ZA465	Panavia Tornado GR1 [FK]	RAF No 16 Sqn, Laarbruch	
ZA466	Panavia Tornado GR1 [FH]	RAF No 16 Sqn, Laarbruch	
ZA467	Panavia Tornado GR1 [FF]	RAF No 16 Sqn, Laarbruch	
ZA468	Panavia Tornado GR1 [FN]	RAF No 16 Sqn, Laarbruch	
ZA469	Panavia Tornado GR1 [GD]	RAF No 20 Sqn, Laarbruch	
ZA470	Panavia Tornado GR1 [FL]	RAF No 16 Sqn, Laarbruch	
ZA471	Panavia Tornado GR1 [FJ]	RAF No 16 Sqn, Laarbruch	
ZA472	Panavia Tornado GR1 [EE]	RAF No 15 Sqn, Laarbruch	
ZA473	Panavia Tornado GR1 [FM]	RAF No 16 Sqn, Laarbruch	
ZA474	Panavia Tornado GR1 [FG]	RAF No 16 Sqn, Laarbruch	
ZA475	Panavia Tornado GR1 [FC]	RAF No 16 Sqn, Laarbruch	
ZA490	Panavia Tornado GR1 [GG]	RAF No 20 Sqn, Laarbruch	
ZA491	Panavia Tornado GR1 [GC]	RAF No 20 Sqn, Laarbruch	
ZA492	Panavia Tornado GR1 [FE]	RAF No 16 Sqn, Laarbruch	
ZA493	Panavia Tornado GR1 [GH]	RAF No 20 Sqn, Laarbruch	
ZA494	Panavia Tornado GR1 [15]	RAF Honington BDRT	
ZA540	Panavia Tornado GR1T	RAF No 27 Sqn, Marham	
ZA541	Panavia Tornado GR1T [S]	RAF No 617 Sqn, Marham	
ZA542	Panavia Tornado GR1 [04]	RAF No 27 Sqn, Marham	
ZA543	Panavia Tornado GR1	RAF TWCU/45 Sqn, Honington	
ZA544	Panavia Tornado GR1T	RAF TWCU/45 Sqn, Honington	
ZA545	Panavia Tornado GR1	RAF TWCU/45 Sqn, Honington	
ZA546	Panavia Tornado GR1 [05]	RAF No 27 Sqn, Marham	
ZA547	Panavia Tornado GR1 [03]	RAF No 27 Sqn, Marham	
ZA548	Panavia Tornado GR1T [B-10]	RAF TTTE, Cottesmore	
ZA549	Panavia Tornado GR1T	RAF No 27 Sqn, Marham	
ZA550	Panavia Tornado GR1 [08]	RAF No 27 Sqn, Marham	
ZA551	Panavia Tornado GR1T [T]	RAF No 617 Sqn, Marham	
ZA552	Panavia Tornado GR1T	RAF TWCU/45 Sqn, Honington	
ZA553	Panavia Tornado GR1 [01]	RAF No 27 Sqn, Marham	
ZA554	Panavia Tornado GR1 [11]	RAF No 27 Sqn, Marham	
ZA555	Panavia Tornado GR1T	RAF TWCU/45 Sqn, Honington	
ZA556	Panavia Tornado GR1	RAF TWCU/45 Sqn, Honington	
ZA557	Panavia Tornado GR1 [15]	RAF No 27 Sqn, Marham	
ZA559	Panavia Tornado GR1 [U]	RAF No 9 Sqn, Bruggen	
ZA560	Panavia Tornado GR1 [C]	RAF No 617 Sqn, Marham	
ZA561	Panavia Tornado GR1 [02]	RAF No 27 Sqn, Marham	
ZA562	Panavia Tornado GR1T [B-15]	RAF TTTE, Cottesmore	
ZA563	Panavia Tornado GR1 [10]	RAF No 27 Sqn, Marham	
ZA564	Panavia Tornado GR1	RAF TWCU/45 Sqn, Honington	
ZA585	Panavia Tornado GR1 [L]	RAF No 617 Sqn, Marham	
ZA587	Panavia Tornado GR1 [B]	RAF St Athan	
ZA588	Panavia Tornado GR1 [C]	RAF No —	
ZA589	Panavia Tornado GR1 [D]	RAF St Athan	
ZA590	Panavia Tornado GR1 [E]	RAF No —	
ZA591	Panavia Tornado GR1	RAF TWCU/45 Sqn, Honington	
ZA592	Panavia Tornado GR1 [B]	RAF No 617 Sqn, Marham	
ZA593	Panavia Tornado GR1	RAF TWCU/45 Sqn, Honington	
ZA594	Panavia Tornado GR1T	RAF TWCU/45 Sqn, Honington	
ZA595	Panavia Tornado GR1T	RAF TWCU/45 Sqn, Honington	
ZA596	Panavia Tornado GR1 [L]	RAF No —	
ZA597	Panavia Tornado GR1 [M]	RAF No —	
ZA598	Panavia Tornado GR1T	RAF TWCU/45 Sqn, Honington	
ZA599	Panavia Tornado GR1T [B-16]	RAF TTTE, Cottesmore	

Notes	Serial	Type (alternative identity)	Owner, Operator or Location
	ZA600	Panavia Tornado GR1 [07]	RAF No 27 Sqn, Marham
	ZA601	Panavia Tornado GR1 [M]	RAF No 617 Sqn, Marham
	ZA602	Panavia Tornado GR1T [B-13]	RAF TTTE, Cottesmore
	ZA604	Panavia Tornado GR1T	RAF TWCU/45 Sqn, Honington
	ZA605	Panavia Tornado GR1 [G]	RAF No 617 Sqn, Marham
	ZA606	Panavia Tornado GR1 [09]	RAF No 27 Sqn, Marham
	ZA607	Panavia Tornado GR1 [P]	RAF No 617 Sqn, Marham
	ZA608	Panavia Tornado GR1 [Z]	RAF No 617 Sqn, Marham
	ZA609	Panavia Tornado GR1 [J]	RAF No 617 Sqn, Marham
	ZA611	Panavia Tornado GR1 [A]	RAF No 617 Sqn, Marham
	ZA612	Panavia Tornado GR1T	RAF TWCU/45 Sqn, Honington
	ZA613	Panavia Tornado GR1 [N]	RAF No 617 Sqn, Marham
	ZA614	Panavia Tornado GR1 [E]	RAF No 617 Sqn, Marham
	ZA625	Slingsby Venture T2 [1]	RAF No 616 VGS, Henlow
	ZA626	Slingsby Venture T2 [C]	RAF No 624 VGS, Chivenor
	ZA627	Slingsby Venture T2	RAF No 612 VGS, Benson
	ZA628	Slingsby Venture T2 [B]	RAF No 637 VGS, Little Rissington
	ZA629	Slingsby Venture T2 [9]	RAF No 663 VGS, Kinloss
	ZA630	Slingsby Venture T2	RAF No 616 VGS, Henlow
	ZA631	Slingsby Venture T2 [1]	RAF ACCGS, Syerston
	ZA632	Slingsby Venture T2 [2]	RAF No 632 VGS, Ternhill
	ZA633	Slingsby Venture T2 [3]	RAF No 616 VGS, Henlow
	ZA634	Slingsby Venture T2 [C]	RAF No 635 VGS, Samlesbury
	ZA652	Slingsby Venture T2 [6]	RAF No 642 VGS, Linton-on-Ouse
	ZA653	Slingsby Venture T2 [1]	RAF No 612 VGS, Benson
	ZA654	Slingsby Venture T2 [2]	RAF No 611 VGS, Swanton Morley
	ZA655	Slingsby Venture T2 [V]	RAF No 644 VGS, Syerston
	ZA656	Slingsby Venture T2 [6]	RAF No 624 VGS, Chivenor
	ZA657	Slingsby Venture T2	RAF No 644 VGS, Syerston
	ZA658	Slingsby Venture T2	RAF ACCGS/644 VGS, Syerston
	ZA659	Slingsby Venture T2	RAF No 642 VGS, Linton-on-Ouse
	ZA660	Slingsby Venture T2 [6]	RAF No 612 VGS, Benson
	ZA661	Slingsby Venture T2 [3]	RAF No 637 VGS, Little Rissington
	ZA662	Slingsby Venture T2 [62]	RAF No 633 VGS, Cosford
	ZA663	Slingsby Venture T2 [3]	RAF ACCGS, Syerston
	ZA664	Slingsby Venture T2 [4]	RAF ACCGS, Syerston
	ZA665	Slingsby Venture T2	RAF No 637 VGS, Little Rissington
	ZA666	Slingsby Venture T2 [6]	RAF No 613 VGS, Halton
	ZA670	B-V Chinook HC1 [BG]	RAF No 18 Sqn, Gutersloh
	ZA671	B-V Chinook HC1 [EO]	RAF No 7 Sqn, Odiham
	ZA672	B-V Chinook HC1 [BH]	RAF No 18 Sqn, Gutersloh
	ZA673	B-V Chinook HC1 [BQ]	RAF No 18 Sqn, Gutersloh
	ZA674	B-V Chinook HC1 [BA]	RAF No 18 Sqn, Gutersloh
	ZA675	B-V Chinook HC1 [BB]	RAF No 18 Sqn, Gutersloh
	ZA676	B-V Chinook HC1 [FG]	RAF store, Wroughton
	ZA677	B-V Chinook HC1 [BR]	RAF No 18 Sqn, Gutersloh
	ZA678	B-V Chinook HC1 [EZ]	RAF No 7 Sqn, Odiham
	ZA679	B-V Chinook HC1 [BC]	RAF No 18 Sqn, Gutersloh
	ZA680	B-V Chinook HC1 [J]	RAF No 78 Sqn, Mount Pleasant, Fl
	ZA681	B-V Chinook HC1 [ES]	RAF No 7 Sqn, Odiham
	ZA682	B-V Chinook HC1 [BY]	RAF No 18 Sqn, Gutersloh
	ZA683	B-V Chinook HC1 [EW]	RAF No 7 Sqn, Odiham
	ZA684	B-V Chinook HC1 [F]	RAF No 78 Sqn, Mount Pleasant, Fl
	ZA704	B-V Chinook HC1 [BJ]	RAF No 18 Sqn, Gutersloh
	ZA705	B-V Chinook HC1	RAF No 7 Sqn, Odiham
	ZA707	B-V Chinook HC1 [EV]	RAF No 7 Sqn, Odiham
	ZA708	B-V Chinook HC1 [BK]	RAF No 18 Sqn, Gutersloh
	ZA709	B-V Chinook HC1 [A]	RAF No 78 Sqn, Mount Pleasant, Fl
	ZA710	B-V Chinook HC1 [EY]	RAF No 7 Sqn, Odiham
	ZA711	B-V Chinook HC1 [ET]	RAF No 7 Sqn, Odiham
	ZA712	B-V Chinook HC1 [ER]	RAF No 7 Sqn, Odiham
	ZA713	B-V Chinook HC1 [EN]	RAF No 7 Sqn, Odiham
	ZA714	B-V Chinook HC1 [EX]	RAF No 7 Sqn, Odiham
	ZA717	B-V Chinook HC1 [B]	RAF No 78 Sqn, Mount Pleasant, Fl
	ZA718	B-V Chinook HC1 [EQ]	RAF No 7 Sqn, Odiham
	ZA720	B-V Chinook HC1 [BN]	RAF No 18 Sqn, Gutersloh
	ZA721	B-V Chinook HC1 [EP]	RAF No 7 Sqn, Odiham
	ZA726	WS Gazelle AH1	AAC No 663 Sqn, Soest
	ZA727	WS Gazelle AH1	AAC No 661 Sqn, Hildesheim
	ZA728	WS Gazelle AH1 [33D]	RM 3 CBAS, Yeovilton
	ZA729	WS Gazelle AH1	AAC No 652 Sqn, Hildesheim
	ZA730	WS Gazelle AH1 [F]	RM store, Wroughton
	ZA731	WS Gazelle AH1 [C]	AAC No 29 Flt, Suffield, Canada
	ZA732	WS Gazelle AH1 [D]	AAC No 29 Flt, Suffield, Canada

Serial	Type (alternative identity)	Owner, Operator or Location	Notes
ZA733	WS Gazelle AH1 [J]	AAC No 665 Sqn, Aldergrove	
ZA734	WS Gazelle AH1	AAC No 25 Flt, Belize	
ZA735	WS Gazelle AH1	AAC store, Wroughton	
ZA736	WS Gazelle AH1 [A]	AAC No 29 Flt, Suffield, Canada	
ZA737	WS Gazelle AH1 [V]	AAC ARWS, Middle Wallop	
ZA765	WS Gazelle AH1	AAC No 25 Flt, Belize	
ZA766	WS Gazelle AH1	AAC No 663 Sqn, Soest	
ZA767	WS Gazelle AH1	AAC No 25 Flt, Belize	
ZA768	WS Gazelle AH1 [F]	AAC ARWS, Middle Wallop	
ZA769	WS Gazelle AH1 [K]	AAC ARWS, Middle Wallop	
ZA771	WS Gazelle AH1 [Z]	AAC ARWS, Middle Wallop	
ZA772	WS Gazelle AH1	AAC No 656 Sqn, Netheravon	
ZA773	WS Gazelle AH1	AAC No 655 Sqn, Aldergrove	
ZA774	WS Gazelle AH1	AAC No 655 Sqn, Aldergrove	
ZA775	WS Gazelle AH1	AAC No 656 Sqn, Netheravon	
ZA776	WS Gazelle AH1 [13D]	RM 3 CBAS, Yeovilton	
ZA777	WS Gazelle AH1	AAC No 661 Sqn, Hildesheim	
ZA801	WS Gazelle HT3 [V]	RAF Abingdon Fire Section	
ZA802	WS Gazelle HT3 [W]	RAF No 2 FTS, Shawbury	
ZA803	WS Gazelle HT3 [X]	RAF No 2 FTS, Shawbury	
ZA804	WS Gazelle HT3 [I]	RAF No 2 FTS, Shawbury	
ZA934	WS Puma HC1 [FC]	RAF No 240 OCU, Odiham	
ZA935	WS Puma HC1 [CT]	RAF No 33 Sqn, Odiham	
ZA936	WS Puma HC1 [CU]	RAF No 33 Sqn, Odiham	
ZA937	WS Puma HC1 [CV]	RAF No 33 Sqn, Odiham	
ZA938	WS Puma HC1 [CW]	RAF No 33 Sqn, Odiham	
ZA939	WS Puma HC1 [CX]	RAF No 33 Sqn, Odiham	
ZA940	WS Puma HC1 [CY]	RAF No 1563 Flt, Belize	
ZA941	WS Puma HC1	MoD(PE) RAE Farnborough	
ZA947	Douglas Dakota C3 (KG661)	MoD(PE) RAE Farnborough	
ZB500	WS Lynx (G-LYNX)	Westlands, Yeovil	
ZB506	WS61 Sea King Mk 4X	MoD(PE) RAE Bedford	
ZB507	WS61 Sea King Mk 4X	MoD(PE) RAE Farnborough	
ZB600	BAe Harrier T4A [R]	RAF No 4 Sqn, Gutersloh	
ZB601	BAe Harrier T4A [X]	RAF No 233 OCU, Wittering	
ZB602	BAe Harrier T4A [Y]	RAF No 233 OCU, Wittering	
ZB603	BAe Harrier T4A [AZ]	RAF No 3 Sqn, Gutersloh	
ZB604	BAe Harrier T4N [717/VL]	RN No 899 Sqn, Yeovilton	
ZB605	BAe Harrier T4N [718/VL]	RN No 899 Sqn, Yeovilton	
ZB615	SEPECAT Jaguar T2	MoD(PE) IAM Farnborough	
ZB625	WS Gazelle HT3 [N]	RAF No 2 FTS, Shawbury	
ZB626	WS Gazelle HT3 [L]	RAF No 2 FTS, Shawbury	
ZB627	WS Gazelle HT3 [A]	RAF No 2 FTS, Shawbury	
ZB628	WS Gazelle HT3 [V]	RAF No 2 FTS, Shawbury	
ZB629	WS Gazelle HT3	RAF No 32 Sqn, Northolt	
ZB646	WS Gazelle HT2 [CU]	RN store, Wroughton	
ZB647	WS Gazelle HT2 [CU]	RN store, Wroughton	
ZB648	WS Gazelle HT3	MoD(PE) RAE Farnborough	
ZB649	WS Gazelle HT2 [CU]	RNAY Fleetlands	
ZB665	WS Gazelle AH1	AAC store, Wroughton	
ZB666	WS Gazelle AH1 [G]	AAC ARWS, Middle Wallop	
ZB667	WS Gazelle AH1	AAC No 664 Sqn, Detmold	
ZB668	WS Gazelle AH1	AAC store, Wroughton	
ZB669	WS Gazelle AH1	AAC store, Wroughton	
ZB670	WS Gazelle AH1	AAC No 655 Sqn, Aldergrove	
ZB671	WS Gazelle AH1 [E]	AAC No 29 Flt, Suffield, Canada	
ZB672	WS Gazelle AH1	AAC Garrison Air Sqn, Falklands	
ZB673	WS Gazelle AH1 [P]	AAC ARWS, Middle Wallop	
ZB674	WS Gazelle AH1	AAC Garrison Air Sqn, Falklands	
ZB675	WS Gazelle AH1	AAC Garrison Air Sqn, Falklands	
ZB676	WS Gazelle AH1	AAC store, Wroughton	
ZB677	WS Gazelle AH1	AAC No 661 Sqn, Hildesheim	
ZB678	WS Gazelle AH1	AAC store, Wroughton	
ZB679	WS Gazelle AH1	AAC store, Wroughton	
ZB680	WS Gazelle AH1 [B]	AAC No 29 Flt, Suffield, Canada	
ZB681	WS Gazelle AH1 [G]	AAC No 655 Sqn, Aldergrove	
ZB682	WS Gazelle AH1	AAC No 655 Sqn, Aldergrove	
ZB683	WS Gazelle AH1	AAC No 655 Sqn, Aldergrove	
ZB684	WS Gazelle AH1	AAC No 655 Sqn, Aldergrove	
ZB685	WS Gazelle AH1 [H]	AAC No 655 Sqn, Ballykelly	
ZB686	WS Gazelle AH1	AAC No 655 Sqn, Ballykelly	
ZB687	WS Gazelle AH1	AAC No 655 Sqn, Ballykelly	
ZB688	WS Gazelle AH1	AAC store, Wroughton	

Notes	Serial	Type (alternative identity)	Owner, Operator or Location
	ZB689	WS Gazelle AH1	AAC store, Wroughton
	ZB690	WS Gazelle AH1	AAC store, Wroughton
	ZB691	WS Gazelle AH1	AAC store, Wroughton
	ZB692	WS Gazelle AH1	AAC store, Wroughton
	ZB693	WS Gazelle AH1	AAC store, Wroughton
	ZD230	BAC Super VC10 (G-ASGA)	RAF Abingdon, store
	ZD231	BAC Super VC10 (G-ASGB)	RAF Abingdon, store
	ZD232	BAC Super VC10 (G-ASGD) (8699M)	RAF Brize Norton, JATE
	ZD233	BAC Super VC10 (G-ASGE)	RAF FF&SS, Catterick
	ZD234	BAC Super VC10 (G-ASGF) (8700M)	RAF Brize Norton
	ZD235	BAC Super VC10 (G-ASGG)	RAF Abingdon, store
	ZD236	BAC Super VC10 (G-ASGH)	RAF Abingdon, store
	ZD237	BAC Super VC10 (G-ASGI)	RAF Abingdon, store
	ZD238	BAC Super VC10 (G-ASGJ)	RAF Abingdon, store
	ZD239	BAC Super VC10 (G-ASGK)	RAF Abingdon, store
	ZD240	BAC Super VC10 (G-ASGL)	RAF Abingdon, store
	ZD241	BAC Super VC10 (G-ASGM)	RAF Abingdon, store
	ZD242	BAC Super VC10 (G-ASGP)	RAF Abingdon, store
	ZD243	BAC Super VC10 (G-ASGR)	RAF Abingdon, store
	ZD249	WS Lynx HAS3	MoD(PE) Westlands, Yeovil
	ZD250	WS Lynx HAS3 [376/XB]	RN No 829 Sqn, Portland
	ZD251	WS Lynx HAS3 [631/PO]	RN No 702 Sqn, Portland
	ZD252	WS Lynx HAS3 [301/PO]	RN No 815 Sqn, Portland
	ZD253	WS Lynx HAS3 [304/PO]	RN No 815 Sqn, Portland
	ZD254	WS Lynx HAS3 [632/PO]	RN No 702 Sqn, Portland
	ZD255	WS Lynx HAS3 [479]	RN No 815 Sqn, Portland
	ZD256	WS Lynx HAS3 [432/SC]	RN No 815 Sqn, Portland
	ZD257	WS Lynx HAS3 [346/BW]	RN No 815 Sqn, Portland
	ZD258	WS Lynx HAS3 [GIB]	RN No 815 Sqn (208 Flt), Gibraltar
	ZD259	WS Lynx HAS3 [323/AB]	RN No 815 Sqn, Portland
	ZD260	WS Lynx HAS3 [303]	RN No 815 Sqn, Portland
	ZD261	WS Lynx HAS3 [GW]	RN NATIU, Lee-on-Solent
	ZD262	WS Lynx HAS3 [376/XB]	RN No 815 Sqn, Portland
	ZD263	WS Lynx HAS3 [630]	RN No 702 Sqn, Portland
	ZD264	WS Lynx HAS3 [411/EB]	RN No 815 Sqn, Portland
	ZD265	WS Lynx HAS3 [328/BA]	RN No 829 Sqn, Portland
	ZD266	WS Lynx HAS3	MoD(PE) Westlands, Yeovil
	ZD267	WS Lynx HAS3	MoD(PE) A&AEE Boscombe Down
	ZD268	WS Lynx HAS3 [342/BT]	RN No 829 Sqn, Portland
	ZD272	WS Lynx AH1 [A]	AAC No 663 Sqn, Soest
	ZD273	WS Lynx AH1	AAC No 656 Sqn, Netheravon
	ZD274	WS Lynx AH1	AAC No 656 Sqn, Netheravon
	ZD275	WS Lynx AH1	AAC No 657 Sqn, Oakington
	ZD276	WS Lynx AH1	AAC No 652 Sqn, Hildesheim
	ZD277	WS Lynx AH1	AAC No 655 Sqn, Aldergrove
	ZD278	WS Lynx AH1	AAC store, Wroughton
	ZD279	WS Lynx AH1	AAC store, Wroughton
	ZD280	WS Lynx AH1	AAC No 663 Sqn, Soest
	ZD281	WS Lynx AH1	AAC No 657 Sqn, Oakington
	ZD282	WS Lynx AH1 [24A]	RM 3 CBAS, Yeovilton
	ZD283	WS Lynx AH1 [M]	AAC ARW/LCF, Middle Wallop
	ZD284	WS Lynx AH1 [24B]	RM 3 CBAS, Yeovilton
	ZD285	WS Lynx AH1/5	MoD(PE) RAE Farnborough
	ZD318	BAe Harrier GR5	MoD(PE) BAe Dunsfold
	ZD319	BAe Harrier GR5	MoD(PE) BAe Dunsfold
	ZD320	BAe Harrier GR5	MoD(PE) A&AEE, Boscombe Down
	ZD476	WS61 Sea King HC4 [ZA]	RN No 707 Sqn, Yeovilton
	ZD477	WS61 Sea King HC4 [VC]	RN No 846 Sqn, Yeovilton
	ZD478	WS61 Sea King HC4 [VE]	RN No 846 Sqn, Yeovilton
	ZD479	WS61 Sea King HC4 [ZE]	RN No 707 Sqn, Yeovilton
	ZD480	WS61 Sea King HC4 [VG]	RN No 846 Sqn, Yeovilton
	ZD485	FMA IA58 Pucara (A-515)	RAF Cosford Aerospace Museum
	ZD493	BAC VC10 (G-ARVJ)	RAF Brize Norton
	ZD559	WS Lynx AH1/5	MoD(PE) RAE Bedford
	ZD560	WS Lynx HAS3	MoD(PE) ETPS Boscombe Down
	ZD565	WS Lynx HAS3	RNAS Portland
	ZD566	WS Lynx HAS3	RN Portland
	ZD567	WS Lynx HAS3 [636/PO]	RN No 702 Sqn, Portland
	ZD574	B-V Chinook HC1 [FH]	RAF No 240 OCU, Odiham
	ZD575	B-V Chinook HC1 [FF]	RAF No 240 OCU, Odiham
	ZD576	B-V Chinook HC1 [FG]	RAF No 240 OCU, Odiham

Serial	Type (alternative identity)	Owner, Operator or Location	Notes
ZD578	BAe Sea Harrier FRS1 [711]	RN No 899 Sqn, Yeovilton	
ZD579	BAe Sea Harrier FRS1 [710]	RN No 899 Sqn, Yeovilton	
ZD580	BAe Sea Harrier FRS1 [004/R]	RN No 801 Sqn, Yeovilton	
ZD581	BAe Sea Harrier FRS1 [721]	RN No 899 Sqn, Yeovilton	
ZD582	BAe Sea Harrier FRS1 [124/L]	RN No 800 Sqn, Yeovilton	
ZD607	BAe Sea Harrier FRS1 [712]	RN No 899 Sqn, Yeovilton	
ZD608	BAe Sea Harrier FRS1	RN No — Sqn, Yeovilton	
ZD609	BAe Sea Harrier FRS1 [122/L]	RN No 800 Sqn, Yeovilton	
ZD610	BAe Sea Harrier FRS1	RN No — Sqn, Yeovilton	
ZD611	BAe Sea Harrier FRS1	RN No — Sqn, Yeovilton	
ZD612	BAe Sea Harrier FRS1	RN No 899 Sqn, Yeovilton	
ZD613	BAe Sea Harrier FRS1	RN No — Sqn, Yeovilton	
ZD614	BAe Sea Harrier FRS1	RN No — Sqn, Yeovilton	
ZD615	BAe Sea Harrier FRS1	RN No — Sqn, Yeovilton	
ZD620	BAe 125 CC3	RAF No 32 Sqn, Northolt	
ZD621	BAe 125 CC3	RAF No 32 Sqn, Northolt	
ZD625	WS61 Sea King HC4 [ZF]	RN No 707 Sqn, Yeovilton	
ZD626	WS61 Sea King HC4 [ZG]	RN No 707 Sqn, Yeovilton	
ZD627	WS61 Sea King HC4 [ZH]	RN No 707 Sqn, Yeovilton	
ZD630	WS61 Sea King HAS5 [013/R]	RN No 820 Sqn, Culdrose	
ZD631	WS61 Sea King HAS5 [019/R]	RN No 820 Sqn, Culdrose	
ZD632	WS61 Sea King HAS5 [010/R]	RN No 820 Sqn, Culdrose	
ZD633	WS61 Sea King HAS5 [018/R]	RN No 820 Sqn, Culdrose	
ZD634	WS61 Sea King HAS5 [702/PW]	RN No 819 Sqn, Prestwick	
ZD635	WS61 Sea King HAS5 [703]	RN Predannack Fire School	
ZD636	WS61 Sea King HAS5 [704/PW]	RN No 819 Sqn, Prestwick	
ZD637	WS61 Sea King HAS5 [704]	RN No 819 Sqn, Prestwick	
ZD643	Schleicher Vanguard TX1 (BGA2884)	RAF No 618 VGS, West Malling	
ZD644	Schleicher Vanguard TX1 (BGA2883)	RAF No 618 VGS, West Malling	
ZD645	Schleicher Vanguard TX1 (BGA2885)	RAF No 618 VGS, West Malling	
ZD646	Schleicher Vanguard TX1 (BGA2886)	RAF No 618 VGS, West Malling	
ZD647	Schleicher Vanguard TX1 (BGA2887)	RAF No 618 VGS, West Malling	
ZD648	Schleicher Vanguard TX1 (BGA2888)	RAF No 618 VGS, West Malling	
ZD649	Schleicher Vanguard TX1 (BGA2889)	RAF No 618 VGS, West Malling	
ZD650	Schleicher Vanguard TX1 (BGA2890)	RAF No 618 VGS, West Malling	
ZD651	Schleicher Vanguard TX1 (BGA2891)	RAF No 618 VGS, West Malling	
ZD652	Schleicher Vanguard TX1 (BGA2892)	RAF No 618 VGS, West Malling	
ZD657	Schleicher Valiant TX1 (BGA2893)	RAF ACCGS, Syerston	
ZD658	Schleicher Valiant TX1 (BGA2894)	RAF No 625 VGS, South Cerney	
ZD659	Schleicher Valiant TX1 (BGA2895)	RAF No 618 VGS, West Malling	
ZD660	Schleicher Valiant TX1 (BGA2896)	RAF No 662 VGS, Arbroath	
ZD661	Schleicher Valiant TX1 (BGA2897)	RAF ACCGS, Syerston	
ZD667	BAe Harrier GR5 [U]	RAF No 4 Sqn, Gutersloh	
ZD668	BAe Harrier GR5	MoD(PE) for RAF	
ZD669	BAe Harrier GR5	MoD(PE) for RAF	
ZD670	BAe Harrier GR5	MoD(PE) for RAF	
ZD671	BAe Harrier T4	MoD(PE) for RAF	
ZD672	BAe Harrier T4	MoD(PE) for RAF	
ZD673	BAe Harrier T4	MoD(PE) for RAF	
ZD674	BAe Harrier T4	MoD(PE) for RAF	
ZD703	BAe 125 CC3	RAF No 32 Sqn, Northolt	
ZD704	BAe 125 CC3	RAF No 32 Sqn, Northolt	
ZD707	Panavia Tornado GR1 [BK]	RAF No 14 Sqn, Bruggen	
ZD708	Panavia Tornado GR1	MoD(PE) BAe Warton	
ZD709	Panavia Tornado GR1 [AM]	RAF No 9 Sqn, Bruggen	
ZD710	Panavia Tornado GR1 [BJ]	RAF No 14 Sqn, Bruggen	
ZD711	Panavia Tornado GR1T [DZ]	RAF No 31 Sqn, Bruggen	
ZD712	Panavia Tornado GR1T [BY]	RAF No 14 Sqn, Bruggen	
ZD713	Panavia Tornado GR1T [DY]	RAF No 31 Sqn, Bruggen	

Notes	Serial	Type (alternative identity)	Owner, Operator or Location
	ZD714	Panavia Tornado GR1	MoD(PE) BAe Warton
	ZD715	Panavia Tornado GR1 [DB]	RAF No 31 Sqn, Bruggen
	ZD716	Panavia Tornado GR1 [T]	MoD(PE) TOEU Boscombe Down
	ZD717	Panavia Tornado GR1 [CD]	RAF No 17 Sqn, Bruggen
	ZD718	Panavia Tornado GR1 [BH]	RAF No 14 Sqn, Bruggen
	ZD719	Panavia Tornado GR1 [AD]	RAF No 9 Sqn, Bruggen
	ZD720	Panavia Tornado GR1 [CK]	RAF No 17 Sqn, Bruggen
	ZD738	Panavia Tornado GR1 [DD]	RAF No 31 Sqn, Bruggen
	ZD739	Panavia Tornado GR1 [AC]	RAF No 9 Sqn, Bruggen
	ZD740	Panavia Tornado GR1 [DA]	RAF No 31 Sqn, Bruggen
	ZD741	Panavia Tornado GR1T [AU]	RAF No 9 Sqn, Bruggen
	ZD742	Panavia Tornado GR1T [CY]	RAF No 17 Sqn, Bruggen
	ZD743	Panavia Tornado GR1T [CZ]	RAF No 17 Sqn, Bruggen
	ZD744	Panavia Tornado GR1 [BD]	RAF No 14 Sqn, Bruggen
	ZD745	Panavia Tornado GR1 [AB]	RAF No 9 Sqn, Bruggen
	ZD746	Panavia Tornado GR1 [DJ]	RAF No 31 Sqn, Bruggen
	ZD747	Panavia Tornado GR1 [DK]	RAF No 31 Sqn, Bruggen
	ZD748	Panavia Tornado GR1 [DG]	RAF No 31 Sqn, Bruggen
	ZD749	Panavia Tornado GR1 [U]	MoD(PE) TOEU Boscombe Down
	ZD788	Panavia Tornado GR1 [CB]	RAF No 17 Sqn, Bruggen
	ZD789	Panavia Tornado GR1 [CE]	RAF No 17 Sqn, Bruggen
	ZD790	Panavia Tornado GR1 [DL]	RAF No 31 Sqn, Bruggen
	ZD791	Panavia Tornado GR1 [BG]	RAF No 14 Sqn, Bruggen
	ZD792	Panavia Tornado GR1 [CF]	RAF No 17 Sqn, Bruggen
	ZD793	Panavia Tornado GR1 [CA]	RAF No 17 Sqn, Bruggen
	ZD808	Panavia Tornado GR1 [CJ]	RAF No 17 Sqn, Bruggen
	ZD809	Panavia Tornado GR1 [AA]	RAF No 9 Sqn, Bruggen
	ZD810	Panavia Tornado GR1 [CG]	RAF No 17 Sqn, Bruggen
	ZD811	Panavia Tornado GR1 [DF]	RAF No 31 Sqn, Bruggen
	ZD812	Panavia Tornado GR1T [FV]	RAF No 16 Sqn, Laarbruch
	ZD842	Panavia Tornado GR1T [BZ]	RAF No 14 Sqn, Bruggen
	ZD843	Panavia Tornado GR1 [DH]	RAF No 31 Sqn, Bruggen
	ZD844	Panavia Tornado GR1 [DE]	RAF No 31 Sqn, Bruggen
	ZD845	Panavia Tornado GR1 [BA]	RAF No 14 Sqn, Bruggen
	ZD846	Panavia Tornado GR1 [BL]	RAF No 14 Sqn, Bruggen
	ZD847	Panavia Tornado GR1 [CH]	RAF No 17 Sqn, Bruggen
	ZD848	Panavia Tornado GR1 [BC]	RAF No 14 Sqn, Bruggen
	ZD849	Panavia Tornado GR1 [CC]	RAF No 17 Sqn, Bruggen
	ZD850	Panavia Tornado GR1 [CL]	RAF No 17 Sqn, Bruggen
	ZD851	Panavia Tornado GR1 [DC]	RAF No 31 Sqn, Bruggen
	ZD890	Panavia Tornado GR1 [AE]	RAF No 9 Sqn, Bruggen
	ZD891	Panavia Tornado GR1 [BB]	RAF No 14 Sqn, Bruggen
	ZD892	Panavia Tornado GR1 [AF]	RAF No 9 Sqn, Bruggen
	ZD893	Panavia Tornado GR1 [AG]	RAF No 9 Sqn, Bruggen
	ZD894	Panavia Tornado GR1 [BE]	RAF No 14 Sqn, Bruggen
	ZD895	Panavia Tornado GR1 [BF]	RAF No 14 Sqn, Bruggen
	ZD899	Panavia Tornado F2T	MoD(PE) BAe Warton
	ZD900	Panavia Tornado F2T	MoD(PE) BAe Warton
	ZD901	Panavia Tornado F2T [AA]	RAF No 229 OCU/65 Sqn, Coningsby
	ZD902	Panavia Tornado F2T [AC]	RAF No 229 OCU/65 Sqn, Coningsby
	ZD903	Panavia Tornado F2T [AB]	RAF No 229 OCU/65 Sqn, Coningsby
	ZD904	Panavia Tornado F2T [AE]	RAF No 229 OCU/65 Sqn, Coningsby
	ZD905	Panavia Tornado F2 [AV]	RAF No 229 OCU/65 Sqn, Coningsby
	ZD906	Panavia Tornado F2 [AN]	RAF store, St Athan
	ZD932	Panavia Tornado F2 [AM]	RAF No 229 OCU/65 Sqn, Coningsby
	ZD933	Panavia Tornado F2 [AO]	RAF store, St Athan
	ZD934	Panavia Tornado F2T [AD]	RAF No 229 OCU/65 Sqn, Coningsby
	ZD935	Panavia Tornado F2T [AF]	RAF No 229 OCU/65 Sqn, Coningsby
	ZD936	Panavia Tornado F2 [AP]	RAF No 229 OCU/65 Sqn, Coningsby
	ZD937	Panavia Tornado F2 [AQ]	RAF No 229 OCU/65 Sqn, Coningsby
	ZD938	Panavia Tornado F2 [AR]	RAF No 229 OCU/65 Sqn, Coningsby
	ZD939	Panavia Tornado F2 [AS]	RAF No 229 OCU/65 Sqn, Coningsby
	ZD940	Panavia Tornado F2 [AT]	RAF No 229 OCU/65 Sqn, Coningsby
	ZD941	Panavia Tornado F2 [AU]	RAF No 229 OCU/65 Sqn, Coningsby
	ZD948	Lockheed TriStar KC1 (G-BFCA)	RAF No 216 Sqn, Brize Norton
	ZD949	Lockheed TriStar K1 (G-BFCB)	MoD(PE) Marshalls, Cambridge
	ZD950	Lockheed TriStar KC1 (G-BFCC)	RAF No 216 Sqn, Brize Norton
	ZD951	Lockheed TriStar K1 (G-BFCD)	MoD(PE) Marshalls, Cambridge
	ZD952	Lockheed TriStar KC1 (G-BFCE)	RAF No 216 Sqn, Brize Norton
	ZD953	Lockheed TriStar KC1 (G-BFCF)	RAF No 216 Sqn, Brize Norton
	ZD974	Schleicher Janus C (BGA2875)	RAF ACCGS, Syerston
	ZD975	Schleicher Janus C (BGA2876)	RAF ACCGS, Syerston
	ZD980	B-V Chinook HC1 [FJ]	RAF No 240 OCU, Odiham
	ZD981	B-V Chinook HC1 [BD]	RAF No 18 Sqn, Gutersloh

Serial	Type (alternative identity)	Owner, Operator or Location	Notes
ZD982	B-V Chinook HC1 [FI]	RAF No 240 OCU, Odiham	
ZD983	B-V Chinook HC1 [BF]	RAF No 18 Sqn, Gutersloh	
ZD984	B-V Chinook HC1 [BE]	RAF No 18 Sqn, Gutersloh	
ZD990	BAe Harrier T4A	MoD(PE) for RAF	
ZD991	BAe Harrier T4A	MoD(PE) for RAF	
ZD992	BAe Harrier T4A	MoD(PE) for RAF	
ZE154	Panavia Tornado F3T	RAF No 229 OCU/65 Sqn, Coningsby	
ZE155	Panavia Tornado F3	MoD(PE), BAe Warton	
ZE156	Panavia Tornado F3	MoD(PE), BAe Warton	
ZE157	Panavia Tornado F3T [AH]	RAF No 229 OCU/65 Sqn, Coningsby	
ZE158	Panavia Tornado F3	MoD(PE), BAe Warton	
ZE159	Panavia Tornado F3 [AW]	RAF No 229 OCU/65 Sqn, Coningsby	
ZE160	Panavia Tornado F3T [AG]	RAF No 229 OCU/65 Sqn, Coningsby	
ZE161	Panavia Tornado F3 [AX]	RAF No 229 OCU/65 Sqn, Coningsby	
ZE162	Panavia Tornado F3 [AY]	RAF No 229 OCU/65 Sqn, Coningsby	
ZE163	Panavia Tornado F3T	RAF No 229 OCU/65 Sqn, Coningsby	
ZE164	Panavia Tornado F3 [AN]	RAF No 229 OCU/65 Sqn, Coningsby	
ZE165	Panavia Tornado F3 [AZ]	RAF No 229 OCU/65 Sqn, Coningsby	
ZE166	Panavia Tornado F3T [AI]	RAF No 229 OCU/65 Sqn, Coningsby	
ZE167	Panavia Tornado F3 [AL]	RAF No 229 OCU/65 Sqn, Coningsby	
ZE168	Panavia Tornado F3	MoD(PE), BAe Warton	
ZE199	Panavia Tornado F3T	MoD(PE), BAe Warton	
ZE200	Panavia Tornado F3	MoD(PE), BAe Warton	
ZE201	Panavia Tornado F3	MoD(PE), BAe Warton	
ZE202	Panavia Tornado F3T	RAF No 229 OCU/65 Sqn, Coningsby	
ZE203	Panavia Tornado F3 [AO]	RAF No 229 OCU/65 Sqn, Coningsby	
ZE204	Panavia Tornado F3	RAF No 229 OCU/65 Sqn, Coningsby	
ZE205	Panavia Tornado F3T [AJ]	RAF No 229 OCU/65 Sqn, Coningsby	
ZE206	Panavia Tornado F3	MoD(PE), BAe Warton	
ZE207	Panavia Tornado F3	MoD(PE), BAe Warton	
ZE208	Panavia Tornado F3T	MoD(PE), BAe Warton	
ZE209	Panavia Tornado F3	MoD(PE), BAe Warton	
ZE210	Panavia Tornado F3	MoD(PE), BAe Warton	
ZE250	Panavia Tornado F3T	MoD(PE), BAe Warton	
ZE251	Panavia Tornado F3	MoD(PE), BAe Warton	
ZE252	Panavia Tornado F3	MoD(PE), BAe Warton	
ZE253	Panavia Tornado F3T	MoD(PE), BAe Warton	
ZE254	Panavia Tornado F3	MoD(PE), BAe Warton	
ZE255	Panavia Tornado F3	MoD(PE), BAe Warton	
ZE256	Panavia Tornado F3T	MoD(PE), BAe Warton	
ZE257	Panavia Tornado F3	MoD(PE), BAe Warton	
ZE258	Panavia Tornado F3	MoD(PE), BAe Warton	
ZE287	Panavia Tornado F3T	MoD(PE), BAe Warton	
ZE288	Panavia Tornado F3	MoD(PE), BAe Warton	
ZE289	Panavia Tornado F3	MoD(PE), BAe Warton	
ZE290	Panavia Tornado F3T	MoD(PE), BAe Warton	
ZE291	Panavia Tornado F3	MoD(PE), BAe Warton	
ZE292	Panavia Tornado F3	MoD(PE), BAe Warton	
ZE293	Panavia Tornado F3T	MoD(PE), BAe Warton	
ZE294	Panavia Tornado F3	MoD(PE), BAe Warton	
ZE295	Panavia Tornado F3	MoD(PE), BAe Warton	
ZE296	Panavia Tornado F3T	MoD(PE), BAe Warton	
ZE338	Panavia Tornado F3	MoD(PE), BAe Warton	
ZE339	Panavia Tornado F3	MoD(PE), BAe Warton	
ZE340	Panavia Tornado F3T	MoD(PE), BAe Warton	
ZE341	Panavia Tornado F3	MoD(PE), BAe Warton	
ZE342	Panavia Tornado F3	MoD(PE), BAe Warton	
ZE343	Panavia Tornado F3T	MoD(PE), BAe Warton	
ZE350	McD Phantom F3 [T]	RAF No 74 Sqn, Wattisham	
ZE351	McD Phantom F3 [I]	RAF No 74 Sqn, Wattisham	
ZE352	McD Phantom F3 [G]	RAF No 74 Sqn, Wattisham	
ZE353	McD Phantom F3 [E]	RAF No 74 Sqn, Wattisham	
ZE354	McD Phantom F3 [R]	RAF No 74 Sqn, Wattisham	
ZE355	McD Phantom F3 [S]	RAF No 74 Sqn, Wattisham	
ZE356	McD Phantom F3 [Q]	RAF No 74 Sqn, Wattisham	
ZE357	McD Phantom F3 [N]	RAF No 74 Sqn, Wattisham	
ZE358	McD Phantom F3 [H]	RAF No 74 Sqn, Wattisham	
ZE359	McD Phantom F3 [J]	RAF No 74 Sqn, Wattisham	
ZE360	McD Phantom F3 [O]	RAF No 74 Sqn, Wattisham	
ZE361	McD Phantom F3 [P]	RAF No 74 Sqn, Wattisham	
ZE362	McD Phantom F3 [V]	RAF No 74 Sqn, Wattisham	
ZE363	McD Phantom F3	RAF No 74 Sqn, Wattisham	
ZE364	McD Phantom F3 [Z]	RAF No 74 Sqn, Wattisham	

Notes	Serial	Type (alternative identity)	Owner, Operator or Location
	ZE368	WS61 Sea King HAR3	RAF No 202 Sqn SAR*
	ZE369	WS61 Sea King HAR3	RAF No 202 Sqn SAR*
	ZE370	WS61 Sea King HAR3	RAF No 202 Sqn SAR*
	ZE375	WS Lynx AH5	MoD(PE) Rolls-Royce, Filton
	ZE376	WS Lynx AH7	MoD(PE) Westlands, Yeovil
	ZE377	WS Lynx AH7	AAC
	ZE378	WS Lynx AH7	AAC
	ZE379	WS Lynx AH7	AAC
	ZE380	WS Lynx AH7	AAC
	ZE381	WS Lynx AH7	AAC
	ZE382	WS Lynx AH7	AAC
	ZE383	WS Lynx AH7	AAC
	ZE395	BAe 125 CC3	RAF No 32 Sqn, Northolt
	ZE396	BAe 125 CC3	RAF No 32 Sqn, Northolt
	ZE410	Agusta A109A (AE-334)	AAC 7 Regt HQ Flt, Netheravon
	ZE411	Agusta A109A (AE-331)	AAC 7 Regt HQ Flt, Netheravon
	ZE412	Agusta A109A	AAC 7 Regt HQ Flt, Netheravon
	ZE413	Agusta A109A	AAC 7 Regt HQ Flt, Netheravon
	ZE418	WS61 Sea King HAS5 [707]	RN No 819 Sqn, Prestwick
	ZE419	WS61 Sea King HAS5 [014/R]	RN No 820 Sqn, Culdrose
	ZE420	WS61 Sea King HAS5 [254]	RN No 824 Sqn, Culdrose
	ZE421	WS61 Sea King HAS5 [502]	RN No 810 Sqn, Culdrose
	ZE422	WS61 Sea King HAS5	RN NASU, Culdrose
	ZE425	WS61 Sea King HC4 [A]	RN No 845 Sqn, Yeovilton
	ZE426	WS61 Sea King HC4 [B]	RN No 845 Sqn, Yeovilton
	ZE427	WS61 Sea King HC4 [C]	RN No 845 Sqn, Yeovilton
	ZE428	WS61 Sea King HC4 [D]	RN No 845 Sqn, Yeovilton
	ZE432	BAC 1-11/479 (DQ-FBV)	MoD(PE) ETPS Boscombe Down
	ZE433	BAC 1-11/479 (DQ-FBQ)	MoD(PE) RAE Bedford
	ZE438	BAe Jetstream T3 [576]	RN No 750 Sqn, Culdrose
	ZE439	BAe Jetstream T3 [577]	RN No 750 Sqn, Culdrose
	ZE440	BAe Jetstream T3 [578]	RN No 750 Sqn, Culdrose
	ZE441	BAe Jetstream T3 [579]	RN No 750 Sqn, Culdrose
	ZE449	Sud SA330L Puma HC1 (PA-12)	MoD(PE) Westlands, Weston-super-Mare
	ZE472	HS Hawk T63 (104)	BAe/Abu Dhabi AF, Dunsfold
	ZE477	WS Lynx 3	MoD(PE) Westlands, Yeovil
	ZE495	Grob Viking T1 (BGA3000)	RAF No 644 VGS, Syerston
	ZE496	Grob Viking T1 (BGA3001)	RAF No 631 VGS, Sealand
	ZE497	Grob Viking T1 (BGA3002)	RAF No 622 VGS, Upavon
	ZE498	Grob Viking T1 (BGA3003)	RAF ACCGS, Syerston
	ZE499	Grob Viking T1 (BGA3004)	RAF ACCGS, Syerston
	ZE500	Grob Viking T1 (BGA3005)	RAF No 631 VGS, Sealand
	ZE501	Grob Viking T1 (BGA3006)	RAF ACCGS, Syerston
	ZE502	Grob Viking T1 (BGA3007)	RAF No 645 VGS, Catterick
	ZE503	Grob Viking T1 (BGA3008)	RAF No 625 VGS, South Cerney
	ZE504	Grob Viking T1 (BGA3009)	RAF No 645 VGS, Catterick
	ZE520	Grob Viking T1 (BGA3010)	RAF No 645 VGS, Catterick
	ZE521	Grob Viking T1 (BGA3011)	RAF No 662 VGS, Arbroath
	ZE522	Grob Viking T1 (BGA3012)	RAF No 662 VGS, Arbroath
	ZE523	Grob Viking T1 (BGA3013)	RAF No 631 VGS, Sealand
	ZE524	Grob Viking T1 (BGA3014)	RAF store, Kemble
	ZE525	Grob Viking T1 (BGA3015)	RAF No 622 VGS, Upavon
	ZE526	Grob Viking T1 (BGA3016)	RAF No 631 VGS, Sealand
	ZE527	Grob Viking T1 (BGA3017)	RAF
	ZE528	Grob Viking T1 (BGA3018)	RAF No 631 VGS, Sealand
	ZE529	Grob Viking T1 (BGA3019)	RAF No 631 VGS, Sealand
	ZE530	Grob Viking T1 (BGA3020)	RAF No 645 VGS, Catterick
	ZE531	Grob Viking T1 (BGA3021)	RAF No 645 VGS, Catterick
	ZE532	Grob Viking T1 (BGA3022)	RAF ACCGS, Syerston
	ZE533	Grob Viking T1 (BGA3023)	RAF No 622 VGS, Upavon
	ZE534	Grob Viking T1 (BGA3024)	RAF No 662 VGS, Arbroath
	ZE550	Grob Viking T1 (BGA3025)	RAF No 622 VGS, Upavon
	ZE551	Grob Viking T1 (BGA3026)	RAF store, Kemble
	ZE552	Grob Viking T1 (BGA3027)	RAF No 662 VGS, Arbroath
	ZE553	Grob Viking T1 (BGA3028)	RAF No 643 VGS, Scampton
	ZE554	Grob Viking T1 (BGA3029)	RAF No 631 VGS, Sealand
	ZE555	Grob Viking T1 (BGA3030)	RAF No 631 VGS, Sealand
	ZE556	Grob Viking T1 (BGA3031)	RAF No 622 VGS, Upavon
	ZE557	Grob Viking T1 (BGA3032)	RAF No 661 VGS, Kirknewton
	ZE558	Grob Viking T1 (BGA3033)	RAF store, Shawbury
	ZE559	Grob Viking T1 (BGA3034)	RAF No 661 VGS, Kirknewton
	ZE560	Grob Viking T1 (BGA3035)	RAF store, Kemble
	ZE561	Grob Viking T1 (BGA3036)	RAF No 661 VGS, Kirknewton

Serial	Type (alternative identity)	Owner, Operator or Location	Notes
ZE562	Grob Viking T1 (BGA3037)	RAF store, Kemble	
ZE563	Grob Viking T1 (BGA3038)	RAF store, Kemble	
ZE564	Grob Viking T1 (BGA3039)	RAF No 661 VGS, Kirknewton	
ZE584	Grob Viking T1 (BGA3040)	RAF store, Kemble	
ZE585	Grob Viking T1 (BGA3041)	RAF ACCGS, Syerston	
ZE586	Grob Viking T1 (BGA3042)	RAF No 625 VGS, South Cerney	
ZE587	Grob Viking T1 (BGA3043)	RAF No 614 VGS, Wethersfield	
ZE588	Grob Viking T1 (BGA3044)	RAF No 614 VGS, Wethersfield	
ZE589	Grob Viking T1 (BGA3045)	RAF store, Shawbury	
ZE590	Grob Viking T1 (BGA3046)	RAF store, Shawbury	
ZE591	Grob Viking T1 (BGA3047)	RAF store, Shawbury	
ZE592	Grob Viking T1 (BGA3048)	RAF No 614 VGS, Wethersfield	
ZE593	Grob Viking T1 (BGA3049)	RAF No 614 VGS, Wethersfield	
ZE594	Grob Viking T1 (BGA3050)	RAF No 661 VGS, Kirknewton	
ZE595	Grob Viking T1 (BGA3051)	RAF No 625 VGS, South Cerney	
ZE600	Grob Viking T1 (BGA3052)	RAF No 626 VGS, Predannack	
ZE601	Grob Viking T1 (BGA3053)	RAF No 625 VGS, South Cerney	
ZE602	Grob Viking T1 (BGA3054)	RAF store, Kemble	
ZE603	Grob Viking T1 (BGA3055)	RAF store, Kemble	
ZE604	Grob Viking T1 (BGA3056)	RAF store, Kemble	
ZE605	Grob Viking T1 (BGA3057)	RAF store, Shawbury	
ZE606	Grob Viking T1 (BGA3058)	RAF No 626 VGS, Predannack	
ZE607	Grob Viking T1 (BGA3059)	RAF store, Shawbury	
ZE608	Grob Viking T1 (BGA3060)	RAF No 625 VGS, South Cerney	
ZE609	Grob Viking T1 (BGA3061)	RAF No 626 VGS, Predannack	
ZE610	Grob Viking T1 (BGA3062)	RAF No 621 VGS, Weston-super-Mare	
ZE611	Grob Viking T1 (BGA3063)	RAF No 621 VGS, Weston-super-Mare	
ZE612	Grob Viking T1 (BGA3064)	RAF No 621 VGS, Weston-super-Mare	
ZE613	Grob Viking T1 (BGA3065)	RAF No 621 VGS, Weston-super-Mare	
ZE614	Grob Viking T1 (BGA3066)	RAF No 621 VGS, Weston-super-Mare	
ZE625	Grob Viking T1 (BGA3067)	RAF No 643 VGS, Scampton	
ZE626	Grob Viking T1 (BGA3068)	RAF store, Kemble	
ZE627	Grob Viking T1 (BGA3069)	RAF store, Kemble	
ZE628	Grob Viking T1 (BGA3070)	RAF No 643 VGS, Scampton	
ZE629	Grob Viking T1 (BGA3071)	RAF No 662 VGS, Arbroath	
ZE630	Grob Viking T1 (BGA3072)	RAF store, Kemble	
ZE631	Grob Viking T1 (BGA3073)	RAF No 643 VGS, Scampton	
ZE632	Grob Viking T1 (BGA3074)	RAF store, Kemble	
ZE633	Grob Viking T1 (BGA3075)	RAF store, Kemble	
ZE634	Grob Viking T1 (BGA3076)	RAF No —	
ZE635	Grob Viking T1 (BGA3077)	RAFC Cranwell Glider Flight	
ZE636	Grob Viking T1 (BGA3078)	RAF Halton Glider Flight	
ZE637	Grob Viking T1 (BGA3079)	RAF No —	
ZE650	Grob Viking T1 (BGA3080)	RAF No 614 VGS, Wethersfield	
ZE651	Grob Viking T1 (BGA3081)	RAF No 645 VGS, Catterick	
ZE652	Grob Viking T1 (BGA3082)	RAF ACCGS, Syerston	
ZE653	Grob Viking T1 (BGA3083)	RAF ACCGS, Syerston	
ZE654	Grob Viking T1 (BGA3084)	RAF No —	
ZE655	Grob Viking T1 (BGA3085)	RAF No —	
ZE656	Grob Viking T1 (BGA3086)	RAF No 617 VGS, Manston	
ZE657	Grob Viking T1 (BGA3087)	RAF No —	
ZE658	Grob Viking T1 (BGA3088)	RAF ACCGS, Syerston	
ZE659	Grob Viking T1 (BGA3089)	RAF No 615 VGS, Kenley	
ZE677	Grob Viking T1 (BGA3090)	RAF No 615 VGS, Kenley	
ZE678	Grob Viking T1 (BGA3091)	RAF No 615 VGS, Kenley	
ZE679	Grob Viking T1 (BGA3092)	RAF No 615 VGS, Kenley	
ZE680	Grob Viking T1 (BGA3093)	RAF No 617 VGS, Manston	
ZE681	Grob Viking T1 (BGA3094)	RAF No 615 VGS, Kenley	
ZE682	Grob Viking T1 (BGA3095)	RAF No 643 VGS, Scampton	
ZE683	Grob Viking T1 (BGA3096)	RAF No 617 VGS, Manston	
ZE684	Grob Viking T1 (BGA3097)	RAF No 617 VGS, Manston	
ZE685	Grob Viking T1 (BGA3098)	RAF No 617 VGS, Manston	
ZE686	Grob Viking T1 (BGA3099)	RAF No 617 VGS, Manston	
ZE690	BAe Sea Harrier FRS2	MoD(PE) for RN	
ZE691	BAe Sea Harrier FRS2	MoD(PE) for RN	
ZE692	BAe Sea Harrier FRS2	MoD(PE) for RN	
ZE693	BAe Sea Harrier FRS2	MoD(PE) for RN	
ZE694	BAe Sea Harrier FRS2	MoD(PE) for RN	
ZE695	BAe Sea Harrier FRS2	MoD(PE) for RN	
ZE696	BAe Sea Harrier FRS2	MoD(PE) for RN	
ZE697	BAe Sea Harrier FRS2	MoD(PE) for RN	
ZE698	BAe Sea Harrier FRS2	MoD(PE) for RN	
ZE700	BAe 146 CC2	RAF Queen's Flight, Benson	
ZE701	BAe 146 CC2	RAF Queen's Flight, Benson	

Notes	Serial	Type (alternative identity)	Owner, Operator or Location
	ZE704	Lockheed TriStar K2 (N508PA)	RAF No 216 Sqn, Brize Norton
	ZE705	Lockheed TriStar K2 (N509PA)	RAF No 216 Sqn, Brize Norton
	ZE706	Lockheed TriStar K2 (N503PA)	MoD(PE) Marshalls, Cambridge
	ZE728	Panavia Tornado F3T	MoD(PE), BAe Warton
	ZE729	Panavia Tornado F3	MoD(PE), BAe Warton
	ZE730	Panavia Tornado F3	MoD(PE), BAe Warton
	ZE731	Panavia Tornado F3	MoD(PE), BAe Warton
	ZE732	Panavia Tornado F3	MoD(PE), BAe Warton
	ZE733	Panavia Tornado F3	MoD(PE), BAe Warton
	ZE734	Panavia Tornado F3	MoD(PE), BAe Warton
	ZE735	Panavia Tornado F3T	MoD(PE), BAe Warton
	ZE736	Panavia Tornado F3	MoD(PE), BAe Warton
	ZE737	Panavia Tornado F3	MoD(PE), BAe Warton
	ZE755	Panavia Tornado F3	MoD(PE), BAe Warton
	ZE756	Panavia Tornado F3	MoD(PE), BAe Warton
	ZE757	Panavia Tornado F3	MoD(PE), BAe Warton
	ZE758	Panavia Tornado F3	MoD(PE), BAe Warton
	ZE759	Panavia Tornado F3T	MoD(PE), BAe Warton
	ZE760	Panavia Tornado F3	MoD(PE), BAe Warton
	ZE761	Panavia Tornado F3	MoD(PE), BAe Warton
	ZE762	Panavia Tornado F3	MoD(PE), BAe Warton
	ZE763	Panavia Tornado F3	MoD(PE), BAe Warton
	ZE764	Panavia Tornado F3	MoD(PE), BAe Warton
	ZE785	Panavia Tornado F3	MoD(PE), BAe Warton
	ZE786	Panavia Tornado F3T	MoD(PE), BAe Warton
	ZE787	Panavia Tornado F3	MoD(PE), BAe Warton
	ZE788	Panavia Tornado F3	MoD(PE), BAe Warton
	ZE789	Panavia Tornado F3	MoD(PE), BAe Warton
	ZE790	Panavia Tornado F3	MoD(PE), BAe Warton
	ZE791	Panavia Tornado F3	MoD(PE), BAe Warton
	ZE792	Panavia Tornado F3	MoD(PE), BAe Warton
	ZE793	Panavia Tornado F3T	MoD(PE), BAe Warton
	ZE794	Panavia Tornado F3	MoD(PE), BAe Warton
	ZE808	Panavia Tornado F3	MoD(PE), BAe Warton
	ZE809	Panavia Tornado F3	MoD(PE), BAe Warton
	ZE810	Panavia Tornado F3	MoD(PE), BAe Warton
	ZE811	Panavia Tornado F3	MoD(PE), BAe Warton
	ZE812	Panavia Tornado F3	MoD(PE), BAe Warton
	ZE830	Panavia Tornado F3T	MoD(PE), BAe Warton
	ZE831	Panavia Tornado F3	MoD(PE), BAe Warton
	ZE832	Panavia Tornado F3	MoD(PE), BAe Warton
	ZE833	Panavia Tornado F3	MoD(PE), BAe Warton
	ZE834	Panavia Tornado F3	MoD(PE), BAe Warton
	ZE835	Panavia Tornado F3	MoD(PE), BAe Warton
	ZE836	Panavia Tornado F3	MoD(PE), BAe Warton
	ZE837	Panavia Tornado F3T	MoD(PE), BAe Warton
	ZE838	Panavia Tornado F3	MoD(PE), BAe Warton
	ZE839	Panavia Tornado F3	MoD(PE), BAe Warton
	ZE858	Panavia Tornado F3	MoD(PE), BAe Warton
	ZE859	Panavia Tornado F3	MoD(PE), BAe Warton
	ZE860	Panavia Tornado F3	MoD(PE), BAe Warton
	ZE861	Panavia Tornado F3	MoD(PE), BAe Warton
	ZE862	Panavia Tornado F3T	MoD(PE), BAe Warton
	ZE882	Panavia Tornado F3	MoD(PE), BAe Warton
	ZE883	Panavia Tornado F3	MoD(PE), BAe Warton
	ZE884	Panavia Tornado F3	MoD(PE), BAe Warton
	ZE885	Panavia Tornado F3	MoD(PE), BAe Warton
	ZE886	Panavia Tornado F3	MoD(PE), BAe Warton
	ZE887	Panavia Tornado F3	MoD(PE), BAe Warton
	ZE888	Panavia Tornado F3T	MoD(PE), BAe Warton
	ZE889	Panavia Tornado F3	MoD(PE), BAe Warton
	ZE890	Panavia Tornado F3	MoD(PE), BAe Warton
	ZE891	Panavia Tornado F3	MoD(PE), BAe Warton
	ZE905	Panavia Tornado F3	MoD(PE) BAe Warton
	ZE906	Panavia Tornado F3	MoD(PE) BAe Warton
	ZE907	Panavia Tornado F3	MoD(PE) BAe Warton
	ZE908	Panavia Tornado F3T	MoD(PE) BAe Warton
	ZE909	Panavia Tornado F3	MoD(PE) BAe Warton
	ZE910	Panavia Tornado F3	MoD(PE) BAe Warton
	ZE911	Panavia Tornado F3	MoD(PE) BAe Warton
	ZE912	Panavia Tornado F3	MoD(PE) BAe Warton
	ZE913	Panavia Tornado F3	MoD(PE) BAe Warton
	ZE914	Panavia Tornado F3	MoD(PE) BAe Warton
	ZE934	Panavia Tornado F3T	MoD(PE) BAe Warton

Serial	Type (alternative identity)	Owner, Operator or Location	Notes
ZE935	Panavia Tornado F3	MoD(PE) BAe Warton	
ZE936	Panavia Tornado F3	MoD(PE) BAe Warton	
ZE937	Panavia Tornado F3	MoD(PE) BAe Warton	
ZE938	Panavia Tornado F3	MoD(PE) BAe Warton	
ZE939	Panavia Tornado F3	MoD(PE) BAe Warton	
ZE940	Panavia Tornado F3	MoD(PE) BAe Warton	
ZE941	Panavia Tornado F3T	MoD(PE) BAe Warton	
ZE942	Panavia Tornado F3	MoD(PE) BAe Warton	
ZE943	Panavia Tornado F3	MoD(PE) BAe Warton	
ZE960	Panavia Tornado F3	MoD(PE) BAe Warton	
ZE961	Panavia Tornado F3	MoD(PE) BAe Warton	
ZE962	Panavia Tornado F3	MoD(PE) BAe Warton	
ZE963	Panavia Tornado F3	MoD(PE) BAe Warton	
ZE964	Panavia Tornado F3T	MoD(PE) BAe Warton	
ZE965	Panavia Tornado F3	MoD(PE) BAe Warton	
ZE966	Panavia Tornado F3	MoD(PE) BAe Warton	
ZE967	Panavia Tornado F3	MoD(PE) BAe Warton	
ZE968	Panavia Tornado F3	MoD(PE) BAe Warton	
ZE969	Panavia Tornado F3	MoD(PE) BAe Warton	
ZE982	Panavia Tornado F3	MoD(PE) BAe Warton	
ZE983	Panavia Tornado F3	MoD(PE) BAe Warton	
ZF115	WS61 Sea King Mk 4	MoD(PE) RAE Farnborough	
ZF116	WS61 Sea King HC4	RN NASU, Yeovilton	
ZF117	WS61 Sea King HC4	MoD(PE) A&AEE Boscombe Down	
ZF118	WS61 Sea King HC4 [H]	RN No 845 Sqn, Yeovilton	
ZF119	WS61 Sea King HC4	RN NASU, Yeovilton	
ZF120	WS61 Sea King HC4	MoD(PE) for RN	
ZF121	WS61 Sea King HC4	MoD(PE) for RN	
ZF122	WS61 Sea King HC4	MoD(PE) for RN	
ZF123	WS61 Sea King HC4	MoD(PE) for RN	
ZF124	WS61 Sea King HC4	MoD(PE) for RN	
ZF130	BAe 125-600B (G-BLUW)	MoD(PE) BAe Woodford	
ZF135	Short Tucano T1	MoD(PE) Short Bros, Belfast	
ZF136	Short Tucano T1	MoD(PE) Short Bros, Belfast	
ZF137	Short Tucano T1	MoD(PE) Short Bros, Belfast	
ZF138	Short Tucano T1	MoD(PE) Short Bros, Belfast	
ZF139	Short Tucano T1	MoD(PE) Short Bros, Belfast	
ZF140	Short Tucano T1	MoD(PE) Short Bros, Belfast	
ZF141	Short Tucano T1	MoD(PE) Short Bros, Belfast	
ZF142	Short Tucano T1	MoD(PE) Short Bros, Belfast	
ZF143	Short Tucano T1	MoD(PE) Short Bros, Belfast	
ZF144	Short Tucano T1	MoD(PE) Short Bros, Belfast	
ZF145	Short Tucano T1	MoD(PE) Short Bros, Belfast	
ZF444	BN2A Islander (G-WOTG)	RAF Parachute Association, Weston-on-the-Green	
ZF520	Piper PA-31 Navajo Chieftain (N35823/G-BLZK)	MoD(PE) RAE Farnborough	
ZF521	Piper PA-31 Navajo Chieftain (N27509)	MoD(PE) RAE Farnborough	
ZF522	Piper PA-31 Navajo Chieftain (N4261A/G-RNAV/N27728)	MoD(PE) RAE Farnborough	
ZF534	BAe EAP	BAe Warton	
ZF577	BAC Lightning F53	BAe Warton stored	
ZF578	BAC Lightning F53	BAe Warton stored	
ZF579	BAC Lightning F53	BAe Warton stored	
ZF580	BAC Lightning F53	BAe Warton stored	
ZF581	BAC Lightning F53	BAe Warton stored	
ZF582	BAC Lightning F53	BAe Warton stored	
ZF583	BAC Lightning F53	BAe Warton stored	
ZF584	BAC Lightning F53	BAe Warton stored	
ZF585	BAC Lightning F53	BAe Warton stored	
ZF586	BAC Lightning F53	BAe Warton stored	
ZF587	BAC Lightning F53	BAe Warton stored	
ZF588	BAC Lightning F53	BAe Warton stored	
ZF589	BAC Lightning F53	BAe Warton stored	
ZF590	BAC Lightning F53	BAe Warton stored	
ZF591	BAC Lightning F53	BAe Warton stored	
ZF592	BAC Lightning F53	BAe Warton stored	
ZF593	BAC Lightning F53	BAe Warton stored	
ZF594	BAC Lightning F53	BAe Warton stored	
ZF595	BAC Lightning T55	BAe Warton stored	
ZF596	BAC Lightning T55	BAe Warton stored	
ZF597	BAC Lightning T55	BAe Warton stored	

Notes	Serial	Type (alternative identity)	Owner, Operator or Location
	ZF598	BAC Lightning T55	BAe Warton stored
	ZF622	Piper Navajo Chieftain	MoD(PE) A&AEE Boscombe Down
	ZF641	WS EH-101	MoD(PE) Westlands, Yeovil
	ZF644	WS EH-101	MoD(PE) Westlands, Yeovil
	ZF649	WS EH-101	MoD(PE) Westlands, Yeovil
	Z....	Embraer EMB312 Tucano (G-14-007/G-BTUC)	MoD(PE), Short Bros, Belfast

Supermarine S5 replica N220/G-BDFF. *APM*

WR965 Shackleton AEW2 of No 8 Squadron. *PRM*

RN Historic Flight's Sea Hawk WV908. *PRM*

Hunter FGA9 XE601, ETPS Boscombe Down. *PRM*

ETPS Scout AH1 XP849. *PRM*

Andover C1 XS597, No 32 Squadron, Northolt. *PRM*

The A&AEE's Phantom FG1 XT597. *PRM*

Hercules W2 XV208 from RAE Farnborough. *PRM*

Sea King Mk 4X ZB507 is flown from Farnborough. *PRM*

Chinook HC1 ZD574 from No 240 OCU, Odiham. *PRM*

BAe's EAP demonstrator ZF534. *PRM*

Stephen Grey's P-47D Thunderbolt 226671/N47DD. *PRM*

NA T-6G Texan 2807/G-BHTH in USN colours. *PRM*

Irish Air Corps Magister 215. *David Marsh*

HS125 238 taking off from Baldonnel. *Dave Marsh*

FIGHTER SQUADRON
ROYAL AIR FORCE
IN OMNIBUS PRINCEPS
Squadron badges and other stickers. Send SAE for leaflet.
Squadron Prints
Full colour lithos 11½″ × 17¼″ from our original paintings. Over 160 different aircraft and warship subjects in stock. New titles added regularly. Start your collection now.
Tornado GR.1
17(F) Squadron
ZD789/CE
RAF Bruggen
F-16A Fighting Falcon
614th TFS
Torrejon Air Base
82-1007
401st TFW
Spain
Squadron Prints Sales
48 Station Road
Waddington
Lincoln
LN5 9QN
Trade enquiries welcome
617 SQUADRON
ROYAL AIR FORCE
APRES MOI LE DELUGE

Gloster Gladiator L8032 flying with the Shuttleworth Trust at Old Warden. *PRM*

The FAA Historic Aircraft Flight's Swordfish LS326. *PRM*

Miles Messenger G-AIEK flies as 'Monty's' RG333. *PRM*

Auster AOP9 XR244 survives with the AAC Historic Flight at Middle Wallop. *PRM*

The Battle of Britain Memorial Flight's Hurricane LF363. *APM*

Hawker Hunter T7 XL564 in the raspberry ripple colour scheme of the ETPS at Boscombe Down. *PRM*

WH453 a Meteor D16 is used by the MoD at Llanbedr. *PRM*

Sea King AEW2 XV714 flying with No 849 Sqn from RNAS Culdrose. *PRM*

An RAF Gazelle HT3, XZ932 [S], from No 2 FTS at Shawbury. *PRM*

Panavia Tornado GR1 ZA542 wearing the colours of No 27 Squadron, RAF Marham. *PRM*

ZD950 the first TriStar K1 in service with No 214 Sqn. *PRM*

Tornado F3 ZE161 in the colours of No 229 OCU, RAF Coningsby. *PRM*

CZL Super Aero 45 painted to represent a Luftwaffe Heinkel He111 A1+BT. *APM*

One of the ex-Swiss AF Venom FB50s, J1632, is preserved at Cranfield. *PRM*

French Navy Alize No 56. *PRM*

A C-5A Galaxy painted in USAF 'European' camouflage. *PRM*

Deletions

The following British serials of aircraft which were shown in the seventh edition of *Military Aircraft Markings* have been omitted from the 1987 edition. The reason for the deletion has been given where possible.

Serial	*Type (alternative identity)*	*Owner, operator and location*	*Notes*
X4936	VS Spitfire VB	Re-instated as AB910	
N6532	DH Tiger Moth (G-ANTS)	Exported to Hong Kong	
RH378	Miles Messenger IIA	To G-AJOE	
RM694	VS Spitfire XIV	Not imported	
SL574	VS Spitfire XVIe	To American Eagle Association, San Diego	
TE184	VS Spitfire XVIe	To USA	
TW511	Auster 5	To G-CMAL	
VT745	Fairey Firefly AS5	Exported	
WA669	Gloster Meteor T7	Written off 25 May 1986	
WB534	DH Devon C2 (G-BLPZ)	To Denmark as OY-BHZ	
WB645	DH Chipmunk T10 PAX	Scrapped at Bicester 1985	
WF379	Vickers Varsity T1	Burned at West Freugh	
WH856	EE Canberra TT18	Scrapped Abingdon November 1986	
WH872	EE Canberra T17	Scrapped at Bedford	
WJ349	Percival Sea Prince C2	Scrapped at Weybridge	
WJ627	EE Canberra B2	Burned at Bedford	
WK144	EE Canberra B2	Burned at St Athan	
WL678	Vickers Varsity T1	Burned at Leeds-Bradford Airport	
WL801	Avro Shackleton MR2C	Scrapped at Cosford	
WZ544	DH Vampire T11	Scrapped	
WZ672	Auster AOP9	To USA as N803KB	
XA536	EE Canberra T19	Burned at Abingdon	
XA868	WS55 Whirlwind HAR1	Scrapped (?)	
XA900	Avro Vulcan B1	Scrapped at Cosford	
XD220	VS Scimitar F1	To New York	
XD527	DH Vampire T11	Burned at Manston	
XD601	DH Vampire T11	Scrapped at Tinwald Downs	
XE860	DH Vampire T11	Burned at Markfield	
XE950	DH Vampire T11		
XF730	Avro Shackleton MR3	Scrapped at Kinloss	
XG496	DH Devon C2	To G-ANDX	
XH304	DH Vampire T11	Written off 25 May 1986	
XH563	Avro Vulcan B2MRR	Scrapped at Scampton, November 1986	
XJ572	DH Sea Vixen FAW2	Burned at Catterick	
XJ695	Hawker Hunter FGA9	See XF519	
XL321	Avro Vulcan B2	Burned at Catterick	
XL566	Hawker Hunter T7	To Bruggen as 8891M	
XL583	Hawker Huntor T7	Scrapped at Brawdy	
XL735	Saro Skeeter AOP12	Burned at Manston	
XL839	WS55 Whirlwind HAR9	Burned at Lee-on-Solent	
XM275	EE Canberra B(I)8	Burned atr Wattisham	
XN261	WS55 Whirlwind HAS7	Scrapped at Lee-on-Solent	
XN652	DH Sea Vixen D3	Burned at Catterick 23 April 1986	
XN965	HS Buccaneer S1	To Pendine Ranges	
XP286	Auster AOP9	Reduced to parts at Thruxton	
XP341	WS55 Whirlwind HAR10	Burned at Cranwell	
XP409	AW Argosy C1	Scrapped at Winterbourne Gunner	
XP531	HS Gnat T1	Scrapped at Coltishall	
XP564	Hunting Jet Provost T4	Scrapped at Brawdy	
XP826	DHC Beaver AL1	To Canada as C-BGWS	
XR455	WS55 Whirlwind HAR10	Burned at Manston	
XR760	EE Lightning F6	Written off 15 July 1986	
XS150	WS58 Wessex HAS1	Burned at Lee-on-Solent	
XT199	Westland Sioux AH1	To Panama as HP-850	
XT242	Westland Sioux AH1	See XW179	
XT248	Westland Sioux AH1	To Australia as VH-	
XT431	Westland Wasp HAS1	See XS463 (the second)	
XV434	McD Phantom FGR2	Written off 7 January 1986	

Notes	Serial	Type (alternative identity)	Owner, operator and location
	XV471	McD Phantom FGR2	Written off 3 July 1986
	XW407	BAC Jet Provost T5A	Written off 6 June 1986
	XW411	BAC Jet Provost T5A	Written off 6 June 1986
	XW769	HS Harrier GR3	Written off Chievres 28 June 1986
	XW916	HS Harrier GR3	Written off 17 June 1986
	XX514	SA Bulldog T1	Written off 29 September 1986 near Thirsk
	XX761	SEPECAT Jaguar GR1	Scrapped
	XZ491	BAe Sea Harrier FRS1	Written off 16 April 1986
	XZ640	WS Lynx AH1	Written off 17 September 1986
	ZA715	B-V Chinook HC1	Written off 13 May 1986
	ZG200	BAe Hawk 200	Written off 2 July 1986

The Grob Viking T1 glider has replaced the Slingsby Sedbergh and Cadet gliders which have all been taken out of service. The following subsequent identities of those disposed of to the civil market have so far been reported:

Sedbergh TX1:			
WB920 to BGA 3221	WB939 to BGA 3220	WB941 to BGA 3219	WB944 to BGA 3160
WB958 to BGA 3243	WB981 to BGA 3238	WB993 to BGA 3225	WG496 to BGA 3242
WG498 to BGA 3245	WJ306 to BGA 3240	XN151 to BGA 3235	XN156 to BGA 3250
Cadet TX3:			
WT904 to Swedish AF GC	WT913 to BGA 3239	WT914 to BGA 3194	WT918 to BFA 3241
XA308 to BGA 3249	XE795 to BGA 3251	XE800 to BGA 3229	

RAF Maintenance Command/ Support Command 'M' number cross-reference for serials listed in Military Aircraft Markings

1746M/K4972	7060M/VF301	7293M/RW393	7525M/WT619	7622M/WV606
4354M/BL614	7090M/EE531	7323M/VV217	7530M/WT648	7625M/WD356
5377M/EP120	7118M/LA198	7325M/R5868	7532M/WT651	7630M/VZ304
5405M/LF738	7119M/LA226	7362M/475081 (VP546)	7533M/WT680	7641M/XA634
5466M/LF751	7150M/PK683	7416M/WN907	7543M/WN901	7645M/WD293
5690M/MK356	7151M/VT229	7421M/WT660	7544M/WN904	7646M/VX461
5713M/BM597	7154M/WB188	7422M/WT684	7548M/PS915	7648M/XF785
5758M/DG202	7174M/VX272	7428M/WK198	7564M/XE982	7656M/WJ573
6372M/EE549	7175M/VV106	7432M/WZ724	7570M/XD674	7663M/XA571
6457M/ML427	7200M/VT812	7443M/WX853	7582M/WP180	7673M/WV332
6490M/LA255	7241M/TE311	7451M/TE476	7583M/WP185	7688M/WW421
6709M/TE356	7243M/TE462	7458M/WX905	7602M/WE600	7693M/WV483
6944M/RW386	7244M/TB382	7464M/XA564	7604M/XD542 (XD429)	7696M/WV493
6947M/RW388	7245M/RW382	7467M/WP978	7605M/WS692	7697M/WV495
6948M/DE673	7246M/TD248	7470M/XA553	7606M/WV562	7698M/WV499
6960M/MT847	7256M/TB752	7473M/XE946	7607M/TJ138	7700M/WV544
7000M/TE392	7257M/TB252	7491M/WT569	7615M/WV679	7703M/WG725
7001M/TE356	7279M/TB752	7496M/WT612	7616M/WW388	7704M/TW536
7008M/EE549	7281M/TB252	7499M/WT555	7618M/WW442	7705M/WL505
7014M/N6720	7285M/VV119	7510M/WT694	7621M/WV686	7706M/WB584
7015M/NL985	7288M/PK724			7709M/WT933

7711M/PS915
7712M/WK281
7715M/XK724
7716M/WS776
7717M/XA549
7718M/WA577
7719M/WK277
7729M/WB758
7734M/XD536
7736M/WZ559
7737M/XD602
7739M/XA801
7750M/WL168
7751M/WL131
7755M/WG760
7758M/PM651
7759M/PK664
7761M/XH318
7762M/XE670
7770M/WT746
7796M/WJ676
7805M/TW117
7806M/TA639
7809M/XA699
7816M/WG763
7817M/TX214
7822M/XP248
7825M/WK991
7827M/XA917
7829M/XH992
7839M/WV781
7840M/XK482
7841M/WV783
7847M/WV276
7849M/XF319
7851M/WZ706
7852M/XG506
7854M/XM191
7855M/XK416
7859M/XP283
7860M/XL738
7862M/XR246
7864M/XP244
7865M/TX226
7866M/XH278
7867M/XH980
7868M/WZ736
7869M/WK935
7870M/XM556
7881M/WD413
7883M/XT150
7887M/XD375
7890M/XD453
7891M/XM693
7894M/XD818
7895M/WF784
7898M/XP854
7899M/XG540
7900M/WA576
7902M/WZ550
7906M/WH132
7917M/WA591
7920M/WL360
7923M/XT133
7928M/XE849
7930M/WH301
7931M/RD253
7932M/WZ744
7933M/XR220
7937M/WS843
7938M/XH903
7939M/XD596
7940M/XL764
7949M/XF974
7955M/XH767
7957M/XF545
7959M/WS774
7960M/WS726
7961M/WS739
7964M/WS760
7965M/WS792
7967M/WS844
7969M/WS840
7970M/WP907
7971M/XK699
7972M/XH764
7973M/WS807
7976M/XK418
7979M/XM529
7980M/XM561
7982M/XH892
7983M/XD506
7984M/XN597
7986M/WG777
7988M/XL149
7990M/XD452
7997M/XG452
7998M/XD515
8005M/WG768
8007M/XF990
8009M/XG518
8010M/XG547
8011M/XV269
8012M/VS562
8017M/XL762
8018M/XN344
8019M/WZ869
8020M/WB847
8021M/XL824
8022M/XN341
8023M/XD463
8025M/XH124
8027M/XM555
8032M/XH837
8033M/XD382
8034M/XL703
8040M/XR493
8041M/XF690
8043M/XF836
8046M/XL770
8049M/WE168
8050M/XG329
8051M/XN929
8052M/WH166
8053M/WK968
8054AM/XM410
8054BM/XM417
8055AM/XM402
8055BM/XM404
8056M/XG337
8057M/XR243
8060M/WW397
8062M/XR669
8063M/WT536
8070M/EP120
8071M/TE476
8072M/PK624
8073M/TB252
8075M/RW382
8076M/XM386
8077M/XN594
8078M/XM351
8079M/XN492
8080M/XM480
8081M/XM468
8082M/XM409
8083M/XM367
8084M/XM369
8085M/XM467
8086M/TB752
8087M/XN925
8088M/XN602
8090M/XM698
8092M/WK654
8094M/WT520
8099M/WD355
8101M/WH984
8102M/WT486
8103M/WR985
8106M/WR982
8108M/WV703
8113M/WV753
8114M/WL798
8117M/WR974
8118M/WZ549 (WZ475)
8119M/WR971
8122M/XD613
8128M/WH775
8139M/XJ582
8140M/XJ571
8141M/XN688
8142M/XJ560
8143M/XN691
8147M/XR526
8151M/WV795
8153M/WV903
8154M/WV908
8155M/WV797
8156M/XE339
8158M/XE369
8159M/XD528
8160M/XD622
8161M/XE993
8162M/WM913
8163M/XP919
8164M/WF299
8169M/WH364
8171M/XJ607
8172M/XJ609
8173M/XN685
8174M/WZ576
8177M/WM224
8179M/XN928
8180M/XN930
8182M/XN953
8183M/XN962
8184M/WT520
8186M/WR977
8187M/WH791
8188M/XG327
8189M/WD646
8190M/XJ918
8192M/XR658
8194M/XK862
8196M/XE920
8197M/WT346
8198M/WT339
8203M/XD377
8205M/XN819
8206M/WG419
8207M/WD318
8208M/WG303
8209M/WG418
8210M/WG471
8211M/WK570
8212M/WK587
8213M/WK626
8215M/WP869
8216M/WP927
8217M/WZ866
8222M/XJ604
8224M/XN699
8226M/XP921
8229M/XM355
8230M/XM362
8231M/XM375
8232M/XM381
8233M/XM408
8234M/XN458
8235M/XN549
8236M/XP573
8237M/XS179
8238M/XS180
8239M/XS210
8344M/WH960
8345M/XG540
8346M/XN734
8350M/WH840
8352M/XN632
8355M/KG374 /KN645
8357M/WK576
8359M/WF825
8360M/WP863
8361M/WB670
8362M/WG477
8363M/WG463
8364M/WG464
8365M/XK421
8366M/XG454
8367M/XG474
8368M/XF926
8369M/WE139
8370M/N1671
8371M/XA847
8372M/K8042
8373M/P2617
8375M/NX611
8376M/RF398
8377M/R9125
8378M/T9707
8379M/DG590
8380M/Z7197
8382M/VR930
8383M/K9942
8384M/X4590
8385M/N5912
8386M/NV778
8387M/T6296
8388M/XL993
8389M/VX573
8390M/SL542
8392M/SL674
8393M/XK987
8394M/WG422
8395M/WF408
8396M/XK740
8398M/WR967
8399M/WR539
8401M/XP686
8402M/XN769
8403M/XK531
8406M/XP831
8407M/XP585
8408M/XS186
8409M/XS209
8410M/XR662
8411M/XM139
8412M/XM147
8413M/XM192
8414M/XM173
8415M/XM181
8416M/XM183
8417M/XM144
8418M/XM178
8422M/XM169
8427M/XM172
8428M/XH593
8429M/XH592
8431M/XR651
8434M/XM411
8435M/XN512
8436M/XN554
8437M/WG362
8438M/XP761
8439M/WZ846
8440M/WD935
8441M/XR107
8442M/XP411
8444M/XP400
8445M/XK968
8446M/XP748
8447M/XP359
8453M/XP745
8454M/XP442
8455M/XP444
8457M/XS871
8458M/XP672
8459M/XR650
8460M/XP680
8462M/XX477
8463M/XP355
8465M/W1048
8466M/L-866
8467M/WP912
8470M/PN999
8472M/VH513
8473M/WP180
8487M/J-1172
8488M/WL627
8489M/XN816
8490M/WH703
8491M/WJ880
8492M/WJ872
8493M/XR571
8494M/XP557
8495M/XR672
8497M/XM698
8498M/XR670
8499M/XP357
8501M/XP640
8502M/XP686
8503M/XS451
8505M/XL384
8506M/XR704
8507M/XS215
8508M/XS218
8509M/XT141
8510M/XP567
8511M/WT305
8513M/XN724
8514M/XS176
8515M/WH869
8516M/XR643
8517M/XA932
8531M/XS418
8532M/XS423
8533M/XS449
8534M/XS450

RAF Maintenance cross-reference

8535M/XS454
8538M/XN781
8546M/XN728
8548M/WT507
8549M/WT534
8550M/XT595
8551M/XN774
8554M/TG511
8556M/XN855
8558M/XP439
8559M/XN467
8560M/XR569
8561M/XS100
8562M/XS110
8564M/XN387
8565M/E-408 (XF979)
8566M/(XV279) XV555
8567M/WL738
8568M/XP503
8569M/XR535
8570M/XR954
8571M/XR984
8572M/XM706
8573M/XM708
8574M/XM705
8575M/XP542
8576M/XP502
8577M/XP532
8578M/XR534
8579M/XR140
8580M/XP516
8581M/WJ775
8582M/XE874
8584M/WH903
8585M/XE670
8586M/XE643
8587M/XP677
8588M/XR681
8589M/XR700
8590M/XM191
8591M/XA893
8592M/XM969
8595M/XH278
8598M/WP270
8602M/XR541
8603M/XR951
8604M/XS104
8606M/XP530
8607M/XP538
8608M/XP540
8609M/XR953
8610M/XL502
8611M/WF128
8612M/XD182
8613M/XJ724
8614M/XP515
8615M/XP532
8616M/XP541
8617M/XM709
8618M/XP504
8619M/XP511
8620M/XP534
8621M/XR538
8622M/XR980
8623M/XR998
8624M/XS102
8625M/XS105
8626M/XS109
8627M/XP558
8628M/XJ380
8630M/WG362
8631M/XR574
8632M/XP533
8634M/WP314
8635M/XP514
8636M/XR540
8637M/XR991
8638M/XS101
8639M/XS107
8640M/XR977
8641M/XR987
8642M/XR537
8643M/WJ867
8645M/XD163
8646M/XK969
8647M/XP338
8648M/XK526
8650M/XP333
8652M/WH794
8653M/XS120
8654M/XL898
8655M/XN126
8656M/XP405
8657M/VZ634
8660M/XW538
8661M/XJ727
8662M/XR458
8664M/WJ603
8665M/WL754
8667M/WP972
8668M/WJ821
8670M/XL384
8671M/XJ435
8672M/XP351
8673M/XD165
8674M/XP395
8676M/XL577
8677M/XJ695 (XF519)
8678M/XE656
8679M/XF526
8680M/XF527
8681M/XG164
8682M/XP404
8683M/WJ870
8684M/XJ634
8685M/XF516
8686M/XG158
8687M/XJ639
8689M/WK144
8691M/WT518
8692M/WL741
8693M/WH863
8695M/WJ817
8696M/WH773
8697M/WJ825
8699M/ZD232
8700M/ZD234
8701M/XP352
8702M/XG196
8703M/VW453
8704M/XN643
8705M/XT281
8706M/XF383
8707M/XF386
8708M/XF509
8709M/XG209
8710M/XG274
8711M/XG290
8712M/XF439
8713M/XG225
8714M/XK149
8715M/XG264 (XF445)
8716M/XV155
8718M/XX396
8719M/XT257
8721M/XP354
8722M/WJ640
8723M/XL567
8724M/XW923
8726M/XP299
8727M/XR486
8728M/WT532
8729M/WJ815
8730M/XD186
8731M/XP361
8732M/XJ729
8733M/XL318
8734M/XM657
8735M/WJ681
8736M/XF375
8738M/XJ695 (XF519)
8739M/XH170
8740M/WE173
8741M/XW329
8743M/WD790
8745M/XL392
8746M/XH171
8747M/WJ629
8749M/XH537
8751M/XT255
8752M/XR509
8753M/WL795
8754M/XG882
8755M/WJ637 (WH699)
8756M/XL427
8757M/XM656
8760M/XL386
8761M/WJ977
8762M/WH740
8763M/WH665
8764M/XP344
8766M/XJ782
8767M/XX635
8768M/A-522
8769M/A-528
8770M/XL623
8771M/XM602
8772M/WR960
8773M/XV156
8774M/XV338
8776M/XV152
8777M/XX914
8778M/XM598
8779M/XM607
8780M/WK102
8781M/WE982
8782M/XH136
8783M/XW272
8784M/VP976
8785M/XS642
8786M/XN495
8791M/XP329
8792M/XP345
8793M/XP346
8794M/XP398
8795M/VP958
8796M/XK943
8797M/XX947
8798M/XG151
8799M/WV787
8800M/XG226
8801M/XS650
8802M/XJ608
8805M/XT772
8806M/XP140
8807M/XL587
8808M/XP695
8810M/XJ825
8811M/XL445
8813M/VT260
8814M/XM927
8815M/XX118
8816M/XX734
8819M/XS479
8820M/VP952
8821M/XX115
8822M/VP957
8823M/VP965
8824M/VP971
8825M/WB530
8826M/XV638
8827M/XX300
8828M/XS587
8829M/XE653
8830M/XF515
8831M/XG160
8832M/XG172
8833M/XL569
8834M/XL572
8835M/XL576
8836M/XL592
8837M/XL617
8838M/429366
8839M/XG194
8840M/XG252
8844M/XJ676
8845M/XS572
8846M/XE673
8847M/XX344
8848M/XZ135
8850M/XV436
8851M/XT595
8852M/XV337
8853M/XT277
8854M/XV154
8855M/XT284
8856M/XT274
8857M/XW544
8858M/XW541
8859M/XW545
8860M/XW549
8861M/XW528
8862M/XN473
8863M/XG154
8864M/WJ678
8865M/XN641
8866M/XL609
8867M/XK532
8868M/WH775
8869M/WH957
8870M/WH964
8871M/WJ565
8873M/XR453
8874M/XE597
8875M/XE624
8876M/VN791 (XA312)
8877M/XP159
8878M/XR993
8879M/XX948
8880M/XF435
8881M/XG254
8882M/XR396
8883M/XX946
8884M/VX275
8885M/XW922
8886M/XA243
8887M/WK162
8888M/XA231
8889M/XN239
8890M/WT532
8892M/XL618
8893M/WT745
8894M/XT669
8895M/XX746
8896M/XX821
8897M/XX969
8898M/XX109
8899M/XX786
8900M/XZ368
8901M/XZ383
8902M/XX739
8903M/XX747
8904M/XX966
8905M/XX975
8906M/XX976
8907M/XZ371
8908M/XZ382
8909M/XV784
8910M/XL160
8911M/XH673
8912M/XL189
8913M/
8914M/
8915M/
8916M/
8917M/
8918M/
8919M/
8920M/
8921M/
8922M/
8923M/
8924M/
8925M/
8926M/
8927M/
8928M/
8929M/
8930M/
8931M/
8932M/
8933M/
8934M/
8935M/
8936M/
8937M/
8938M/
8939M/
8940M/
8941M/
8942M/
8943M/
8944M/
8945M/
8946M/
8947M/
8948M/
8949M/
8950M/

RN engineerings 'A' airframe number cross-reference for serials listed in Military Aircraft Markings

A646/SX300
A680/DE373
A2001/W5984 (HS618)
A2054/SX300
A2055/SX336
A2127/DE373
A2439/WF219
A2472/XA508
A2483/WF259
A2503/WM994
A2509/WF299
A2510/WM913
A2511/WM983 (XE364)
A2517/WM961
A2522/WM993
A2525/XN334
A2526/WV911
A2527/XP107
A2530/WM969
A2531/WG718
A2532/WV826
A2534/XE368
A2538/XJ393
A2539/XG831
A2540/WN464
A2542/XA862
A2543/XA870
A2556/XE327
A2557/WV798
A2571/XG577
A2572/XJ402
A2574/XD332
A2575/XG574
A2576/WV198
A2577/XB480
A2579/XN332
A2580/XE369
A2581/XK532
A2597/XS509
A2598/XJ482
A2600/XN934
A2602/XN925
A2603/XK911
A2605/XN308
A2607/XK944
A2608/XA459
A2609/XM329
A2610/XN647
A2611/XJ575
A2612/XN650
A2614/XN314
A2615/XT256
A2616/XN651
A2618/XP116
A2619/XS695
A2620/XN650
A2621/XJ584
A2622/XJ602
A2623/XN697
A2624/XN692
A2625/XL846
A2626/XL847
A2627/XN967
A2628/XP558
A2629/XM667
A2630/XL853
A2632/WV903
A2633/XE369
A2635/XF339
A2637/WV797
A2639/XN650
A2640/XP155
A2642/XL836
A2643/XN311 (XN296)
A2645/WF225
A2646/XK988
A2647/XS463
A2648/XS125
A2649/XS869
A2650/XP160
A2651/XG596
A2653/XK943
A2654/XN302
A2655/XN953
A2658/XP984
A2659/XV669
A2660/WV908
A2661/WV795
A2662/WF299
A2663/XN309
A2664/XV644
A2666/XS872
A2667/XP226
A2668/XS885
A2669/XP149
A2670/XS128
A2671/XS867
A2672/XS537
A2673/WF122
A2674/WF125
A2675/XS881
A2676/XR572
A2677/XR993
A2678/XR955
A2679/XP535
A2680/XP157
A2681/XP117
A2682/XM845
A2683/XS878
A2684/XP151
A2685/XS886
A2686/XS873
A2687/XS877
A2688/XP158
A2689/XM874
A2690/XS887
A2691/XS868
A2692/XM917
A2693/XM843
A2694/XS865
A2695/XS876
A2696/XS882
A2697/XS870
A2699/XS570
A2700/XP980
A2701/XL500
A2702/XS545
A2703/XT441
A2705/XS866
A2706/XM868
A2707/XS122
A2708/XR540
A2709/XR991
A2710/
A2712/XN359
A2713/XN386
A2714/XL880
A2715/
A2716/
A2717/
A2718/
A2719/
A2720/
A2721/
A2722/XT757
A2723/XT487
A2724/
A2725/
A2726/
A2727/
A2728/
A2729/
A2730/
A2731/
A2732/
A2733/
A2734/
A2735/
A2736/
A2737/
A2738/
A2739/
A2740/
A2741/
A2742/
A2743/
A2744/
A2745/
A2746/
A2747/
A2748/
A2749/
A2750/

RAF Gliding and Soaring Association Markings

Notes	Identity	Type, Previous Identity and Competition Number	Club and Location
	R1	Schempp-Hirth Janus C (BGA 2723)	Cranwell GC, RAF Cranwell
	R2	Schempp-Hirth Janus C	RAFG&SA Centre, RAF Bicester
	R3	Schleicher ASK-13	RAFG&SA Centre, RAF Bicester
	R4	Schleicher ASK-13	Anglia GC, RAF Wattisham
	R5	Schleicher Ka-7	Four Counties GC, RAF Syerston
	R7	Schleicher ASK-13	Clevelands GC, RAF Dishforth
	R8	Grob G102 Astir CS (OY-XGE)	RAFG&SA Centre, RAF Bicester
	R9	Schempp-Hirth Janus B	Four Counties GC, RAF Syerston
	R10	Schempp-Hirth Discus B [R10]	RAFG&SA Centre, RAF Bicester
	R11	Schempp-Hirth Discus	Chilterns GC, RAF Halton
	R15	Schleicher Ka-7	RAFG&SA Centre, RAF Bicester
	R16	Schempp-Hirth Ventus [16]	Bannerdown GC, RAF Hullavington
	R18	Schleicher ASW-19 [R18]	Fenlands GC, RAF Marham
	R20	Schleicher ASK-21	Bannerdown GC, RAF Hullavington
	R21	Schleicher ASK-21	RAFG&SA Centre, RAF Bicester
	R22	Schleicher ASK-21	Wrekin GC, RAF Cosford
	R25	Schleicher ASK-21	Fulmar GC, RAF Kinloss
	R26	Schempp-Hirth Nimbus 3 [26]	RAFG&SA Centre, RAF Bicester
	R27	Schempp-Hirth Ventus [27]	RAFG&SA Centre, RAF Bicester
	R29	Schleicher Ka-7	Humber GC, RAF Scampton
	R30	Glaser-Dirks DG-300 [R30]	Humber GC, RAF Scampton
	R32	Schleicher ASK-18	Fulmar GC, RAF Kinloss
	R33	Schleicher ASK-18	RAFG&SA Centre, RAF Bicester
	R34	Schleicher ASK-21	Bannerdown GC, RAF Hullavington
	R36	Schleicher ASK-18	Four Counties GC, RAF Syerston
	R37	Schleicher ASK-13	Wrekin GC, RAF Cosford
	R40	Schleicher ASK-21	RAFG&SA Centre, RAF Bicester
	R41	Schleicher ASK-13	Chilterns GC, RAF Halton
	R42	Schleicher K-8b	Anglia GC, RAF Wattisham
	R43	Schleicher ASK-18	Wrekin GC, RAF Cosford
	R44	Schleicher K-8b	RAFG&SA Centre, RAF Bicester
	R45	Schleicher K-8b	Fulmar GC, RAF Kinloss
	R46	Schleicher ASK-13	Fenlands GC, RAF Marham
	R47	Schleicher K-8b	Cranwell GC, RAF Cranwell
	R49	Schleicher ASK-18	Bannerdown GC, RAF Hullavington
	R50	Grob G103 Acro	RAFG&SA Centre, RAF Bicester
	R57	Grob G102 Astir	Four Counties GC, RAF Syerston
	R58	Grob G103a Twin Astir Acro (BGA 2873)	Four Counties GC, RAF Syerston
	R60	Grob G102 Astir	Clevelands GC, RAF Dishforth
	R63	Grob G102 Astir	Humber GC, RAF Scampton
	R66	Grob G102 Astir	Cranwell GC, RAF Cranwell
	R67	Grob G102 Astir	Anglia GC, RAF Wattisham
	R68	Grob G102 Astir	Wrekin GC, RAF Cosford
	R69	Grob G102 Astir	Fenlands GC, RAF Marham
	R75	Schleicher K-8b	Fenlands GC, RAF Marham
	R77	Grob G102 Astir	RAFG&SA Centre, RAF Bicester
	R78	Grob G102 Astir	Bannerdown GC, RAF Hullavington
	R82	Grob G102 Astir	Fulmar GC, RAF Kinloss
	R84	Grob G102 Astir	Chilterns GC, RAF Halton
	R85	Schleicher K-8b	Fenlands GC, RAF Marham
	R86	Schleicher ASK-13	Fenlands GC, RAF Marham
	R87	Schempp-Hirth Ventus [87]	Four Counties GC, RAF Syerston
	R88	Schleicher ASK-13	Humber GC, RAF Scampton
	R95	Schleicher K-8b	Clevelands GC, RAF Dishforth
	R96	Schleicher K-8b	Chilterns GC, RAF Halton
	R98	Schleicher K-8b	Humber GC, RAF Scampton
	232	Rolladen-Schneider LS4 [232]	Cranwell GC, RAF Cranwell

RN Gliding and Soaring Association Markings

Identity	*Type, Previous Identity and Competition Number*	*Club and Location*	*Notes*
N1	Eiri PiK-20D (BGA 2537/786)	Portsmouth Naval GC, RNAS Lee-on-Solent	
N11	Schleicher K-8b (BGA 2142)	Portsmouth Naval GC, RNAS Lee-on-Solent	
N12	Grob G102 Astir II (BGA 2630)	Portsmouth Naval GC, RNAS Lee-on-Solent	
N14	Slingsby T50 Skylark 4 (BGA 1239/103)	Portsmouth Naval GC, RNAS Lee-on-Solent	
N21	Slingsby T21B Sedbergh (BGA 673)	Portsmouth Naval GC, RNAS Lee-on-Solent	
N22	Omnipol L-13 Blanik (BGA 2407)	Portsmouth Naval GC, RNAS Lee-on-Solent	
N23	Slingsby T49B Capstan (BGA 1196)	Portsmouth Naval GC, RNAS Lee-on-Solent	
N27	Schleicher Ka-7 (BGA 1157)	Portsmouth Naval GC, RNAS Lee-on-Solent	
N29	Schleicher ASK-13 (BGA 3254)	Portsmouth Naval GC, RNAS Lee-on-Solent	
N51	Centrair 101A Pegasus (BGA 2987/EVM)	Seahawk GC, RNAS Culdrose	
N52	SZD-30 Pirat II (BGA 1551/CHG)	Seahawk GC, RNAS Culdrose	
N53	LET L-13 Blanik (BGA 2263/DPC)	Seahawk GC, RNAS Culdrose	
N54	Slingsby T.49B Capstan (BGA 1360/BZG)	Seahawk GC, RNAS Culdrose	
N55	Slingsby T.49B Capstan (BGA 1118/BPD)	Seahawk GC, RNAS Culdrose	

RN Landing Platform and Shore Station Code-letters

Alpha-Numeric Sequence

Notes	Sqn code	Deck letters	Name and Pennant Number	Type/task
	323	AB	HMS *Ambuscade* (F172)	Type 21
	430	AC	HMS *Achilles* (F12)	Leander
	455	AE	HMS *Ariadne* (F72)	Leander
	341	AG	HMS *Avenger* (F185)	Type 21
	421	AJ	HMS *Ajax* (F114)	Leander
	327	AL	HMS *Alacrity* (F174)	Type 21
	472	AM	HMS *Andromeda* (F57)	Leander
	470	AP	HMS *Apollo* (F70)	Leander
	426	AR	HMS *Arethusa* (F38)	Leander
	466	AT	HMS *Argonaut* (F56)	Leander
	422	AU	HMS *Aurora* (F10)	Leander
	322	AV	HMS *Active* (F171)	Type 21
	326	AW	HMS *Arrow* (F173)	Type 21
	320	AZ	HMS *Amazon* (F169)	Type 21
	328	BA	HMS *Brave* (F94)	Type 22
	—	BD	RFA *Sir Bedivere* (L3004)	Landing ship
	—	BE	RFA *Blue Rover* (A270)	Fleet tanker
	440	BK	HMS *Berwick* (F115)	Type 12
	333	BM	HMS *Birmingham* (D86)	Type 42
	334	BS	HMS *Bristol* (D23)	Type 82
	342	BT	HMS *Brilliant* (F90)	Type 22
	—	BV	HMS *Black Rover* (A273)	Fleet tanker
	346	BW	HMS *Broadsword* (F88)	Type 22
	403	BX	HMS *Battleaxe* (F89)	Type 22
	330	BZ	HMS *Brazen* (F91)	Type 22
	335	CF	HMS *Cardiff* (D108)	Type 42
	—	CH	HMS *Challenger* (K07)	Seabed ops
	463	CP	HMS *Cleopatra* (F28)	Leander
	—	CU	RNAS Culdrose (HMS *Seahawk*)	
	—	CW	HMS *Cornwall* (F99)	Type 22
	431	CY	HMS *Charybdis* (F75)	Leander
	—	DC	HMS *Dumbarton Castle* (P268)	Fishery protection
	—	DG	RFA *Diligence* (A132)	Maintenance
	423	DM	HMS *Diomede* (F16)	Leander
	464	DN	HMS *Danae* (F47)	Leander
	411	EB	HMS *Edinburgh* (D97)	Type 42
	434/5	ED	HMS *Endurance* (A171)	Ice Patrol
	—	EN	RFA *Engadine* (K08)	Helicopter support
	433	EU	HMS *Euryalus* (F15)	Leander
	420	EX	HMS *Exeter* (D89)	Type 42
	342	FA	RFA *Fort Austin* (A386)	Support ship
	404	FF	HMS *Fife* (D20)	County
	343	FG	RFA *Fort Grange* (A385)	Support ship
	—	FL	RNAY Fleetlands	
	—	FS	HMS *Fearless* (L10)	Assault
	461	GA	HMS *Galatea* (F18)	Leander
	410	GC	HMS *Gloucester* (D96)	Type 42
	—	GN	RFA *Green Rover* (A268)	Fleet tanker
	—	GR	RFA *Sir Geraint* (L3027)	Landing ship
	—	GV	RFA *Gold Rover* (A271)	Fleet tanker
	344	GW	HMS *Glasgow* (D88)	Type 42
	—	GY	RFA *Grey Rover* (A269)	Fleet tanker
	416	HL	HMS *Hecla* (A133)	Hecla
	475	HM	HMS *Hermione* (F58)	Leander
	325	HR	HMS *Herald* (A138)	Hecla
	414	HT	HMS *Hecate* (A137)	Hecla
	—	ID	HMS *Intrepid* (L11)	Assault
	465	JO	HMS *Juno* (F52)	Leander
	443	JP	HMS *Jupiter* (F60)	Leander
	—	L	HMS *Illustrious* (R06)	Carrier
	—	LC	HMS *Leeds Castle* (P258)	Fishery protection

Sqn code	*Deck letters*	*Name and Pennant Number*	*Type/task*	*Notes*
—	LN	RFA *Sir Lancelot* (L3029)	Landing ship	
332	LP	HMS *Liverpool* (D92)	Type 42	
—	LS	RNAS Lee-on-Solent (HMS *Daedalus*)		
360	MC	HMS *Manchester* (D95)	Type 42	
424	MV	HMS *Minerva* (F45)	Leander	
—	N	HMS *Invincible* (R05)	Carrier	
324	NA	HMS *Naiad* (F39)	Leander	
345	NC	HMS *Newcastle* (D87)	Type 42	
417	NM	HMS *Nottingham* (D91)	Type 42	
347	OD	RFA *Olmeda* (A124)	Fleet tanker	
347	ON	RFA *Olna* (A123)	Fleet tanker	
347	OW	RFA *Olwen* (A122)	Fleet tanker	
471	PB	HMS *Phoebe* (F42)	Leander	
445	PL	HMS *Plymouth* (F126)	Type 12	
454	PN	HMS *Penelope* (F127)	Leander	
—	PO	RNAS Portland (HMS *Osprey*)		
—	PV	RFA *Sir Percival* (L3036)	Landing ship	
—	PW	Prestwick Airport (HMS *Gannet*)		
—	R	HMS *Ark Royal* (R09)	Carrier	
436	RG	RFA *Regent* (A486)	Support ship	
462	RO	HMS *Rothesay* (F107)	Type 12	
437	RS	RFA *Resource* (A480)	Support ship	
432	SC	HMS *Scylla* (F71)	Leander	
334	SN	HMS *Southampton* (D90)	Type 42	
450	SS	HMS *Sirius* (F40)	Leander	
—	TM	RFA *Sir Tristram* (L3505)	Landing ship	
347	TS	RFA *Tidespring* (A75)	Fleet tanker	
375	VB	HMS *Beaver* (F93)	Type 22	
—	VL	RNAS Yeovilton (HMS *Heron*)		
—	WU	RNAY Wroughton		
376	XB	HMS *Boxer* (F92)	Type 22	
407	YK	HMS *York* (D98)	Type 42	
456	YM	HMS *Yarmouth* (F101)	Type 12	
405		HMS *London* (F95)	Type 22	
		HMS *Sheffield* (F96)	Type 22	
		HMS *Coventry* (F98)	Type 22	
		RFA *Oakleaf*	Fleet tanker	
		RFA *Orangeleaf*		
		HMS *Norfolk*	Type 23	
		HMS *Argyll*	Type 23	
		HMS *Lancaster*	Type 23	
		HMS *Marlborough*	Type 23	

Ships' Numeric Code — Deck Letters Analysis

	0	1	2	3	4	5	6	7	8
32	AZ		AV	AB	NA	HR	AW	AL	BA
33	BZ		LP	BM	BS SN	CF			
34		AG	BJ FA	FG	GW	NC	BW	OD ON OW TS	
36	MC								
37						VB	XB		
40				BX	FF			YK	
41	GC	EB			HT		HL	NM	
42	EX	AJ	AU	DM	MV		AR		
43	AC	CY	SC	EU	ED	ED	RG	RS	
44	BK			JP		PL			
45	SS				PN	AE	YM		
46		GA	RO	CP	DN	JO	AT		
47	AP	PB	AM			HM			

RN Code-Squadron-Base-Aircraft Cross-check

Code Numbers	*Deck/Base Letters*	*Unit*	*Location*	*Aircraft Type(s)*
000 – 005	R	801 Sqn	Yeovilton	Sea Harrier FRS1
010 – 019	N	820 Sqn	Culdrose	Sea King HAS5
123 – 127	L	800 Sqn	Yeovilton	Sea Harrier FRS1
130 – 139	—	826 Sqn	Culdrose	Sea King HAS5
180 – 187	—	849 Sqn	Culdrose	Sea King AEW2
252 – 254	—	824 Sqn	Culdrose	Sea King HAS5
264 – 274	—	814 Sqn	Culdrose	Sea King HAS5
300 – 306	PO	815 Sqn	Portland	Lynx HAS2/HAS3
320 – 479	*	815/829 Sqns	Portland	Lynx HAS2/HAS3/Wasp HAS1
500 – 511	—	810 Sqn	Culdrose	Sea King HAS5
538 – 559	CU	705 Sqn	Culdrose	Gazelle HT2
560 – 575	CU	750 Sqn	Culdrose	Jetstream T2
576 – 579	—	750 Sqn	Culdrose	Jetstream T3
582 – 597	—	706 Sqn	Culdrose	Sea King HAS5
600 – 604	PO	829 Sqn	Portland	Lynx HAS2/HAS3
605 – 612	PO	829 Sqn	Portland	Wasp HAS1
620 – 628	PO	772 Sqn	Portland	Wessex HU5
630 – 638	PO	702 Sqn	Portland	Lynx HAS2/HAS3
640 – 648	PO	702 Sqn	Portland	Lynx HAS2/HAS3
701 – 707	PW	819 Sqn	Prestwick	Sea King HAS5
710 – 718	VL	899 Sqn	Yeovilton	Sea Harrier FRS1/T4N
719 – 720	VL	899 Sqn	Yeovilton	Hunter T8M
816 – 817	CU	771 Sqn	Culdrose	Chipmunk T10
818 – 819	CU	771 Sqn	Culdrose	Sea Devon C20
820 – 826	CU	771 Sqn	Culdrose	Wessex HU5
830 – 838	VL	FRADU	Yeovilton	Hunter GA11
840 – 848	VL	FRADU	Yeovilton	Canberra TT18
850 – 856	VL	FRADU	Yeovilton	Canberra T22
860 – 868	VL	FRADU	Yeovilton	Hunter GA11
869 – 880	VL	FRADU	Yeovilton	Hunter T7/T8
901 – 912	—	FGF	Plymouth	Chipmunk T10

*See foregoing separate ships' Deck Letter analysis

British-based Historic Aircraft in Overseas Markings

Some 'Historic' aircraft carry the markings of overseas air arms and can be seen in the UK, mainly preserved in museums and collections or taking part in air shows.

Serial	*Type (alternative identity)*	*Owner, operator and location*	*Notes*
Argentina			
A-517	FMA IA58 Pucara (G-BLRP)	Privately owned, Headcorn	
A-522	FMA IA58 Pucara (8768M)	FAA Museum, RNAS Yeovilton	
A-528	FMA IA58 Pucara (8769M)	Museum of Army Flying, Middle Wallop	
A-533	FMA IA58 Pucara (ZD486)	Museum of Army Flying, Middle Wallop	
A-549	FMA IA58 Pucara (ZD487)	Imperial War Museum, Duxford	
AE-406	Bell UH-1H [656]	Museum of Army Flying, Middle Wallop	
AE-409	Bell UH-1H	Museum of Army Flying, Middle Wallop	
AE-422	Bell UH-1H	FAA Museum, RNAS Yeovilton	
AE-424	Bell UH-1H (G-BMLA)	Privately owned, Headcorn	
AE-520	Vertol CH-47C Chinook	RAF store, Wroughton	
0729	Beech T-34C Turbo Mentor [1-A-411]	FAA Museum, RNAS Yeovilton	
0767	Macchi MB339AA [4-A-116]	FAA Museum, RNAS Yeovilton	
Australia			
A2-4	Supermarine Seagull V (VH-ALB)	Battle of Britain Museum, Hendon	
A16-199	Lockheed Hudson IV (G-BEOX) (FH174) [SF-R]	RAF Museum, Hendon	
Belgium			
FT-36	Lockheed T-33A	Dumfries & Galloway Aviation Museum, Tinwald Downs	
FT-37	Lockheed T-33A	RAF Alconbury	
HD-75	Hanriot HD1 (OO-APJ/G-AFDX/N75)	RAF Museum, Hendon	
Canada			
920	VS Stranraer (CF-BXO) [Q-N]	RAF Museum, Hendon	
5547	Hawker Hurricane II (G-HURI)	Privately owned, Coventry	
9059	Bristol Bolingbroke IVT	Privately owned, Portsmouth	
9893	Bristol Bolingbroke IVT	Privately owned, Duxford	
9940	Bristol Bolingbroke IVT	Royal Scottish Museum of Flight, East Fortune	
10038	Bristol Bolingbroke IVT (G-MKIV)	Privately owned, Duxford	
10201	Bristol Bolingbroke IVT	Strathallan Aircraft Collection	
18393	Avro Canada CF-100 (G-BCYK)	Imperial War Museum, Duxford	
20385	CCF AT-16 Harvard IV (G-BGPB)	Harvard Formation Team, North Weald	
5481	Hawker Hurricane	Privately owned, Sandown	
Denmark			
E-402	Hawker Hunter F51	Lovaux, Hurn	
E-407	Hawker Hunter F51	Privately owned, Lutterworth	
E-419	Hawker Hunter F51	North East Aircraft Museum, Usworth	
E-421	Hawker Hunter F51	Brooklands College of Technology, Surrey	
E-423	Hawker Hunter F51	Second World War Aircraft Preservation Society, Lasham	
E-424	Hawker Hunter F51	Lincolnshire Aviation Museum, East Kirkby	
E-425	Hawker Hunter F51	Midland Air Museum, Coventry	
E-427	Hawker Hunter F51 (G-9-447)	BAe OTD, Hull	
E-430	Hawker Hunter F51	Privately owned, Faygate	
ET-273	Hawker Hunter T7	Lovaux, Macclesfield	
L866	Consolidated Catalina (8466M)	RAF Cosford Aerospace Museum	
Eire			
177	Percival Provost T1 (G-BLIW)	Privately owned, Shoreham	
178	Percival Provost T1 (G-BKOS)	Privately owned, Kingsclere	

Historic Aircraft

Notes	Serial	Type (alternative identity)	Owner, operator and location
	Finland		
	VI-3	Valtion Viima (G-BAAY)	Privately owned, White Waltham
	France		
	9	Dassault Mystere IVA	RAF Bentwaters
	16	Dassault Mystere IVA	RAF Lakenheath
	19	Deperdussin Replica (BAPC136)	Leisure Sport, Thorpe Park
	25	Dassault Mystere IVA	RAF Woodbridge
	36	Dassault Mystere IVA [EABDR 8]	RAF Upper Heyford
	37	Nord 3400 [MAB]	Privately owned, Coventry
	39	Nord 3400 [MOC]	Privately owned, Coventry
	45	SNCAN Stampe SV4C (G-BHFG)	Privately owned, Enstone
	46	Dassault Mystere IVA [EABDR 6]	RAF Upper Heyford
	50	Dassault Mystere IVA	RAF Woodbridge
	57	Dassault Mystere IVA [8-MT]	Imperial War Museum, Duxford
	59	Dassault Mystere IVA [314-TH]	Wales Aircraft Museum, Cardiff
	60	Dassault Mystere IVA [8-MT]	RAF Lakenheath Fire Section
	65	Nord 3202 (G-BMBF)	Privately owned, Breighton
	68	Nord 3400 [MHA]	Privately owned, Coventry
	70	Dassault Mystere IVA	Midland Air Museum, Coventry
	75	Dassault Mystere IVA	RAF Lakenheath
	79	Dassault Mystere IVA [8-NB]	Norfolk & Suffolk Aviation Museum, Flixton
	83	Dassault Mystere IVA [8-MS]	Newark Air Museum, Winthorpe
	84	Dassault Mystere IVA	Lashenden Air Warfare Museum, Headcorn
	85	Dassault Mystere IVA [8-MV]	Confederate Air Force, Coventry
	92	MH Broussard (G-BJGW) [31-GW]	Privately owned, Duxford
	97	Dassault Mystere IVA	RAF Lakenheath
	99	Dassault Mystere IVA	RAF Lakenheath
	101	Dassault Mystere IVA [8-MN]	Bomber County Aviation Museum, Cleethorpes
	103	Nord Norecrin (G-BHXJ)	Privately owned, Popham
	104	Dassault Mystere IVA	RAF Bentwaters
	113	Dassault Mystere IVA	RAF Lakenheath
	120	Stampe SV4C (G-AZGC)	Privately owned, Booker
	121	Dassault Mystere IVA [8-MY]	City of Norwich Aviation Museum
	121	Nord 3400 [MJA]	Privately owned, Coventry
	124	Nord 3400 [MOO]	Privately owned, Coventry
	126	Dassault Mystere IVA	RAF Lakenheath
	127	Dassault Mystere IVA [EABDR 7]	RAF Upper Heyford
	133	Dassault Mystere IVA	RAF Woodbridge
	139	Dassault Mystere IVA [EABDR 9]	RAF Upper Heyford
	145	Dassault Mystere IVA	RAF Lakenheath
	146	Dassualt Mystere IVA [8-MC]	North East Aircraft Museum, Usworth
	184	Dassault Mystere IVA	RAF Lakenheath, BDRT
	217	MH Broussard (G-BKPU)	Privately owned, Shawdene
	241	Dassault Mystere IVA	RAF Lakenheath
	276	Dassault Mystere IVA	RAF Woodbridge
	285	Dassault Mystere IVA	RAF Lakenheath
	300	Dassault Mystere IVA	RAF Lakenheath
	309	Dassault Mystere IVA	RAF Lakenheath
	318	Dassault Mystere IVA	Dumfries & Galloway Aviation Museum, Tinwald Downs
	319	Dassault Mystere IVA [8-ND]	Rebel Air Museum, Andrewsfield
	1076	Morane MS230 (G-AVEB)	Privately owned, Booker
	3398	Spad XIII Replica (G-BFYO) [2]	FAA Museum, RNAS Yeovilton
	133722	Vought F4U-7 Corsair (NX1337A) [15F22]	Privately owned, Duxford/Sutton Bridge
	Germany		
	C19/18	Albatros Replica (BAPC 118)	Privately owned, North Weald
	D5397/17	Albatros D.VA Replica (G-BFXL)	FAA Museum, RNAS Yeovilton
	5036	Bucker Jungmann (G-ATJX) [AT+JX]	Privately owned, Stapleford Tawney
	D2+600	CASA 352L (G-BFHG)	Aces High, North Weald
	N7+AA	CASA 352L (G-BFHF)	Privately owned, Coventry
	N8+AA	CASA 352L (G-BFHD)	Privately owned, Hurn
	A1+BT	CZL Super Aero (G-APRR)	Privately owned, Elstree
	13064	NA P-47	RAF Museum restoration, Cardington
	475081	Fieseler Fi156C Storch (VP546/ 7362M)	RAF St Athan Historic Aircraft Collection
	28368	Flettner Fl282V Kolibri	Midland Air Museum, Coventry

Serial	Type (alternative identity)	Owner, operator and location	Notes
100143	Focke-Achgelis Fa330	Imperial War Museum, Duxford	
100502	Focke-Achgelis Fa330	Lincolnshire Aviation Museum, East Kirkby	
100509	Focke-Achgelis Fa330	Science Museum, South Kensington	
100545	Focke-Achgelis Fa330	Torbay Aircraft Museum, Paignton	
100549	Focke-Achgelis Fa330	Greater Manchester Museum of Science and Industry	
8	Focke Wulf FW190 Replica (G-WULF)	Privately owned, Elstree	
7334	Focke Wulf FW190 Replica (G-SYFW) [2+1]	Privately owned, Guernsey	
584219/38	Focke Wulf FW190F-8/UI (PN999/8470M)	RAF St Athan Historic Aircraft Collection	
733682	Focke Wulf FW190A-8/R6	Imperial War Museum, Duxford	
4253/18	Fokker D.VII (G-BFPL)	Privately owned, Lower Upham	
5125/18	Fokker D.VII Replica (BAPC 110)	Leisure Sport, Thorpe Park	
8417/18	Fokker D.VII	RAF Museum Restoration Centre, Cardington	
102/18	Fokker Dr.1 Dreidekker Replica (BAPC 88)	FAA Museum, RNAS Yeovilton	
150/17	Fokker Dr.1 Dreidekker Replica (BAPC 139)	Leisure Sport, Thorpe Park	
152/17	Fokker Dr.1 Dreidekker Replica (G-ATJM)	Privately owned, North Weald	
425/17	Fokker Dr.1 Dreidekker Replica (BAPC 133)	Torbay Aircraft Museum, Paignton	
425/17	Fokker Dr.1 Dreidekker Replica (G-BEFR)	Privately owned, St Athan	
422/15	Fokker EIII replica (G-AVJO)	Privately owned, Booker	
22912	Hansa Brandenburg W.29 Replica (BAPC 138)	Leisure Sport, Thorpe Park	
701152	Heinkel He111H-23 (8471M) [NT+SL]	Battle of Britain Museum, Hendon	
120227	Heinkel He162A Salamander (VH513/8472M) [2]	RAF St Athan Historic Aircraft Collection	
120235	Heinkel He162A Salamander	Imperial War Museum, Duxford	
14	Hispano HA1112 (C4K-235/ G-BJZZ)	Privately owned, Sandown	
1Z+NK	Junkers Ju52/3M (6316)	Imperial War Museum, Duxford	
494083	Junkers Ju87D-3 (8474M) [RI+JK]	Battle of Britain Museum, Hendon	
360043	Junkers Ju88R-1 (PJ876/8475M) [D5+EV]	Battle of Britain Museum, Hendon	
7198/18	LVG C.VI (G-AANJ)	Shuttleworth Collection, Old Warden	
6	Messerschmitt Bf109 Replica (BAPC74)	Torbay Aircraft Museum	
14	Messerschmitt Bf109 Replica (BAPC67)	Midland Air Museum, Coventry	
1190	Messerschmitt Bf109E-3	Privately owned, Hurn	
4101	Messerschmitt Bf109E-3 (DG200/ 8477M) [12]	Battle of Britain Museum, Hendon	
10639	Messerschmitt Bf109G-6 (RN228/ 8478M)	RAF Benson, under restoration	
730301	Messerschmitt Bf110G-4 (AX772/ 8479M) [D5+RL]	Battle of Britain Museum, Hendon	
191316	Messerschmitt Me163B Komet	Science Museum, South Kensington	
191614	Messerschmitt Me163B Komet (8481M)	RAF Cosford Aerospace Museum	
191659	Messerschmitt Me163B Komet	Royal Scottish Museum of Flight, East Fortune	
191660	Messerschmitt Me163B Komet [3]	Imperial War Museum, Duxford	
191904	Messerschmitt Me163B Komet (8480M) [25]	RAF St Athan Historic Aircraft Collection	
112372	Messerschmitt Me262A-1 (VK893/ 8482M)	RAF St Athan Historic Aircraft Collection	
420430	Messerschmitt Me410A-1/U2 (8483M) [PD+VO]	RAF St Athan Historic Aircraft Collection	
ZA+WN	Morane-Saulnier MS500 (G-AZMH)	Privately owned, Booker	
FI+S	Morane-Saulnier MS505 (G-BIRW) Criquet	Royal Scottish Museum of Flight, East Fortune	
17	Nord 1002 (G-ATBG)	Privately owned, Sutton Bridge	
1C+RF	Pilatus P-2 (U-110/G-PTWO)	Privately owned, Duxford	
1480	Bf109 Replica (BAPC66)	Hawkinge Aeronautical Trust	
Greece			
52-6541	Republic F-84F Thunderflash	North East Aircraft Museum, Usworth	

Historic Aircraft

Notes	Serial	Type (alternative identity)	Owner, operator and location
	51-6151	Canadair F-86D Sabre	North East Aircraft Museum, Usworth
	India		
	Q497	EE Canberra T4 (WH847)	BAe Samlesbury, stored
	Iraq		
	333	DH Vampire T55 (pod only)	Military Aircraft Preservation Group, Hadfield, Derbys
	Israel		
	28	P-51D	Privately owned, Fowlmere, Cambs
	Italy		
	MM19607	Canadair F-86E Sabre (XB733/ G-ATBF)	Privately owned, Much Hoole, Lancs
	MM5701	Fiat CR42 (BT474/8468M) [13-95]	Battle of Britain Museum, Hendon
	MM53211	Fiat G.46-4 (BAPC 79)	Privately owned, Lympne
	MM53432	NA T-6D [RM-11]	Privately owned, South Wales
	MM53795	NA Harvard IV (G-BJST) [SC-66]	Privately owned, RAF Kemble
	MM53796	NA Harvard IV [SC-52]	Privately owned, RAF Kemble
	MM54137	NA T-6G Texan (G-CTKL)	Privately owned, Dorchester
	MM542540	Piper Super Cub	RAF Woodbridge, stored
	Netherlands		
	E-15	Fokker S-11 Instructor (G-BIYU)	Privately owned, Denham
	R-163	Piper Super Cub (G-BIRH)	Privately owned, Lee-on-Solent
	204/V	Lockheed SP-2H Neptune	RAF Cosford Aerospace Museum
	N-250	Hunter F6 (nose only) [G-9-185]	Science Museum, South Kensington
	Norway		
	56321	Saab Safir (G-BKPY)	Newark Air Museum, Winthorpe
	Poland		
	1420	MiG-15 (G-BMZF)	Aces High, North Weald
	1120	MiG-15	RAF Museum, Hendon
	Portugal		
	3460	Dornier 27 (G-BMFG)	Privately owned, Booker
	3497	Dornier 27 (G-BMFH)	Privately owned, Booker
	South Africa		
	6130	Lockheed Ventura II (AJ469)	RAF Museum Store, Henlow
	Spain		
	T2B-272	CASA C.352L	RAF Cosford Aerospace Museum
	HD5-1	Dornier Do24T-3 [58-1]	RAF Museum, Hendon
	C6-88	Hispano HA.1112	Privately owned, Stubbington
	T2-124	Bf-109K [FE-124]	Warbirds of GB, Bitteswell
	Sweden		
	35075	Saab J-35J Draken [40]	Imperial War Museum, Duxford
	29640	Saab J-29F [08]	Midland Air Museum, Coventry
	32028	A-32A Lansen (G-BMSG)	Privately owned, Cranfield
	Switzerland		
	J-108	Pilatus P-2 (G-BJAX)	Privately owned, Duxford
	U-125	Pilatus P-2 (G-BLKZ)	Privately owned, Goodwood
	U-142	Pilatus P-2 (G-BONE)	Privately owned, Southend
	U-143	Pilatus P-2 (G-CJCI)	Privately owned, Micheldever
	J-1008	DH Vampire FB6	Mosquito Aircraft Museum, London Colney
	J-1172	DH Vampire FB6 (8487M)	Greater Manchester Museum of Science and Industry
	J-1523	DH Venom FB50 (G-VENI)	Privately owned, Cranfield
	J-1601	DH Venom FB50 (G-VIDI)	Privately owned, Cranfield
	J-1605	DH Venom FB50 (G-BLID)	Aces High, Duxford
	J-1614	DH Venom FB50 (G-BLIE)	Privately owned, Glasgow
	J-1632	DH Venom FB50 (G-VNOM)	Privately owned, Cranfield
	J-1704	DH Venom FB54	RAF Cosford Aerospace Museum
	USA		
	0-17899	Convair VT-29B	Imperial War Museum, Duxford

Serial	Type (alternative identity)	Owner, operator and location	Notes
111989	Cessna L-19A Bird Dog (N33600)	Museum of Army Flying, Middle Wallop	
115042	NA T-6G Texan (G-BGHU) [TA-042]	Privately owned, Wellesbourne Mountford	
115302	Piper L-18C (G-BJTP)	Privately owned, Stoke Orchard, Glos	
121714	Grumman F8F-2B Bearcat (NX700H) [S/100]	Privately owned, Duxford	
12392	NA AT-6D Harvard IIB (FE905/LN-BNM)	RAF Museum store, Cardington	
13064	NA P-47	RAF Museum restoration, Cardington	
133854	NA Harvard III (G-SUES)	Privately owned, Biggin Hill	
14060	Lockheed T-33A [LN]	RAF Lakenheath BDRT	
1411	Grumman Widgeon (N444M)	Privately owned, Biggin Hill	
14286	Lockheed T-33A [WK]	Imperial War Museum, Duxford	
14419	Lockheed T-33A [30-QC]	Midland Air Museum, Coventry	
140547	NA T-28C Trojan (N2800Q)	Privately owned, Duxford	
146289	NA T-28C Trojan (N99153)	Norfolk & Suffolk Aviation Museum, Flixton	
150225	Westland Wessex (G-AYNC)	Privately owned, Hurn	
151632	NA TB-25N Mitchell (NL9494Z)	Privately owned, Coventry	
153008	McD F-4N Phantom	RAF Alconbury, BDRT	
155848	McD F-4S Phantom (WS-11/VMFA-232]	FAA Museum, RNAS Yeovilton	
164	Beech 18 (G-BKGL)	British Aerial Museum, Duxford	
16718	Lockheed T-33A	City of Norwich Aviation Museum	
16769	Lockheed T-33A	RAF Mildenhall Fire Section	
17473	Lockheed T-33A	RAF Cosford Aerospace Museum	
17657	Douglas A-26K Invader (FY64)	Privately owned, Southend	
181528	Piper J-3C-65 Cub	Privately owned, Southampton	
18-2001	Piper L-18 Super Cub (G-BIZV)	Privately owned, Compton Abbas	
19252	Lockheed T-33A [314-UY]	Tangmere Military Aviation Museum	
226671	NA P-47D (N47DD) [MX-X]	Privately owned, Duxford	
231983	Boeing B-17G (F-BDRS) [IY-GS]	Imperial War Museum, Duxford	
236800	Piper J-3C-65 Cub (G-BHPK) [A-44]	Privately owned, Sywell	
24535	Kaman HH-43F Huskie	Midland Air Museum, Coventry	
26	Boeing Stearman (G-BAVO)	Privately owned, Liverpool	
27767	Aeronca L-3A (G-BIHW)	Privately owned, Swansea	
2807	NA T-6G Texan (G-BHTH) [111-VE]	Privately owned, Liverpool	
29963	Lockheed T-33A	Wales Aircraft Museum, Cardiff	
315509	Douglas C-47A (G-BHUB)	Imperial War Museum, Duxford	
329417	Piper J-3C-65 Cub (G-BDHK)	Privately owned, Coleford	
329601	Piper J-3C-65 Cub (G-AXHR) [D-44]	Privately owned, Old Warden	
329934	Piper J-3C-65 Cub (G-BCPH) [72-B]	Privately owned, Booker	
413048	Piper J-3C-65 Cub (G-BCXJ) [39-E]	Privately owned, Compton Abbas	
41386	Thomas-Morse S4 Scout Replica (G-MJTD)	Privately owned, Hitchin	
42157	NA F-100D Super Sabre	North East Aviation Museum, Usworth	
42163	NA F-100D Super Sabre [11-YG]	Dumfries & Galloway Aviation Museum, Tinwald Downs	
42165	NA F-100D Super Sabre [11-ML]	Imperial War Museum, Duxford	
42174	NA F-100D Super Sabre	Midland Air Museum, Coventry	
42196	NA F-100D Super Sabre [LT]	Norfolk & Suffolk Aviation Museum, Flixton	
42204	NA F-100D Super Sabre [11-MQ]	RAF Alconbury	
42212	NA F-100D Super Sabre [LN]	RAF Sculthorpe	
42223	NA F-100D Super Sabre	Newark Air Museum, Winthorpe	
42239	NA F-100D Super Sabre [FW-239]	Confederate Air Force, Coventry	
429366	NA TB-25N Mitchell (N9115Z/151645/8838M)	Bomber Command Museum, Hendon	
431171	NA B-25J Mitchell (N7614C)	Imperial War Museum, Duxford	
44	Piper L-18 Super Cub (G-BJLH) [K-33]	Privately owned, Liverpool	
454537	Piper L-4J Cub (G-BFDL) [04-J]	Privately owned, Prestwick	
461748	Boeing B-29A Superfortress (G-BHDK) [Y]	Imperial War Museum, Duxford	
463221	NA P-51D Mustang (N6340T) (really 473149) [G4-S]	Privately owned, Duxford	
472028	NA P-51D Mustang (41 IAF)	Privately owned, Teesside	
472216	NA P-51D Mustang (G-BIXL)	Privately owned, North Weald	

Notes	Serial	Type (alternative identity)	Owner, operator and location
	472258	NA P-51D Mustang (really 473979) [WZ-I]	Imperial War Museum, Duxford
	473877	NA P-51D Mustang (N167F) [B6-S]	Privately owned, Duxford
	479609	Piper J-3C-65 Cub (G-BHXY) [PR]	Privately owned, Barton
	480015	Piper J-3C-65 Cub (G-AKIB)	Privately owned, White Waltham
	480133	Piper J-3C-65 Cub (G-BDCD) [44-B]	Privately owned, Slinfold
	480594	Piper J-3C-65 Cub (G-BEDJ)	Privately owned, Ashford Hill
	483009	NA AT-6 Harvard (really 244450)	Epping Museum, North Weald
	483868	Boeing B-17G Fortress (N5237V) [A-N]	Bomber Command Museum, Hendon
	485784	Boeing B-17G (G-BEDF) [K-G]	Privately owned, Duxford
	51-15227	NA T-6G Harvard (G-BKRA) [10]	Privately owned, Shoreham
	540	Piper L-4 Cub (G-BCNX)	Privately owned, Monewden
	54048	NA F-100D Super Sabre (really 42269) [LN]	RAF Lakenheath, at gate
	542265	NA F-100D Super Sabre [FW-2265]	RAF Wethersfield, at gate
	542447	Piper PA18-135 Super Cub (G-SCUB)	Privately owned, Anwick
	542457	Piper PA18-135 Super Cub (G-LION/R-167)	Privately owned, Orsett
	542474	Piper PA18-135 Super Cub (G-PCUB/R-184)	Privately owned, Redhill
	54433	Lockheed T-33A [WD]	Norfolk & Suffolk Aviation Museum, Flixton
	54439	Lockheed T-33A	North East Aviation Museum, Usworth
	5547	Lockheed T-33A (really 19036)	Newark Air Museum, Winthorpe
	60312	McDonnell F-101F Voodoo [AR]	RAF Alconbury, BDRT
	60689	Boeing B-52D Stratofortress	Imperial War Museum, Duxford
	612414	Boeing CH47A Chinook	RAF Odiham, instructional use
	62-494	Republic F-105G Thunderchief [LN] (really 24434)	RAF Lakenheath, BDRT
	63000	NA F-100D Super Sabre (really 42160) [FW-000]	Wales Aircraft Museum, Cardiff
	63-414	McD F-4C Phantom (37414)	RAF Woodbridge BDRT
	63-419	McD F-4C Phantom (37419)	RAF Alconbury BDRT
	63-428	Republic F-105G Thunderchief [JB] (really 24428)	RAF Upper Heyford
	63-449	McD F-4C Phantom (37449) [SA]	RAF Upper Heyford BDRT
	63-471	McD F-4C Phantom (37471) [LN]	RAF Lakenheath BDRT
	63-610	McD F-4C Phantom (37610)	RAF Lakenheath BDRT
	63-699	McD F-4C Phantom (37699)	RAF Upper Heyford BDRT
	63935	NA F-100F Super Sabre [11-MN]	RAF Alconbury
	63938	NA F-100F Super Sabre [11-MU]	Lashenden Air Warfare Museum, Headcorn
	64-707	McD F-4C Phantom (40707)	RAF Mildenhall BDRT
	6771	Republic F-84F Thunderstreak (52-7133/FU-6)	RAF Museum/RAeS Medway Branch, Rochester
	68-060	GD F111E (pod)	Dumfries & Galloway Aviation Museum, Tinwald Downs
	70270	McDonnell F-101B Voodoo	RAF Woodbridge
	7797	Aeronca L-16A (G-BFAF)	Privately owned, Finmere
	80260	McDonnell F-101B Voodoo	RAF Bentwaters
	82062	DHC U-6A Beaver	Midland Air Museum, Coventry
	88297	Goodyear FG-1D Corsair (N8297) [29]	Privately owned, Duxford
	897	Aeronca Chief (G-BJEV)	Privately owned, Little Gransden
	91007	Lockheed T33A (G-TJET) [TR-007]	Privately owned, Cranfield
	P51D	NA P-51D Mustang (G-PSID) (really 4472258)	Warbirds of GB, Bitteswell

Irish Army Air Corps Military Aircraft Markings

Serial	Type (alternative identity)	Owner, operator and location	Notes
34	Miles Magister	Irish Aviation Museum Store, Castlemoate House, Dublin	
141	Avro Anson	Irish Aviation Museum Store, Castlemoate House, Dublin	
164	DH Chipmunk	Engineering Wing, Baldonnel (stored)	
168	DH Chipmunk	Training Wing, Gormanston	
172	DH Chipmunk	Engineering Wing, Baldonnel	
173	DH Chipmunk	South East Aviation Enthusiasts, Waterford	
176	DH Dove	Civil Defence, Phoenix Park, Dublin	
183	Percival Provost T51	Irish Aviation Museum Store, Castlemoate House, Dublin	
187	DH Vampire T11	Aviation Society of Ireland, stored, Baldonnel	
191	DH Vampire T11	Irish Aviation Museum Store, Castlemoate House, Dublin	
192	DH Vampire T11	Institute of Technology, Bolton Street, Dublin, in store, Baldonnel	
195	Sud Alouette III	No 1 Support Wing, Baldonnel	
196	Sud Alouette III	No 1 Support Wing, Baldonnel	
197	Sud Alouette III	No 1 Support Wing, Baldonnel	
198	DH Vampire T11 (XE977)	On display, Baldonnel	
199	DH Chipmunk	Training Wing, Gormanston	
202	Sud Alouette III	No 1 Support Wing, Baldonnel	
203	Cessna FR172H	No 2 Support Wing, Gormanston	
205	Cessna FR172H	No 2 Support Wing, Gormanston	
206	Cessna FR172H	No 2 Support Wing, Gormanston	
207	Cessna FR172H	No 2 Support Wing, Gormanston	
208	Cessna FR172H	No 2 Support Wing, Gormanston	
209	Cessna FR172H	No 2 Support Wing, Gormanston	
210	Cessna FR172H	No 2 Support Wing, Gormanston	
211	Sud Alouette III	No 1 Support Wing, Baldonnel	
212	Sud Alouette III	No 1 Support Wing, Baldonnel	
213	Sud Alouette III	No 1 Support Wing, Baldonnel	
214	Sud Alouette III	No 1 Support Wing, Baldonnel	
215	Fouga Super Magister	No 1 Support Wing, Baldonnel	
216	Fouga Super Magister	No 1 Support Wing, Baldonnel	
217	Fouga Super Magister	No 1 Support Wing, Baldonnel	
218	Fouga Super Magister	No 1 Support Wing, Baldonnel	
219	Fouga Super Magister	No 1 Support Wing, Baldonnel	
220	Fouga Super Magister	No 1 Support Wing, Baldonnel	
221	Fouga Super Magister [3-KE]	Engineering Wing, Baldonnel	
222	SIAI SF-260W Warrior	Training Wing, Baldonnel	
223	SIAI SF-260W Warrior	Training Wing, Baldonnel	
225	SIAI SF-260W Warrior	Training Wing, Baldonnel	
226	SIAI SF-260W Warrior	Training Wing, Baldonnel	
227	SIAI SF-260W Warrior	Training Wing, Baldonnel	
228	SIAI SF-260W Warrior	Training Wing, Baldonnel	
229	SIAI SF-260W Warrior	Training Wing, Baldonnel	
230	SIAI SF-260W Warrior	Training Wing, Baldonnel	
231	SIAI SF-260W Warrior	Training Wing, Baldonnel	
232	Beech King Air 200 (EI-BCY)	Maritime Squadron, Baldonnel	
233	SIAI SF-260MC	Engineering Wing, Baldonnel (stored)	
234	Beech King Air 200 (EI-BFJ)	Maritime Squadron, Baldonnel	
235	SIAI SF-260W Warrior	Training Wing, Baldonnel	
237	Aerospatiale Gazelle	Advanced Flying Training School, Baldonnel	
238	HS125/700B	Transport Squadron, Baldonnel	
240	Beech King Air 200	Transport Squadron, Baldonnel	
241	Aerospatiale Gazelle	Advanced Flying Training School, Baldonnel	
243	Cessna FR172P	No 2 Support Wing, Gormanston	
244	SA365F Dauphin II	Naval Squadron, Baldonnel	
245	SA365F Dauphin II	Naval Squadron, Baldonnel	
246	SA365F Dauphin II	Naval Squadron, Baldonnel	

Overseas Military Aircraft Markings

Aircraft included in this section are a selection of those likely to be seen visiting UK civil and military airfields on transport flights, exchange visits, exercises and for air shows. It is not a comprehensive list of *all* aircraft operated by the air arms concerned.

Serial

AUSTRALIA
Royal Australian Air Force

Boeing 707-338C
33 Sqn, Canberra
A20-623
A20-624
A20-627
A20-629
Lockheed C-130H Hercules
36 Sqn, Richmond
A97-001
A97-002
A97-003
A97-004
A97-005
A97-006
A97-007
A97-008
A97-009
A97-010
A97-011
A97-012
Lockheed C130E Hercules
37 Sqn, Richmond
A97-159
A97-160
A97-167
A97-168
A97-171
A97-172
A97-177
A97-178
A97-180
A97-187
A97-189
A97-190
Lockheed P-3C Orion
Edinburgh, NSW
10 Sqn
11 Sqn †
A9-656†
A9-657†
A9-658†
A9-659†
A9-660†
A9-661†
A9-662†
A9-663†
A9-664†
A9-665†
A9-751*
A9-752*
A9-753*
A9-754*
A9-755*
A9-756*

Serial

A9-757*
A9-758*
A9-759*
A9-760*

AUSTRIA
Oesterreichische Luftstreitkrafte

Saab 105ÖE (yellow)
1101/A
1102/B
1104/D
1105/E
1106/F
1107/G
1108/H
1109/I
1110/J
Saab 105ÖE (green)
1111/A
1112/B
1114/D
1116/F
1117/G
1119/I
1120/J
Saab 105ÖE (red)
1122/B
1123/C
1124/D
1125/E
1126/F
1127/G
1128/H
1129/I
1130/J
Saab 105ÖE (blue)
1131/A
1132/B
1133/C
1134/D
1135/E
1136/F
1137/G
1139/I
1140/J
Short SC7 Skyvan 3M
Tullin
5S-TA
5S-TB

Serial

BELGIUM
Force Aerienne Belge/ Belgische Luchtmacht

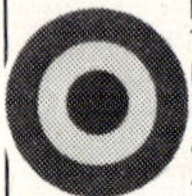

D-BD Alpha Jet
7/11 Smaldeel, Brustem
AT01
AT02
AT03
AT05
AT06
AT08
AT09
AT10
AT11
AT12
AT13
AT14
AT15
AT16
AT17
AT18
AT19
AT20
AT21
AT22
AT23
AT24
AT25
AT26
AT27
AT28
AT29
AT30
AT31
AT32
AT33
Dassault Mirage 5BA
1/8 Smaldeel, Bierset
2/42 Smaldeel, Florennes
BA01 2 Sm
BA03 8 Sm
BA04 1 Sm
BA05 1 Sm
BA08 8 Sm
BA10 1 Sm
BA11 2 Sm
BA15 8 Sm
BA16 1 Sm
BA17 2 Sm
BA18 8 Sm
BA20 8 Sm
BA21 2 Sm
BA22 1 Sm
BA23 8 Sm
BA26 1 Sm
BA27 8 Sm

Serial
BA30 2 Sm
BA31 1 Sm
BA33 8 Sm
BA37 1 Sm
BA39 1 Sm
BA42 8 Sm
BA43 1 Sm
BA44 1 Sm
BA45 8 Sm
BA46 1 Sm
BA48 1 Sm
BA50 2 Sm
BA51 8 Sm
BA52 1 Sm
BA53 2 Sm
BA54 2 Sm
BA56 2 Sm
BA57 1 Sm
BA59 2 Sm
BA60 8 Sm
BA62 1 Sm
BA63 8 Sm
Dassault Mirage 5BD
BD01 8 Sm
BD03 8 Sm
BD04 2 Sm
BD07 1 Sm
BD09 1 Sm
BD10 1 Sm
BD11 2 Sm
BD12 2 Sm
BD13 2 Sm
BD14 2 Sm
BD15 2 Sm
Dassault Mirage 5BR
BR03 42 Sm
BR04 42 Sm
BR07 42 Sm
BR08 42 Sm
BR09 42 Sm
BR10 42 Sm
BR12 42 Sm
BR13 42 Sm
BR14 42 Sm
BR15 42 Sm
BR16 42 Sm
BR17 42 Sm
BR19 42 Sm
BR20 42 Sm
BR21 42 Sm
BR22 42 Sm
BR23 42 Sm
BR24 42 Sm
BR25 42 Sm
BR26 42 Sm
BR27 42 Sm
Boeing 727-29C
21 Smaldeel, Melsbroek
CB01 21 Sm
CB02 21 Sm
Swearingen Merlin IIIA
21 Smaldeel, Melsbroek
CF01 21 Sm
CF02 21 Sm
CF04 21 Sm
CF05 21 Sm
CF06 21 Sm

Serial
Lockheed C-130H Hercules
20 Smaldeel, Melsbroek
CH01 20 Sm
CH02 20 Sm
CH03 20 Sm
CH04 20 Sm
CH05 20 Sm
CH06 20 Sm
CH07 20 Sm
CH08 20 Sm
CH09 20 Sm
CH10 20 Sm
CH11 20 Sm
CH12 20 Sm
Dassault Mystere 20
21 Smaldeel, Melsbroek
CM01 21 Sm
CM02 21 Sm
Hawker-Siddeley HS748 srs 2A
21 Smaldeel, Melsbroek
CS01 21 Sm
CS02 21 Sm
CS03 21 Sm
General Dynamics F-16A
349/350 Smaldeel, Bevekom (1 Wg) 23/31 Smaldeel, Kleine Brogel (10 Wg)
FA01 349 Sm
FA02 350 Sm
FA03 349 Sm
FA04 350 Sm
FA05 349 Sm
FA09 349 Sm
FA10 350 Sm
FA12 350 Sm
FA15 350 Sm
FA16 349 Sm
FA17 349 Sm
FA18 350 Sm
FA19 350 Sm
FA20 349 Sm
FA21 349 Sm
FA22 350 Sm
FA23 350 Sm
FA25 349 Sm
FA26 349 Sm
FA27 349 Sm
FA28 350 Sm
FA30 350 Sm
FA31 349 Sm
FA32 350 Sm
FA34 349 Sm
FA36 350 Sm
FA37 350 Sm
FA38 350 Sm
FA39 350 Sm
FA40 349 Sm
FA43 349 Sm
FA44 350 Sm
FA45 349 Sm
FA46 349 Sm
FA47 350 Sm
FA48 350 Sm
FA49 349 Sm

Serial
FA50 349 Sm
FA51 350 Sm
FA52 350 Sm
FA53 350 Sm
FA54 350 Sm
FA55 349 Sm
FA56 31 Sm
FA57 23 Sm
FA58 31 Sm
FA60 31 Sm
FA61 23 Sm
FA62 31 Sm
FA63 23 Sm
FA64 31 Sm
FA65 23 Sm
FA66 31 Sm
FA67 23 Sm
FA68 31 Sm
FA69 23 Sm
FA70 31 Sm
FA71 23 Sm
FA72 31 Sm
FA73 23 Sm
FA74 31 Sm
FA75 23 Sm
FA76 31 Sm
FA77 23 Sm
FA78 31 Sm
FA80 31 Sm
FA81 23 Sm
FA82 31 Sm
FA83 23 Sm
FA84 31 Sm
FA85 23 Sm
FA86 31 Sm
FA87 23 Sm
FA88 31 Sm
FA89 23 Sm
FA90 31 Sm
FA91 23 Sm
FA92 31 Sm
FA93 23 Sm
FA94 31 Sm
FA95 23 Sm
FA96 31 Sm
General Dynamics F-16B
1 Wing, Bevekom; 10 Wing, Kleine Brogel
FB01 1 Wg
FB02 1 Wg
FB03 1 Wg
FB04 1 Wg
FB05 1 Wg
FB06 1 Wg
FB07 10 Wg
FB08 1 Wg
FB09 1 Wg
FB10 10 Wg
FB11 1 Wg
FB12 1 Wg
FB13 10 Wg
FB14 10 Wg
FB15 10 Wg
FB17 10 Wg
FB18 10 Wg
FB19 10 Wg
FB20 10 Wg

Overseas Serials

Serial

Westland Sea King Mk48
40 Smaldeel, Koksijde
RS01
RS02
RS03
RS04
RS05
Siai Marchetti SF.260MB
Ecole de Pilotage Elementaire, Gossoncourt
ST02
ST03
ST04
ST06
ST07
ST09
ST11
ST12
ST14
ST15
ST16
ST17
ST18
ST19
ST20
ST21
ST22
ST23
ST24
ST25
ST26
ST27
ST29
ST30
ST31
ST32
ST33
ST34
ST35
ST36

Belgische Landmacht
Britten-Norman BN-2A Islander
*15/16 Smaldeel, Brasschaat
†ECOLE LT AVN, Brasschaat
B01/LA*
B02/LB*
B03/LC*
B04/LD†
B05/LE†
B06/LF†
B07/LG†
B08/LH†
B09/LI*
B10/LJ†
B11/LK†
B12/LL†
Sud Alouette II
16, 17 and 18 Smaldeel and SvHLV
A04
A05
A08
A09
A11

Serial

A12
A13
A14
A15
A16
A18
A20
A21
A22
A23
A25
A26
A27
A29
A30
A31
A32
A34
A35
A37
A40
A41
A42
A43
A44
A45
A46
A47
A48
A49
A50
A53
A54
A55
A56
A57
A59
A61
A62
A63
A64
A65
A66
A67
A68
A69
A70
A72
A73
A74
A75
A76
A77
A78
A79
A80
A81
A90
A92
A93
A94
A95

Belgische Zeemacht
Sud Alouette III
40 Smaldeel, Koksijde
M1 (OT-ZPA)
M2 (OT-ZPB)
M3 (OT-ZPC)

Serial

BRAZIL
Forca Aerea Brazileira

Lockheed C-130E Hercules
1 GT 1 Esq Afonsos
C-130 2451
C-130 2452
C-130 2454
C-130 2455
C-130 2456
C-130 2458
C-130 2460
Lockheed KC-130H Hercules
1 GT 2 Esq Afonsos
C-130 2461
C-130 2462
Lockheed C-130H Hercules
1 GT 1 Esq Afonsos
C-130 2463
C-130 2464
C-130 2465
Lockheed RC-130E Hercules
6 GAV 1 Esq Recife
C-130 2459

CANADA
Canadian Armed Forces

1st CAG, Sollingen West Germany
McDonnell Douglas CF-18A Hornet
188728
188729
188730
188731
188732
188733
188734
188735
188736
188738
188739
188740
188741
188742
188743
188744
188745
188746
188747
188748
188749
188750
188751
188752
188753
188754
188755
188756
188757
188758
188759
188760
188761
188762
McDonnell Douglas CF-18B Hornet
188918

Serial

188919
188922

Lockheed
C-130E Hercules
*429 Sqn, Winnipeg
†435 Sqn, Edmonton
‡436 Sqn, Trenton
130305
130306*
130307*
130308‡
130309
130310*
130311
130313†
130314‡
130315‡
130316
130317‡
130318
130319†
130320‡
130321‡
130322‡
130323‡
130324‡
130325‡
130326‡
130327‡
130328‡

Lockheed
C-130H Hercules
130332
130333
130334
130335†

Canadair CT-133
Silver Star
1st CAG, Sollingen
West Germany
133052
133094
133315
133345
133542

Boeing CC-137
(B.707-374C)
437 Sqn, Ottawa
13701
13702
13703
13704
13705

Lockheed
CP-140 Aurora
140101 407 Sqn
140102 404 Sqn
140103 405 Sqn
140104 404 Sqn
140105 404 Sqn
140106 404 Sqn
140107 404 Sqn
140108 405 Sqn
140109 407 Sqn
140110 415 Sqn
140111 415 Sqn
140112 415 Sqn
140113 415 Sqn
140114 415 Sqn
140115 404 Sqn
140116 407 Sqn
140117 407 Sqn
140118 407 Sqn

Serial

Canadair CC-144
Challenger
No 412 Sqn, Lahr
West Germany
144601
144602
144606
144608
144609
144610

CHILE
Fuerza Aérea de Chile

Lockheed
C-130H Hercules
Grupo 10, Santiago
995
996

DENMARK
Kongelige Danske
Flyvevaabnet

Saab A-35XD
Draken
*Eskadrille 725,
Karup
†Eskadrille 729,
Karup
A001*
A002*
A004†
A005*
A006*
A007*
A008*
A009*
A010*
A011*
A012†
A014*
A017*
A018*
A019*
A020*

Saab S-35XD
Draken
Eskadrille 729, Karup
AR102
AR104
AR105
AR106
AR107
AR108
AR109
AR110
AR111
AR112
AR113
AR114
AR115
AR116
AR117
AR118
AR119
AR120

Saab Sk-35XD
Draken
Karup
AT151 Esk 729
AT152 Esk 729
AT153 Esk 725
AT154 Esk 725
AT155 Esk 729

Serial

AT156 Esk 729
AT157 Esk 725
AT158 Esk 725
AT160 Esk 725

Lockheed
C-130H Hercules
Eskadrille 721,
Vaerlose
B678
B679
B680

Saab 17
Supporter
*Flyveskolen, Avno
(FLSK), †Haerens
Flyvetjaeneste
(Danish Army),
Vandel, ‡Eskadrille
721, Vaerlose
T401 Aalborg Stn Flt
T402 Skystrup Stn Flt
T403 Karup Stn Flt
T404 Karup Stn Flt
T405 Karup Stn Flt
T407 Karup Stn Flt
T408‡
T409‡
T410†
T411†
T412†
T413†
T414†
T415†
T417†
T418†
T419‡
T420‡
T421*
T422*
T423*
T424*
T425*
T426*
T427*
T428*
T429*
T430*
T431*
T432*

Grumman
Gulfstream III
Eskadrille 721,
Vaerlose
F249
F313
F330

General Dynamics
F-16A
*Eskadrille 723,
Aalborg;
†Eskadrille 727,
Skrydstrup;
‡Eskadrille 730,
Skrydstrup
E174‡
E176*
E177†
E178†
E180*
E181†
E182‡
E183*
E184*

Serial

E185‡
E187†
E188*
E189*
E190†
E191‡
E192‡
E193*
E194‡
E195*
E196*
E197*
E198*
E199†
E200‡
E201*
E202‡
E203*
E596*
E597‡
E598‡
E599*
E600†
E601†
E602‡
E603‡
E604*
E605‡
E606‡
E607*
E608*
E609‡
E610†
E611†

General Dynamics F-16B

ET204†
ET205†
ET206‡
ET208‡
ET210*
ET612†
ET613†
ET614*
ET615†

Sikorsky S-61A

Eskadrille 722, Vaerlose

U240
U275
U276
U277
U278
U279
U280
U481

Sovaernets Flyvetjaeneste (Navy)

Westland Lynx HAS80

Eskadrille 722, Vaerlose

S134
S142
S170
S175
S181
S187
S191

Serial

Haerens Flyvetjaeneste (Army)

Hughes 500M

Vandel

H201
H202
H203
H205
H206
H207
H209
H210
H211
H212
H244
H245
H246

ECUADOR

Lockheed C-130H Hercules

FAE-812
FAE-893

EGYPT

Al Quwwat al-Jawwiya Ilmisriya

Lockheed C-130H Hercules

16 Sqn, Cairo West

1271/SU-BAB
1272/SU-BAC
1273/SU-BAD
1274/SU-BAE
1275/SU-BAF
1277/SU-BAI
1278/SU-BAJ
1279/SU-BAK
1280/SU-BAL
1281/SU-BAM
1282/SU-BAN
1283/SU-BAP
1284/SU-BAQ
1285/SU-BAR
1286/SU-BAS
1287/SU-BAT
1288/SU-BAU
1289/SU-BAV
1290/SU-BEW
1291/SU-BEX
1292/SU-BEY

FRANCE

Armee de l'Air

Aerospatiale TB-30 Epsilon

GE315, Cognac

1 UA
2 UB
3 FZ
4 UC
5 UD
6 UE
7 UF
8 UG
9 UH
10 UI
11 UJ
12 UK
13 UL
14 UM

Serial

15 UN
16 UO
17 UP
18 UQ
19 UR
20 US
21 UT
22 UU
23 UV
24 UW
25 UX
26 UY
27 UZ
28 VA
29 VB
30 VC
31 VD
32 VE
33 VF
34 VG
35 VH
36 VI
37 VJ
38 VK
39 VL
40 VM
41 VN
42 VO
43 VP
44 VQ
45 VR
46 VS
47 VT
48 VU
49 VV
50 VW
52 VX
53 VY
54 VZ
56 WA
58 WB
60 WC
61 WD
62 WE
63 WF
64 WG
66 WI
68 WJ
69 WL
70 WM
71 WN
72 WO
73 WP
74 WQ
75 WR
76 WS
77 WT
78 WU
79 WV
80 WW
81 WX
82 WY
83 WZ
84 XA
85 XB
86 XC
87 XD
88 XE
89 XF
90 XG
91 XH

Serial

Boeing KC-135F/ *KC-135FR
ERV 93, Avord and Mont de Marsan
38470/CA*
38471/CB
38472/CC
38474/CE
38475/CF
312735/CG
312736/CH
312737/CI*
312738/CJ
312739/CK
312740/CL

CAARP CAP-20
GI 312, Salon de Provence
1 VU
02 VV
3 VW
4 VX
5 VY
6 VZ

Cessna 310
CEV
045 AU
046 AV
185 AC
186 BI
187 BJ
188 BK
190 BL
192 BM
193 BG
194 BH
242 BW
244 AX
820 CL

Cessna 404
692 DX
815 DY

Cessna 411
CEV
185 AC
248 AB
F006 AD
F008 AE

D-BD Alpha Jet
*Patrouille de France
EC 8, Cazaux, GE 314, Tours; CEAM (118), Mont de Marsan
01
02 F-ZWRU
E1 8-NP
E3 118-BR
E4 314-LP
E5 118-BU
E6 8-NW
E7 314-LB
E8 314-LL
E9 8-NN
E10 8-MU
E11 8-MP
E12 8-NO
E13 314-LH
E14
E15 314-LJ
E17 8-MR
E18 314-LM

Serial

E19 8-MK
E20 314-LO
E21 8-NY
E22 314-LQ
E23 8-MQ
E24 8-MA
E25 314-LT
E26 314-TK
E27 8-MU
E28 314-TL
E29 314-LV
E30 314-LW
E31 314-LX
E32 314-LY
E33 8-NL
E34 314-LZ
E35 314-TH
E36 314-TC
E37 314-TD
E38 314-TE
E39 314-TF
E40 8-MD
E41 8-MH
E42 314-TI
E43 314-LI
E44
E45 314-TP
E46
E47 8-ND
E48 8-NZ
E49 314
E50 314-TS
E51 F-TERA*
E53 F-TERC*
E55 F-TERE* (4)
E58 F-TERH* (5)
E59 F-TERI* (3)
E60
E61 F-TERJ* (8)
E63 F-TERL* (6)
E64 314-TT
E65 314-LL
E66 314-TV
E67 314-TW
E68 314-TX
E69 314-TO
E70 314-TY
E72 314-LF
E73 118-BT
E74 8-ND
E75 314-UF
E76 314-UE
E77 8-NA
E79 8-NS
E80
E81 8-NK
E82 8-NX
E83 314-UJ
E84 314-LL
E85 314-LW
E86 314-LN
E87 314-LS
E88 8-MG
E89 314-UQ
E90 314-TH
E91 314-TG
E92 314-TB
E93 8-NT
E94 8-MO
E95 8-MI
E96 8-MJ
E97 314-LF
E98

Serial

E99 8-MW
E100
E101 8-NG
E102 8-ME
E103 314-TO
E104 314-LC
E105 314-TF
E106 314-VB
E107 F-TERK* (4)
E108 314-UD
E109 314-LK
E110 8-NB
E112 8-NQ
E113 8-NJ
E114 8-NN
E115 314-UF
E116 8-NV
E117 314-TZ
E118 314-TM
E119 314-TR
E120 314-TJ
E121 314-VK
E122 314-VG
E123 314-VM
E124 8-MC
E125 314-TN
E126 314-TQ
E127 8-MY
E128 314-TX
E129 314-VP
E130 8-MT
E131 314-TY
E132 314-TL
E133 314-TY
E134 8-NE
E135 314
E136 314-LO
E137 8-MF
E138 8-NF
E139 8-MM
E140 314-UB
E141 314
E142 8-ML
E143 314-TX
E144 314-VW
E145 8-MM
E146 314-VZ
E147 314-LA
E148 314-LC
E149 314-TR
E150 8-NO
E151 314-VD
E152
E153 314-LL
E154 314-LN
E155 F-TERF*
E156 F-TERG* (9)
E157 8-NI
E158 314-LR
E159 8-MD
E160 314-TJ
E161 8-MN
E162 314-TA
E163 314-LS
E164 8-MS
E165 314-UA
E166 314-UC
E167 8-MV
E168 314
E169 314-LG
E170 F-TERM* (2)
E171 F-TERN* (5)
E172 F-TERO* (0)

Serial

E173 F-TERP* (7)
E174 F-TERQ* (1)
E175 314-LU
E176
E177
E178
E179
E180

Dassault Falcon 20C

*EDT 60
†EDC57
1 CV
22 CS
49 OA*
79 CT
86 CG
93 N*
104 B†
115 339-WL
124 CC
131 CD
138 CR
145 CV
167 L*
188 CU
238 M*
260 A
268 K
291 P†
309 U*
422 L*
451 338-WN
463 339-WM
483 338-

Dassault Falcon 50

5 F-RAFI EDT 60
147 F-RAFJ EDT-60

Dassault Mirage IVA/IVP*

EB 1/91, Mont-de-Marsan; EB 2/91, Cazaux; EB 1/94 Istres; EB 2/94, St Dizier; CIFAS 328 Bordeaux-Merignac

1 AP
2 AA
4 AC
5 AD
6 AE
7 AF
8/01* AG
9 AH
11 AJ
12 AK
13* AL
14 AM
16 AO
18 AQ
19 AR
20 AS
21 AT
23 AV
24 AW
25 AX
26/02* AY
27 AZ
29 BB
31 BD
32 BE
33 CR
34 BG

Serial

36 BI
37 BJ
39 BL
42 BO
43 BP
44 BQ
45 BR
46 BS
47 BT
48 BU
49 BV
51 BX
52 BY
53 BZ
54 CA
55 CB
56 CC
57 CD
59 CF
61 CH
62 CI

Dassault Mirage F.1C

EC 5, Orange; EC 12, Cambrai; EC 30, Rheims; EC 118/24, Mont de Marsan

2 30-MC
3 30-MB
4 118-AM
5
6 30-MA
8 5-OK
9 12-KB
10 12-KH
12 30-FL
13 30-SF
14 30-MS
15 12-ZD
16 12-YA
17
18 30-ME
19 12
20 12-YD
21 30-MI
22 12-ZD
23
24
25 12-ZC
26 30-FH
27 30-SQ
29 12-YM
30 30-FA
31 12-ZA
32 12-KD
33 12-ZE
35
36 12-ZB
37 30-YB
38 30-MG
39 12-KM
40 12-YA
41 30-SG
42 30-FK
43 12-YK
44 12-KB
45 30-SR
47
48 13-SO
49 12-ZF
50 30-SA
52 12-YG
54 30-MF

Serial

55 12-KH
60 12-KA
62 12-ZH
63 12-YJ
64 30-SP
67
68 12-ZK
69 30-FJ
70 30-FO
71 12-KJ
72 30-MO
73 12-KP
74 12-ZJ
75 12-KO
76 30-MM
77 12-KF
78 12-ZL
79 30-MR
80 30-FP
81 12-KK
82 30-FI
83 12-YE
84 12-YO
85 12-ZQ
87 10-SL
90 12-YN
100 30-MQ
101 30-SC
102 10-SM
103 12-YC
201 118-AK
202 5-NE
203 5-NC
204
205 30-FI
206 5-OA
207 30-FE
208 5-NO
210 30-SE
211 5-NN
213 12-ZR
214 5-OG
216 5-OL
217 30-MK
218 5-OM
219 12-KI
220 12-KL
221 30-FF
223 5-NM
224 5-OI
225 118-AO
226 5-OD
227 12-KP
228 5-OH
229 5-ND
230 118-AP
231 12-YH
232 5-OC
233 30-MJ
234 30-SM
235 30-FP
236 5-NJ
237 5-ND
238 5-NR
239 30-FC
240 12-YP
241 5-NE
242 5-NA
243 12-KC
244 5-OQ
245 5-NI
246 5-OK
247 30-FR

Serial	
248	12-YF
249	12-ZG
251	30-MH
252	5-ON
253	
254	12-ZM
255	5-NQ
256	30-FQ
257	12-YI
258	12-YL
259	30-FA
260	5-OB
261	12-ZI
262	10-SB
264	12-KN
265	5-NB
266	12-KG
267	30-MP
268	5-OO
270	12-KE
271	30-FM
272	5-NG
273	12-ZN
274	5-OF
275	5-NH
277	
278	5-OE
279	5-NK
280	5-NF
281	5-AU
282	5-AW
283	12-ZO

Dassault Mirage F.1CR
ER 33 Strasbourg

Serial	
601	Istres
602	CV
603	33-NR
604	33-NK
605	33-NF
606	33-CD
607	33-CP
608	33-CN
609	33-CC
610	33-CH
611	33-CA
612	33-NJ
613	33-CE
614	33-CQ
615	33-NB
616	33-NN
617	33-NO
618	118-AA
619	118-AC
620	33-CJ
621	33-CM
622	33-NC
623	33-ND
624	33-NE
625	33-NF
626	33-NG
627	33-NH
628	33-NI
629	33-NJ
630	33-NL
631	33
632	33-NM
633	33-NN
634	33-NO
635	33-NP
636	33-NQ
637	118-AB
638	118-AR
639	33-NA
640	33-NS
641	33-CA
642	33-NE
643	33-CO
644	33-NG
645	33-CE
646	33-NH
647	
648	
649	33-CF
650	33-CG
651	33-CL
652	33-CK
653	33-CB
654	33-CL
655	33-NN
656	33-NI
657	33-NS
658	
659	
660	
661	
662	
663	

Dassault Mirage 2000C
EC 2, Dijon; CEAM (118), Mont de Marsan

Serial	
01	
03	
04	
1	2-EP
2	
3	118-AV
4	118-AW
5	118-AS
6	118-AY
8	2-EC
9	2-ED
10	2-EE
11	2-EF
12	2-EH
13	2-EI
14	2-EJ
15	2-EK
16	2-EL
17	2-EM
18	2-EN
19	2-LA
20	2-LE
21	2-LF
22	2-LG
23	2-LH
24	2-LI
25	2-LK
27	2-LM
28	2-LN
29	2-LO
30	2-EO
31	2-LP

Dassault Mirage 2000B
EC 2, Dijon

Serial	
501	
502	2-ER
503	118-AX
504	2-FA
505	2-ER
506	2-EQ
507	2-LC
508	2-LD
509	2-FF
510	2-LJ

DHC6 Twin Otter
CEAM (118) Mont de Marsan; ET 63 Toulouse
GAM 56: Evreux

Serial	
292	OW
296	OV
298	OY
300	OZ
603	82-PU
730	52-LF
742	52-LG
743	118-ID
745	63-VY
786	63-VV
790	63-VW

Douglas DC8F

Serial	
45570	F-RAFE
45819	F-RAFC
45820	F-RAFA
46013	F-RAFG
46043	F-RAFD
46130	F-RAFF
46132	F-RAFB

Embraer Xingu
CEAM (118) Mont de Marsan; * GE 319 Avord; † ETT 43 Bordeaux; ‡ETT 44 Aix-en-Provence

Serial	
054	118-IA
064	118-IB
072	YA*
073	YB*
075	YC*
076	YD*
078	YE*
080	YF*
082	YG*
084	YH*
086	YI*
089	YJ*
091	YK*
092	YL*
095	YM*
096	YN*
098	YO*
099	YP*
100	YR*
101	BW†
102	BX†
103	CT‡
105	CU‡
107	YV*
108	CW‡
109	
110	
111	YQ*

Morane Saulnier Paris
ETT 41 Metz; ETT 43 Bordeaux; ETT 44 Aix-en-Provence; ET 65 Villacoublay; CEAM (118) Mont de Marsan

Serial	
1	118-DB
14	070-MD
19	41-AR
20	

Serial	
23	65-LA
24	65-LW
25	118-DI
26	
27	65-LZ
29	43-BB
30	65-LI
34	65-LD
35	43-BC
36	43-BD
38	41-AT
44	65-LS
45	41-AR
51	
53	GE-314
54	65-LK
56	65-LB
57	65-LP
58	
59	65-LV
60	65-LQ
61	65-LY
62	118-DO
65	65-LZ
68	
70	65-LT
71	65-LC
73	41-AS
75	118-DC
77	118-DE
78	65-LU
79	65-LA
80	65-LM
81	65-LL
82	65-LN
83	316-DB
91	65-LJ
93	65-LD
94	65-LH
96	
97	43-BA
100	NG
113	NI
114	NJ
115	OV
116	ON
117	AZ
118	NQ
119	NL

Nord 262 Fregate
Esc 70 Chateaudun; *ET 65 Villacoublay

Serial	
3	OH
58	MH
64	AA*
66	AB*
67	MI
68	AC*
76	118 AD
77	AK*
78	AF*
80	AG*
81	AH*
83	AI*
86	316-DD
87	AN*
88	
89	118-IR
91	70-MB
92	316-DE
93	AP*
94	AU
95	AQ*
105	AE*
106	70-MA
107	AX*
108	
109	AM*
110	AS*

Nord Noratlas
ET 63 Toulouse; CEAM (118) Mont de Marsan; CIFAS (328) Bordeaux
EE54: Metz*

Serial	
18	CR
28*	
41	
66*	
94	VF*
96	63-VH
100	63-VC
104	118-IF
105	63-VM
113	63-VN
146	63-WV
153	328-EH
157	63-WK
162	63-VP
165	63-VK
169	63-VL
180	63-VB
185	63-VG
193	316-FU
196	316-FO
200	328-EK
201	63-VJ

C-160 Transall
ET 61 Orleans (C160A/F); ET 64 Evreux (C160NG)

Serial	
A02	61-MI
A04	
A06	61-ZB
F1	61-MA
F2	61-MB
F3	61-MC
F4	61-MD
F5	61-ME
F11	61-MF
F12	61-MG
F13	61-MH
F14	61-MI
F15	61-MJ
F16	61-MK
F17	61-ML
F18	61-MM
F42	61-MN
F43	61-MO
F44	61-MP
F45	61-MQ
F46	61-MR
F47	61-MS
F48	61-MT
F49	61-MU
F50	61-MV
F51	61-MW
F52	61-MX
F53	61-MY
F54	61-MZ
F55	61-ZC
F86	61-ZD
F87	61-ZE
F88	61-ZF
F89	61-ZG
F90	61-ZH
F91	61-ZI
F92	61-ZJ
F93	61-ZK
F94	61-ZL
F95	61-ZM
F96	61-ZN
F97	61-ZO
F98	61-ZP
F99	61-ZQ
F100	61-ZR
F153	61-ZS
F154	61-ZT
F155	61-ZU
F157	61-ZW
F158	61-ZX
F159	61-ZY
F160	61-ZZ
F201	64-GA
F202	64-GB
F203	64-GC
F204	64-GD
F205	64-GE
F206	64-GF
F207	64-GG
F208	64-GH
F210	64-GJ
F211	64-GK
F212	64-GL
F213	64-GM
F214	64-GN
F215	64-GO
F216	AMD-BA
F217	64-GQ
F218	64-GR
F219	64-GS
F220	ELINT
F221	ELINT
F222	64-GV
F223	64-GW
F224	64-GX
(Command Post Prototype)	
F225	64-GY
F226	64-GZ
F227	64-GP

SEPECAT Jaguar A
EC 3 Nancy; EC 7 St Dizier; EC 11 Toul

Serial	
A1	3-XP
A2	3-XN
A3	
A5	3-XP
A7	3-XK
A8	3-XL
A9	3-XD
A10	3-XH
A11	3-XA
A12	11-YH
A13	3-XN
A14	3-XF
A15	7-IE
A16	3-XJ
A17	7
A19	3-XE
A20	7-NN
A21	7-IA
A22	7-HC
A23	7-HO
A24	7-HH
A25	7-IB
A26	7-HQ
A27	3-XP

Serial	
A28	7-NK
A29	7-HA
A31	7-NJ
A32	7-NL
A33	
A34	7-IL
A35	7-HG
A36	7-II
A37	7-PA
A38	7-IC
A39	7-IP
A40	7-NF
A41	7-ND
A43	7-HD
A44	7-ID
A46	7-IM
A47	7-HP
A48	7-NH
A49	
A50	11-YM
A53	7-PG
A54	7-HM
A55	7-HN
A56	7-HK
A58	7-NN
A59	7-HB
A60	7-HF
A61	7-IF
A64	11-RO
A65	7-IO
A66	7-NC
A67	7-NB
A70	7-NI
A72	7-HJ
A73	7-PB
A74	7-NA
A75	11-YH
A76	7-HL
A79	7-NP
A80	7-IN
A82	11-YB
A83	118-AH
A84	11-YJ
A85	11-MG
A86	11-MG
A87	11-RX
A88	11-RQ
A89	
A90	11-RJ
A91	11-YJ
A92	11-MS
A93	11-MV
A94	11-ED
A95	11-EC
A96	11-MW
A97	11-YD
A98	11-EH
A99	11-MQ
A100	11-MP
A101	11-RV
A103	11-EB
A104	11-MT
A107	11
A108	
A110	11-MD
A112	11-RM
A113	
A115	11-RH
A117	11-MH
A118	11-YI
A119	11-YG
A120	11-MG
A121	11-YN

Serial	
A122	11-YA
A123	11-YC
A124	
A126	11-RB
A127	11-EJ
A128	11-MF
A129	11-MK
A130	11-MC
A131	
A133	11-EF
A135	11-RJ
A136	
A137	7-NK
A138	11-EG
A139	11-EL
A140	11-EE
A141	11-RN
A142	7-NL
A143	
A144	11-RW
A145	11-RG
A146	118-AI
A148	11-YL
A149	11-EK
A150	11-YK
A151	11-EA
A152	118-AG
A153	11-EX
A154	11-RT
A155	
A156	7-ND
A157	11-EN
A158	11-EU
A159	11-EV
A160	

SEPECAT Jaguar E

E1	7-PK
E2	3-XO
E3	7-PN
E4	7-HK
E5	3-XD
E6	11-ME
E7	
E8	7-PP
E9	7-PH
E10	11-YY
E11	7-IG
E12	7-IJ
E13	7-PD
E15	11-YZ
E16	11-RF
E17	
E18	7-NG
E19	11-MB
E20	11-RU
E21	7-PO
E22	7-PC
E23	11-EI
E24	11-EM
E25	7-PE
E27	11-MA
E28	7-PK
E29	7-PJ
E30	11-EH
E31	7-HI
E32	7-NE
E33	11-RC
E35	7-PF
E36	7-PL
E37	7-PQ
E38	7-PM
E39	11-YX
E40	11-YY

Serial

Aeronavale/Marine

Morane Saulnier Paris

ES 57, Landivisiau

32	
33	
40	
41	
42	
46	
47	
48	
85	
87	
88	

Nord 262 Fregate

ES 2, Lann Bihoue;
ES 3, Hyeres;
ES 55, Aspretto;
ES 56, Nimes-Garons;
ES 11, Le Bourget

16	
28	(3S)
43	
45	
46	
51	(56S)
52	(2S)
53	
59	(2S)
60	(56S)
61	(3S)
62	(3S)
63	(2S)
65	(2S)
69	
70	(56S)
71	(2S)
72	(56S)
73	(56S)
75	(2S)
79	
100	(56S)
102	(3S)
104	(11S)

SA.321G Super Frelon

ES 20, St Raphael;
ES 27, Mururoa;
32 F, Lanveoc;
33 F, San Mandrier

101	(27S)
102	
105	
106	(27S)
118	
120	
122	
134	
137	
141	
144	
148	
149	
160	
162	
163	
164	
165	

Overseas Serials

Serial	Serial	Serial
Breguet 1050 Alizé 4F, Lann Bihoue; 6F, Nimes-Garons; ES 59, Hyeres 11 (59S) 12 17 22 (6F) 24 25 (4F) 26 (59S) 28 30 (6F) 31 33 36 (6F) 41 43 (4F) 44 45 47 (6F) 48 (4F) 50 (59S) 51 (4F) 52 (20S) 53 55 56 (4F) 59 60 64 (59S) 65 (6F) 68 76 (4F) 87 (4F) **Breguet 1150 Atlantic** *21F/22F, Nimes-Garons; †23F/24F, Lann Bihoue 01* 1* 3* 5† 7* 9 11* 15 17† 21† 23† 25 27* 31† 35* 38* 41* 44† 45* 47† 48 49* 51 52 54* 55† 56 57* 61 63† 65 66*	67* 68 ANG.01 ANG.02 ANG.03 ANG.04 **Dassault Etendard IVM** *16F, Landivisiau; †ES 59, Hyeres 2* 3* 4* 5* 6* 7* 9* 11† 13* 14* 15† 16† 21* 22* 26* 29† 30* 32* 34† 36† 37† 40† 41† 42 52† 53* 56* 57† 59† 60* 62* 63* 66* **Dassault Etendard IVP** 16F Landivisiau 101 107 108 109 114 115 117 118 120 **Dassault Super Etendard** *11F, Landivisiau; †14F, Landivisiau; ‡17F, Hyeres 1‡ 2* 3 4 5 6* 7* 8‡ 9 10* 11* 12 13†	14† 15† 16 17 18 19 20 21 23† 24‡ 25† 26* 27 28* 29* 30 31† 32† 33‡ 34 35* 37* 38* 39 40* 41† 42 43 44† 45 46‡ 47* 48† 49* 50† 51 52‡ 53‡ 54* 55* 57‡ 59‡ 60* 61 62‡ 63* 64‡ 66‡ 68 69 70† 71* **Dassault Falcon 10(MER)** ES3, Hyeres; ES 57 Landivisiau 32 101 129 133 143 185 **Dassault Falcon Guardian** 48 65 72 77 80

Serial

Embraer Xingu
ES 11, Le Bourget; ES 20, Frejus; ES 52, Lann Bihoue; ERC, Cuers
55
65
66 ERC
67
68
69
70
71 (20S)
74
77
79
81
83
85
87
90

LTV F-8E (FN) Crusader
12F, Landivisiau
1
2
3
4
5
6
7
8
10
11
12
16
17
18
19
23
25
27
28
29
32
33
34
35
37
39
40
41

Piper Navajo
*ES 2, Lann Bihoue; †ES 3, Hyeres; ‡ES 20 Frejus
227*
232*
903†
904†
906†
912†
914†
916†
925*
927‡
929*
931†

Westland Lynx HAS2 (FN)*; HAS4 (FN)†
31F, San Mandrier; 34F, Lanveoc; 35F, Lanveoc; ES 20 St Raphael
03*
260*
262*
263*
264*
265*
266*
267*
268*
270*
271*
272*
273*
274*
275*
276*
278*
621*
622*
623*
624*
625*
626*
627*
801†
802†
803†
804†
805†
806†
807†
808†
809†
810†
811†
812†
813†
814†

GREECE
Elliniki Aeroporia

Lockheed C-130H Hercules
356 Elefis
741
742
743
744
745
746
747
748
749
750
751
752

ISRAEL
Heyl ha'avir

Lockheed C-130H Hercules
4X-FBA/102
4X-FBB/006
4X-FBC/305

Lockheed C-130E Hercules
4X-FBD/311
4X-FBE/304
4X-FBF/301
4X-FBG/310
4X-FBH/312
4X-FBI/314
4X-FBK/318
4X-FBL/313
4X-FBM/316
4X-FBN/307
4X-FBO/420
4X-FBP/208

Lockeed C-130H Hercules
4X-FBQ/420
4X-FBS/427
4X-FBT/435
4X-FBU/448
4X-FBW/436
4X-FBX/428

Lockheed KC-130H Hercules
4X-FBY/422
4X-FBZ/445

ITALY
Aeronautica Militare Italiano

Aeritalia G222
46 Brigata Aerea, Pisa
MM62101 RS-36
MM62102 46-20
MM62104 46-91
MM62105 46-82
MM62107
MM62108 46-30
MM62109 46-96
MM62110 46-81
MM62111 46-83
MM62112 46-85
MM62113 46-34
MM62114 46-80
MM62115 46-22
MM62116 46-35
MM62117 46-25
MM62118 46-24
MM62119 46-21
MM62120 46-90
MM62121 46-86
MM62122 46-23
MM62123 46-93
MM62124 46-88
MM62125 46-87
MM62126 46-26
MM62127 46-27
MM62128 RS-34
MM62129 46-29
MM62130 46-31
MM62132 46-32
MM62133 46-93
MM62134 46-33
MM62143 46-36
MM62144 46-98

Aeritalia G222TCM
46 Brigata Aerea, Pisa
MM62103 RS-35
MM62135 46-94
MM62136 46-97
MM62137 46-95
MM62138 46

Aeritalia G222RM
14° Stormo, Practica di Mare
MM62139 14-20

Overseas Serials

Serial

MM62140 14-21
MM62141 14-22

Aermacchi MB339
*Frecce Tricolori
† Scuola Volo Basico Iniziale Aviogetti, Lecce; ‡14° Stormo, Pratica di Mare

MM54438 14-32
MM54439* 11
MM54440† 00
MM54442 RS-45
MM54443† 50
MM54445† RS-45
MM54446 RS-50
MM54447† 02
MM54448† 03
MM54449† 04
MM54450‡ 14-30
MM54451‡ 14-31
MM54452‡
MM54453† 61-72
MM54454† 61-73
MM54455† 07
MM54456† 10
MM54457† 11
MM54458† 12
MM54459† 13
MM54460† 14
MM54461† 15
MM54462† 16
MM54463† 17
MM54464† 20
MM54465† 21
MM54467† 23
MM54468† 24
MM54469† 25
MM54470† 26
MM54471† 27
MM54472† 30
MM54473* 10
MM54474* 6
MM54475*
MM54476* 1
MM54477* 4
MM54478*
MM54479* 9
MM54480* 8
MM54481* 7
MM54482* 3
MM54483*
MM54484* 2
MM54485* 12
MM54486* 5
MM54487‡ 31
MM54488† 32
MM54489† 33
MM54490† 34
MM54491† 35
MM54492† 36
MM54493† 37
MM54494† 40
MM54495† 41
MM54496† 42
MM54497† 43
MM54498† 44
MM54499† 45
MM54500† 46
MM54501† 47
MM54503† 51
MM54504† 52
MM54505† 53
MM54506† 54

Serial

MM54507† 55
MM54508† 56
MM54509† 57
MM54510† 60
MM54511† 61
MM54512† 62
MM54513† 63
MM54514† 64
MM54515† 65
MM54516† 66
MM54517† 67
MM54518† 70
MM54533 61-72
MM54534 61-73
MM54535
MM54536* 11
MM54537* 1
MM54538
MM54539
MM54540 61-77

Dassault Falcon 50
31° Stormo, Roma Ciampino

MM62020 31-20
MM62021 31-21

Grumman Gulfstream III
31° Stormo, Ciampino

MM62022 SI-22

Lockheed C-130H Hercules
46 Brigata Aerea, Pisa

MM61988 46-02
MM61989 46-03
MM61990 46-04
MM61991 46-05
MM61992 46-06
MM61993 46-07
MM61994 46-08
MM61995 46-09
MM61997 46-11
MM61998 46-12
MM61999 46-13
MM62001 46-15

McDonnell Douglas DC9-32
31° Stormo, Roma Ciampino

MM62012 31-12
MM62013 31-13

Panavia Tornado
*TTTE RAF Cottesmore
6° Stormo, Ghedi
36° Stormo, Giola del Colle

MM586
MM587
MM7001 RS-01
MM7002* I-92
MM7003* I-93
MM7004* I-90
MM7005* I-91
MM7006*
MM7007 I-94
MM7008
MM7009 6-04
MM7010 6-03
MM7011 6-10
MM7012 6-11
MM7013 6-05

Serial

MM7014 6-12
MM7015 6-01
MM7016 6-23
MM7017 6-14
MM7018 6-24
MM7019 6-22
MM7020 6-21
MM7021 6-30
MM7022 6-26
MM7023 6-27
MM7024 6-25
MM7025 6-31
MM7026 6-33
MM7027 6-32
MM7028 6-34
MM7029 6-35
MM7030 6-36
MM7031 6-37
MM7033 6-42
MM7034 6-41
MM7035 36-30
MM7036 36-31
MM7037
MM7038 36-33
MM7039
MM7040 36-35
MM7041 (RSV)
MM7042 36-50
MM7043 36-36
MM7044 36-42
MM7046 36-34
MM7047 36-37
MM7048
MM7049 36-40
MM7050 36-44
MM7051 36-43
MM7052 36-41
MM7053 36-45
MM7054 36-46
MM7055 36-47
MM7056
MM7057
MM7058
MM7059 36-55
MM7060
MM7061
MM7062 6-53
MM7063 6-52
MM7064 6-54
MM7065 6-55
MM7066 6-56
MM7067 6-57
MM7068 6-60
MM7069 6-61
MM7070 6-62
MM7071 6-63
MM7072 6-64
MM7073
MM7074
MM7075
MM7076
MM7077
MM7078
MM7079
MM7080
MM7081
MM7082
MM7083
MM7084
MM7085
MM7086
MM7087
MM7088

Serial

MM55000* I-42
MM55001* I-40
MM55002* I-41
MM55003* I-43
MM55004* I-44
MM55005 36-56
MM55006 6-15
MM55007 36-55
MM55008 6-20
MM55009 6-16
MM55010 6-50
MM55011 6-51

Piaggio-Douglas PD-808/ *PD-808-RM

14° Gruppo, Treviso-San Angelo;
31° Stormo, Roma-Ciampino

MM61948 31-48
MM61949 31-49
MM61950 31-50
MM61951 31-51
MM61952 14-65
MM61953 31-53
MM61954 31-54
MM61955 31-55
MM61956 31-56
MM61957 31-57
MM61958 14-
MM61959 14-
MM61960 31-60
MM61961 31-61
MM61962 14-
MM61963 31-63
MM62014* 14-53
MM62015* 14-54
MM62016* 14-55
MM62017* 14-56

JORDAN
Al Quwwat Al-Jawwiya Alamalakiya Al-Urduniya

Lockheed C-130B Hercules

3 Sqn, Amman

340
341

Lockheed C-130H Hercules

3 Sqn, Amman

344
345
346
347

KUWAIT
Kuwait Air Force

McDonnell Douglas DC9-32

KAF 320
KAF 321

Lockheed L100-30 Hercules

KAF 322
KAF 323
KAF 324
KAF 325

LUXEMBOURG
NATO — Geilenkirchen

Boeing E-3A

LX-N90442
LX-N90443
LX-N90444
LX-N90445
LX-N90446
LX-N90447
LX-N90448
LX-N90449
LX-N90450
LX-N90451
LX-N90452
LX-N90453
LX-N90454
LX-N90455
LX-N90456
LX-N90457
LX-N90458
LX-N90459

NETHERLANDS
Koninklijke Luchmacht

Fokker F-27-100 Friendship

334 Sqn, Soesterberg

C-1
C-2
C-3

Fokker F-27-300M Troopship

334 Sqn, Soesterberg

C-4
C-5
C-6
C-7
C-8
C-9
C-10
C-11
C-12

F-27-200MPA

M-1
M-2

General Dynamics F-16A/F16B*

306 Sqn, Volkel;
311 Sqn, Volkel;
312 Sqn, Volkel;
315 Sqn, Twente;
322 Sqn, Leeuwarden;
323 Sqn, Leeuwarden
Operational Conversion Unit (TCA), Leeuwarden

J192 311 Sqn
J193 311 Sqn
J194 311 Sqn
J195 311 Sqn
J196 312 Sqn
J197 315 Sqn
J198 315 Sqn
J199 315 Sqn
J200 315 Sqn
J201 315 Sqn
J202 315 Sqn
J203 315 Sqn
J204 315 Sqn
J205 315 Sqn
J206 315 Sqn
J207 315 Sqn
J208* 315 Sqn
J209* 315 Sqn
J210* 315 Sqn
J211* 315 Sqn
J212 323 Sqn
J213 323 Sqn
J214 323 Sqn
J215 322 Sqn
J218 322 Sqn
J219 322 Sqn
J220 322 Sqn
J221 322 Sqn
J222 322 Sqn
J223 322 Sqn
J226 322 Sqn
J228 322 Sqn
J229 322 Sqn
J230 322 Sqn
J231 323 Sqn
J232 323 Sqn
J234 323 Sqn
J235 323 Sqn
J236 323 Sqn
J238 322 Sqn
J239 322 Sqn
J240 322 Sqn
J241 322 Sqn
J242 322 Sqn
J243 322 Sqn
J245 323 Sqn
J246 323 Sqn
J247 323 Sqn
J248 312 Sqn
J249 323 Sqn
J250 323 Sqn
J251 322 Sqn
J253 323 Sqn
J254 323 Sqn
J255 323 Sqn
J256 323 Sqn
J257 322 Sqn
J258 311 Sqn
J259* 322 Sqn
J260* 322 Sqn
J261* 322 Sqn
J262* 323 Sqn
J263* 323 Sqn
J264* 323 Sqn
J265* 323 Sqn
J266* 323 Sqn
J267* 323 Sqn
J268* 323 Sqn
J269* 323 Sqn
J270* 312 Sqn
J358 315 Sqn
J359 315 Sqn
J360 315 Sqn
J361
J362
J363
J364
J365
J366
J367
J368*
J369*
J616 306 Sqn
J617 311 Sqn
J618 311 Sqn
J619 311 Sqn
J620 311 Sqn
J622 311 Sqn
J623 311 Sqn
J624 311 Sqn

Overseas Serials

Serial	
J625	311 Sqn
J627	305 Sqn
J628	306 Sqn
J630	306 Sqn
J631	306 Sqn
J632	306 Sqn
J633	306 Sqn
J635	306 Sqn
J636	306 Sqn
J637	306 Sqn
J638	306 Sqn
J639	306 Sqn
J640	306 Sqn
J641	306 Sqn
J642	306 Sqn
J643	306 Sqn
J644	306 Sqn TGP
J645	306 Sqn
J646	306 Sqn TGP
J647	306 Sqn
J648	306 Sqn
J649*	306 Sqn
J650*	311 Sqn
J651*	311 Sqn
J652*	311 Sqn
J653*	306 Sqn TGP
J654*	311 Sqn
J655*	306 Sqn
J656*	312 Sqn
J657*	311 Sqn
J864	312 Sqn
J866	312 Sqn
J867	311 Sqn
J868	311 Sqn
J869	312 Sqn
J870	312 Sqn
J871	312 Sqn
J872	312 Sqn
J873	312 Sqn
J874	312 Sqn
J875	312 Sqn
J876	312 Sqn
J877	312 Sqn
J878	312 Sqn
J879	312 Sqn
J880	312 Sqn
J881	312 Sqn
J882*	312 Sqn
J883*	TCA
J884*	312 Sqn
J885*	315 Sqn

Northrop NF-5A

313 Sqn, Twente;
314 Sqn, Eindhoven;
315 Sqn, Twente;
316 Sqn, Gilze-Rijen

Serial	
K3001	313 Sqn
K3003	313 Sqn
K3004	313 Sqn
K3005	313 Sqn
K3008	314 Sqn
K3011	313 Sqn
K3012	313 Sqn
K3013	314 Sqn
K3014	313 Sqn
K3015	314 Sqn
K3016	316 Sqn
K3017	316 Sqn
K3018	316 Sqn
K3019	314 Sqn
K3021	314 Sqn
K3023	316 Sqn
K3024	313 Sqn
K3025	313 Sqn
K3026	314 Sqn
K3027	316 Sqn
K3028	313 Sqn
K3030	313 Sqn
K3031	316 Sqn
K3032	313 Sqn
K3033	316 Sqn
K3035	314 Sqn
K3036	314 Sqn
K3039	313 Sqn
K3040	313 Sqn
K3041	313 Sqn
K3042	313 Sqn
K3044	314 Sqn
K3045	313 Sqn
K3046	316 Sqn
K3047	316 Sqn
K3048	313 Sqn
K3049	314 Sqn
K3051	313 Sqn
K3052	316 Sqn
K5054	316 Sqn
K3055	314 Sqn
K3056	313 Sqn
K3058	313 Sqn
K3062	313 Sqn
K3063	316 Sqn
K3065	314 Sqn
K3066	316 Sqn
K3067	314 Sqn
K3068	314 Sqn
K3069	314 Sqn
K3070	314 Sqn
K3072	316 Sqn
K3073	316 Sqn

Northrop NF-5B

313 Sqn, Twente;
314 Sqn, Eindhoven;
315 Sqn, Twente;
316 Sqn, Gilze-Rijen

Serial	
K4001	313 Sqn
K4003	313 Sqn
K4005	313 Sqn
K4006	316 Sqn
K4007	316 Sqn
K4009	314 Sqn
K4010	313 Sqn
K4011	316 Sqn
K4012	316 Sqn
K4013	313 Sqn
K4014	313 Sqn
K4015	314 Sqn
K4016	313 Sqn
K4017	314 Sqn
K4019	314 Sqn
K4020	314 Sqn
K4021	314 Sqn
K4023	316 Sqn
K4024	316 Sqn
K4025	316 Sqn
K4026	313 Sqn
K4027	313 Sqn
K4028	316 Sqn
K4029	316 Sqn
K4030	313 Sqn

Sud Alouette III

*Grasshoppers
298 Sqn, Soesterberg;
300 Sqn, Deelan

A177
A208
A209
A217
A218
A226
A227
A235
A246
A247
A253
A254
A260
A261
A267
A275
A281
A292
A301
A302
A307
A319
A324
A336
A342
A343
A350*
A351*
A374
A383
A390*
A391
A398
A399
A407
A414
A451
A452
A453
A464
A465*
A471
A482
A483
A488
A489
A494
A495
A499*
A500
A514
A515
A521
A522
A528
A529
A535
A536
A542
A549
A550

Marine Luchtvaartdienst

Lockheed P-3C Orion

320 Sqn, Valkenburg

300
301
302
303
304
305 stored
306
307 stored
308
309

Serial

310
311
312

Westland Lynx
*UH14A
†SH14B
‡SH14C
7/860 Sqns, De Kooij
260* K
261* K
262* K
264* K
265* IS
266† PH
267† K
268† K
269† TR
270† BK
271† CB
272†
273†
274† PF
276‡
277‡
278‡
279‡
280‡ EV
281‡ PH
282† CB
283‡

NEW ZEALAND
Royal New Zealand Air Force

Boeing 727-22C
40 Sqn, Whenuapai
NZ7271
NZ7272

Lockheed C-130H Hercules
40 Sqn, Whenuapai
NZ7001
NZ7002
NZ7003
NZ7004
NZ7005

Lockheed P-3B Orion
5 Sqn, Whenuapai
NZ4201
NZ4202
NZ4203
NZ4204
NZ4205
NZ4206

NIGERIA
Federal Nigerian Air Force

Lockheed C-130H Hercules
NAF-910
NAF-911
NAF-912
NAF-913
NAF-914
NAF-915
NAF-916
NAF-917
NAF-918

NORWAY
Kongelige Norske Luftforsvaret

Dassault Falcon 20 ECM
335 Skv, Gardermoen
041
053
0125

General Dynamics F-16A/*F-16B
331 Skv, Bøsø;
332 Skv, Rygge;
334 Skv, Bodø;
338 Skv, Orland

Serial	
272	332 Skv
273	332 Skv
274	332 Skv
275	332 Skv
276	332 Skv
277	332 Skv
278	332 Skv
279	332 Skv
281	332 Skv
282	332 Skv
284	332 Skv
285	332 Skv
286	332 Skv
287	338 Skv
288	338 Skv
289	338 Skv
290	338 Skv
291	338 Skv
292	338 Skv
293	338 Skv
294	332 Skv
295	332 Skv
296	338 Skv
297	338 Skv
298	338 Skv
299	332 Skv
300	334 Skv
302*	332 Skv
303*	332 Skv
304*	332 Skv
305*	332 Skv
306*	338 Skv
307*	338 Skv
658	334 Skv
659	334 Skv
660	334 Skv
661	334 Skv
662	334 Skv
663	334 Skv
664	334 Skv
665	334 Skv
666	334 Skv
667	334 Skv
668	334 Skv
669	334 Skv
670	334 Skv
671	334 Skv
672	334 Skv
673	331 Skv
674	331 Skv
675	331 Skv
676	331 Skv
677	331 Skv
678	331 Skv
679	331 Skv
680	331 Skv
681	331 Skv
682	331 Skv
683	334 Skv
684	331 Skv
685	331 Skv
686	331 Skv
687	331 Skv
688	331 Skv
689*	331 Skv
690*	332 Skv
691*	334 Skv
692*	334 Skv
693*	332 Skv

Lockheed C-130H Hercules
335 Skv, Gardermoen
952
953
954
955
956
957

Lockheed P-3B Orion
333 Skv, Andøya
576
583
599
600
601
602
603

Northrop F-5A
336 Skv, Rygge;
338 Skv, Orland

Serial	
125	336 Skv
128	336 Skv
129	338 Skv
130	338 Skv
131	336 Skv
132	336 Skv
133	336 Skv
134	336 Skv
207	336 Skv
208	336 Skv
210	336 Skv
214	338 Skv
215	336 Skv
220	336 Skv
222	336 Skv
225	336 Skv
369	336 Skv
370	33[illegible] Skv
372	338 Skv
373	338 Skv
374	336 Skv
375	338 Skv
563	338 Skv
565	336 Skv
568	338 Skv
571	338 Skv
573	338 Skv
575	336 Skv
895	336 Skv
896	338 Skv
897	336 Skv
898	336 Skv
901	338 Skv
902	336 Skv
904	338 Skv

Northrop F-5B
336 Skv, Ryge; 135
135

Serial

136
241
242
243
244
387
594
595
906
907
908

Westland
Sea King Mk43
330 Skv, Bødø
060
062
066
068
069
070
071
072
073
074
189

Westland Lynx
Mk86
337 Skv
207
216
228
232
235
237

OMAN
Al Quwwat al Jawwiya al Saltanat Oman

BAC 1-11
srs 485GD
45 Sqn, Seeb
551
552
553

Lockheed
C-130H Hercules
45 Sqn, Seeb
501
502
503

Short Skyvan 3M
25 Sqn, Seeb
901
902
903
904
906
907
908
910
911
912
913
914
915
916

PORTUGAL
Forca Aerea Portuguesa

Cessna T-37C
*Asas de Portugal
102 Esq, Sintra
2401

Serial

2402
2403
2404*
2407*
2410
2411
2412
2415*
2417
2418
2419
2420
2421*
2422
2423*
2424
2425
2426*
2427
2428
2429*
2430

Lockheed
C-130H Hercules
501 Esq, Montijo
6801
6802
6803
6804
6805

Falcon 20C
504 Esq, Lisbon
8101
8102
8103

SAUDI ARABIA
Al Quwwat Al-Jawwiya as Sa' udiya

Grumman
Gulfstream III
1 Sqn, Riyadh
103 (HZ-109)
107

Lockheed
C-130 Hercules
4 Sqn, Jeddah
16 Sqn, Jeddah

451 C-130E
452 C-130E
455 C-130E
456 KC-130H
457 KC-130H
458 KC-130H
459 KC-130H
460 C-130H
461 C-130H
462 C-130H
463 C-130H
464 C-130H
465 C-130H
466 C-130H
467 C-130H
468 C-130H
469 C-130H
470 C-130H
1601 C-130H
1602 C-130H
1603 C-130H
1604 C-130H
1605 C-130H
1606 C-130E
1607 C-130E

Serial

1608 C-130E
1609 C-130E
1610 C-130E
1611 C-130E
1612 C-130H
1614 C-130H
1615 C-130H
1616 KC-130H
1617 KC-130H
1618 C-130H
1619 C-130H
1620 KC-130H
1621 KC-130H

Lockheed Jetstar
1 Sqn, Riyadh
101
102

SINGAPORE
Republic of Singapore Air Force

Lockheed
C-130B Hercules
122 Sqn, Changi
720
721

Lockheed
C-130H Hercules
122 Sqn, Changi
724
725
730
731
732
733

SPAIN
Ejercito del Aire

CASA 101 Aviojet
411/412 Esc, Zaragoza
793 Esc, San Javier

XE.25-02 793-02
XE.25-03 793-03
XE.25.04 793.04
E.25-05 793-05
E.25-06 793-06
E.25-07 793-07
E.25-08 793-08
E.25-09 793-09
E.25-10 793-10
E.25-11 793-11
E.25-12 793-12
E.25-13 793-13
E.25-14 793-14
E.25-15 793-15
E.25-16 793-16
E.25-17 793-17
E.25-18 793-18
E.25-19 793-19
E.25-20 793-20
E.25-21 793-21
E.25-22 793-22
E.25-23 793-23
E.25-24 793-24
E.25-25 793-25
E.25-26 793-26
E.25-27 793-27
E.25-28 793-28
E.25-29 793-29
E.25-30 793-30
E.25-31 793-31
E.25-32 411-01

Serial	
E.25-33	412-25
E.25-34	411-02
E.25-35	412-26
E.25-36	411-03
E.25-37	412-27
E.25-38	411-04
E.25-39	412-28
E.25-40	411-05
E.25-41	412-29
E.25-42	793-32
E.25-43	793-33
E.25-44	793-34
E.25-45	793-35
E.25-46	793-36
E.25-47	793-37
E.25-48	793-38
E.25-49	793-39
E.25-50	793-40
E.25-51	411-06
E.25-52	412-30
E.25-53	411-07
E.25-54	412-31
E.25-55	411-08
E.25-56	412-32
E.25-57	411-09
E.25-58	412-33
E.25-59	411-10
E.25-60	412-34
E.25-61	411-11
E.25-62	412-35
E.25-63	411-12
E.25-64	412-36
E.25-65	411-13
E.25-66	412-37
E.25-67	411-14
E.25-68	412-38
E.25-69	411-15
E.25-70	412-39
E.25-71	411-16
E.25-72	412-40
E.25-73	411-17
E.25-74	412-41
E.25-75	411-18
E.25-76	412-42
E.25-77	411-19
E.25-78	412-43
E.25-79	411-20
E.25-80	412-44
E.25-81	411-21
E.25-82	412-45
E.25-83	411-22
E.25-84	793-41
E.25-85	411-23
E.25-86	412-47
E.25-87	411-24
E.25-88	412-48

Casa 212 Aviocar

212 (XT.12),
212A (T.12B),
212B (TR.12A),
212D (TE.12B),
212E (T.12C).
351/352 Esc Getafe;
403 Esc Cuatro Vientos;
406 Esc Torrejon;
461 Esc Gando, Las Palmas;
721 Esc Alcantarilla;
744/745 Esc Matacan;
792 Esc San Javier.

Serial	
XT.12-1	406-10
XT.12-2	406-11
TR.12A-3	403-11
TR.12A-4	403-12
TR.12A-5	403-13
TR.12A-6	403-14
TR.12A-7	403-15
TR.12A-8	792-3
TE.12B-9	792-5
TE.12B-10	745-10
T.12B-12	352-12
T.12B-13	745-13
T.12B-14	461-14
T.12B-15	351-15
T.12B-16	744-16
T.12B-17	352-17
T.12B-18	461-18
T.12B-19	461-19
T.12B-20	351-20
T.12B-21	352-21
T.12B-22	352-22
T.12B-23	721-23
T.12B-24	252-24
T.12B-25	744-25
T.12B-26	721-26
T.12B-27	461-27
T.12B-28	721-28
T.12B-29	352-29
T.12B-30	744-30
T.12B-31	461-31
T.12B-32	352-32
T.12B-33	721-33
T.12B-34	744-34
T.12B-35	461-35
T.12B-36	351-36
T.12B-37	721-37
T.12B-38	352-38
T.12B-39	745-39
T.12B-40	792-2
T.12B-41	792-4
T.12B-42	792-6
T.12B-43	461-43
T.12B-44	405-44
T.12B-46	745-46
T.12B-47	721-47
T.12B-48	352-48
T.12B-49	352-49
T.12B-50	745-50
T.12B-51	744-51
T.12B-52	721-52
T.12B-53	351-53
T.12B-54	351-54
T.12B-55	461-55
T.12B-56	745-56
T.12B-57	721-57
T.12B-58	461-58
T.12B-59	352-59
T.12B-60	351-60
T.12B-61	351-61
T.12B-63	351-63
T.12B-64	461-64
T.12B-65	745-65
T.12B-66	721-66
T.12B-67	745-67
T.12B-68	351-68
T.12B-69	351-69
T.12B-70	352-70
T.12B-71	351-71
TR.12D-72	408-01
TR.12D-73	408-02
TR.12D-74	408-03

Dassault Falcon 20

401 Esc, Madrid

Serial
TM.11-1/401-02
TM.11-2/401-03
TM.11-3/401-04
TM.11-4/401-05

Dassault Falcon 50

401 Esc, Madrid

T.16-1/401-09

Douglas DC8-52

401 Esc, Madrid

T.15-1/401-01
T.15-2/401-07

Fokker F.27M Friendship 400MPA

802 Esc, Gando

D.2-01
D.2-02
D.2-03

Lockheed C-130H Hercules

311 Esc/312 Esc, Zaragoza

T.10-2/311-02
T.10-3/311-03
T.10-4/311-04
T.10-8/311-05
T.10-9/311-06
T.10-10/312-04

Lockheed KC-130H Hercules

312 Esc, Zaragosa

TK.10-5/312-01
TK.10-6/312-02
TK.10-7/312-03
TK.10-11/312-05
TK.10-12/312-06

SWEDEN

Kungl Svenska Flygvapnet

Lockheed C-130E Hercules

F7, Satenäs

84001/841
84002/842

Lockheed C-130H Hercules

F7, Satenäs

84003/843
84004/844
84005/845
84006/846
84007/847
84008/848

Cessna 404

87001/871
87002/872
87003/873

Metro III

88001/881
88002/882
88003/883

SWITZERLAND

Schweizerische Flugwaffe

Beech E-50 Twin Bonanza

A-711
A-712
A-713

THAILAND

Royal Thai Air Force

DC.8-62AF

60112 (HS-TGO)

Serial

TURKEY
Turk Hava Kuvvetleri
Lockheed C-130D Hercules
221 Sqn
019
020
021
022
023
024
026
027
028
029
030
031
032
033
034
035
036
038
039
040
Lockheed C-130E Hercules
222 Sqn, Erkilet
ETI-00991
ETI-01468
ETI-12186
ETI-12947
ETI-13187
ETI-13188
ETI-13189
ETI-17949
Vickers V794 Viscount
8th VIP Unit, Yesilkoy
246
430
431

UNITED ARAB EMIRATES
United Arab Emirates Air Force
Abu Dhabi
Lockheed C-130H Hercules
1212
1213
1214
Dubai
Lockheed C-130H Hercules
311
312

WEST GERMANY
Luftwaffe
Boeing 707-307C
FBS, Cologne/Bonn
10+01
10+02
10+03
10+04
Canadair CL601 Challenger
FBS, Cologne/Bonn
12+01
12+02
12+03
12+04
12+05
12+06
12+07
HFB 320 Hansa Jet
*FBS, Cologne/Bonn;
†JBG32 Lechfeld;
‡ES 61, Ingolstadt
16+01*
16+02*
16+03*
16+04*
16+05*
16+06*
16+07‡
16+08‡
16+21†
16+22
16+23†
16+24†
16+25†
16+26†
16+27†
16+28†
VFW 614
FBS, Cologne/Bonn
17+01
17+02
17+03
McD RF-4E Phantom
AKG 51, Bremgarten;
AKG 52, Leck;
TSLW 1, Kaufbeuren;
ES 61, Ingolstadt
35+01 ES 61
35+02 AKG 52
35+03 AKG 51
35+04 AKG 51
35+05 AKG 52
35+06 AKG 51
35+07 AKG 51
35+08 AKG 52
35+09 AKG 52
35+10 AKG 52
35+11 AKG 52
35+12 AKG 51
35+13 AKG 52
35+14 AKG 52
35+17 AKG 52
35+18 AKG 52
35+19 AKG 51
35+20 AKG 52
35+21 AKG 52
35+22 AKG 51
35+24 AKG 52
35+25 AKG 51
35+26 AKG 52
35+28 AKG 51
35+29 AKG 51
35+31 AKG 52
35+32 AKG 52
35+33 AKG 51
35+34 AKG 51
35+35 AKG 51
35+36 AKG 52
35+37 AKG 52
35+38 AKG 51
35+39 AKG 52
35+40 AKG 51
35+41 AKG 52
35+42 AKG 52
35+43 AKG 52
35+44 AKG 51
35+46 AKG 51
35+48 AKG 51
35+49 AKG 51
35+50 AKG 51
35+51 AKG 51
35+52 AKG 52
35+53 AKG 52
35+54 AKG 52
35+56 AKG 51
35+57 AKG 51
35+58 AKG 51
35+59 AKG 51
35+60 AKG 52
35+61 AKG 51
35+62 TSLW 1
35+63 AKG 51
35+64 AKG 51
35+65 AKG 52
35+66 AKG 52
35+67 AKG 52
35+68 AKG 51
35+69 AKG 52
35+71 AKG 51
35+72 AKG 52
35+73 AKG 51
35+74 AKG 52
35+75 AKG 52
35+76 AKG 52
35+77 AKG 52
35+78 AKG 51
35+79 AKG 52
35+82 AKG 51
35+83 ES 61
35+84 AKG 52
35+85 AKG 52
35+86 AKG 51
35+87 AKG 52
35+88 AKG 51
McD F-4F Phantom
JBG 35, Pferdsfeld;
JBG 36, Hopsten;
JG 71, Wittmundhaven;
JG 74, Neuberg;
TSLW 1, Kaufbeuren;
ES 61, Ingolstadt
37+01 JBG 36
37+03 JG 71
37+04 TSLW 1
37+05 JG 74
37+06 JG 71
37+07 JBG 36
37+08 JG 71
37+09 JBG 35
37+10 JG 71
37+11 JG 74
37+12 JBG 36
37+13 JBG 35
37+14 TSLW 1
37+15 ES 61
37+16 ES 61
37+17 JBG 36
37+18 JBG 35
37+19 JG 71
37+20 JG 74
37+21 JBG 36
37+22 JBG 35
37+23 JG 71
37+24 JG 74
37+25 JBG 36
37+26 JBG 35

Serial	
37+27	JG 71
37+28	JBG 35
37+29	JBG 36
37+30	JBG 35
37+31	JG 71
37+32	JG 74
37+33	JBG 36
37+34	JBG 35
37+35	JG 71
37+36	JG 74
37+37	JBG 36
37+38	JBG 35
37+39	JG 71
37+40	JG 74
37+41	JBG 36
37+42	JBG 35
37+43	JG 71
37+44	JG 74
37+45	JBG 36
37+46	JBG 35
37+47	JG 71
37+48	JG 74
37+49	JBG 36
37+50	JBG 35
37+51	JG 71
37+52	JBG 35
37+53	JBG 36
37+54	JBG 35
37+55	JBG 36
37+56	JG 74
37+57	JBG 36
37+58	JBG 35
37+60	JG 74
37+61	JG 71
37+63	JG 71
37+64	JG 74
37+65	JBG 36
37+66	JBG 35
37+67	JG 71
37+69	JBG 36
37+70	JBG 35
37+71	JG 71
37+73	JBG 36
37+75	JG 71
37+76	JG 74
37+77	JBG 36
37+78	JBG 35
37+79	JG 71
37+81	JBG 36
37+82	JBG 35
37+83	JG 71
37+84	JG 74
37+85	JBG 36
37+86	JG 71
37+88	JG 74
37+89	JBG 36
37+90	JBG 36
37+91	ES 61
37+92	JG 74
37+93	JBG 36
37+94	JBG 35
37+96	JG 74
37+97	JBG 36
37+98	JBG 35
38+00	JG 74
38+01	JBG 36
38+02	JBG 35
38+03	JG 71
38+04	JG 74
38+05	JBG 36
38+06	JG 74
38+07	JG 71
38+08	JG 74

Serial	
38+09	JBG 36
38+10	JBG 35
38+11	JG 71
38+12	JG 74
38+13	JBG 36
38+14	JBG 35
38+15	JG 71
38+16	JG 74
38+17	JBG 36
38+18	JBG 35
38+20	JG 74
38+21	JBG 36
38+24	JG 74
38+25	JBG 36
38+26	JBG 35
38+27	JG 71
38+28	JG 74
38+29	JBG 36
38+30	JBG 35
38+31	JG 71
38+32	JG 74
38+33	JBG 36
38+34	JBG 35
38+36	JBG 74
38+37	JBG 36
38+38	JBG 35
38+39	JG 71
38+40	JG 74
38+42	JBG 35
38+43	JG 71
38+44	JG 74
38+45	JBG 36
38+46	JBG 35
38+47	JG 71
38+48	JG 74
38+49	JBG 36
38+50	JBG 35
38+51	JG 71
38+52	JG 74
38+53	JBG 36
38+54	JBG 35
38+55	JG 71
38+56	JG 74
38+57	JBG 36
38+58	JBG 35
38+59	JG 71
38+60	JG 74
38+61	JG 71
38+62	JBG 35
38+63	JG 71
38+64	JG 74
38+66	JG 71
38+67	JG 71
38+68	JG 74
38+69	JBG 36
38+70	JBG 35
38+72	JG 74
38+73	JBG 36
38+74	JBG 35
38+75	JBG 35

D-BD Alpha Jet

JBG 41, Husum; JBG 43, Oldenburg; JBG 49, Fürstenfeldbruck; JBG 44, Beja (Portugal)

40+01	ES 61
40+02	ES 61
40+03	JBG 49
40+04	JBG 43
40+05	JBG 49
40+06	JBG 49

Serial	
40+07	JBG 49
40+08	JBG 44
40+09	JBG 41
40+10	JBG 41
40+11	JBG 43
40+12	JBG 49
40+13	JBG 43
40+14	JBG 43
40+15	JBG 41
40+16	JBG 41
40+17	JBG 49
40+18	JBG 49
40+20	JBG 43
40+21	JBG 41
40+22	JBG 41
40+23	JBG 49
40+24	JBG 43
40+25	JBG 49
40+26	JBG 41
40+27	JBG 43
40+28	JBG 41
40+29	JBG 49
40+30	JBG 49
40+31	JBG 43
40+32	JBG 43
40+33	JBG 41
40+34	JBG 41
40+35	JBG 49
40+36	JBG 43
40+37	JBG 49
40+38	JBG 43
40+39	JBG 41
40+40	JBG 49
40+41	JBG 41
40+42	JBG 49
40+43	JBG 43
40+44	JBG 43
40+45	JBG 41
40+46	JBG 43
40+47	JBG 49
40+48	JBG 44
40+49	JBG 49
40+50	JBG 43
40+51	JBG 41
40+52	JBG 44
40+53	JBG 44
40+54	JBG 43
40+56	ES 61
40+57	JBG 43
40+58	JBG 43
40+59	JBG 49
40+60	JBG 41
40+61	JBG 43
40+62	JBG 41
40+63	JBG 41
40+64	JBG 49
40+65	JBG 49
40+66	JBG 44
40+67	JBG 49
40+68	JBG 41
40+69	JBG 43
40+70	JBG 41
40+71	LKO
40+72	JBG 44
40+73	JBG 49
40+74	JBG 41
40+75	JBG 43
40+76	JBG 41
40+77	JBG 49
40+78	JBG 43
40+79	JBG 43
40+80	JBG 43
40+81	JBG 41

Serial	
40+82	JBG 49
40+83	JBG 41
40+84	JBG 49
40+85	JBG 49
40+86	JBG 43
40+87	JBG 43
40+88	JBG 41
40+89	JBG 41
40+90	JBG 49
40+91	JBG 49
40+92	JBG 43
40+93	JBG 44
40+94	JBG 44
40+95	JBG 43
40+96	JBG 49
40+97	JBG 49
40+98	JBG 41
40+99	JBG 41
41+00	JBG 43
41+01	JBG 43
41+02	JBG 41
41+03	JBG 41
41+04	JBG 49
41+05	JBG 43
41+06	JBG 41
41+07	JBG 49
41+08	JBG 49
41+09	JBG 49
41+10	LKO
41+11	JBG 49
41+12	JBG 43
41+13	JBG 43
41+14	JBG 41
41+15	JBG 41
41+16	JBG 44
41+17	JBG 44
41+18	JBG 43
41+19	JBG 43
41+20	JBG 41
41+21	JBG 41
41+22	JBG 44
41+23	JBG 44
41+24	JBG 41
41+25	JBG 49
41+26	JBG 49
41+27	JBG 43
41+28	JBG 43
41+29	JBG 44
41+30	JBG 44
41+31	JBG 41
41+32	JBG 41
41+33	JBG 41
41+34	JBG 43
41+35	JBG 49
41+36	JBG 49
41+37	JBG 49
41+38	JBG 49
41+39	JBG 43
41+40	JBG 43
41+41	JBG 41
41+42	JBG 43
41+43	JBG 43
41+44	JBG 49
41+45	JBG 49
41+46	JBG 43
41+47	JBG 41
41+48	JBG 41
41+49	JBG 49
41+50	JBG 49
41+51	JBG 43
41+52	JBG 43
41+53	JBG 41
41+54	JBG 41
41+55	JBG 49
41+56	JBG 49
41+57	JBG 43
41+58	JBG 43
41+59	JBG 41
41+60	JBG 41
41+61	JBG 49
41+62	JBG 49
41+63	JBG 43
41+64	JBG 43
41+65	JBG 41
41+66	JBG 41
41+67	JBG 49
41+68	JBG 49
41+70	JBG 43
41+71	JBG 41
41+72	JBG 41
41+73	JBG 41
41+74	JBG 41
41+75	JBG 41

Panavia Tornado
***Marinesflieger 1, Schleswig**
†TTTE RAF Cottesmore;
JBG 31, Nörvenich;
JBG 32, Lechfeld;
JBG 33, Büchel;
JBG 38, Jever

Serial	
43+01/G-20†	
43+02/G-21†	
43+03/G-22†	
43+04/G-23†	
43+05/G-24†	
43+06/G-25†	
43+07/G-26†	
43+08/G-27†	
43+09/G-28†	
43+10/G-29†	
43+11/G-30†	
43+12/G-70†	
43+13/G-71†	
43+14/G-72†	
43+15/G-31†	
43+16/G-32†	
43+17/G-33†	
43+18/G-77†	
43+19/G-78†	
43+20/G-73†	
43+22	JBG 38
43+23/G-34†	
43+25/G-75†	
43+26/G-76†	
43+27	MFG 1
43+28	JBG 38
43+29	JBG 31
43+30	JBG 38
43+31/G-36†	
43+32	JBG 38
43+33	JBG 38
43+34	JBG 38
43+35/G-38†	
43+36	JBG 38
43+37/G-37†	
43+38	JBG 38
43+40	JBG 38
43+41	JBG 31
43+42*	MFG 1
43+43*	MFG 1
43+44*	MFG 1
43+45*	MFG 1
43+46*	MFG 1
43+47*	MFG 1
43+48*	MFG 1
43+50*	MFG 1
43+51*	MFG 1
43+52*	MFG 1
43+53*	MFG 1
43+54*	MFG 1
43+55*	MFG 1
43+56*	MFG 1
43+57*	MFG 1
43+58*	MFG 1
43+59*	MFG 1
43+60*	MFG 1
43+61*	MFG 1
43+62*	MFG 1
43+63*	MFG 1
43+64*	MFG 1
43+65*	MFG 1
43+67*	MFG 1
43+68*	MFG 1
43+69*	MFG 1
43+70*	MFG 1
43+71*	MFG 1
43+72*	MFG 1
43+73*	MFG 1
43+74*	MFG 1
43+75*	MFG 1
43+76*	MFG 1
43+77*	MFG 1
43+78*	MFG 1
43+79	JBG 38
43+80*	MFG 1
43+81*	MFG 1
43+82*	MFG 1
43+83*	MFG 1
43+84*	MFG 1
43+85*	MFG 1
43+86*	TSLW
43+87*	MFG 1
43+88*	MFG 1
43+89*	MFG 1
43+90	JBG 38
43+91	JBG 38
43+92	JBG 31
43+94	JBG 31
43+95	JBG 32
43+96	JBG 31
43+97	JBG 31
43+98	JBG 38
43+99	JBG 31
44+00	JBG 31
44+01	JBG 38
44+02	JBG 31
44+03	JBG 31
44+04	JBG 31
44+05	JBG 38
44+06	JBG 31
44+07	JBG 31
44+08	JBG 38
44+09	JBG 31
44+10	JBG 38
44+11	JBG 38
44+12	JBG 31
44+13	JBG 38
44+14	JBG 31
44+15	JBG 38
44+16	JBG 31
44+17	JBG 38
44+18	JBG 31
44+19	JBG 31
44+20	JBG 38
44+21	JBG 31
44+22	JBG 31
44+23	JBG 31

Serial	
44+24	JBG 38
44+25	JBG 33
44+26	JBG 31
44+27	JBG 31
44+28	JBG 31
44+29	JBG 31
44+30	JBG 31
44+31	JBG 31
44+32	JBG 31
44+33	JBG 31
44+34	JBG 31
44+35	JBG 31
44+36	JBG 32
44+37	JBG 32
44+38	JBG 32
44+39	JBG 32
44+40	JBG 33
44+41	JBG 31
44+42	JBG 32
44+43	JBG 32
44+44	JBG 31
44+46	JBG 32
44+48	JBG 31
44+49	JBG 31
44+50	JBG 32
44+51	JBG 32
44+52	JBG 31
44+53	JBG 32
44+54	JBG 32
44+55	JBG 32
44+56	JBG 32
44+57	JBG 32
44+58	JBG 32
44+59	JBG 32
44+60	JBG 32
44+61	JBG 31
44+62	JBG 32
44+63	JBG 32
44+64	JBG 32
44+65	TSLW
44+66	JBG 32
44+67	JBG 32
44+68	JBG 32
44+69	JBG 32
44+70	JBG 32
44+71	JBG 32
44+72	JBG 33
44+73	JBG 33
44+74	JBG 33
44+75	JBG 33
44+76	JBG 32
44+77	JBG 32
44+78	JBG 32
44+79	JBG 32
44+80	JBG 32
44+81	JBG 32
44+82	JBG 32
44+83	JBG 32
44+84	JBG 32
44+85	JBG 32
44+86	JBG 33
44+87	JBG 33
44+88	JBG 33
44+89	JBG 33
44+90	
44+91	JBG 33
44+92	JBG 33
44+94	JBG 33
44+95	JBG 33
44+96	JBG 33
44+97	JBG 33
44+98	JBG 33
44+99	JBG 33

Serial	
44+00	JBG 33
45+01	JBG 33
45+02	JBG 33
45+03	JBG 33
45+04	JBG 33
45+05	JBG 33
45+06	JBG 33
45+07	JBG 33
45+08	JBG 33
45+09	JBG 33
45+10	JBG 33
45+11	JBG 33
45+12*	MFG 2
45+13	
45+14	JBG 33
45+15	JBG 33
45+16*	MFG2
45+17	JBG 33
45+18	JBG 33
45+19	JBG 33
45+20	JBG 33
45+21	JBG 33
45+22	JBG 33
45+23	JBG 33
45+24	JBG 33
45+25	JBG 33
45+26*	MFG 2
45+27	
45+28	
45+29	
45+30	
45+31	
45+32	
45+33	
45+34	
45+35	
45+36	
45+37	
45+38	
45+39	
45+40	
45+41	
45+42	
45+43	
45+44	
45+45	
45+46	
45+47	
45+48	
45+49	
45+50	
45+51	
45+52	
45+53	
45+54	
45+55	
45+56	
45+57	
45+58	
45+59	
45+60	

Transall C-160

LTG 61, Landsberg;
LTG 62, Wunstorf;
LTG 63, Hohn
ES61 Ingolstadt

50+06	LTG 61
50+07	LTG 61
50+08	LTG 61
50+09	LTG 62
50+10	LTG 62
50+17	LTG 62
50+29	LTG 62

Serial	
50+33	LTG 63
50+34	LTG 62
50+35	LTG 62
50+36	LTG 62
50+37	LTG 62
50+38	LTG 62
50+39	LTG 62
50+40	LTG 61
50+41	LTG 63
50+42	LTG 63
50+43	LTG 61
50+44	LTG 61
50+45	LTG 63
50+46	LTG 62
50+47	LTG 61
50+48	
50+49	LTG 61
50+50	LTG 63
50+51	LTG 61
50+52	LTG 62
50+53	LTG 62
50+54	LTG 63
50+55	LTG 62
50+56	LTG 63
50+57	LTG 61
50+58	LTG 63
50+59	LTG 63
50+60	LTG 62
50+61	LTG 63
50+62	LTG 61
50+64	LTG 61
50+65	LTG 62
50+66	LTG 61
50+67	LTG 63
50+68	LTG 61
50+69	LTG 63
50+70	ES 61
50+71	LTG 63
50+72	LTG 61
50+73	LTG 62
50+74	LTG 61
50+75	ES 61
50+76	LTG 63
50+77	LTG 63
50+78	LTG 62
50+79	LTG 63
50+80	LTG 61
50+81	LTG 62
50+82	LTG 63
50+83	LTG 62
50+84	LTG 63
50+85	LTG 61
50+86	LTG 61
50+87	LTG 63
50+88	LTG 61
50+89	LTG 62
50+90	LTG 63
50+91	LTG 62
50+92	LTG 61
50+93	LTG 61
50+94	LTG 62
50+95	LTG 63
50+96	LTG 61
50+97	LTG 62
50+98	LTG 61
50+99	LTG 61
51+00	LTG 63
51+01	LTG 61
51+02	LTG 63
51+03	LTG 62
51+04	LTG 61
51+05	LTG 62
51+06	LTG 63

Overseas Serials

Serial		Serial		Serial
51+07	LTG 62	58+78	JBG 31	**Westland Lynx Mk88**
51+08	LTG 63	58+79	LTG 62	Marinesflieger 3, Nordholz
51+09	LTG 63	58+80	JBG 33	83+01
51+10	LTG 61	58+81	LTG 62	83+02
51+11	LTG 62	58+82	JBG 43	83+03
51+12	LTG 63	58+83	LTG 62	83+04
51+13	LTG 61	58+84	JBG 43	83+05
51+14	LTG 63	58+85	JG 74	83+06
51+15	LTG 61	58+86	JBG 49	83+07
Dornier Do.28D-2 Skyservant		58+87	JBG 49	83+08
*Marinesflieger, Kiel		58+89	JBG 49	83+09
58+05		58+90	JBG 49	83+10
58+06		58+91		83+11
58+08	LTG 62	58+92	AKG 52	83+12
58+09	LTG 62	58+93		83+13
58+10		58+94	JBG 35	83+14
58+11		58+95		83+15
58+13		58+96		83+16
58+14	LTG 62	58+97		83+17
58+15	JBG 31	58+98	AKG 52	**Westland Sea King HAS.41**
58+16		58+99	JG 71	Marinesflieger 5, Kiel
58+17		59+00	FBS	89+50
58+18	LTG 63	59+01	FBS	89+51
58+20	JGB 31	59+02	FBS	89+52*
58+21		59+03	FBS	89+53
58+23	LTG 61	59+04	FBS	89+54
58+24		59+05	FBS	89+55
58+26	LTG 63	59+06*		89+56
58+27		59+07*		89+57
58+28	JBG 35	59+08*		89+58
58+29	LTG 61	59+09*		89+59
58+30	LTG 63	59+10*		89+60
58+31		59+11*		89+61
58+32	JG 74	59+12*		89+62
58+33		59+13*		89+63
58+34	LTG 62	59+14*		89+65
58+36	LTG 62	59+15*		89+66
58+37		59+16*		89+67
58+38	LTG 62	59+17*		89+68
58+39	LTG 62	59+18*		89+69
58+40		59+19*		89+70
58+41		59+20*		89+71
58+42		59+21*		**English Electric Canberra B2**
58+43		59+22*		ES 61, Manching
58+44		59+23*		99+34
58+46	LTG 62	59+24*		99+35
58+47		59+25*		
58+49	JBG 49	**Dornier Do228**		
58+50	JBG 33	Marinesflieger 5, Kiel		
58+51	JBG 31	98+78		
58+52	LTG 62	**Breguet 1151 Atlantic**		
58+53	JBG 32	Marinesflieger 3 Nordholz		
58+54	AKG 51	61+01		
58+55	JBG 32	61+02		
58+58	JBG 33	61+03		
58+59	JBG 34	61+04		
58+60	AKG 52	61+05		
58+61	JBG 34	61+06		
58+62	JBG 36	61+07		
58+64		61+08		
58+65	JG 71	61+09		
58+66	JBG 38	61+10		
58+67	JBG 38	61+11		
58+68	LTG 62	61+12		
58+69	LTG 62	61+13		
58+70	LTG 62	61+14		
58+71	LTG 61	61+15		
58+72	AKG 51	61+16		
58+73	JBG 31	61+17		
58+74	JBG 41	61+19		
58+76	JBG 41	61+20		
58+77	JBG 49			

Spanish AF CASA101 Aviojet E25-47. *PRM*

Swedish Navy B-V107 (Hkp-4) 04063. *APM*

United Arab Emirates C-130H Hercules 1214. *PRM*

USAFE F-16C Fighting Falcon 84-386 from Hahn. *PRM*

Gates C-21A Learjet 40085, a USAFE VIP transport. *APM*

US Army Beech U-21A 0-18021. *PRM*

US Military Aircraft Markings

All USAF aircraft have been allocated a fiscal year (FY) number since 1921. Individual aircraft are given a serial according to the fiscal year in which they are ordered. The numbers commence at 0001 and are prefixed with the year of allocation. For example F-111E 68-0001 was the first aircraft ordered in 1968. The fiscal year (FY) serial is carried on the technical bloc which is usually stencilled on the left-hand side of the aircraft just below the cockpit. The number displayed on the fin is a corruption of the FY serial. Most tactical aircraft carry the fiscal year in small figures followed by the last three digits of the serial in large figures. For example F-111F 70-2362 carries 70362 on its tail. An exception to this practice is the F-5E which carries the five digits of the production serial without the fiscal year. For example the FY serial of the F-5E which displays 01532 is 74-01532. Large transport and tanker aircraft such as C-130s and KC-135s usually display a five-figure number commencing with the last digit of the appropriate fiscal year and four figures of the production number. An example of this is EC-135H 61-0282 which displays 10282 on its fin. Aircraft of more than 10 years vintage which might duplicate a five-figure number of a more modern type in service, are prefixed 0-.

USN serials follow a straightforward numerical sequence which commenced, for the present series, with the allocation of 00001 to an SB2C Helldiver by the Bureau of Aeronautics in 1940. Numbers in the 163000 series are presently being issued. They are usually carried in full on the rear fuselage of the aircraft and displayed either as a four- or five-figure sequence or in full on the fin.

UK based USAF Aircraft

The following aircraft are normally based in the UK. They are listed in numerical order of type with individual aircraft in serial number order, as depicted on the aircraft. The number in brackets is either the alternative presentation of the five-figure number commencing with the last digit of the fiscal year, or the fiscal year where a five-figure serial is presented on the aircraft. Where it is possible to identify the allocation of aircraft to individual squadrons by means of colours carried on fin or cockpit edge, this is also provided.

Serial	*Notes*
Lockheed TR-1A	
(95RS/17RW, RAF Alconbury)	
01068 (FY80)	
01069 (FY80)	
01070 (FY80)	
01077 (FY80)	
01078 (FY80)	
01079 (FY80)	
01081 (FY80)	
01083 (FY80)	
01084 (FY80)	
01085 (FY80)	
McDonnell-Douglas RF-4C Phantom	
AR: 1TRS/10TRW, RAF Alconbury	
68-554 (80554)	
68-561 (80561)	
68-563 (80563)	
68-565 (80565)	
68-567 (80567) [10 TRW]	
68-568 (80568)	
68-580 (80580)	
68-589 (80589)	
69-369 (90369)	
69-370 (90370)	
69-378 (90378)	
69-380 (90380)	
69-381 (90381)	
69-382 (90382)	
69-383 (90383)	
69-384 (90384)	
71-259 (10259)	

Notes	Serial
	Northrop F-5E Tiger II
	527AS/10TRW, RAF Alconbury
	FY74
	01532
	01534
	01534 Replica at Alconbury gate
	01535
	01543
	01544
	01545
	01547
	01549
	01551
	01553
	01554
	01556
	01559
	01560
	01563
	01566
	01568
	01569
	Fairchild A-10A Thunderbolt II
	WR: 81TFW:
	78TFS red (r) Woodbridge
	91TFS blue (bl) Woodbridge
	92TFS yellow (y) Bentwaters
	509TFS grey (gy) Bentwaters
	510TFS purple (pr) Bentwaters
	511TFS black (bk) Bentwaters
	79-217 (90217)
	79-218 (90218) y
	79-219 (90219) bk
	79-220 (90220) gy
	79-221 (90221) pr
	79-224 (90224) gy
	79-225 (90225) bl
	80-143 (00143) r
	80-144 (00144) gy
	80-145 (00145) y
	80-146 (00146) bk
	80-147 (00147) pr
	80-155 (00155) pr
	80-156 (00156) bk
	80-157 (00157) bk
	80-158 (00158) bl
	80-159 (00159) y
	80-160 (00160) pr
	80-167 (00167) r
	80-168 (00168) y
	80-169 (00169) pr
	80-170 (00170) gy
	80-171 (00171) bl
	80-172 (00172) bk
	80-179 (00179) r
	80-180 (00180) bl
	80-181 (00181) y
	80-183 (00183) pr
	80-184 (00184) bk
	80-185 (00185)
	80-192 (00192) y
	80-194 (00194) gy
	80-195 (00195) pr
	80-196 (00196) bk
	80-203 (00203) r
	80-204 (00204) bl
	80-205 (00205) bl
	80-206 (00206) y
	80-207 (00207) y
	80-208 (00208) gy
	80-215 (00215) pr

Notes	Serial
	80-216 (00216) pr
	80-217 (00217) y
	80-218 (00218) gy
	80-219 (00219) gy
	80-220 (00220) bl
	80-227 (00227) gy
	80-228 (00228) pr
	80-229 (00229) bk
	80-230 (00230) bk
	80-231 (00231) gy
	80-232 (00232) bl
	80-233 (00233) r
	80-234 (00234) bl
	80-235 (00235) r
	80-236 (00236) r
	80-237 (00237) bk
	80-270 (00270) r
	80-271 (00271) bl
	80-272 (00272) y
	80-273 (00273) gy
	80-274 (00274) pr
	80-275 (00275) bk
	80-276 (00276) y
	80-277 (00277) bk
	80-278 (00278) r
	80-279 (00279) pr
	80-280 (00280) bl
	80-281 (00281) y
	81-939 (10939) gy
	81-940 (10940) bk
	81-941 (10941) r
	81-942 (10942) bl
	81-943 (10943) y
	81-944 (10944) pr
	81-947 (10947) gy
	81-948 (10948) gy
	81-949 (10949) bk
	81-950 (10950) bl
	81-951 (10951) bl
	81-952 (10952) pr
	81-953 (10953) gy
	81-954 (10954) y
	81-955 (10955) bk
	81-956 (10956) bl
	81-957 (10957) y
	81-960 (10960) r
	81-961 (10961) r
	81-962 (10962) bl
	81-963 (10963) y
	81-964 (10964) gy
	81-965 (10965) pr
	81-966 (10966) pr
	81-967 (10967) bk
	81-976 (10976) bl
	81-977 (10977) y
	81-978 (10978) r
	81-979 (10979) gy
	81-980 (10980) pr
	81-981 (10981) bk
	81-982 (10982) bl
	81-983 (10983) bl
	81-984 (10984) r
	81-985 (10985) y
	81-986 (10986) bk
	81-987 (10987) gy
	81-988 (10988) pr
	81-990 (10990) gy
	819-91 (10991) bl
	81-992 (10992) y
	82-646 (20646) pr
	82-647 (20647) bk
	82-649 (20649) bl
	82-650 (20650) pr

Serial	Notes
82-654 (20654) r	
82-655 (20655) bl '	
82-656 (20656) y	
82-657 (20657) gy	
82-658 (20658) r	
82-659 (20659) bk	

Sikorsky HH-53C
67 ARRS, RAF Woodbridge

Serial	Notes
5784 (FY69)	
5785 (FY69)	
5796 (FY69)	
5797 (FY69)	
8284 (FY68)	

General Dynamics EF-111A Raven
UH: RAF Upper Heyford
66ECIO/42ECS grey

Serial	Notes
66-030 (60030)	
66-033 (60033)	
66-037 (60037)	
66-039 (60039)	
66-041 (60041)	
66-055 (60055)	
66-056 (60056)	
66-057 (60057)	
67-032 (70032)	
67-034 (70034)	
67-035 (70035)	
67-041 (70041)	
67-052 (70052)	

General Dynamics F-111E
UH: 20TFW, RAF Upper Heyford
55TFS blue/white (bl)
77TFS red (r)
79TFS yellow/black (y)

Serial	Notes
67-119 (70119) bl	
67-120 (70120) r	
67-121 (70121) bl	
67-122 (70122) y	
67-123 (70123) y	
68-001 (80001) r	
68-002 (80002) y	
68-004 (80004) bl	
68-005 (80005) bl	
68-006 (80006) bl	
68-007 (80007) r	
68-009 (80009) r	
68-010 (80010) y	
68-011 (80011) r	
68-013 (80013) y	
68-014 (80014) bl	
68-015 (80015) bl	
68-016 (80016) bl	
68-017 (80017) r	
680-20 TFW (80020) multi	
68-021 (80021) r	
68-022 (80022) y	
68-023 (80023) y	
68-025 (80025) bl	
68-026 (80026) bl	
68-027 (80027) r	
68-028 (80028) r	
68-029 (80029) r	
68-030 (80030) y	
68-031 (80031) r	
68-032 (80032) y	
68-033 (80033) y	
68-034 (80034) bl	
68-035 (80035) bl	
68-036 (80036) bl	
68-037 (80037) r	
68-038 (80038) r	
68-039 (80039) r	
68-040 (80040) y	
68-041 (80041) r	
68-043 (80043) y	
68-044 (80044) bl	
68-046 (80046) bl	
68-047 (80047) r	
68-048 (80048) r	
68-049 (80049) r	
68-050 (80050) y	
68-051 (80051) r	
68-052 (80052) y	
68-053 (80053) y	
68-054 (80054) bl	
680-55 (80055) bl	
68-056 (80056) bl	
68-059 (80059) r	
68-061 (80061) r	
68-062 (80062) y	
68-063 (80063) y	
68-064 (80064) bl	
68-065 (80065) bl	
68-066 (80066) bl	
68-067 (80067) r	
68-068 (80068) r	
68-069 (80069) r	
68-071 (80071) r	
68-072 (80072) y	
68-073 (80073) y	
68-074 (80074) bl	
68-075 (80075) bl	
68-076 (80076) bl	
68-077 (80077) r	
68-078 (80078) r	
68-079 (80079) y	
68-080 (80080) y	
68-082 (80082) y	
68-083 (80083) y	
68-084 (80084) bl	

General Dynamics F-111F
LN: 48TFW, RAF Lakenheath
492 TFS blue (bl)
493 TFS yellow (y)
494 TFS red (r)
495 TFS green (gn)

Serial	Notes
70-362 (02362) bl	
70-363 (02363) y	
70-364 (02364) bl	
70-365 (02365) bl	
70-368 (02368) bl	
70-369 (02369) bl	
70-370 (02370) bl	
70-371 (02371) gn	
70-372 (02372) r	
70-373 (02373) bl	
70-374 (02374) y	
70-375 (02375) bl	
70-376 (02376) y	
70-378 (02378) r	
70-379 (02379) r	
70-381 (02381) y	
70-382 (02382) y	
70-383 (02383) y	
70-384 (02384) r	
70-385 (02385) gn	
70-386 (02386) y	
70-387 (02387) gn	
70-390 (02390) multi	
70-391 (02391) gn	

USAF (UK based)

Notes	Serial	Notes	Serial
	70-392 (02392) gn 70-394 (02394) bl 70-396 (02396) bl 70-397 (02397) y 70-398 (02398) gn 70-399 (02399) bl 70-401 (02401) r 70-402 (02402) y 70-403 (02403) bl 70-404 (02404) y 70-405 (02405) r 70-406 (02406) bl 70-408 (02408) r 70-409 (02409) r 70-411 (02411) bl 70-412 (02412) gn 70-413 (02413) r 70-414 (02414) gn 70-415 (02415) y 70-416 (02416) r 70-417 (02417) r 70-418 (02418) bl 70-419 (02419) gn 71-883 (10883) y 71-884 (10884) gn 71-885 (10885) gn 71-886 (10886) bl 71-887 (10887) y 71-888 (10888) bl 71-889 (10889) y 71-890 (10890) y 71-891 (10891) y 71-892 (10892) y 71-893 (10893) bl 71-894 (10894) gn 72-442 (21442) bl 72-443 (21443) r 72-444 (21444) r 72-445 (21445) gn 72-446 (21446) gn		72-448 (21448) multi 72-449 (21449) y 72-450 (21450) y 72-451 (21451) y 72-452 (21452) y 73-707 (30707) r 73-708 (30708) r 73-710 (30710) r 73-711 (30711) gn 73-712 (30712) gn 73-713 (30713) gn 73-715 (30715) r 74-177 (40177) bl 74-178 (40178) gn 74-180 (40180) bl 74-181 (40181) bl 74-182 (40182) y 74-183 (40183) gn 74-184 (40184) r 74-185 (40185) r **Lockheed C-130 Hercules** 67ARRS/39 ARRW, RAF Woodbridge 50962 (FY65) HC-130H 60220 (FY66) HC-130P 95820 (FY69) HC-130N 95823 (FY69) HC-130N 95826 (FY69) HC-130N 95827 (FY69) HC-130N **Boeing EC-135H** 513TAW/10 ACCS, RAF Mildenhall *FY61* 10282 EC-135H 10285 EC-135H 10286 EC-135H 10291 EC-135H

UK based US Navy Aircraft

Notes	Serial	Notes	Serial
	Beech UC-12B **8G:** Naval Air Facility, RAF Mildenhall 1322/8D (161322) 1503/8G (161503)		

European based USAF Aircraft

These aircraft are normally based in Western Europe with the USAFE. They are shown in numerical order of type designation, with individual aircraft in serial number order as carried on the aircraft. An alternative five-figure presentation of the serial is shown in brackets where appropriate. Fiscal year (FY) details are also provided if necessary. The unit allocation and operating bases are given for most aircraft.

Serial

Bell UH-1N
67ARRS
Det 2 Ramstein*
Det 9 Zaragoza†
FY69
96603†
96606*
96607*
96608*
96609*
96611†
96630†

McDonnell Douglas
RF-4C Phantom
ZR: 26TRW/38TRS
Zweibrucken green/white

Serial	
66-400 (60400)	
67-443 (70443)	
67-451 (70451)	
68-569 (80569)	
68-577 (80577)	
68-587 (80587)	
68-590 (80590)	
69-358 (90358)	
69-360 (90360)	
69-361 (90361)	
69-365 (90365)	
69-366 (90366)	
69-367 (90367)	
69-368 (90368)	[26 TRW]
69-371 (90371)	
69-372 (90372)	
69-374 (90374)	
71-249 (10249)	
71-251 (10251)	
71-254 (10254)	
72-152 (20152)	
72-153 (20153)	

McDonnell Douglas
F-4E Phantom
SP: 52TFW
Spangdahlem
23 TFS blue/white (bl)
81 TFS yellow/black (y)
480 TFS red/white (r)
*=TFS
†=TFW

Serial		
7-1247 (10247)	SP	y
71-079 (11079)	SP	r
72-122 (20122)	SP	r
72-139 (20139)	SP	bl
72-159 (20159)	SP	y
72-160 (20160)	SP	bl
72-165 (20165)	SP	r
72-166 (20166)	SP	y
72-167 (20167)	SP	r
72-407 (21407)	SP	bl
72-477 (21477)	SP	r
72-482 (21482)	SP	bl
72-483 (21483)	SP	r
72-485 (21485)	SP	r
74-038 (41038)	SP	r
74-044 (41044)	SP	bl
74-045 (41045)	SP	y
740-480 (41048)*	SP	r
74-049 (41049)	SP	r
74-050 (41050)	SP	r
740-52 (41052)†	SP	r
74-053 (41053)	SP	y
74-055 (41055)	SP	bl
74-056 (41056)	SP	y
74-057 (41057)	SP	y
74-059 (41059)	SP	bl
74-060 (41060)	SP	bl
74-622 (41622)	SP	bl
74-628 (41628)	SP	r
74-633 (41633)	SP	bl
74-634 (41634)	SP	y
74-635 (41635)	SP	r
74-636 (41636)	SP	y
74-638 (41638)	SP	bl
74-639 (41639)	SP	y
74-641 (41641)	SP	bl
74-642 (41642)	SP	y
74-644 (41644)	SP	bl
74-645 (41645)	SP	y
74-648 (41648)	SP	y
74-650 (40650)	SP	bl
74-650 (41650)	SP	y
74-651 (41651)	SP	bl
74-652 (40652)	SP	r
74-652 (41652)	SP	y
74-653 (40653)	SP	r
74-653 (41653)	SP	bl
74-654 (40654)	SP	bl
74-656 (40656)	SP	r
74-657 (40657)	SP	y
74-659 (40659)	SP	r
74-662 (40662)	SP	bl
74-663 (40663)	SP	y
74-664 (40664)	SP	bl

McDonnell Douglas
F-4G Phantom
SP: 52TFW
Spangdahlem
23 TFS blue/white (bl)
81 TFS yellow/black (y)
480 TFS red/white (r)

Serial	
69-202 (97202)	y
69-209 (97209)	r
69-210 (97210)	r
69-212 (97212)	bl
69-228 (97228)	bl
69-232 (97232)	r
69-234 (97234)	r
69-236 (97236)	r
69-237 (97237)	
69-241 (90241)	bl
69-242 (90242)	bl
69-245 (90245)	bl
69-247 (90247)	y
69-248 (90248)	r
69-250 (90250)	r
69-253 (90253)	r
69-255 (90255)	bl
69-258 (90258)	y
69-259 (90259)	bl
69-262 (97262)	bl
69-263 (97263)	y
69-268 (97268)	bl
69-269 (90269)	r
69-270 (97270)	r
69-274 (90274)	r
69-277 (97277)	
69-285 (90285)	y
69-286 (90286)	r
69-291 (97291)	bl
69-293 (97293)	y
69-295 (97295)	y
69-546 (97546)	bl
69-556 (97556)	y
69-558 (97558)	r
69-566 (97566)	bl
69-571 (97571)	bl
69-579 (97579)	r
69-582 (97582)	y
69-587 (97587)	y

McDonnell Douglas
C-9A Nightingale
*VIP 435TAW/55AAS Rhein Main
FY71
10875
10876*
10878*
10879
10880
10881
10882*

Fairchild A-10A
Thunderbolt II
WR: 81 TFW: RAF Woodbridge/Bentwaters, Forward Operating Locations (FOL) in West Germany

Det 1 Sembach AB
Det 2 WGAF Leipheim
Det 3 WGAF Ahlhorn
Det 4 WGAF Norvenich

At each, eight aircraft on rotation from the six UK-based Squadrons at RAF Woodbridge/Bentwaters — see USAF/UK-based section.

USAF (EUR based)

Beech C-12
(*58 MAS Ramstein
†7005ABS Stuttgart
‡JUSMG Torrejon
**MAAG Athens
§ MAAG, Ankara
‡‡JUSMG Turkey)

Serial		
22549 (FY76)†	C-12A	
22550 (FY76)†	C-12A	
22932 (FY77)†	C-12A	
22933 (FY77)†	C-12A	
30498 (FY83)**	C-12A	
31212 (FY83)‡	C-12A	
31216 (FY73)§	C-12A	
31218 (FY73)**	C-12A	
40161 (FY84)*	C-12F	
40162 (FY84)*	C-12F	
40163 (FY84)*	C-12F	
40164 (FY84)*	C-12F	
40165 (FY84)*	C-12F	
40166 (FY84)*	C-12F	
60173 (FY70)§	C-12A	

McDonnell Douglas F-15C/‡F-15D Eagle
CR: 32TFS Soesterberg
green/orange (gn)
orange/green (or)
BT: 36TFW Bitburg
22TFS red (r)
53TFS yellow/black (y)
525TFS blue (bl)
IS: 57FIS Keflavik

Serial		
78-549 (80549)	BT	bl
78-550 (80550)	BT	bl
79-004 (90004)‡	CR	or
79-005 (90005)‡	CR	gn
79-006 (90006)‡	BT	bl
79-007 (90007)‡	BT	y
79-008 (90008)‡	BT	bl
79-009 (90009)‡	BT	y
79-010 (90010)‡	BT	y
79-011 (90011)‡	BT	r
79-012 (90012)‡	BT	r
79-015 (90015)	CR	or
79-016 (90016)	CR	or
79-017 (90017)	CR	or
79-018 (90018)	CR	or
79-019 (90019)	CR	or
79-020 (90020)	CR	or
79-021 (90021)	CR	or
79-022 (90022)	BT	r
79-023 (90023)	CR	or
79-024 (90024)	CR	or
79-025 (90025)	BT	bl
79-026 (90026)	CR	gn
79-027 (90027)	CR	gn
79-028 (90028)	CR	gn
79-029 (90029)	CR	gn
79-030 (90030)	CR	gn
79-031 (90031)	CR	gn
79-032 (90032)	CR	gn
79-033 (90033)	CR	gn
79-034 (90034)	CR	gn
79-035 (90035)	BT	bl
79-036 (90036)	BT	
79-037 (90037)	BT	bl
79-038 (90038)	BT	bl
79-039 (90039)	BT	bl
79-041 (90041)	BT	bl
79-042 (90042)	BT	bl
79-043 (90043)	BT	bl
79-045 (90045)	BT	bl
79-046 (90046)	BT	bl
79-047 (90047)	BT	bl
79-048 (90048)	BT	y
79-049 (90049)	BT	r
79-050 (90050)	BT	bl
79-051 (90051)	BT	r
79-052 (90052)	BT	r
790-53 (90053)	BT	y
79-054 (90054)	BT	r
79-055 (90055)	BT	bl
79-056 (90056)	BT	r
79-057 (90057)	BT	r
79-058 (90058)	BT	bl
79-059 (90059)	BT	r
79-060 (90060)	BT	r
79-062 (90062)	BT	bl
79-063 (90063)	BT	r
79-064 (90064)	BT	r
79-065 (90065)	BT	r
79-066 (90066)	BT	y
79-067 (90067)	BT	y
79-068 (90068)	BT	y
79-069 (90069)	BT	y
79-070 (90070)	BT	y
79-072 (90072)	BT	y
79-073 (90073)	BT	y
79-074 (90074)	BT	y
79-075 (90075)	BT	y
79-076 (90076)	BT	y
79-077 (90077)	BT	y
79-078 (90078)	BT	y
79-079 (90079)	BT	r
79-080 (90080)	BT	y
79-081 (90081)	BT	y
80-002 (00002)	BT	bl
80-003 (00003)	BT	y
80-004 (00004)	BT	r
80-005 (00005)	BT	r
80-006 (00006)	BT	r
80-009 (00009)	BT	r
80-010 (00010)	BT	r
80-011 (00011)	BT	y
80-012 (00012)	BT	y
80-013 (00013)	BT	y
80-014 (00014)	BT	y
80-015 (00015)	BT	y
80-016 (00016)	BT	r
80-017 (00017)	BT	bl
80-018 (00018)	BT	bl
80-019 (00019)	BT	bl
80-020 (00020)	BT	bl
80-021 (00021)	BT	r
80-022 (00022)	BT	r
80-023 (00023)	BT	r
80-024 (00024)	BT	bl
80-026 (00026)	BT	r
80-028 (00028)	BT	y
80-029 (00029)	BT	bl
80-031 (00031)	BT	r
80-033 (00033)	IS	
80-034 (00034)	IS	
80-035 (00035)	IS	
80-038 (00038)	IS	
80-039 (00039)	IS	
80-040 (00040)	IS	
80-041 (00041)	IS	
80-042 (00042)	IS	
80-043 (00043)	IS	
80-044 (00044)	IS	
80-045 (00045)	IS	
80-046 (00046)	IS	
80-047 (00047)	IS	
80-048 (00048)	IS	
80-049 (00049)	IS	
80-050 (00050)	IS	
80-051 (00051)	IS	
80-052 (00052)	IS	
80-056 (00056)‡	IS	
80-057 (00057)‡	IS	
81-027 (10027)	CR	
81-045 (10045)	CR	or
81-046 (10046)	CR	or
81-047 (10047)	CR	or
81-048 (10048)	CR	gn
81-049 (10049)	CR	gn
81-065 (10065)‡	CR	gn

General Dynamics F-16A/‡F-16B
HR: 50TFW Hahn
10TFS blue (bl)
313TFS orange (or)
496TFS yellow (y)
TJ: 401TFW Torrejon
612TFS blue/white (bl)
613TFS yellow/black (y)
614TFS red/black (r)

Serial		
80-543 (00543)	HR	or
80-544 (00544)	HR	
80-545 (00545)	HR	
80-546 (00546)	HR	or
80-555 (00555)	HR	or
80-556 (00556)	HR	bl
80-563 (00563)	HR	or
80-572 (00572)	HR	
80-574 (00574)	HR	or
80-575 (00575)	HR	or
80-576 (00576)	HR	or
80-585 (00585)	HR	or
80-588 (00588)	HR	
80-589 (00589)	HR	bl
80-604 (00604)	HR	
80-605 (00605)	HR	or
80-608 (00608)	HR	
80-612 (00612)	HR	
80-615 (00615)	HR	bl
80-618 (00618)	HR	or
80-619 (00619)	HR	or
80-622 (00622)	HR	
80-636 (00636)‡	HR	or
81-665 (10665)	HR	
81-671 (10671)	HR	or
81-673 (10673)	HR	bl
81-674 (10674)	HR	or
81-680 (10680)	HR	bl
81-682 (10682)	HR	or
81-695 (10695)	HR	
81-696 (10696)	HR	or
81-697 (10697)	HR	or
81-712 (10712)	HR	or
81-713 (10713)	HR	or
81-721 (10721)	HR	
81-731 (10731)	HR	
81-732 (10732)	HR	or
81-738 (10738)	HR	
81-758 (10758)	HR	bl
81-759 (10759)	HR	or
81-788 (10788)	TJ	bl
81-790 (10790)	TJ	bl
81-792 (10792)	TJ	bl
81-794 (10794)	TJ	bl
81-796 (10796)	TJ	bl
81-798 (10798)	TJ	bl
81-800 (10800)	TJ	r
81-802 (10802)	TJ	r
81-804 (10804)	TJ	r

Serial		
81-806 (10806)	TJ	r
81-810 (10810)	TJ	r
81-819 (10819)‡	HR	
81-821 (10821)‡	TJ	r
81-822 (10822)‡	TJ	r
82-002 (21002)	TJ	r
82-004 (21004)	TJ	r
82-007 (21007)	TJ	r
82-009 (21009)	TJ	r
82-011 (21011)	TJ	r
82-013 (21013)	TJ	bl
82-015 (21015)	TJ	bl
82-018 (21018)	TJ	y
82-020 (21020)	TJ	y
82-022 (21022)	TJ	bl
82-024 (21024)	TJ	bl
82-025 (21025)	TJ	bl
82-047 (21047)‡	TJ	r
82-900 (20900)	TJ	r
82-902 (20902)	TJ	r
82-904 (20904)	TJ	r
82-906 (20906)	TJ	r
82-908 (20908)	TJ	r
82-911 (20911)	TJ	r
82-914 (20914)	TJ	y
82-918 (20918)	TJ	r
82-920 (20920)	TJ	r
82-922 (20922)	TJ	r
82-924 (20924)	TJ	r
82-927 (20927)	TJ	r
82-928 (20928)	TJ	bl
82-931 (20931)	TJ	bl
82-933 (20933)	TJ	y
82-936 (20936)	TJ	y
82-938 (20938)	TJ	y
82-941 (20941)	TJ	y
82-943 (20943)	TJ	y
82-944 (20944)	TJ	y
82-946 (20946)	TJ	y
82-948 (20948)	TJ	y
82-949 (20949)	TJ	y
82-952 (20952)	TJ	y
82-954 (20954)	TJ	y
82-957 (20957)	TJ	y
82-962 (20962)	TJ	y
82-964 (20964)	TJ	y
82-965 (20965)	TJ	y
82-968 (20968)	TJ	y
82-970 (20970)	TJ	y
82-975 (20975)	TJ	y
82-977 (20077)	TJ	y
82-980 (20980)	TJ	y
82-981 (20981)	TJ	y
82-982 (20982)	TJ	bl
82-986 (20986)	TJ	bl
82-988 (20988)	TJ	bl
82-991 (20991)	TJ	bl
82-993 (20993)	TJ	bl
82-996 (20996)	TJ	bl
82-998 (20998)	TJ	bl
82-999 (20999)	TJ	r
83-066 (31066)	TJ	bl
83-067 (31067)	TJ	bl
83-068 (31068)	TJ	bl
83-069 (31069)	TJ	bl
83-071 (31071)	TJ	y
83-074 (31074)	TJ	y
83-079 (31079)	TJ	y
83-087 (31087)	TJ	r
83-166 (31166)‡	TJ	y
83-167 (31167)‡	TJ	y
83-168 (31168)‡	TJ	bl
83-169 (31169)‡	TJ	bl

General Dynamics F-16C/F-16D‡
HR: 50TFW Hahn
10TFS blue/yellow (bl)
496TFS yellow (y)
RS: 86TFW Ramstein
512TFS green/black (gn)
526TFS red/black (r)

Serial		
84-238 (41238)	RS	gn
84-239 (41239)	RS	gn
84-240 (41240)	RS	gn
84-250 (41250)	HR	
84-255 (41255)	RS	gn
84-263 (41263)	HR	y
84-264 (41264)	HR	y
84-266 (41266)	RS	gn
84-267 (41267)	RS	gn
84-269 (41269)	RS	gn
84-271 (41271)	RS	gn
84-272 (41272)	RS	gn
84-274 (41274)	HR	y
84-275 (41275)	HR	y
84-276 (41276)	RS	gn
84-277 (41277)	RS	gn
84-278 (41278)	RS	gn
84-279 (41279)	HR	
84-282 (41282)	HR	y
84-283 (41283)	HR	y
84-284 (41284)	HR	y
84-286 (41286)	RS	
84-287 (41287)	RS	gn
84-288 (41288)	RS	gn
84-289 (41289)	RS	gn
84-290 (41290)	RS	gn
84-291 (41291)	RS	gn
84-292 (41292)	HR	
84-293 (41293)	RS	gn
84-294 (41294)	RS	gn
84-295 (41295)	RS	r
84-296 (41296)	HR	
84-297 (41297)	HR	y
84-298 (41298)	HR	y
84-299 (41299)	RS	r
84-300 (41300)	HR	bl
84-301 (41301)	RS	r
84-302 (41302)	RS	gn
84-303 (41303)	RS	r
84-304 (41304)	HR	y
84-305 (41305)	HR	y
84-306 (41306)	HR	y
84-307 (41307)	HR	y
84-300 (41308)	HR	y
84-309 (41309)	HR	y
84-310 (41310)	HR	bl
84-311 (41311)	HR	y
84-312 (41312)	HR	y
84-313 (41313)	HR	y
84-314 (41314)	HR	y
84-315 (41315)	HR	y
84-316 (41316)	RS	
84-317 (41317)	HR	y
84-323 (41323)‡	RS	r
84-324 (41324)‡	HR	
84-325 (41325)‡	HR	y
84-326 (41326)‡	HR	y
84-327 (41327)‡	RS	gn
84-328 (41328)‡	HR	bl
84-329 (41329)‡	RS	gn
84-331 (41331)‡	HR	bl
84-374 (41374)	RS	r
84-375 (41375)	RS	r
84-376 (41376)	RS	r
84-377 (41377)	RS	r

Serial		
84-378 (41378)	HR	y
84-383 (41383)	HR	y
84-384 (41384)	HR	bl
84-385 (41385)	HR	bl
84-386 (41386)	HR	y
84-387 (41387)	HR	bl
84-388 (41388)	HR	
84-389 (41389)	HR	bl
84-390 (41390)	HR	bl
84-391 (41391)	RS	r
84-392 (41392)	HR	
84-393 (41393)	HR	bl
84-394 (41394)	HR	bl
84-395 (41395)	HR	bl
84-396 (41396)	HR	
85-399 (51399)	HR	bl
85-401 (51401)	HR	bl
85-403 (51403)	HR	
85-404 (51404)	RS	r
85-405 (51405)	RS	r
85-407 (51407)	HR	bl
85-408 (51408)	RS	bl
85-409 (51409)	HR	bl
85-410 (51410)	RS	r
85-411 (51411)	HR	bl
85-412 (51412)	HR	r
85-413 (51413)	HR	bl
85-415 (51415)	HR	
85-416 (51416)	HR	
85-417 (51417)	HR	bl
85-422 (51422)	RS	r
85-426 (51426)	RS	r
85-4 (514)		
85-4 (514)		
85-4 (514)		
85-434 (51434)	RS	r
85-436 (51436)	RS	
85-440 (51440)	RS	
85-4 (514)		
85-4 (514)		
85-4 (514)		
85-4 (514)		
85-4 (514)		
85-4 (514)		
85-4 (514)		
85-4 (514)		
85-4 (514)		
85-4 (514)		
85-4 (514)		
85-5 (515)		
85-509 (51509)‡	RS	gn
85-5 (515)‡		
85-5 (515)‡		

Gates C-21A Learjet
*58MAS Ramstein
†7005ABS Stuttgart
FY84
40081†
40082†
40083†
40084*
40085*
40086*

Shorts C-23A Sherpa
322MAW/10MAS Zweibrucken
FY83
30512 *Zweibrucken*
30513 *Ramstein*

USAF (EUR based)

Serial

FY84
40458 *Sembach*
40459 *Spangdahlem*
40460 *Hahn*
40461 *Rhein Main*
40462 *Mildenhall/ Lakenheath*
40463 *Bitburg*
40464 *Zaragosa*
40465 *Alconbury*
40466 *Bentwaters/ Woodbridge*
40467 *Upper Heyford*
40468 *Greenham Common*
40469 *Soesterberg*
40470 *Torrejon*
40471 *Wiesbaden*
40472 *Incirlik*
40473 *Florennes*

North American T-39A/CT-39A
†1868FCS Rhein Main
‡7005ABS Stuttgart
10684 (FY61)‡
24453 (FY62)†

Cessna T-41 Mescalero
FY65
55186 (N5186F) Spangdahlem
55187 (N5187F) Torrejon
55188 (N5188F) Ramstein

Sikorsky CH-53C
601TCW/601 TASS Sembach
01625 (FY70)
01626 (FY70)
01630 (FY70)
10924 (FY68)
10928 (FY68)
10930 (FY68)
10932 (FY68)

Lockheed C-130E Hercules
435TAW Rhein Main: 37TAS;
*7405 OS
01260 (FY70)
01262 (FY70)
01264 (FY70)
01271 (FY70)
01274 (FY70)
10935 (FY68)
10938 (FY68)
10943 (FY68)
10947 (FY68)
17681 (FY64)
18240 (FY64)
21822 (FY62)*
21828 (FY62)*
37885 (FY63)
40502 (FY64)
40527 (FY64)
40550 (FY64)
96566 (FY69)
96582 (FY69)
96583 (FY69)

Lockheed MC-130E Hercules
7SOS Rhein Main
40523 (FY64)
40555 (FY64)
40561 (FY64)
40566 (FY64)

Lockheed VC-140B Jetstar
58MAS Ramstein
12489 (FY61)
12491 (FY61)
24198 (FY62)
24200 (FY62)

European based US Army Aircraft

Bell AH-1S (FM) Cobra
2nd Armoured Cavalry Regiment: Feucht
11th Armoured Cavalry Regiment: Fulda
3rd Aviation Battalion (Combat), 'B' Co: Giebelstadt
3rd Aviation Battalion (Combat), 'C' Co: Schweinfurt
8th Aviation Battalion (Combat), 'B' Co: Mainz-Finthen
8th Aviation Battalion (Combat), 'C' Co: Mainz-Finthen
501st Aviation Battalion (Combat), 'B' Co: Ansbach
501st Aviation Battalion (Combat), 'C' Co: Illesheim
503rd Aviation Battalion (Combat), 'B' Co: Hanau
503rd Aviation Battalion (Combat), 'C' Co: Hanau

FY68
15007 8 B Co
15015 3 C Co
15036 503 C Co
15038 501 B Co
15046 501 B Co
15057 501 C Co
15069 501 B Co
15084 503 B Co
15085 2 ACR
15092 503 B Co
15093 8 B Co
15104 503 C Co
15105 2 ACR
15106 3 B Co
15110 503 B Co
15112 501 C Co
15113 503 C Co
15116 2 ACR
15131 8 C Co
15134 501 B Co
15142 11 ACR
15152 501 B Co
15167 501 B Co
15173 501 B Co
15180 503 B Co
15208 503 C Co

FY66
15249 503 B Co
15250 2 ACR
15252 11 ACR
15254 2 ACR
15261 2 ACR
15263 8 B Co
15264 3 B Co
15266 2 ACR
15273 11 ACR
15275 503 C Co
15286 2 ACR
15289 8 B Co
15290 2 ACR
15292 8 C Co
15293 501 C Co
15295 2 ACR
15315 503 B Co
15316 3 C Co
15321 8 C Co
15322 501 B Co
15324 501 C Co
15328 503 B Co
15335 11 ACR
15348 3 C Co
15350 3 C Co
15356 11 ACR

FY67
15450 2 ACR
15452 8 C Co
15455 2 ACR
15456 501 C Co
15457 503 C Co
15459 2 ACR
15460 8 B Co

Serial	
15470	11 ACR
15473	11 ACR
15475	11 ACR
15477	3 C Co
15479	3 B Co
15480	503 B Co
15489	8 B Co
15490	503 B Co
15491	8 C Co
15497	2 ACR
15506	3 B Co
15508	501 C Co
15512	3 B Co
15520	501 C Co
15522	3 B Co
15528	3 B Co
15530	3 B Co
15535	3 C Co
15540	8 C Co
15548	3 B Co
15551	501 C Co
15565	3 C Co
15571	8 B Co
15572	11 ACR
15587	501 C Co
15593	11 ACR
15610	2 ACR
15613	8 C Co
15614	8 B Co
15617	503 B Co
15621	2 ACR
15624	501 B Co
15633	501 C Co
15642	8 C Co
15643	2 ACR
15650	503 B Co
15652	503 B Co
15658	11 ACR
15659	2 ACR
15662	11 ACR
15664	3 C Co
15665	8 C Co
15666	11 ACR
15675	11 ACR
15679	8 C Co
15682	8 B Co
15683	501 B Co
15701	2 ACR
15710	503 B Co
15716	503 C Co
15717	3 B Co
15721	3 C Co
15736	3 C Co
15741	503 C Co
15745	8 B Co
15757	503 C Co
15762	501 B Co
15764	3 B Co
15769	8 C Co
15771	503 B Co
15772	8 B Co
15775	503 C Co
15776	503 C Co
15784	8 B Co
15789	501 C Co
15790	3 C Co
15805	501 B Co
15815	501 B Co
15822	2 ACR
15829	501 C Co
15833	8 C Co
15842	501 B Co
15852	503 C Co

Serial	
15860	8 C Co
15863	3 C Co
FY70	
15947	501 C Co
15950	501 C Co
15951	503 C Co
15952	11 ACR
15958	11 ACR
15959	8 C Co
15961	8 C Co
15970	3 B Co
15971	3 C Co
15995	2 ACR
16012	3 C Co
16016	3 C Co
16048	3 C Co
16054	501 B Co
16091	501 B Co
FY69	
16411	3 C Co
16422	501 B Co
16426	501 B Co
16429	3 B Co
16431	3 B Co
16432	503 B Co
16433	8 B Co
16434	503 B Co
16436	503 C Co
16445	8 B Co
FY68	
17023	503 C Co
17028	503 B Co
17047	11 ACR
17049	8 B Co
17062	503 C Co
17063	503 B Co
17066	501 C Co
17067	501 C Co
17070	501 C Co
17074	503 C Co
17076	501 B Co
17078	8 B Co
17079	503 B Co
17082	503 C Co
17085	503 C Co
17087	501 C Co
17088	11 ACR
17092	503 B Co
17095	8 C Co
17100	501 B Co
17101	503 C Co
17104	501 B Co
17105	501 C Co
17108	501 C Co
17111	8 C Co
17112	503 B Co
FY71	
20998	11 ACR
21014	503 C Co
21028	503 C Co
21035	2 ACR
FY78	
23118	3 B Co
FY79	
23189	3 B Co
23190	3 B Co
23194	3 B Co

Serial	
23199	3 C Co
23200	3 C Co
23235	3 C Co
FY81	
23526	11 ACR
23527	11 ACR
23528	8 C Co
23529	8 C Co
23530	8 C Co
23531	8 B Co
23532	8 C Co
23533	8 B Co
23534	8 B Co
23535	8 B Co
23536	8 B Co
23537	3 B Co
23538	3 B Co
23539	3 C Co
23540	3 B Co

Grumman V-1 Mohawk

*73CIC, Stuttgart, †2MIB

14239	(FY64)	RV-1D†
14244	(FY64)	OV-1B*
14245	(FY64)	RV-1D†
14246	(FY64)	OV-1B*
14248	(FY64)	OV-1B*
14250	(FY64)	OV-1B*
14256	(FY64)	OV-1B*
14258	(FY64)	OV-1B*
14261	(FY64)	OV-1B*
14263	(FY64)	RV-1D†
14268	(FY64)	OV-1B*
14269	(FY64)	OV-1B*
14270	(FY64)	OV-1B*
15930	(FY68)	OV-1D*
15938	(FY68)	OV-1D*
15940	(FY68)	OV-1D†
15960	(FY68)	OV-1D*
16993	(FY68)	OV-1D*
16996	(FY68)	OV-1D*
17004	(FY69)	OV-1D*
17007	(FY69)	OV-1D*
17008	(FY69)	OV-1D*
17021	(FY69)	OV-1D*
18900	(FY67)	OV-1D*
18905	(FY67)	OV-1C*
18909	(FY67)	OV-1C*
18919	(FY67)	OV-1C*
18921	(FY67)	OV-1C†
25865	(FY62)	OV-1D*
25872	(FY62)	OV-1D*
25878	(FY62)	OV-1D*
25886	(FY62)	OV-1D†
25890	(FY62)	OV-1D*
25891	(FY62)	RV-1D*
25897	(FY62)	RV-1D*

Beech C-12A Super King Air ($=C-12C, †=RC-12D, ‡=C-12F)

25AvCo, Stuttgart;
HQ/USEUCOM;
56AvCo, Vicenza
207AvCo Heidelberg
1MIB, Wiesbaden
2MIB/330 ASACo, Stuttgart

22253	(FY73)	25AvCo
22254	(FY73)	207AvCo
22265	(FY73)	HQ/USEUCOM

Serial		
22260	(FY73)	56AvCo
22261	(FY73)	HQ/USEUCOM
22262	(FY73)	Berlin Bgde
22556	(FY76)	56AvCo
22557	(FY76)	207AvCo
22564	(FY76)	56AvCo
22944	(FY77)	56AvCo
22950	(FY77)	207AvCo
23126$	(FY78)	207AvCo
23127$	(FY78)	207AvCo
23128$	(FY78)	207AvCo
23141†	(FY78)	1MIB
23142†	(FY78)	1MIB
23143†	(FY78)	1MIB
23144†	(FY78)	2MIB/ 330ASA Co
23371†	(FY80)	2MIB/ 330ASA Co
23373†	(FY80)	2MIB/ 330ASA Co
23374†	(FY80)	2MIB/ 330ASA Co
23375†	(FY80)	1MIB
23376†	(FY80)	2MIB/ 330ASA Co
23377†	(FY80)	1MIB
23378†	(FY80)	2MIB/ 330ASA Co
23542†	(FY81)	1MIB
24380†	(FY84)	207AvCo
51264‡	(FY85)	1MIB

Beech U-21A King Air
***EU-21A**

18000*	(FY66)	7th Sigs Bgde
18010	(FY66)	
18013*	(FY66)	7th Sigs Bgde
18014	(FY66)	56th AvCo
18019	(FY66)	56th AvCo
18025	(FY66)	56th AvCo
18027*	(FY66)	7th Sigs Bgde
18037	(FY66)	
18040	(FY66)	
18048	(FY67)	
18049	(FY67)	14th AvCo
18050	(FY67)	
18058	(FY67)	5th Corps
18078	(FY67)	7th Corps
18080	(FY67)	56th AvCo
18116	(FY67)	56th AvCo

Boeing-Vertol
CH-47C Chinook

* 180AvCo, Schwabisch Hall;
† 205AvCo, Mainz-Finthen;
‡ 295AvCo, Coleman Barracks

15002	(FY70)*
15005	(FY70)†
15007	(FY70)†
15012	(FY70)‡
15020	(FY70)*
15028	(FY70)†
15029	(FY70)†
15030	(FY70)†
15032	(FY70)†
15829	(FY68)‡
15831	(FY68)‡
15838	(FY68)†
15846	(FY68)*
15847	(FY68)†
15849	(FY68)‡
15851	(FY68)†
15856	(FY68)*
15865	(FY68)*
15867	(FY68)*
15868	(FY68)*
15990	(FY68)‡
15995	(FY68)*
15997	(FY68)*
16005	(FY68)†
16006	(FY68)*
16008	(FY68)‡
16009	(FY68)†
17106	(FY69)†
17114	(FY69)‡
17116	(FY69)*
17117	(FY69)‡
17118	(FY69)*
17126	(FY69)†
18516	(FY67)‡
18531	(FY67)†
18533	(FY67)‡
18540	(FY67)*
18548	(FY67)*
20946	(FY71)†
20950	(FY71)†
20951	(FY71)†
20952	(FY71)†
20953	(FY71)†
20954	(FY71)‡
22277	(FY74)†
22281	(FY74)*
22283	(FY74)‡
22284	(FY74)‡
22285	(FY74)†
22286	(FY74)†
22291	(FY74)‡
22293	(FY74)‡
22676	(FY76)†
22677	(FY76)‡
22678	(FY76)‡
22679	(FY76)‡
22681	(FY76)*
22683	(FY76)*
22684	(FY76)*
23394	(FY79)*
23395	(FY79)†
23396	(FY79)*
23398	(FY79)‡
24734	(FY85)
24735	(FY85)
24736	(FY85)
24737	(FY85)
24739	(FY85)
24740	(FY85)
24742	(FY85)

Sikorsky UH-60A Blackhawk

3rd Aviation Battalion (Combat), 'D' Co and 'E' Co: Giebelstadt
8th Aviation Battalion (Combat), 'D' Co: Mainz-Finthen
8th Aviation Battalion (Combat), 'E' Co: Wiesbaden
48th Aviation Co: Wiesbaden
203rd Aviation Co: Wertheim
205th AVIM Battalion: Hanau
207th Aviation Co: Heidelburg
394th AVIM Battalion: Nellingen
421st Medical Co, 1st Platoon: Wiesbaden
421st Medical Co, 2nd Platoon: Schweinfurt
421st Medical Co, 3rd Platoon: Wiesbaden
421st Medical Co, 4th Platoon: Darmstadt
501st Aviation Battalion (Combat), 'D' Co and 'E' Co: Ansbach
503rd Aviation Battalion (Combat), 'D' Co and 'E' Co: Hanau

FY80

23425	3 E Co
23427	3 E Co
23428	3 E Co
23431	3 E Co
23432	3 E Co
23433	3 E Co
23436	3 E Co
23438	3 E Co
23439	3 E Co
23440	3 E Co
23441	3 E Co
23442	3 E Co
23443	3 E Co
23489	394
23490	394

FY81

23551	159 Med Co
23568	205
23571	3 E Co
23572	205
23573	205
23575	48
23578	48
23579	48
23580	48
23581	503 E Co
23582	48
23583	503 E Co
23584	503 E Co
23585	357 Avn Det
23586	503 E Co
23587	48
23588	48
23589	48
23590	48
23591	48
23592	48
23593	48
23594	501 E Co
23595	501 E Co
23596	48
23597	48
23598	48
23599	48
23602	503 E Co
23603	503 E Co
23604	503 E Co
23605	503 E Co
23606	503 E Co
23607	8 E Co
23608	501 E Co
23609	503 E Co
23610	503 E Co
23613	501 E Co
23614	503 E Co
23615	503 E Co
23616	8 E Co
23617	503 D Co
23618	503 E Co
23622	8 E Co

Serial	
23623	8 D Co
23624	8 E Co
23625	8 E Co
23626	8 E Co
FY82	
23660	501 E Co
23661	501 E Co
23662	501 E Co
23663	501 E Co
23664	501 E Co
23665	8 E Co
23666	8 E Co
23667	8 E Co
23668	8 E Co
23669	8 E Co
23672	203
23673	203
23674	203
23675	421 4 Pl
23676	421 2 Pl
23682	8 E Co
23683	8 E Co
23684	8 E Co
23685	8 E Co
23686	8 E Co
23690	501 E Co
23691	501 E Co
23692	501 E Co
23693	501 E Co
23694	501 E Co
23695	203
23696	203
23697	203
23698	203
23699	203
23700	—
23701	207
23702	207
23703	203
23704	203
23705	203
23706	203
23707	203
23721	203
23722	203
23723	421 4 Pl
23726	421 4
23727	421 4
23729	421 2 Pl
23730	421 2 Pl
23731	—
23733	421 4 Pl
23735	421
23736	—
23737	421 4 Pl
23738	421 2 Pl
23739	421 4 Pl
23740	—
23741	421 2 Pl
23743	421 2 Pl
23744	501 D Co
23745	394
23746	421 2 Pl
23749	421
23750	421
23751	421
23752	421
23753	421
23754	421
23755	421
23756	421

European based US Navy Aircraft

Grumman C-1A Trader
(VR-24 Sigonella)
136756 [JM46]
136757 [JM45]
146025 [JM41]
146028 [JM42]
146034 [JM43]
146049 [JM44]
146051 [JM51]

Grumman C-2A Greyhound
(VR-24 Sigonella)
148148 [JM20]
155123 [JM25]
155124 [JM24]
162142 [JM22]
162143 [JM23]
162144 [JM24]
162145 [JM25]
162153 [JM21]

Lockheed EP-3E/ *UP-3A Orion
Rota NAS (Spain)
VQ-2
148888 [JQ-23]
149668 [JQ-21]
149677 [JQ-20]*
150494 [JQ-25]
150502 [JQ-22]
150503 [JQ-26]
150505 [JQ-24]
151368 [JQ-27]

Beech UC-12B Super King Air
8C: NAF Sigonella;
8D: NAF Rota
1197 [8D] (161197)
1323 [8C] (161323)
1517 [8D] (161517)

NA CT-39G Sabreliner
(VR-24 Sigonella)
159361 [JM30]
159362 [JM31]
159363 [JM32]

Lockheed C-130F/ KC-130F* Hercules
(VR-22: Rota)
149790 [JL00]
149794 [JL01]
149797 [JL02]
149801 [JL03]
150687 [JL04]*

US based USAF Aircraft

The following aircraft are normally based in the USA but are likely to be seen visiting the UK from time to time. They are listed in numerical progression by the serial actually carried on the aircraft externally. Fiscal year information is provided, together with details of mark variations and in some cases operating units. The types are also in numerical order, commencing with the E-**3**B and concluding with the C-**141**B.

Serial *Wing*

Boeing E-3 Sentry
552 AW&CW
963 AW&CS (bk)
964 AW&CS(r)
965 AW&CS(y)
966 AW&CS(TS) (bl)
00137 (FY80) E-3A y
00138 (FY80) E-3A y
00139 (FY80) E-3C y
10004 (FY81) E-3A y
10005 (FY81) E-3A y
11407 (FY71) E-3B bk
11408 (FY71) E-3A bl
20006 (FY82) E-3A y
20007 (FY82) E-3A y
30008 (FY83) E-3C
30009 (FY83) E-3C y
31674 (FY73) E-3C (Boeing)
31675 (FY73) E-3A r
50556 (FY75) E-3A r
50557 (FY75) E-3A r
50558 (FY75) E-3A
50559 (FY75) E-3A r
50560 (FY75) E-3A r
61604 (FY76) E-3A r
61605 (FY76) E-3A r
61606 (FY76) E-3A r
61607 (FY76) E-3A bk
70351 (FY77) E-3A bk
70352 (FY77) E-3B
70353 (FY77) E-3B bk
70354 (FY77) E-3B bk
70355 (FY77) E-3A bk
70356 (FY77) E-3A bk
80576 (FY78) E-3A bk
80577 (FY78) E-3A r
80578 (FY78) E-3A bk
90001 (FY79) E-3A
90002 (FY79) E-3A bl
90003 (FY79) E-3A r

Boeing E-4B
1ACCS
31676 (FY73)
31677 (FY73)
40787 (FY74)
50125 (FY75)

Lockheed C-5A Galaxy
(*ANG, Air National Guard
†AFRES, Air Force Reserve)
60 MAW: Travis AFB, California; 433 MAW/68 TAS AFRES: Kelly AFB, Texas; 436 MAW: Dover AFB, Delaware; 443 MAW: Altus AFB, Oklahoma; 105MAG: New York ANG, Stewart AFB

Serial	Wing
FY70	
00445	433 MAW†
00446	60 MAW
00447	436 MAW
00448	436 MAW
00449	60 MAW
00450	60 MAW
00451	60 MAW
00452	436 MAW
00453	436 MAW
00454	436 MAW
00455	436 MAW
00456	436 MAW
00457	60 MAW
00458	60 MAW
00459	60 MAW
00460	436 MAW
00461	60 MAW
00462	443 MAW
00463	436 MAW
00464	436 MAW
00465	436 MAW
00466	443 MAW
00467	436 MAW
FY66	
68304	436 MAW
68305	60 MAW
68306	60 MAW
68307	436 MAW
FY67	
70167	436 MAW
70168	433 MAW†
70169	60 MAW
70170	105 MAG*
70171	433 MAW†
70173	436 MAW
70174	436 MAW
FY68	
80211	60 MAW
80212	105 MAG*
80213	60 MAW
80214	436 MAW
80215	436 MAW
80216	60 MAW
80217	436 MAW
80219	60 MAW
80220	436 MAW
80221	60 MAW
80222	436 MAW
80223	60 MAW
80224	436 MAW
80225	436 MAW
80226	60 MAW
80228	60 MAW
FY69	
90001	443 MAW
90002	433 MAW†
90003	436 MAW
90004	436 MAW
90005	60 MAW
90006	436 MAW
90007	60 MAW
90008	436 MAW
90009	60 MAW
90010	60 MAW
90011	60 MAW
90012	60 MAW
90013	60 MAW
90014	443 MAW
90015	137 MAS/105 MAG*
90016	433 MAW/68 TAS†
90017	436 MAW
90018	60 MAW
90019	443 MAW
90020	60 MAW
90021	436 MAW
90022	60 MAW
90023	60 MAW
90024	60 MAW
90025	60 MAW
90026	436 MAW
90027	436 MAW

Lockheed C-5B Galaxy

Serial	Wing
FY83	
31285	443 MAW
FY84	
40059	443 MAW
40060	443 MAW
40061	443 MAW
40062	60 MAW
FY85	
50001	
50002	
50003	
50004	
50005	
50006	
50007	
50008	
50009	
50010	
FY86	
60011	

Serial	Wing
60012	
60013	
60014	
60015	
60016	
60017	
60018	
60019	
60020	
60021	
60022	
60023	
60024	
60025	
60026	
FY87	
70027	
70028	
70029	
70030	
70031	
70032	
70033	
70034	
70035	
70036	
70037	
70038	
70039	
70040	
70041	
70042	
70043	
70044	
70045	

Boeing C-18A/EC-18B*
(Air Force Systems Command)

Serial	Wing
FY81	
10891*	
10892	
10893	
10894	
10895	4950 TW
10896*	
10897	
10898*	

Grumman C-20A Gulfstream III
89 MAW Andrews AFB

FY83
30500
30501
30502

McDonnell-Douglas KC-10A Extender
2 BW* 22 ARW† 68 ARG‡

20190 (FY82)*
20191 (FY82)†
20192 (FY82)*
20193 (FY82)†
30075 (FY83)*
30076 (FY83)†
30077 (FY83)*
30078 (FY83)†
30079 (FY83)*
30080 (FY83)†
30081 (FY83)*
30082 (FY83)*
40185 (FY84)†
40186 (FY84)*
40187 (FY84)†
40188 (FY84)*
40189 (FY84)†
40190 (FY84)*
40191 (FY84)†
40192 (FY84)*
50027 (FY85)†
50028 (FY85)*
50029 (FY85)*
50030 (FY85)*
50031 (FY85)‡
50032 (FY85)*
50033 (FY85)
50034 (FY85)
60027 (FY86)‡
60028 (FY86)
60029 (FY86)
60030 (FY86)
60031 (FY86)
60032 (FY86)
60033 (FY86)
60034 (FY86)
60035 (FY86)
60036 (FY86)
60037 (FY86)
60038 (FY86)
90433 (FY79)*
90434 (FY79)*
91710 (FY79)*
91711 (FY79)*
91712 (FY79)*
91713 (FY79)*
91946 (FY79)†
91947 (FY79)†
91948 (FY79)†
91949 (FY79)†
91950 (FY79)†
91951 (FY79)†

Boeing B-52G Stratofortress

Serial	Wing
FY57	
76468	42 BW
76469	320 BW
76470	416 BW
76471	379 BW
76472	93 BW
76473	42 BW
76474	379 BW
76475	92 BW
76476	42 BW
76477	92 BW
76478	42 BW
76480	319 BW
76483	92 BW
76484	42 BW
76485	97 BW
76486	93 BW
76487	93 BW
76488	43 SW
76489	2 BW
76490	416 BW
76491	97 BW
76492	93 BW
76495	92 BW
76497	2 BW
76498	416 BW
76499	92 BW
76500	2 BW
76501	416 BW
76502	320 BW
76503	319 BW
76504	97 BW
76505	92 BW
76506	2 BW
76508	319 BW
76509	319 BW
76510	43 SW
76511	97 BW
76512	2 BW
76513	320 BW
76514	319 BW
76515	93 BW
76516	379 BW
76517	97 BW
76518	97 BW
76519	2 BW
76520	2 BW
FY58	
80158	319 BW
80159	320 BW
80160	416 BW
80162	97 BW
80163	2 BW
80164	93 BW
80165	319 BW
80166	319 BW
80167	97 BW
80168	379 BW
80170	416 BW
80171	92 BW
80172	43 SW
80173	379 BW
80175	379 BW
80176	416 BW
80177	93 BW
80178	2 BW
80179	379 BW
80181	319 BW
80182	379 BW
80183	97 BW
80184	92 BW
80185	97 BW
80186	43 SW
80189	43 SW
80190	92 BW
80191	93 BW
80192	43 SW
80193	93 BW
80194	319 BW
80195	320 BW
80197	320 BW
80199	97 BW
80200	319 BW
80202	42 BW
80203	93 BW
80204	319 BW
80205	92 BW
80206	93 BW
80207	92 BW
80210	2 BW
80211	92 BW

USAF (US based)

Serial	Wing
80212	2 BW
80213	320 BW
80214	2 BW
80216	2 BW
80217	379 BW
80218	2 BW
80219	2 BW
80220	92 BW
80221	43 SW
80222	92 BW
80223	319 BW
80224	2 BW
80225	2 BW
80226	320 BW
80227	319 BW
80229	379 BW
80230	320 BW
80231	416 BW
80232	2 BW
80233	43 SW
80234	43 SW
80235	93 BW
80236	379 BW
80237	379 BW
80238	319 BW
80239	416 BW
80240	2 BW
80241	2 BW
80242	2 BW
80243	97 BW
80244	379 BW
80245	416 BW
80247	92 BW
80248	2 BW
80249	379 BW
80250	93 BW
80251	2 BW
80252	97 BW
80253	320 BW
80254	416 BW
80255	93 BW
80257	93 BW
80258	42 BW
FY59	
92564	93 BW
92565	42 BW
92566	416 BW
92567	416 BW
92568	93 BW
92569	2 BW
92570	42 BW
92571	93 BW
92572	2 BW
92573	43 SW
92575	93 BW
92577	97 BW
92578	43 SW
92579	319 BW
92580	319 BW
92581	93 BW
92582	92 BW
92583	93 BW
92584	416 BW
92585	320 BW
92586	2 BW
92587	93 BW
92588	2 BW
92589	379 BW
92590	93 BW
92591	93 BW
92592	43 SW
92593	43 SW
92594	319 BW
92595	43 SW
92596	43 SW
92598	42 BW
92599	2 BW
92601	416 BW
92602	416 BW

Boeing B-52H Stratofortress

Serial	Wing
FY60	
00001	410 BW
00002	7 BW
00003	5 BW
00004	7 BW
00005	5 BW
00007	92 BW
00008	5 BW
00009	7 BW
00010	7 BW
00011	5 BW
00012	28 BW
00013	28 BW
00014	7 BW
00015	410 BW
00016	7 BW
00017	7 BW
00018	7 BW
00019	7 BW
00020	
00021	7 BW
00022	410 BW
00023	410 BW
00024	7 BW
00025	7 BW
00026	28 BW
00028	410 BW
00029	7 BW
00030	28 BW
00031	7 BW
00032	7 BW
00033	7 BW
00034	5 BW
00035	7 BW
00036	5 BW
00037	410 BW
00038	7 BW
00040	28 BW
00041	7 BW
00042	92 BW
00043	28 BW
00044	410 BW
00045	410 BW
00046	410 BW
00047	28 BW
00048	28 BW
00049	7 BW
00050	
00051	7 BW
00052	7 BW
00053	5 BW
00054	5 BW
00055	410 BW
00056	5 BW
00057	410 BW
00058	410 BW
00059	5 BW
00060	410 BW
00061	410 BW
00062	7 BW
FY61	
10001	410 BW
10002	410 BW
10003	7 BW
10004	5 BW
10005	7 BW
10006	410 BW
10007	7 BW
10008	7 BW
10009	7 BW
10010	7 BW
10011	5 BW
10012	410 BW
10013	28 BW
10014	7 BW
10015	28 BW
10016	5 BW
10017	7 BW
10018	7 BW
10019	5 BW
10020	28 BW
10021	28 BW
10022	410 BW
10023	410 BW
10024	5 BW
10025	28 BW
10026	5 BW
10027	7 BW
10028	410 BW
10029	5 BW
10031	410 BW
10032	7 BW
10034	410 BW
10035	410 BW
10036	28 BW
10038	7 BW
10039	410 BW
10040	410 BW

Lockheed SR-71A Blackbird

9SRW/99SRS No 4 Det: RAF Mildenhall

FY64

17950
17952
17953
17956
17957
17958
17959
17960
17961
17962
17963
17964
17967
17968
17969
17970
17971
17972
17973
17974
17975
17976

Serial	Wing
17979	
17980	
17981	

Lockheed C-130E/EC-130E$/WC-130E‡/MC-130E§ Hercules
(*ANG, Air National Guard; †AFRES, Air Force Reserve)

Serial	Wing
FY70	
01259	317 TAW
01260	435 TAW
01261	317 TAW
01262	435 TAW
01263	317 TAW
01264	435 TAW
01265	317 TAW
01266	317 TAW
01267	317 TAW
01268	317 TAW
01269	317 TAW
01270	317 TAW
01271	435 TAW
01272	317 TAW
01273	317 TAW
01274	435 TAW
01275	317 TAW
01276	317 TAW
FY68	
10934	317 TAW
10935	435 TAW
10937	317 TAW
10938	435 TAW
10939	317 TAW
10940	317 TAW
10941	317 TAW
10942	317 TAW
10943	435 TAW
10945	317 TAW
10947	435 TAW
10948	314 TAW
10949	314 TAW
10950	314 TAW
FY61	
12358	115 TAS*
12359	115 TAS*
12360†	54 WRS
12361	314 TAW
12362	314 TAW
12363	314 TAW
12364	314 TAW
12365‡	53 WRS
12366‡	54 WRS
12367	115 TAS*
12368	314 TAW
12369	314 TAW
12370	115 TAS*
12371	314 TAW
12372	115 TAS*
12373	115 TAS*
FY64	
17680	314 TAW
17681	435 TAW
18240	435 TAW

Serial	Wing
FY72	
21288	374 TAW
21289	374 TAW
21290	374 TAW
21291	314 TAW
21292	314 TAW
21293	314 TAW
21294	314 TAW
21295	314 TAW
21296	314 TAW
21298	314 TAW
21299	374 TAW
FY62	
21784	130 TAS*
21786	109 TAS*
21787	130 TAS*
21788	130 TAS*
21789	337 TAS†
21790	130 TAS*
21792	115 TAS*
21793	115 TAS*
21794	337 TAS†
21795	130 TAS*
21798	130 TAS*
21799	115 TAS*
21801	115 TAS*
21803	337 TAS†
21804	130 TAS*
21806	756 TAS†
21807	337 TAS†
21808	337 TAS†
21810	337 TAS†
21811	115 TAS*
21812	109 TAS*
21816	337 TAS†
21817	109 TAS*
21820	337 TAS†
21821	314 TAW
21822	7405 OS
21823	337 TAS†
21824	130 TAS*
21826	115 TAS*
21827	314 TAW
21828	7405 OS
21829	109 TAS*
21830	337 TAS†
21833	115 TAS*
21834	756 TAS†
21835	756 TAS†
21837	109 TAS*
21838	337 TAS†
21839	756 TAS†
21842	115 TAS*
21844	756 TAS†
21846	109 TAS*
21847	756 TAS†
21848	756 TAS†
21849	337 TAS†
21850	337 TAS†
21851	115 TAS*
21852	756 TAS†
21855	314 TAW
21856	109 TAS*
21858	337 TAS†
21859	374 TAW
21860	337 TAS†
21862	115 TAS*
21864	109 TAS*
21866	337 TAS†

Serial	Wing
FY63	
37764	357 TAS†
37765	314 TAW
37767	314 TAW
37768	314 TAW
37769	314 TAW
37770	357 TAS†
37771	314 TAW
37773$	193 SOS* [PA]
37776	314 TAW
37777	374 TAW
37778	314 TAW
37779	317 TAW
37781	314 TAW
37782	62 MAW
37783$	193 SOS* [PA]
37784	62 MAW
37786	314 TAW
37788	62 MAW
37790	314 TAW
37791	314 TAW
37792	62 MAW
37793	314 TAW
37794	314 TAW
37795	314 TAW
37796	314 TAW
37799	314 TAW
37800	374 TAW
37803	374 TAW
37804	17 TAS
37805	357 TAS†
37806	314 TAW
37807	317 TAW
37808	314 TAW
37809	317 TAW
37811	374 TAW
37812	374 TAW
37813	317 TAW
37814	62 MAW
37815$	193 SOS* [PA]
37816$	193 SOS* [PA]
37817	357 TAS†
37818	17 TAS
37819	374 TAW
37820	314 TAW
37821	317 TAW
37822	357 TAS†
37823	317 TAW
37824	374 TAW
37825	374 TAW
37826	327 TAS†
37828$	193 SOS* [PA]
37829	17 TAS
37830	17 TAS
37831	17 TAS
37832	327 TAS†
37833	327 TAS†
37834	327 TAS†
37835	314 TAW
37836	314 TAW
37837	17 TAS
37838	314 TAW
37839	314 TAW
37840	374 TAW
37841	314 TAW
37842	62 MAW
37845	317 TAW
37846	17 TAS
37847	314 TAW
37848	327 TAS†

USAF (US based)

Serial	Wing
37849	317 TAW
37850	314 TAW
37851	17 TAS
37852	357 TAS†
37853	327 TAS†
37854	62 MAW
37856	357 TAS†
37857	314 TAW
37858	62 MAW
37859	374 TAW
37860	314 TAW
37861	314 TAW
37863	328 TAS†
37864	314 TAW
37865	374 TAW
37866	314 TAW
37867	327 TAS†
37868	374 TAW
37869$	193 SOS* [PA]
37871	317 TAW
37872	17 TAS
37874	62 MAW
37876	314 TAW
37877	374 TAW
37879	374 TAW
37880	314 TAW
37881	374 TAW
37882	314 TAW
37883	327 TAS†
37884	317 TAW
37885	435 TAW
37887	314 TAW
37888	314 TAW
37889	374 TAW
37890	317 TAW
37891	62 MAW
37892	327 TAS†
37893	62 MAW
37894	314 TAW
37895	374 TAW
37896	314 TAW
37897	374 TAW
37898	314 TAW
37899	317 TAW
39810	317 TAW
39811	314 TAW
39812	314 TAW
39813	314 TAW
39814	314 TAW
39815	314 TAW
39816$	193 SOS* [PA]
39817$	193 SOS* [PA]
FY64	
40495	317 TAW
40496	317 TAW
40497	374 TAW
40498	317 TAW
40499	317 TAW
40500	310 MAS
40501	317 TAW
40502	435 TAW
40503	374 TAW
40504	317 TAW
40510	62 MAW
40512	62 MAW
40513	314 TAW
40514	374 TAW
40515	374 TAW
40517	317 TAW
40518	314 TAW
40519	62 MAW
40520	374 TAW
40521	62 MAW
40523§	7 SOS
40524	62 MAW
40525	317 TAW
40526	314 TAW
40527	435 TAW
40529	317 TAW
40530	314 TAW
40531	317 TAW
40533	314 TAW
40534	374 TAW
40535	314 TAW
40537	317 TAW
40538	314 TAW
40539	317 TAW
40540	317 TAW
40541	317 TAW
40542	317 TAW
40544	374 TAW
40550	435 TAW
40552‡	54 WRS
40553‡	53 WRS
40554‡	54 WRS
40555§	7 SOS
40556	374 TAW
40557	314 TAW
40560	314 TAW
40561§	7 SOS
40566§	7 SOS
40569	314 TAW
40570	317 TAW
FY69	
96566	435 TAW
96579	314 TAW
96580	317 TAW
96582	435 TAW
96583	435 TAW

Lockheed C-130H/EC-130H$/ WC-130H‡/MC-130H§/ LC-130H• Hercules

(*ANG, Air National Guard
†AFRES, Air Force Reserve)

Serial	Wing
FY80	
00320	158 TAS*
00321	158 TAS*
00322	158 TAS*
00323	158 TAS*
00324	158 TAS*
00325	158 TAS*
00326	158 TAS*
00332	158 TAS*
FY81	
10626	700 TAS†
10627	700 TAS†
10628	700 TAS†
10629	700 TAS†
10630	700 TAS†
10631	700 TAS†
FY64	
14861‡	54 WRS
14866‡	920 WRG†
FY82	
20054	144 TAS*
20055	144 TAS*
20056	144 TAS*
20057	144 TAS*
20058	144 TAS*
20059	144 TAS*
20060	144 TAS*
20061	144 TAS*
FY83	
30486	139 TAS*
30487	139 TAS*
30488	139 TAS*
30489	139 TAS*
30490•	139 TAS*
30491•	139 TAS*
30492•	139 TAS*
30493•	139 TAS*
31212§	SOS
FY73	
31580	374 TAW
31581$	41 ECS [DM]
31582	374 TAW
31583$	41 ECS [DM]
31584$	41 ECS [DM]
31585$	41 ECS [DM]
31586$	41 ECS [DM]
31587$	41 ECS [DM]
31588$	41 ECS [DM]
31590	374 TAW
31592$	41 ECS [DM]
31594$	41 ECS [DM]
31595$	41 ECS [DM]
31597	374 TAW
31598	374 TAW
FY84	
40204	700 TAS†
40205	700 TAS†
40206	142 TAS*
40207	142 TAS*
40208	142 TAS*
40209	142 TAS*
40210	142 TAS*
40211	142 TAS*
40212	142 TAS*
40213	142 TAS*
40475§	
40476§	
FY74	
41658	463 TAW
41659	463 TAW
41660	463 TAW
41661	463 TAW
41662	463 TAW
41663	463 TAW
41664	463 TAW
41665	463 TAW
41666	463 TAW
41667	463 TAW
41668	463 TAW
41669	463 TAW
41670	463 TAW
41671	463 TAW
41673	463 TAW
41674	463 TAW
41675	463 TAW

Serial	Wing
41676	463 TAW
41677	463 TAW
41679	463 TAW
41680	463 TAW
41681	463 TAW
41682	463 TAW
41684	463 TAW
41685	463 TAW
41687	463 TAW
41688	463 TAW
41689	463 TAW
41690	463 TAW
41691	463 TAW
41692	463 TAW
42061	463 TAW
42062	463 TAW
42063	463 TAW
42065	463 TAW
42066	463 TAW
42067	463 TAW
42069	463 TAW
42070	463 TAW
42071	463 TAW
42072	463 TAW
42130	463 TAW
42131	463 TAW
42132	463 TAW
42133	463 TAW
42134	463 TAW
FY85	
50011§	
50012§	
50035	†
50036	†
50037	†
50038	†
50039	†
50040	†
50041	†
50042	†
50136	*
50137	*
50138	*
50139	*
50140	*
50141	*
50142	*
50143	*
51301	181 TAS*
51362	181 TAS*
51363	181 TAS*
51364	181 TAS*
FY65	
50963‡	53 WRS
50964‡	815 WRS†
50966‡	53 WRS
50967‡	815 WRS†
50968‡	53 WRS
50969‡	920 WRG†
50972‡	920 WRG†
50976‡	54 WRS
50977‡	920 WRG†
50980‡	920 WRG†
50984‡	54 WRS
50985‡	53 WRS
FY86	
61699§	

Serial	Type	Wing
FY78		
80806		185 TAS*
80807		185 TAS*
80808		185 TAS*
80809		185 TAS*
80810		185 TAS*
80811		185 TAS*
80812		185 TAS*
80813		185 TAS*
FY79		
90473		130 TAS*
90474		130 TAS*
90475		130 TAS*
90476		130 TAS*
90477		130 TAS*
90478		130 TAS*
90479		130 TAS*
90480		130 TAS*

Boeing C-135 Stratotanker

(*ANG, Air National Guard; †AFRES, Air Force Reserve)

Serial	Type	Wing
FY60		
00313	KC-135A	410 BW
00314	KC-135A	410 BW
00315	KC-135A	320 BW
00316	KC-135A	320 BW
00317	KC-135A	93 BW
00318	KC-135A	416 BW
00319	KC-135A	320 BW
00320	KC-135A	379 BW
00321	KC-135R	28 BW
00322	KC-135A	410 BW
00323	KC-135A	28 BW
00324	KC-135A	7 BW
00325	KC-135A	379 BW
00326	KC-135A	379 BW
00327	KC-135A	2 BW
00328	KC-135A	7 BW
00329	KC-135A	379 BW
00330	KC-135A	19 ARW
00331	KC-135A	93 BW
00332	KC-135A	320 BW
00333	KC-135A	319 BW
00334	KC-135A	96 BW
00335	KC-135Q	376 SW
00336	KC-135Q	380 BW
00337	KC-135Q	380 BW
00339	KC-135Q	9 SRW
00341	KC-135A	380 BW
00342	KC-135Q	9 SRW
00343	KC-135Q	380 BW
00344	KC-135Q	376 SW
00345	KC-135Q	9 SRW
00346	KC-135Q	380 BW
00347	KC-135R	
00348	KC-135A	93 BW
00349	KC-135A	509 BW
00350	KC-135A	
00351	KC-135A	340 ARW
00353	KC-135A	96 BW
00355	KC-135A	416 BW
00356	KC-135A	305 ARW
00357	KC-135A	305 ARW
00358	KC-135A	410 BW
00359	KC-135A	410 BW
00360	KC-135A	410 BW
00361	KC-135A	92 BW
00362	KC-135A	305 ARW
00363	KC-135A	
00364	KC-135A	410 BW
00365	KC-135R	28 BW
00366	KC-135A	410 BW
00367	KC-135R	28 BW
00372	C-135E	4950 TW
00374	EC-135E	4950 TW
00375	C-135E	4950 TW
00376	C-135E	8 TDCS/ CinC SC
00377	C-135A	4950 TW
00378	C-135A	55 SRW
FY61		
10261	EC-135L	305 ARW
10262	EC-135A	28 BW
10263	EC-135L	305 ARW
10264	KC-135A	42 BW
10266	KC-135A	97 BW
10267	KC-135A	97 BW
10268	KC-135A	379 BW
10269	EC-135L	305 ARW
10270	KC-135A	319 BW
10271	KC-135A	5 BW
10272	KC-135A	97 BW
10274	EC-135H	6 ACCS
10275	KC-135A	97 BW
10276	KC-135R	384 ARW
10277	KC-135A	97 BW
10278	EC-135A	28 BW
10279	EC-135L	305 ARW
10280	KC-135A	340 ARW
10281	KC-135A	97 BW
10282	EC-135H	10 ACCS
10283	EC-135L	305 ARW
10284	KC-135A	22 ARW
10285	EC-135H	10 ACCS
10286	EC-135H	10 ACCS
10287	EC-135A	28 BW
10288	KC-135A	28 BW
10289	EC-135A	28 BW
10290	KC-135A	97 BW
10291	EC-135H	10 ACCS
10292	KC-135A	97 BW
10293	KC-135R	384 ARW
10294	KC-135A	416 BW
10295	KC-135A	97 BW
10297	EC-135A	28 BW
10298	KC-135A	379 BW
10299	KC-135A	410 BW
10300	KC-135A	22 ARW
10302	KC-135A	93 BW
10303	KC-135A	97 BW
10304	KC-135R	384 ARW
10305	KC-135A	305 ARW
10306	KC-135R	384 ARW
10307	KC-135R	384 ARW
10308	KC-135A	
10309	KC-135R	384 ARW
10310	KC-135R	384 ARW
10311	KC-135R	384 ARW
10312	KC-135R	384 ARW
10313	KC-135R	384 ARW
10314	KC-135A	93 BW
10315	KC-135R	384 ARW
10317	KC-135R	384 ARW
10318	KC-135R	384 ARW
10320	KC-135A	42 BW
10321	KC-135A	410 BW
10323	KC-135A	22 ARW

USAF (US based)

Serial	Type	Wing
10324	KC-135R	384 ARW
10325	KC-135A	42 BW
10326	EC-135E	4950 TW
10327	EC-135E	4950 TW
10329	EC-135E	4950 TW
10330	EC-135E	4950 TW
12662	RC-135S	6 SW
12663	RC-135S	6 SW
12665	WC-135B	55 WRS
12666	WC-135B	55 WRS
12667	WC-135B	55 WRS
12668	C-135C	89 MAW
12669	C-135C	4950 TW
12670	WC-135B	55 WRS
12671	C-135C	89 MAW
12672	WC-135B	55 WRS
12673	WC-135B	55 WRS
12674	WC-135B	55 WRS
FY64		
14828	KC-135A	509 BW
14829	KC-135A	376 SW
14830	KC-135A	5 BW
14831	KC-135A	5 BW
14832	KC-135A	96 BW
14833	KC-135A	97 BW
14834	KC-135A	340 ARW
14835	KC-135A	5 BW
14836	KC-135A	320 BW
14837	KC-135A	319 BW
14838	KC-135A	97 BW
14839	KC-135A	19 ARW
14840	KC-135A	320 BW
14841	RC-135V	55 SRW
14842	RC-135V	55 SRW
14843	RC-135V	55 SRW
14844	RC-135V	55 SRW
14845	RC-135V	55 SRW
14846	RC-135V	55 SRW
14847	RC-135U	55 SRW
14848	RC-135V	55 SRW
14849	RC-135U	55 SRW
FY62		
23497	KC-135A	416 BW
23498	KC-135A	92 BW
23499	KC-135R	19 ARW
23500	KC-135A	380 BW
23501	KC-135A	42 BW
23502	KC-135A	509 BW
23503	KC-135A	42 BW
23504	KC-135A	319 BW
23505	KC-135A	509 BW
23506	KC-135A	380 BW
23507	KC-135A	96 BW
23508	KC-135A	416 BW
23509	KC-135A	28 BW
23510	KC-135A	42 BW
23511	KC-135A	416 BW
23512	KC-135A	93 BW
23513	KC-135A	416 BW
23514	KC-135A	416 BW
23515	KC-135A	410 BW
23516	KC-135A	93 BW
23517	KC-135A	7 BW
23518	KC-135A	340 ARW
23519	KC-135A	416 BW
23520	KC-135A	340 ARW
23521	KC-135A	93 BW
23523	KC-135R	19 ARW
23524	KC-135A	380 BW
23525	KC-135A	340 ARW
23526	KC-135A	416 BW
23527	KC-135A	410 BW
23528	KC-135A	96 BW
23529	KC-135A	509 BW
23530	KC-135A	509 BW
23531	KC-135A	509 BW
23532	KC-135A	509 BW
23533	KC-135R	384 ARW
23534	KC-135R	340 ARW
23537	KC-135A	376 SW
23538	KC-135A	509 BW
23539	KC-135A	340 ARW
23540	KC-135R	28 BW
23541	KC-135A	340 ARW
23542	KC-135A	42 BW
23543	KC-135R	93 BW
23544	KC-135A	2 BW
23545	KC-135A	380 BW
23546	KC-135A	42 BW
23547	KC-135A	42 BW
23548	KC-135A	93 BW
23549	KC-135A	416 BW
23550	KC-135A	340 ARW
23551	KC-135A	19 ARW
23552	KC-135A	96 BW
23553	KC-135A	42 BW
23554	KC-135A	319 BW
23555	KC-135A	410 BW
23556	KC-135A	93 BW
23557	KC-135R	—
23558	KC-135A	96 BW
23559	KC-135A	379 BW
23560	KC-135A	509 BW
23561	KC-135A	96 BW
23562	KC-135A	410 BW
23563	KC-135A	96 BW
23564	KC-135A	—
23565	KC-135A	305 ARW
23566	KC-135A	22 ARW
23567	KC-135A	—
23568	KC-135A	509 BW
23569	KC-135A	19 ARW
23570	EC-135G	28 BW
23571	KC-135A	93 BW
23572	KC-135A	340 ARW
23573	KC-135A	42 BW
23574	KC-135A	305 ARW
23575	KC-135A	42 BW
23576	KC-135A	2 BW
23577	KC-135A	305 ARW
23578	KC-135A	42 BW
23579	EC-135G	28 BW
23580	KC-135A	42 BW
23581	EC-135C	55 SRW
23582	EC-135C	28 BW
23583	EC-135C	55 SRW
23584	EC-135J	9 ACCS
23585	EC-135C	55 SRW
24125	C-135B	58 MAS
24126	C-135B	89 MAW
24127	C-135B	89 MAW
24128	RC-135X	6 SW
24129	C-135B	89 MAW
24130	C-135B	89 MAW
24131	RC-135W	55 SRW
24132	RC-135W	55 SRW
24133	TC-135S	6 SW
24134	RC-135W	55 SRW
24135	RC-135W	55 SRW
24138	RC-135W	55 SRW
24139	RC-135W	55 SRW
26000	VC-137C	89 MAW
FY72		
27000	C-137C	89 MAW
FY63		
37976	KC-135A	93 BW
37977	KC-135A	42 BW
37978	KC-135A	305 ARW
37979	KC-135A	42 BW
37980	KC-135A	305 ARW
37981	KC-135A	19 ARW
37982	KC-135A	379 BW
37983	KC-135A	305 ARW
37984	KC-135A	93 BW
37985	KC-135A	42 BW
37986	KC-135A	320 BW
37987	KC-135A	410 BW
37988	KC-135A	93 BW
37990	KC-135A	305 ARW
37991	KC-135A	—
37992	KC-135A	93 BW
37993	KC-135A	319 BW
37994	EC-135G	305 ARW
37995	KC-135A	410 BW
37996	KC-135A	305 ARW
37997	KC-135R	384 ARW
37998	KC-135A	380 BW
37999	KC-135R	384 ARW
38000	KC-135A	22 ARW
38001	EC-135G	28 BW
38002	KC-135A	28 BW
38003	KC-135A	93 BW
38004	KC-135A	28 BW
38005	KC-135A	2 BW
38006	KC-135A	379 BW
38007	KC-135A	379 BW
38008	KC-135R	19 ARW
38009	KC-135A	305 ARW
38010	KC-135A	22 ARW
38011	KC-135A	410 BW
38012	KC-135A	97 BW
38013	KC-135A	28 BW
38014	KC-135A	22 ARW
38015	KC-135A	97 BW
38016	KC-135A	416 BW
38017	KC-135A	22 ARW
38018	KC-135A	410 BW
38019	KC-135A	22 ARW
38020	KC-135A	22 ARW
38021	KC-135A	5 BW
38022	KC-135A	416 BW
38023	KC-135A	2 BW
38024	KC-135A	22 ARW
38025	KC-135A	305 ARW
38026	KC-135A	22 ARW
38027	KC-135A	42 BW
38028	KC-135A	305 ARW
38029	KC-135A	380 BW
38030	KC-135A	305 ARW
38031	KC-135A	305 ARW
38032	KC-135A	28 BW
38033	KC-135A	305 ARW
38034	KC-135A	28 BW
38035	KC-135A	2 BW
38036	KC-135A	96 BW
38037	KC-135A	93 BW
38038	KC-135A	93 BW
38039	KC-135A	379 BW
38040	KC-135A	305 ARW

Serial	Type	Wing
38041	KC-135A	2 BW
38043	KC-135A	42 BW
38044	KC-135A	2 BW
38045	KC-135A	92 BW
38046	EC-135C	55 SRW
38047	EC-135C	28 BW
38048	EC-135C	28 BW
38049	EC-135C	55 SRW
38050	EC-135C	55 SRW
38051	EC-135C	28 BW
38052	EC-135C	55 SRW
38053	EC-135C	55 SRW
38054	EC-135C	55 SRW
38055	EC-135J	9 ACCS
38056	EC-135J	9 ACCS
38057	EC-135J	9 ACCS
38058	KC-135D	305 ARW
38059	KC-135D	305 ARW
38060	KC-135D	305 ARW
38061	KC-135D	305 ARW
38871	KC-135A	305 ARW
38872	KC-135A	19 ARW
38873	KC-135A	320 BW
38874	KC-135A	319 BW
38875	KC-135A	340 ARW
38876	KC-135A	93 BW
38877	KC-135A	5 BW
38878	KC-135A	5 BW
38879	KC-135A	320 BW
38880	KC-135A	509 BW
38881	KC-135A	380 BW
38883	KC-135A	305 ARW
38884	KC-135A	410 BW
38885	KC-135A	320 BW
38886	KC-135A	96 BW
38887	KC-135A	19 ARW
38888	KC-135A	28 BW
39792	RC-135V	55 SRW
FY55		
53118	EC-135K	8 TDCS
53125	EC-135Y	CinC CC
53129	EC-135P	6 ACCS
53130	KC-135A	7 BW
53136	KC-135A	22 ARW
53137	KC-135A	2 BW
53139	KC-135A	92 BW
53141	KC-135E	154 ARS*
53142	KC-135A	340 ARW
53143	KC-135E	197 ARS*
53145	KC-135A	314 ARS†
53146	KC-135E	145 ARS*
FY85		
56973	C-137C	89 MAW
56974	C-137C	89 MAW
FY56		
63591	KC-135A	380 BW
63592	KC-135A	380 BW
63593	KC-135E	154 ARS*
63594	KC-135A	5 BW
63595	KC-135A	22 ARW
63600	KC-135A	2 BW
63601	KC-135A	93 BW
63603	KC-135A	376 SW
63604	KC-135E	117 ARS*
63606	KC-135E	132 ARS*
63607	KC-135E	151 ARS*
63608	KC-135A	340 ARW
63609	KC-135E	151 ARS*
63610	KC-135A	92 BW
63611	KC-135E	145 ARS*
63612	KC-135E	126 ARS*
63614	KC-135A	19 ARW
63615	KC-135A	19 ARW
63616	KC-135A	93 BW
63617	KC-135A	340 ARW
63619	KC-135A	2 BW
63620	KC-135A	5 BW
63621	KC-135A	7 BW
63622	KC-135E	132 ARS*
63623	KC-135A	336 ARS†
63624	KC-135A	42 BW
63625	KC-135A	305 ARW
63626	KC-135E	147 ARS*
63627	KC-135A	2 BW
63630	KC-135E	154 ARS*
63631	KC-135E	117 ARS*
63632	KC-135A	92 BW
63633	KC-135A	380 BW
63634	KC-135A	19 ARW
63635	KC-135A	96 BW
63636	KC-135A	2 BW
63637	KC-135A	42 BW
63638	KC-135E	197 ARS*
63639	KC-135A	96 BW
63640	KC-135E	132 ARS*
63641	KC-135E	117 ARS*
63642	KC-135A	92 BW
63643	KC-135E	151 ARS*
63644	KC-135A	92 BW
63645	KC-135A	93 BW
63646	KC-135A	92 BW
63647	KC-135A	305 ARW
63648	KC-135E	145 ARS*
63649	KC-135A	2 BW
63650	KC-135E	133 ARS*
63651	KC-135A	92 BW
63652	KC-135A	92 BW
63653	KC-135A	92 BW
63654	KC-135E	132 ARS*
63656	KC-135A	7 BW
63658	KC-135E	117 ARS*
FY57		
71418	KC-135A	42 BW
71419	KC-135A	92 BW
71420	KC-135A	93 BW
71421	KC-135E	116 ARS*
71422	KC-135A	72 ARS†
71423	KC-135A	92 BW
71425	KC-135E	151 ARS*
71426	KC-135E	154 ARS*
71427	KC-135A	376 SW
71428	KC-135E	116 ARS*
71429	KC-135E	117 ARS*
71430	KC-135A	92 BW
71431	KC-135E	126 ARS*
71432	KC-135A	92 BW
71433	KC-135E	197 ARS*
71434	KC-135E	116 ARS*
71435	KC-135A	93 BW
71436	KC-135A	5 BW
71437	KC-135A	92 BW
71438	KC-135E	72 ARS†
71439	KC-135A	92 BW
71440	KC-135R	91 ARS
71441	KC-135A	92 BW
71443	KC-135E	132 ARS*
71445	KC-135E	145 ARS*
71447	KC-135A	92 BW
71448	KC-135E	154 ARS*
71450	KC-135E	132 ARS*
71451	KC-135A	2 BW
71452	KC-135E	197 ARS*
71453	KC-135A	7 BW
71454	KC-135A	376 SW
71455	KC-135E	151 ARS*
71456	KC-135A	340 ARW
71458	KC-135E	108 ARS*
71459	KC-135A	93 BW
71460	KC-135E	117 ARS*
71461	KC-135A	2 BW
71462	KC-135A	—
71463	KC-135E	117 ARS*
71464	KC-135E	145 ARS*
71465	KC-135E	154 ARS*
71467	KC-135A	93 BW
71468	KC-135E	336 ARS†
71469	KC-135A	93 BW
71470	KC-135A	7 BW
71471	KC-135A	19 ARW
71472	KC-135A	22 ARW
71473	KC-135R	384 ARW
71474	KC-135A	509 BW
71475	KC-135E	197 ARS*
71476	KC-135A	305 ARW
71477	KC-135A	340 ARW
71478	KC-135E	151 ARS*
71479	KC-135E	336 ARS†
71480	KC-135E	108 ARS*
71481	KC-135E	154 ARS*
71482	KC-135E	117 ARS*
71483	KC-135R	384 ARW
71484	KC-135E	197 ARS*
71485	KC-135E	151 ARS*
71486	KC-135A	19 ARW
71487	KC-135A	93 BW
71488	KC-135A	2 BW
71490	KC-135A	93 BW
71491	KC-135E	132 ARS*
71492	KC-135A	2 BW
71493	KC-135A	7 BW
71494	KC-135E	154 ARS*
71495	KC-135E	197 ARS*
71496	KC-135E	197 ARS*
71497	KC-135A	92 BW
71499	KC-135A	320 BW
71501	KC-135E	116 ARS*
71502	KC-135R	384 ARW
71503	KC-135E	151 ARS*
71504	KC-135E	72 ARS†
71505	KC-135E	132 ARS*
71506	KC-135A	42 BW
71507	KC-135E	145 ARS*
71508	KC-135A	384 ARW
71509	KC-135E	147 ARS*
71510	KC-135E	191 ARS*
71511	KC-135A	314 ARS†
71512	KC-135A	336 ARS†
71514	KC-135A	340 ARW
72589	KC-135E	55 SRW
72590	KC-135A	68 ARG
72591	KC-135A	410 BW
72592	KC-135A	5 BW
72593	KC-135A	68 ARG
72594	KC-135E	108 ARS*
72595	KC-135E	147 ARS*
72596	KC-135A	5 BW
72597	KC-135A	92 BW

USAF (US based)

Serial	Type	Wing
72598	KC-135A	336 ARS†
72599	KC-135A	319 BW
72600	KC-135E	116 ARS*
72601	KC-135A	97 BW
72602	KC-135A	7 BW
72603	KC-135A	336 ARS†
72604	KC-135E	126 ARS*
72605	KC-135A	19 ARW
72606	KC-135E	150 ARS*
72607	KC-135E	147 ARS*
72608	KC-135E	147 ARS*
72609	KC-135A	19 ARW
FY58		
80001	KC-135A	320 BW
80003	KC-135E	108 ARS*
80004	KC-135A	379 BW
80005	KC-135A	7 BW
80006	KC-135E	191 ARS*
80008	KC-135E	145 ARS*
80009	KC-135A	5 BW
80010	KC-135A	93 BW
80011	KC-135A	305 ARW
80012	KC-135E	191 ARS*
80013	KC-135E	72 ARS†
80014	KC-135A	379 BW
80015	KC-135A	320 BW
80016	KC-135A	92 BW
80017	KC-135E	145 ARS*
80018	KC-135A	305 ARW
80019	EC-135P	6 ACCS
80020	KC-135E	116 ARS*
80021	KC-135A	340 ARW
80022	EC-135P	6 ACCS
80023	KC-135A	68 ARG
80024	KC-135E	126 ARS*
80025	KC-135A	340 ARW
80027	KC-135A	97 BW
80028	KC-135A	410 BW
80029	KC-135A	97 BW
80030	KC-135A	42 BW
80032	KC-135E	150 ARS*
80033	KC-135A	305 ARW
80034	KC-135A	410 BW
80035	KC-135A	379 BW
80036	KC-135A	19 ARW
80037	KC-135A	410 BW
80038	KC-135A	319 BW
80040	KC-135E	150 ARS*
80041	KC-135A	72 ARS†
80042	KC-135Q	380 BW
80043	KC-135E	191 ARS*
80044	KC-135A	19 ARW
80045	KC-135Q	380 BW
80046	KC-135Q	380 BW
80047	KC-135Q	380 BW
80049	KC-135Q	380 BW
80050	KC-135Q	380 BW
80051	KC-135A	93 BW
80052	KC-135E	336 ARS†
80053	KC-135A	314 ARS†
80054	KC-135Q	376 SW
80055	KC-135Q	380 BW
80056	KC-135A	92 BW
80057	KC-135E	108 ARS*
80058	KC-135A	314 ARS†
80059	KC-135A	5 BW
80060	KC-135Q	376 SW
80061	KC-135Q	380 BW
80062	KC-135Q	9 SRW

Serial	Type	Wing
80063	KC-135A	93 BW
80064	KC-135E	314 ARS†
80065	KC-135Q	380 BW
80066	KC-135A	19 ARW
80067	KC-135E	108 ARS*
80068	KC-135E	108 ARS*
80069	KC-135Q	380 BW
80070	KC-135A	376 SW
80071	KC-135Q	9 SRW
80072	KC-135Q	376 SW
80073	KC-135A	96 BW
80074	KC-135Q	9 SRW
80075	KC-135A	93 BW
80076	KC-135A	19 ARW
80077	KC-135Q	9 SRW
80078	KC-135E	150 ARS*
80079	KC-135A	376 SW
80080	KC-135E	191 ARS*
80081	KC-135A	42 BW
80082	KC-135E	116 ARS*
80083	KC-135A	320 BW
80084	KC-135Q	9 SRW
80085	KC-135A	336 ARS†
80086	KC-135Q	9 SRW
80087	KC-135E	150 ARS*
80088	KC-135Q	9 SRW
80089	KC-135Q	9 SRW
80090	KC-135A	314 ARS†
80091	KC-135A	5 BW
80092	KC-135A	379 BW
80093	KC-135A	93 BW
80094	KC-135Q	9 SRW
80095	KC-135Q	9 SRW
80096	KC-135E	314 ARS†
80097	KC-135A	7 BW
80098	KC-135A	—
80099	KC-135Q	9 SRW
80100	KC-135A	7 BW
80102	KC-135A	93 BW
80103	KC-135Q	9 SRW
80104	KC-135A	92 BW
80105	KC-135A	92 BW
80106	KC-135A	93 BW
80107	KC-135E	191 ARS*
80108	KC-135E	314 ARS†
80109	KC-135A	96 BW
80110	KC-135A	319 BW
80111	KC-135E	126 ARS*
80112	KC-135Q	9 SRW
80113	KC-135A	376 SW
80114	KC-135A	93 BW
80115	KC-135E	150 ARS*
80116	KC-135A	96 BW
80117	KC-135Q	9 SRW
80118	KC-135A	19 ARW
80119	KC-135A	5 BW
80120	KC-135R	384 ARW
80121	KC-135A	96 BW
80122	KC-135A	92 BW
80123	KC-135A	379 BW
80124	KC-135A	305 ARW
80125	KC-135Q	9 SRW
80126	KC-135A	305 ARW
80128	KC-135A	5 BW
80129	KC-135Q	9 SRW
80130	KC-135A	7 BW
86970	EC-137B	89 MAW
86971	EC-137B	89 MAW
86972	EC-137B	89 MAW

Serial	Type	Wing
FY59		
91444	KC-135A	92 BW
91445	KC-135E	116 ARS*
91446	KC-135R	28 BW
91447	KC-135A	72 ARS†
91448	KC-135E	133 ARS*
91449	KC-135A	19 ARW
91450	KC-135E	133 ARS*
91451	KC-135A	72 ARS†
91452	KC-135A	116 ARS*
91453	KC-135R	28 BW
91454	KC-135A	319 BW
91455	KC-135R	28 BW
91456	KC-135E	126 ARS*
91457	KC-135E	147 ARS*
91458	KC-135R	384 ARW
91459	KC-135A	—
91460	KC-135Q	376 SW
91461	KC-135A	19 ARW
91462	KC-135Q	380 BW
91463	KC-135A	2 BW
91464	KC-135Q	9 SRW
91466	KC-135R	384 ARW
91467	KC-135Q	380 BW
91468	KC-135Q	9 SRW
91469	KC-135A	380 BW
91470	KC-135Q	9 SRW
91471	KC-135Q	380 BW
91472	KC-135A	97 BW
91473	KC-135E	191 ARS*
91474	KC-135Q	9 SRW
91475	KC-135A	319 BW
91476	KC-135A	319 BW
91477	KC-135E	72 ARS†
91478	KC-135R	93 BW
91479	KC-135E	126 ARS*
91480	KC-135Q	9 SRW
91482	KC-135R	384 ARW
91483	KC-135A	93 BW
91484	KC-135E	147 ARS*
91485	KC-135E	150 ARS*
91486	KC-135A	5 BW
91487	KC-135E	108 ARS*
91488	KC-135A	319 BW
91489	KC-135E	191 ARS*
91490	KC-135Q	9 SRW
91492	KC-135A	319 BW
91493	KC-135A	319 BW
91494	KC-135E	133 ARS*
91495	KC-135E	319 BW
91496	KC-135A	7 BW
91497	KC-135E	150 ARS*
91498	KC-135A	92 BW
91499	KC-135E	133 ARS*
91500	KC-135A	319 BW
91501	KC-135A	92 BW
91502	KC-135A	319 BW
91503	KC-135A	42 BW
91504	KC-135Q	9 SRW
91505	KC-135E	133 ARS*
91506	KC-135E	147 ARS*
91507	KC-135A	42 BW
91508	KC-135A	19 ARW
91509	KC-135E	133 ARS*
91510	KC-135Q	380 BW
91511	KC-135A	42 BW
91512	KC-135Q	9 SRW
91513	KC-135Q	9 SRW
91514	KC-135E	55 SRW
91515	KC-135R	384 ARW
91516	KC-135A	379 BW

Serial	Type	Wing
91517	KC-135R	28 BW
91518	EC-135K	8 TDCS
91519	KC-135E	126 ARS*
91520	KC-135Q	9 SRW
91521	KC-135A	410 BW
91522	KC-135A	410 BW
91523	KC-135Q	9 SRW

Lockheed C-141B Starlifter
(*ANG, Air National Guard
†AFRES, Air Force Reserve)
60 MAW: Travis AFB, California
62 MAW: McChord AFB, Washington
63 MAW: Norton AFB, California
172 MAG: Jackson Field AFB, Mississippi
437 MAW: Charleston AFB, S Carolina
438 MAW: McGuire AFB, New Jersey
443 MAW: Altus AFB, Oklahoma

Serial	Wing
FY61	
12778	438 MAW
FY63	
38075	60 MAW
38076	438 MAW
38078	437 MAW
38079	437 MAW
38080	438 MAW
38081	62 MAW
38082	62 MAW
38083	438 MAW
38084	63 MAW
38085	63 MAW
38086	62 MAW
38087	63 MAW
38088	60 MAW
38089	443 MAW
38090	438 MAW
FY64	
40609	62 MAW
40610	437 MAW
40611	437 MAW
40612	437 MAW
40613	437 MAW
40614	172 MAG*
40615	437 MAW
40616	438 MAW
40617	63 MAW
40618	437 MAW
40619	63 MAW
40620	438 MAW
40621	438 MAW
40622	438 MAW
40623	438 MAW
40625	438 MAW
40626	438 MAW
40627	438 MAW
40628	438 MAW
40629	437 MAW
40630	437 MAW
40631	437 MAW
40632	60 MAW
40633	438 MAW
40634	63 MAW
40635	62 MAW
40636	443 MAW
40637	60 MAW
40638	438 MAW
40639	438 MAW
40640	172 MAG*
40642	60 MAW
40643	60 MAW
40644	437 MAW
40645	60 MAW
40646	437 MAW
40648	60 MAW
40649	437 MAW
40650	438 MAW
40651	437 MAW
40653	63 MAW
FY65	
50216	63 MAW
50217	437 MAW
50218	437 MAW
50219	60 MAW
50220	437 MAW
50221	438 MAW
50222	438 MAW
50223	438 MAW
50224	438 MAW
50225	63 MAW
50226	63 MAW
50227	62 MAW
50228	62 MAW
50229	62 MAW
50230	60 MAW
50231	60 MAW
50232	62 MAW
50233	443 MAW
50234	60 MAW
50235	62 MAW
50236	438 MAW
50237	62 MAW
50238	60 MAW
50239	60 MAW
50240	62 MAW
50241	62 MAW
50242	60 MAW
50243	62 MAW
50244	62 MAW
50245	60 MAW
50246	60 MAW
50247	60 MAW
50248	62 MAW
50249	60 MAW
50250	60 MAW
50251	60 MAW
50252	60 MAW
50253	62 MAW
50254	60 MAW
50255	62 MAW
50256	60 MAW
50257	62 MAW
50258	62 MAW
50259	60 MAW
50260	60 MAW
50261	438 MAW
50262	443 MAW
50263	62 MAW
50264	62 MAW
50265	443 MAW
50266	437 MAW
50267	437 MAW
50268	60 MAW
50269	437 MAW
50270	437 MAW
50271	438 MAW
50272	437 MAW
50273	437 MAW
50275	437 MAW
50276	437 MAW
50277	63 MAW
50278	60 MAW
50279	437 MAW
50280	443 MAW
59397	443 MAW
59398	443 MAW
59399	62 MAW
59400	63 MAW
59401	437 MAW
59402	63 MAW
59403	60 MAW
59404	63 MAW
59405	443 MAW
59406	63 MAW
59408	437 MAW
59409	438 MAW
59410	62 MAW
59411	438 MAW
59412	438 MAW
59413	438 MAW
59414	63 MAW
FY66	
60126	438 MAW
60128	63 MAW
60129	62 MAW
60130	63 MAW
60131	437 MAW
60132	438 MAW
60133	438 MAW
60134	63 MAW
60135	437 MAW
60136	63 MAW
60137	443 MAW
60138	63 MAW
60139	63 MAW
60140	438 MAW
60141	62 MAW
60142	62 MAW
60143	63 MAW
60144	437 MAW
60145	62 MAW
60146	438 MAW
60147	60 MAW
60148	60 MAW
60149	443 MAW
60150	63 MAW
60151	60 MAW
60152	437 MAW
60153	63 MAW
60154	438 MAW
60155	438 MAW
60156	63 MAW
60157	438 MAW
60158	62 MAW
60159	62 MAW
60160	63 MAW
60161	62 MAW
60162	438 MAW
60163	437 MAW
60164	63 MAW
60165	62 MAW
60166	438 MAW
60167	437 MAW
60168	437 MAW
60169	438 MAW
60170	443 MAW

USAF (US based)

Serial	Wing	Serial	Wing	Serial	Wing
60171	63 MAW	60203	437 MAW	70009	63 MAW
60172	63 MAW	60204	438 MAW	70010	437 MAW
60173	438 MAW	60205	63 MAW	70011	437 MAW
60174	438 MAW	60206	62 MAW	70012	437 MAW
60175	63 MAW	60207	443 MAW	70013	438 MAW
60176	62 MAW	60208	63 MAW	70014	437 MAW
60177	63 MAW	60209	437 MAW	70015	63 MAW
60178	437 MAW			70016	437 MAW
60179	63 MAW	67944	60 MAW	70018	62 MAW
60180	63 MAW	67945	437 MAW	70019	438 MAW
60181	63 MAW	67946	63 MAW	70020	438 MAW
60182	63 MAW	67947	437 MAW	70021	438 MAW
60183	438 MAW	67948	438 MAW	70022	63 MAW
60184	63 MAW	67949	63 MAW	70023	63 MAW
60185	438 MAW	67950	438 MAW	70024	438 MAW
60186	443 MAW	67951	62 MAW	70025	443 MAW
60187	437 MAW	67952	63 MAW	70026	437 MAW
60188	60 MAW	67953	438 MAW	70027	438 MAW
60189	443 MAW	67954	438 MAW	70028	63 MAW
60190	437 MAW	67955	437 MAW	70029	63 MAW
60191	60 MAW	67956	437 MAW	70031	60 MAW
60192	62 MAW	67957	63 MAW	70164	62 MAW
60193	63 MAW	67958	63 MAW	70165	438 MAW
60194	437 MAW	67959	63 MAW	70166	443 MAW
60195	437 MAW				
60196	437 MAW	*FY67*			
60197	62 MAW	70001	63 MAW		
60198	63 MAW	70002	438 MAW		
60199	438 MAW	70003	443 MAW		
60200	63 MAW	70004	437 MAW		
60201	63 MAW	70005	63 MAW		
60202	437 MAW	70007	438 MAW		

Civil Registered Aircraft in Military Service

BAC VC10
(Omani Royal Flight)
A40-AB

Boeing B-727
(Government of Saudi Arabia)
HZ122

Grumman Gulfstream III
(Government of Saudi Arabia)

103
107
HZ108

Lockheed C-130H Hercules
(Government of Saudi Arabia)

HZ114
HZ115
HZ116
HZ117

Lockheed P-3 Orion
(NOAA)
N42RF (159773) WP-3D
N43RF (159875) WP-3D

North American Sabre 75A
(Federal Aviation Administration)
N51
N52
N53
N54
N55
N56
N57
N58
N59
N60
N61
N62
N63
N64
N65

North American F-100F Super Sabre
(Flight Refuelling Ltd, Hurn/ Flight Systems, Decimomannu)

N414FS
N415FS
N416FS
N417FS
N418FS
N419FS

Dassault Falcon 20DC
(Flight Refuelling Ltd/FRADU, Hurn)
N900FR
N901FR
N902FR
N903FR
N904FR
N905FR
N906FR
N907FR
N908FR
N909FR